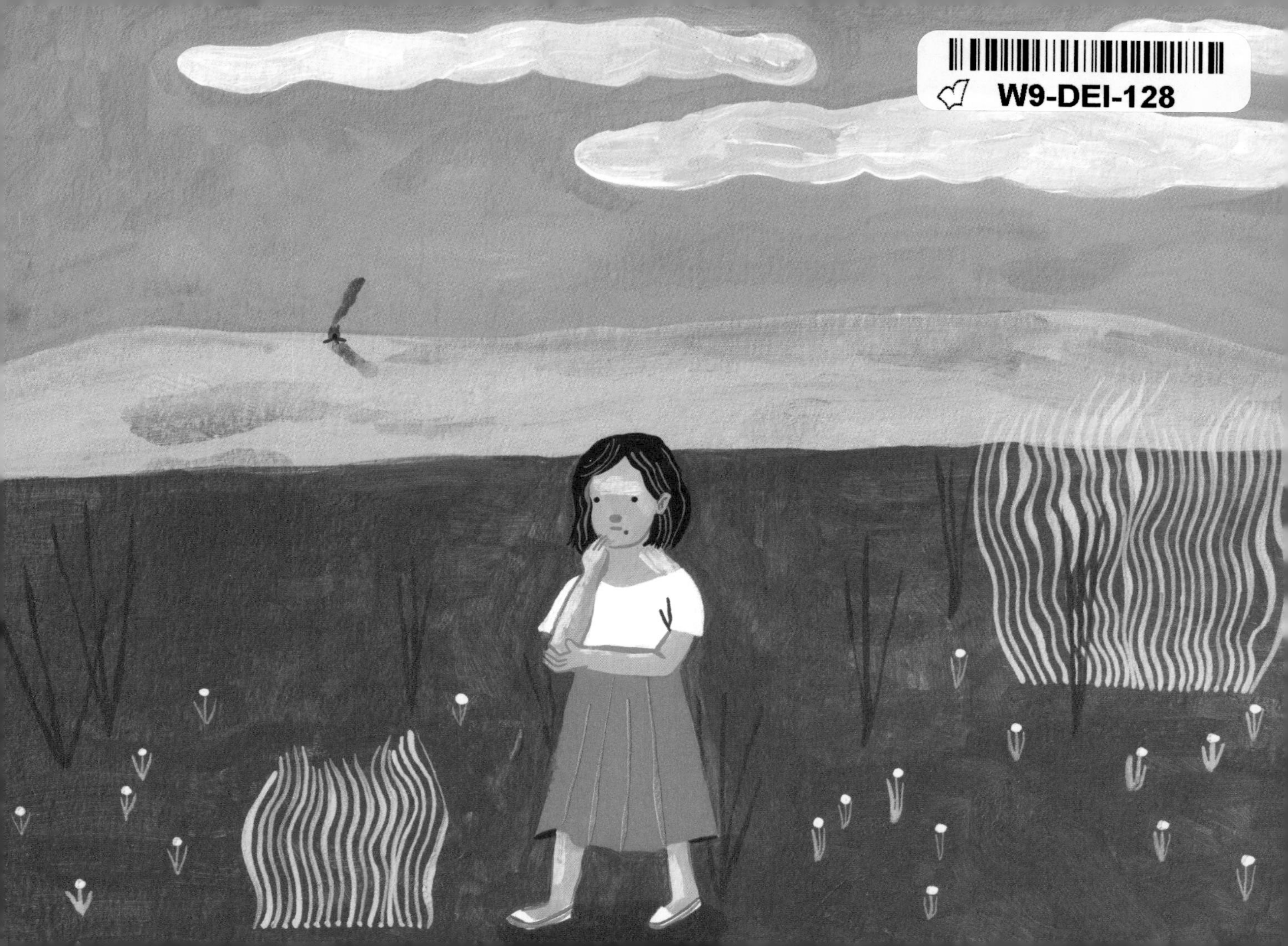

drawnandquarterly.com | pixmadeobjects.com

978-1-77046-462-9 | First edition: June 2021 | Printed in China | 10 9 8 7 6 5 4 3 2 1

Cataloguing data available from Library and Archives Canada

Published in the USA by Drawn & Quarterly, a client publisher of Farrar, Straus and Giroux. Published in Canada by Drawn & Quarterly, a client publisher of Raincoast Books. Published in the United Kingdom by Drawn & Quarterly, a client publisher of Publishers Group UK.

Thank you Paola y Mila, for looking at my work in its early stages & giving me tremendous feedback.
Thank you David, for accepting me into the February 2020 Kuš! Comics Residency. It provided a much needed space & time to finish the comic.

Thank you Jesse, for your support, incredibly helpful drawing advice & lovely ideas for me to consider & put into the comic.

Thank you to the many awesome folks at D+Q, for the final dress-up of the comic, for your suggestions, time & effort into the making of this book.

Last but not least, thank you Dad & Mom, without whom I would not be who I am & what I continually strive to be.

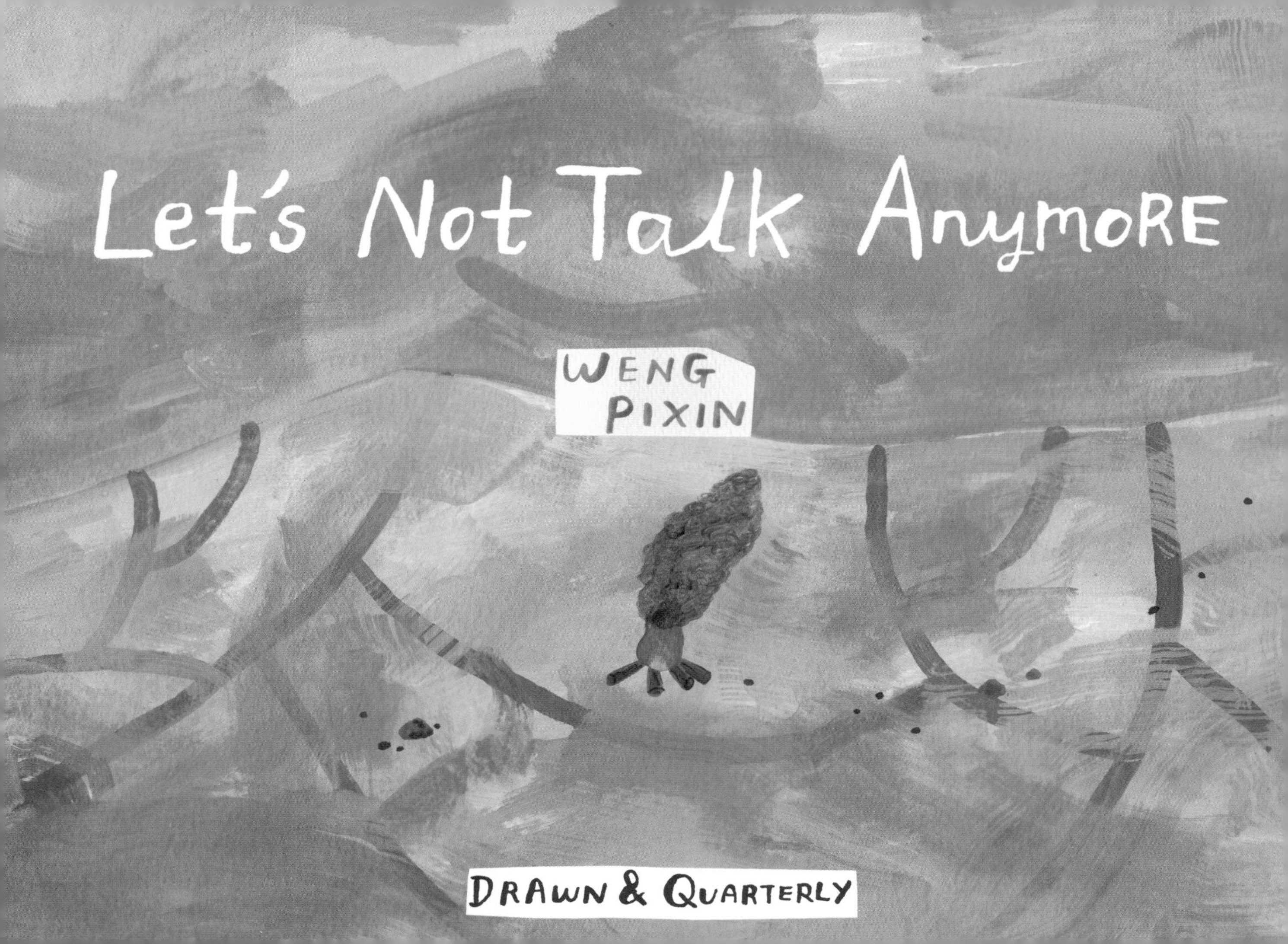
Let's Not Talk Anymore
WENG PIXIN
DRAWN & QUARTERLY

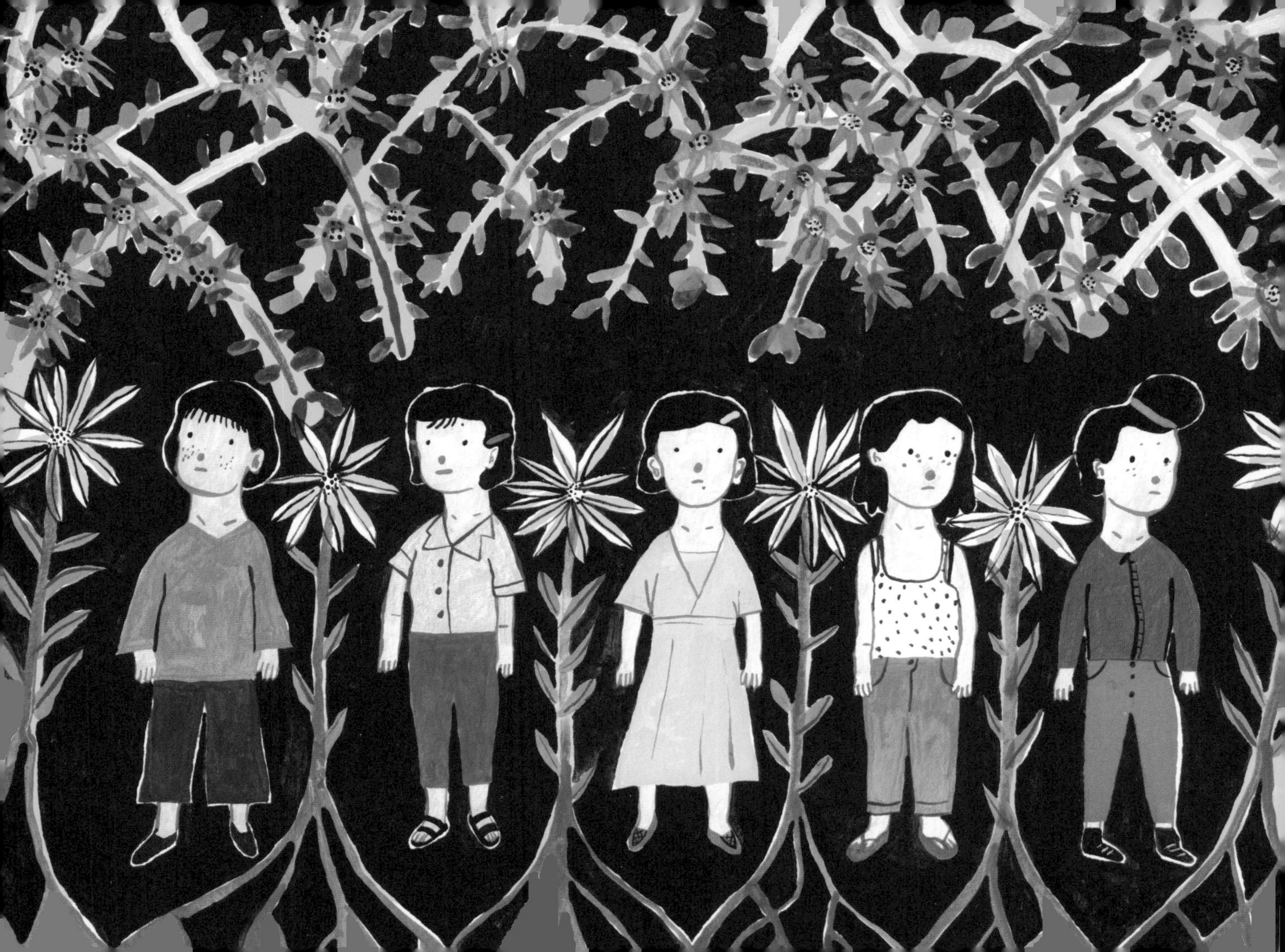

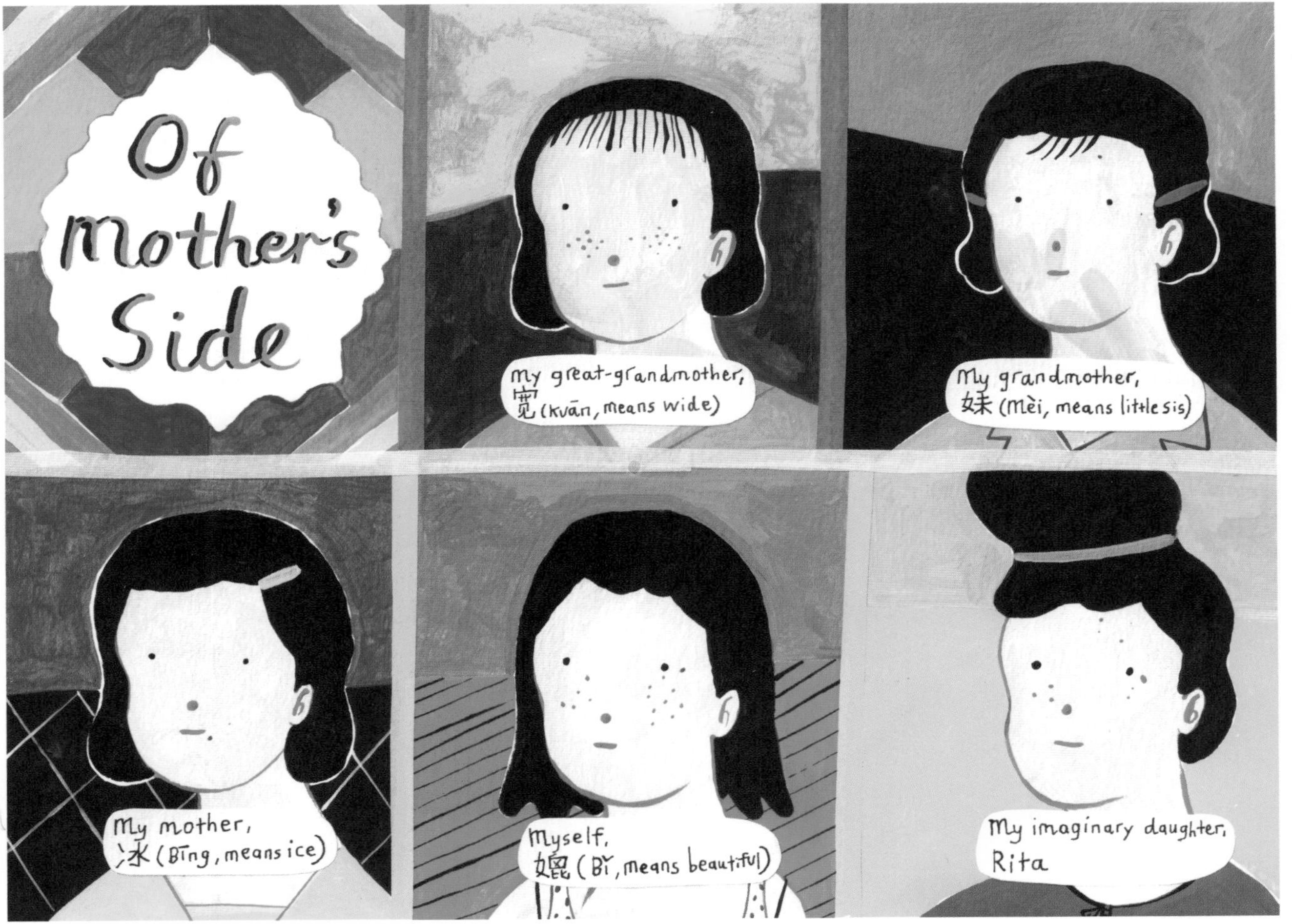
Of Mother's Side
My great-grandmother, 宽 (kvān, means wide)
My grandmother, 妹 (Mèi, means little sis)
My mother, 冰 (Bīng, means ice)
Myself, 媲 (Bǐ, means beautiful)
My imaginary daughter, Rita

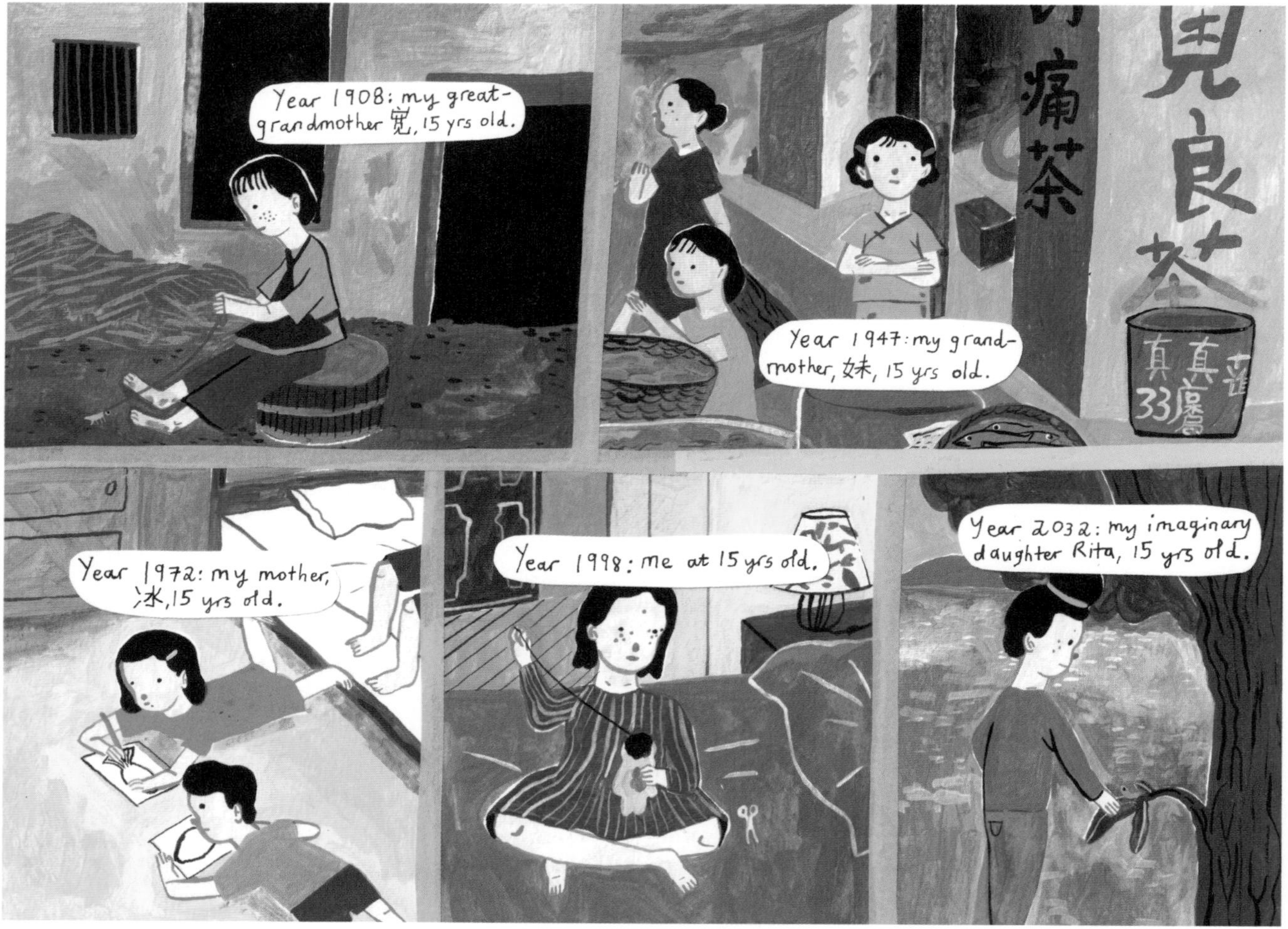
Year 1908: my great-grandmother 宽, 15 yrs old.
痛茶
良茶
Year 1947: my grand-mother, 妹, 15 yrs old.
Year 1972: my mother, 冰, 15 yrs old.
Year 1998: me at 15 yrs old.
Year 2032: my imaginary daughter Rita, 15 yrs old.

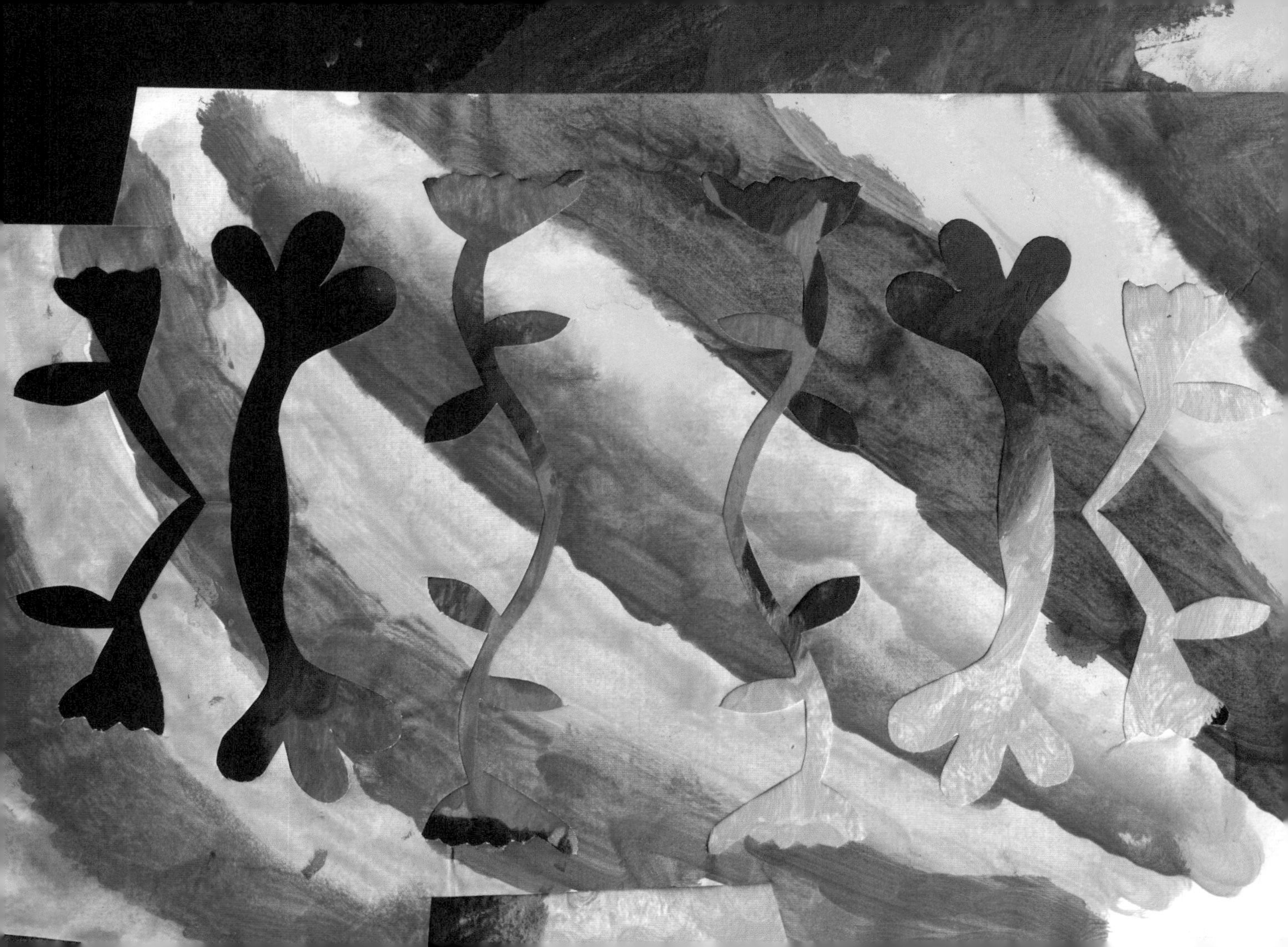

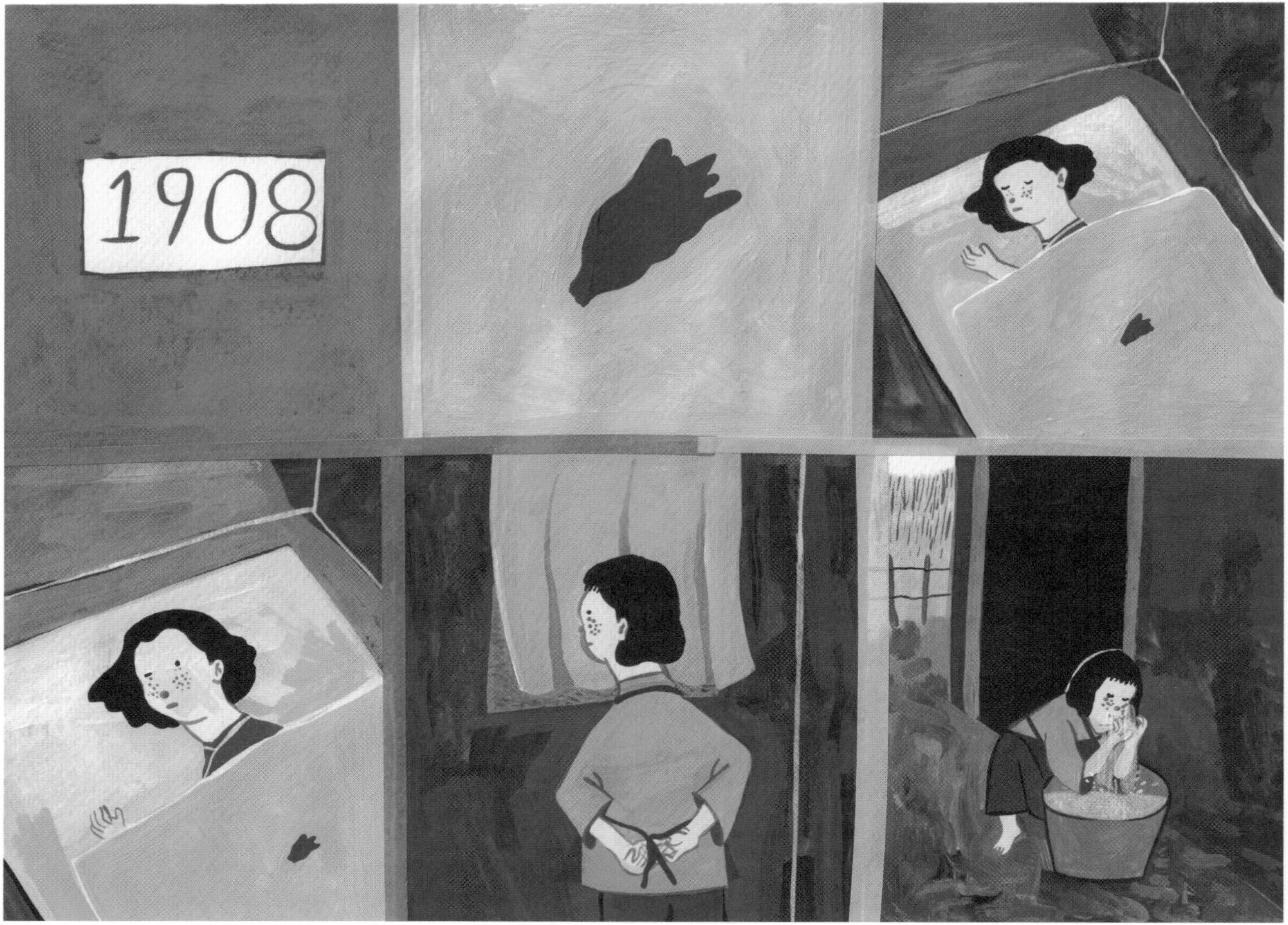
1908

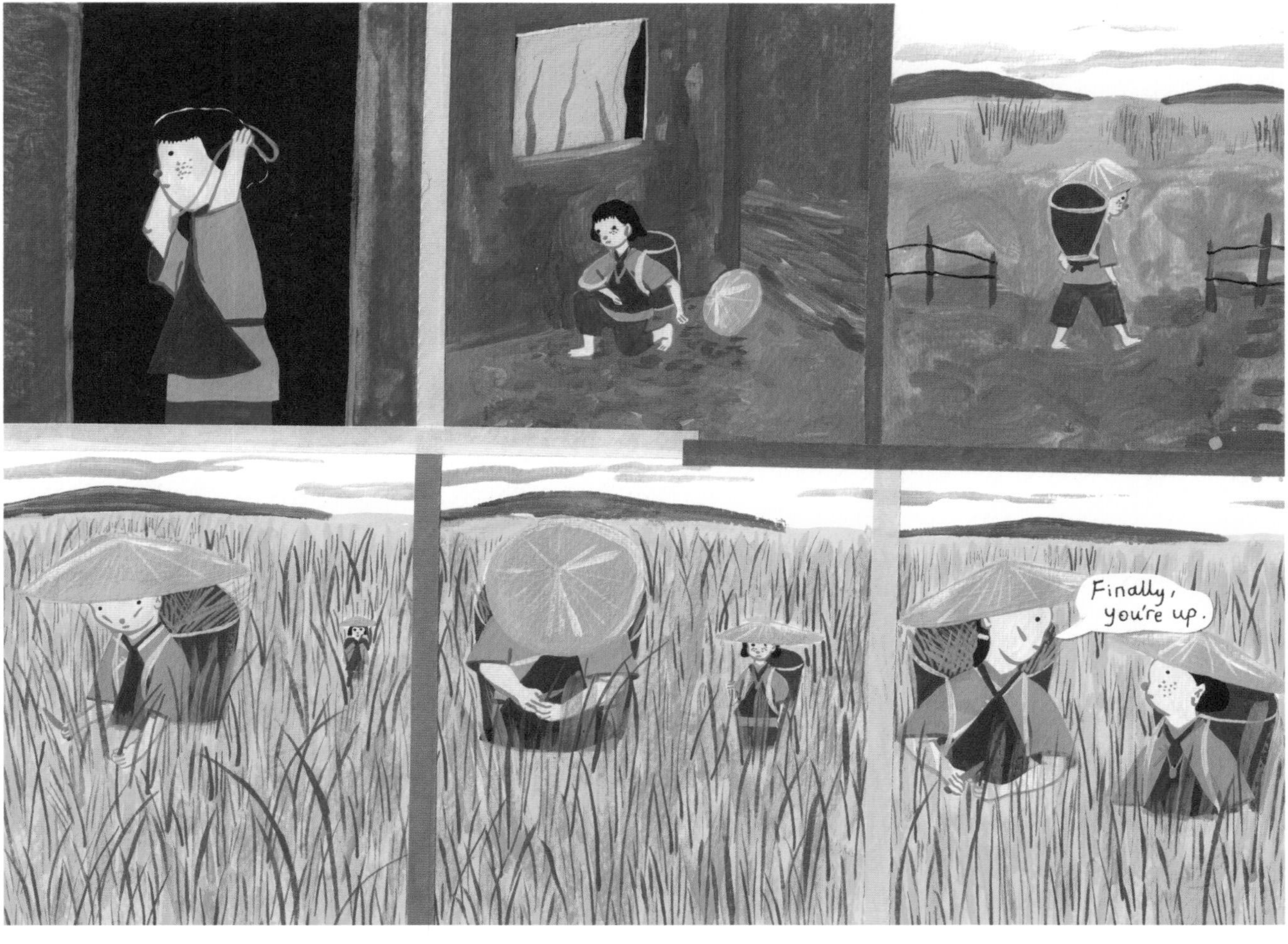
Finally, you're up.

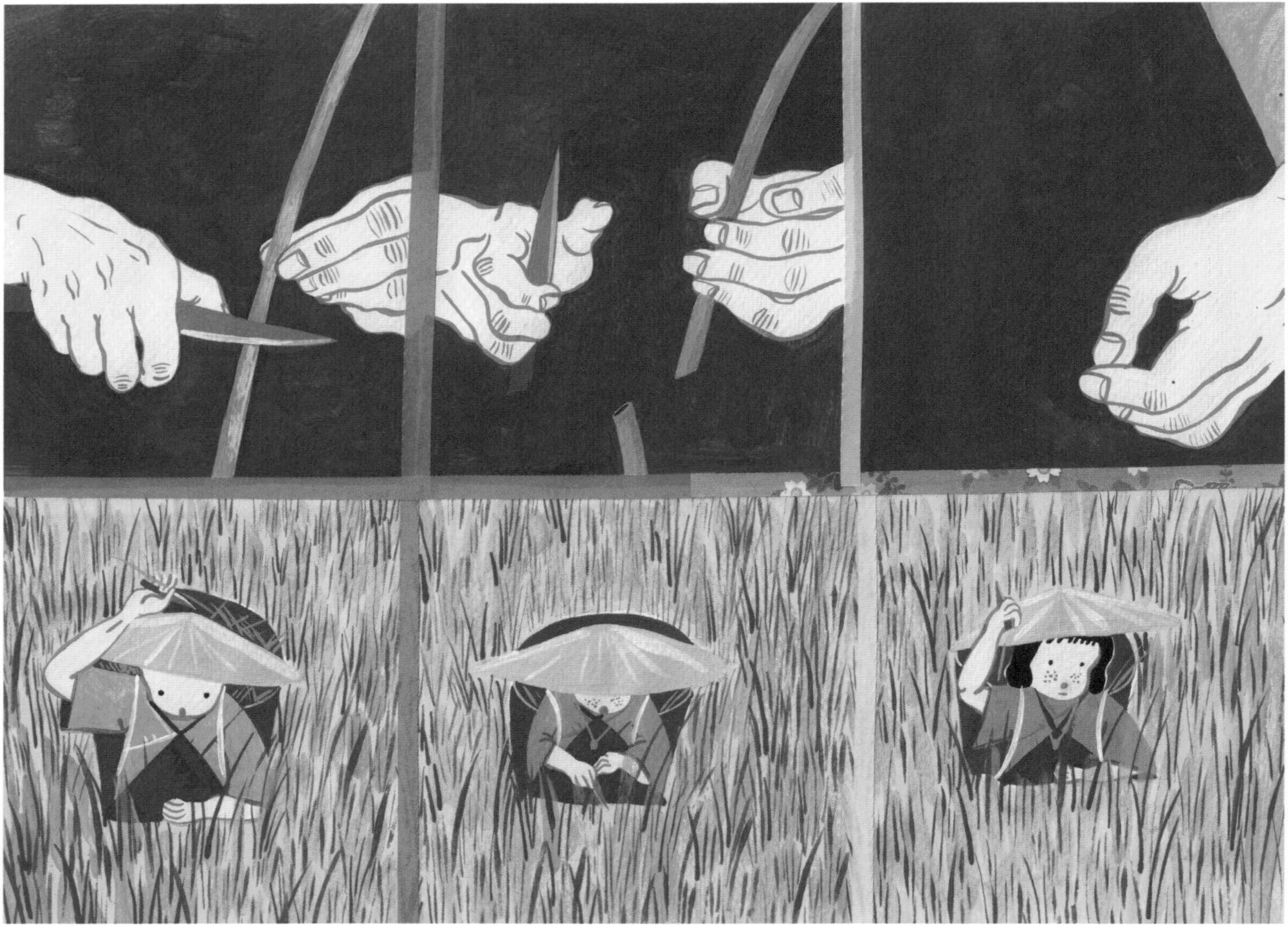

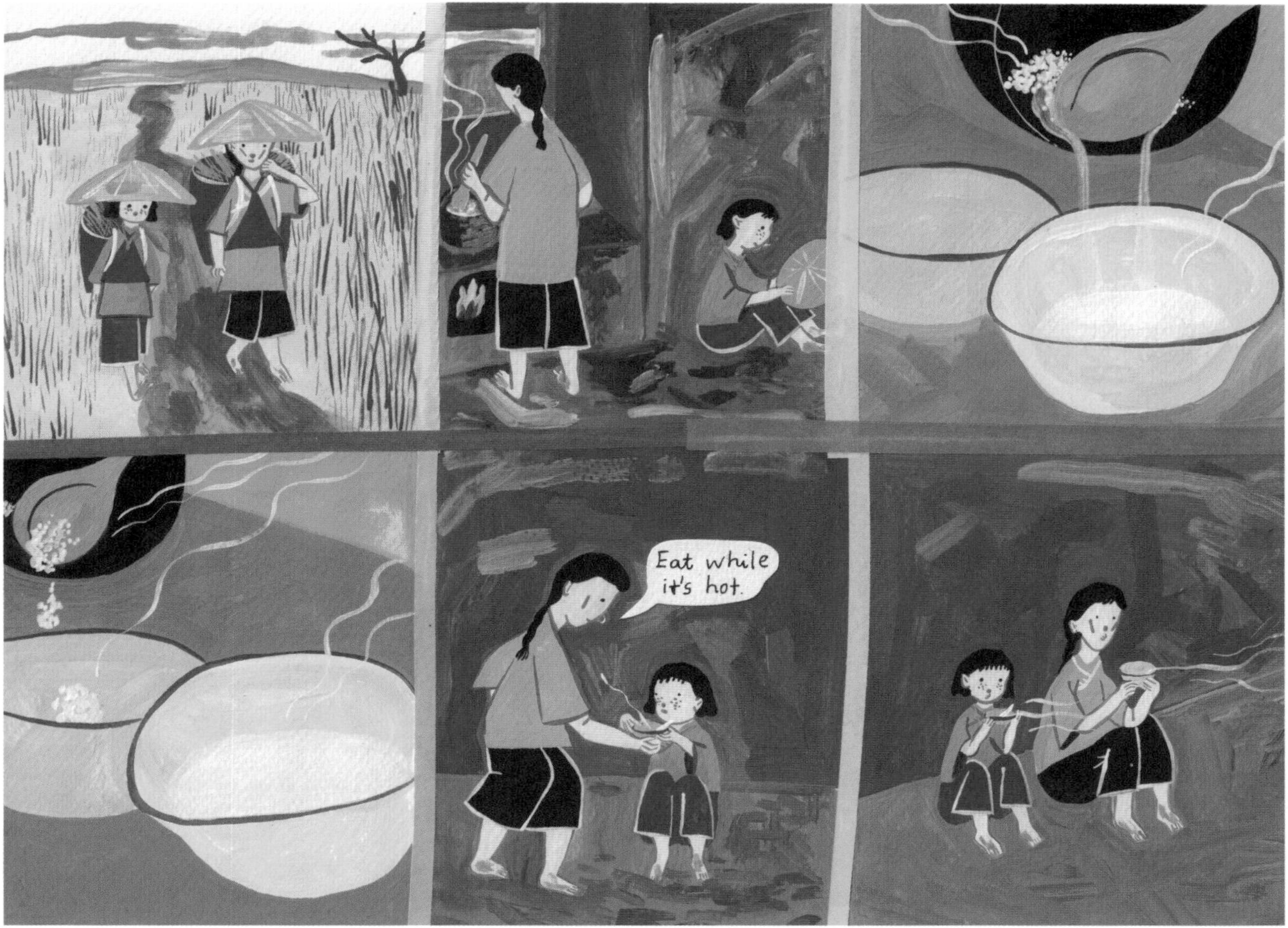
Eat while it's hot.

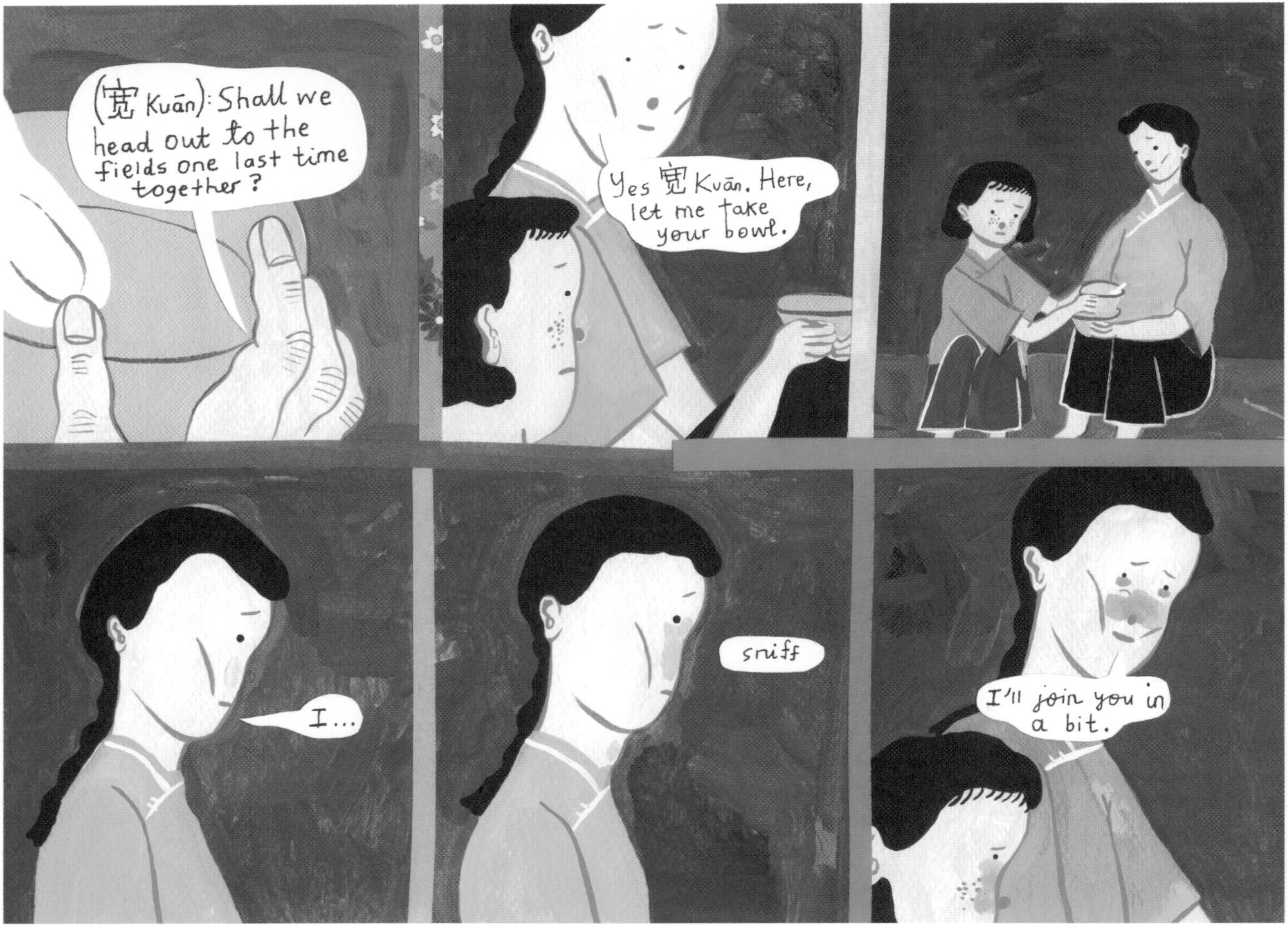
(宽 Kuān): Shall we head out to the fields one last time together?
Yes 宽 Kuān. Here, let me take your bowl.
I...
sniff
I'll join you in a bit.

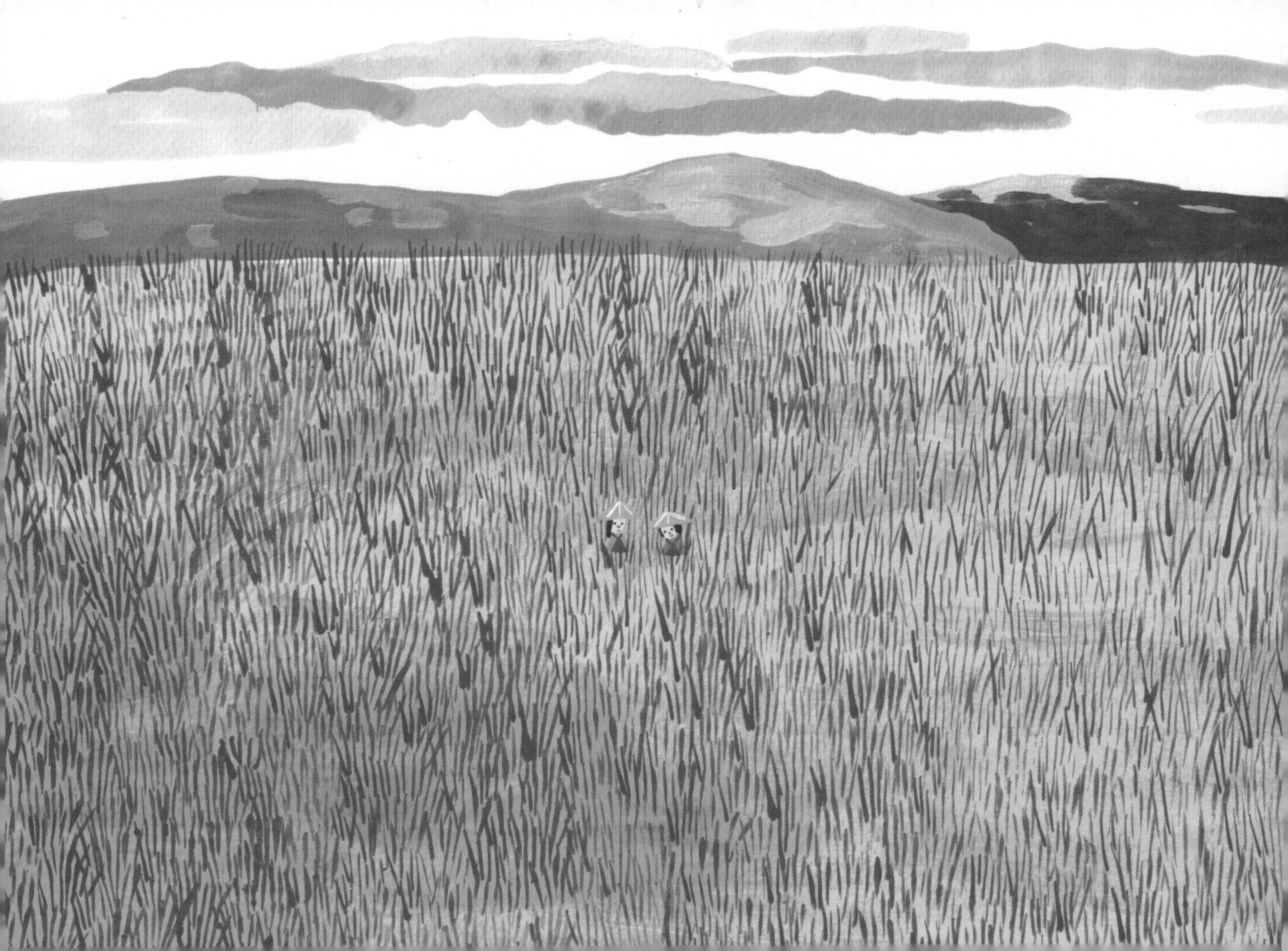

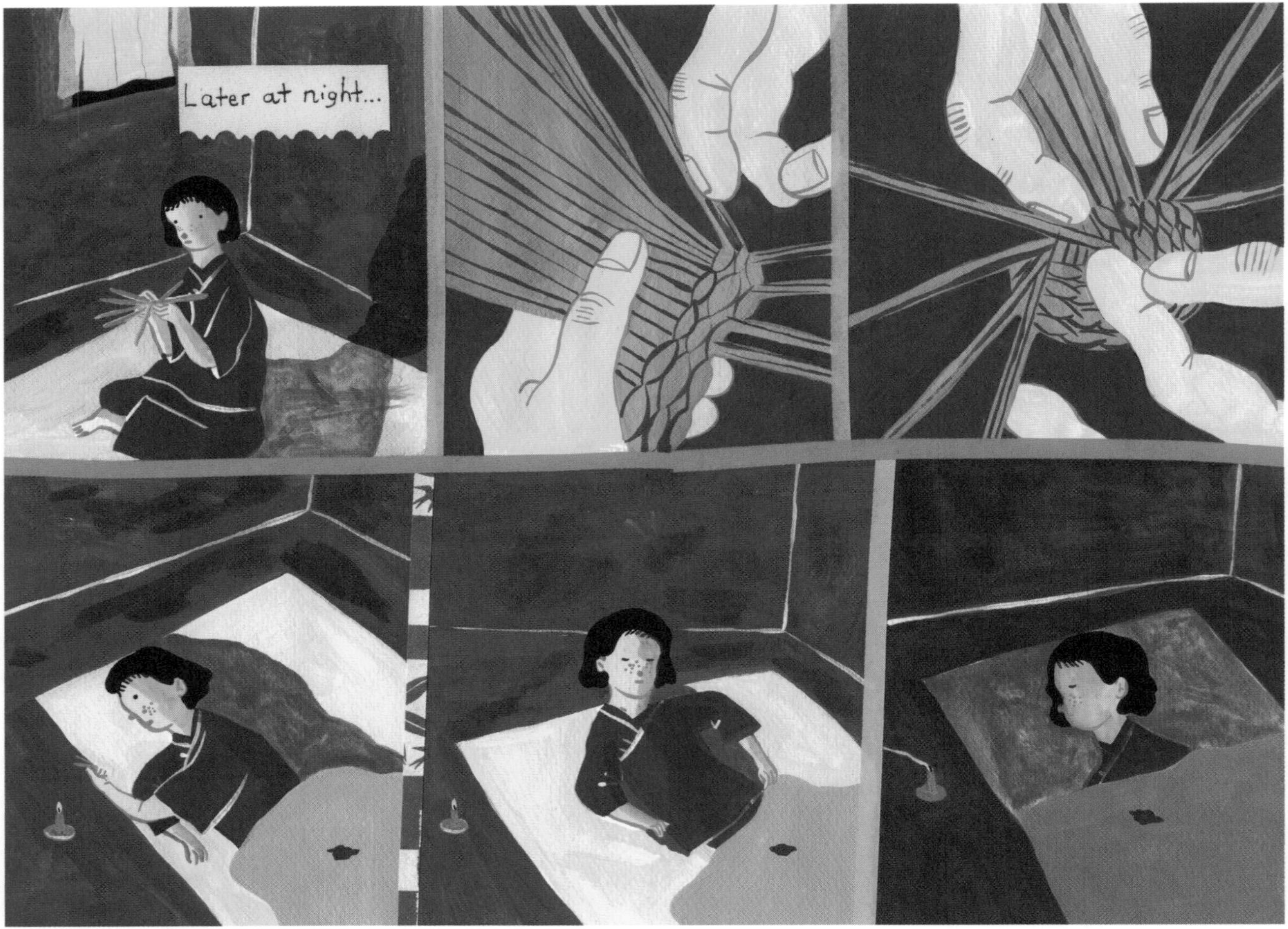
Later at night...

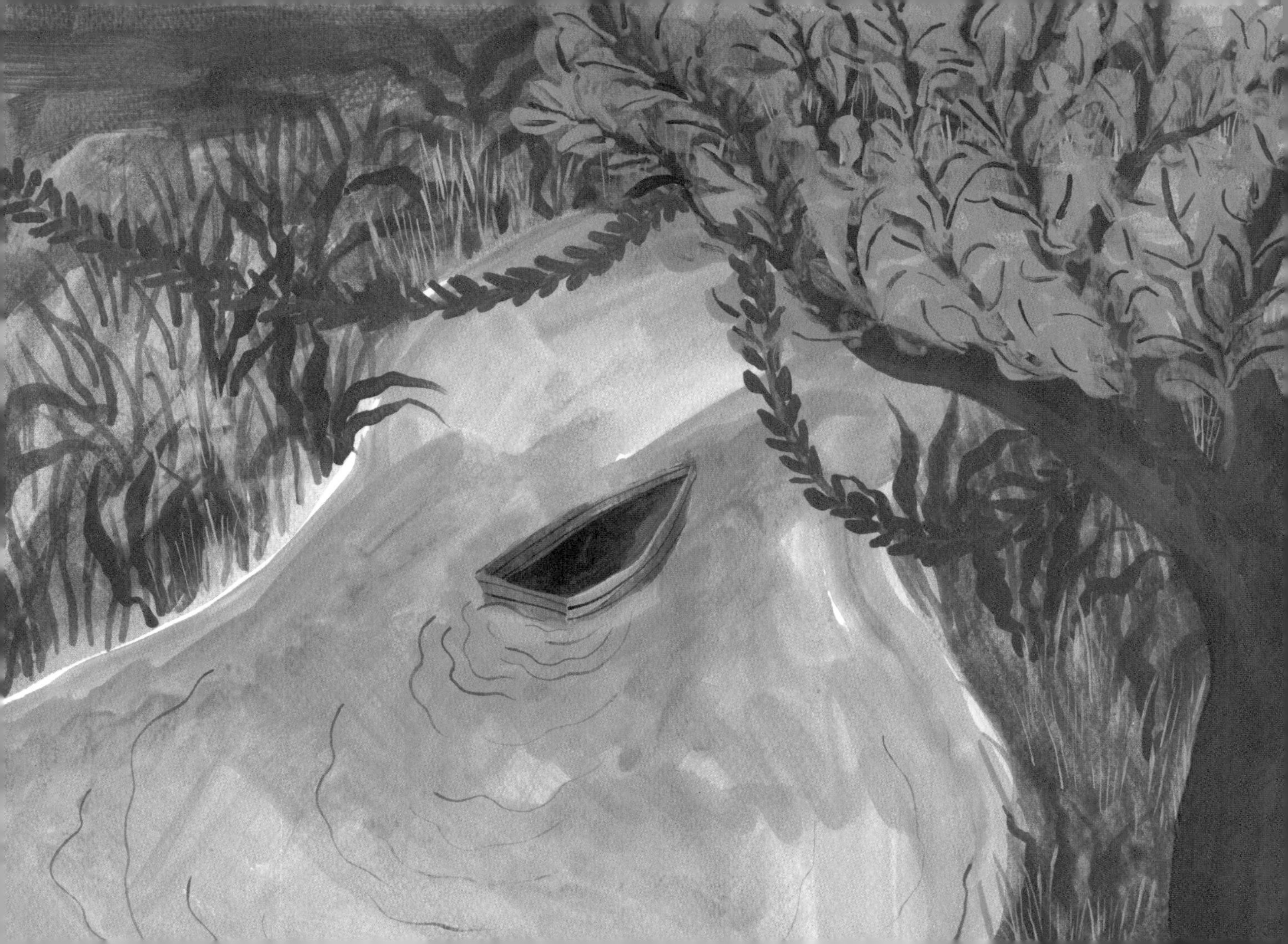

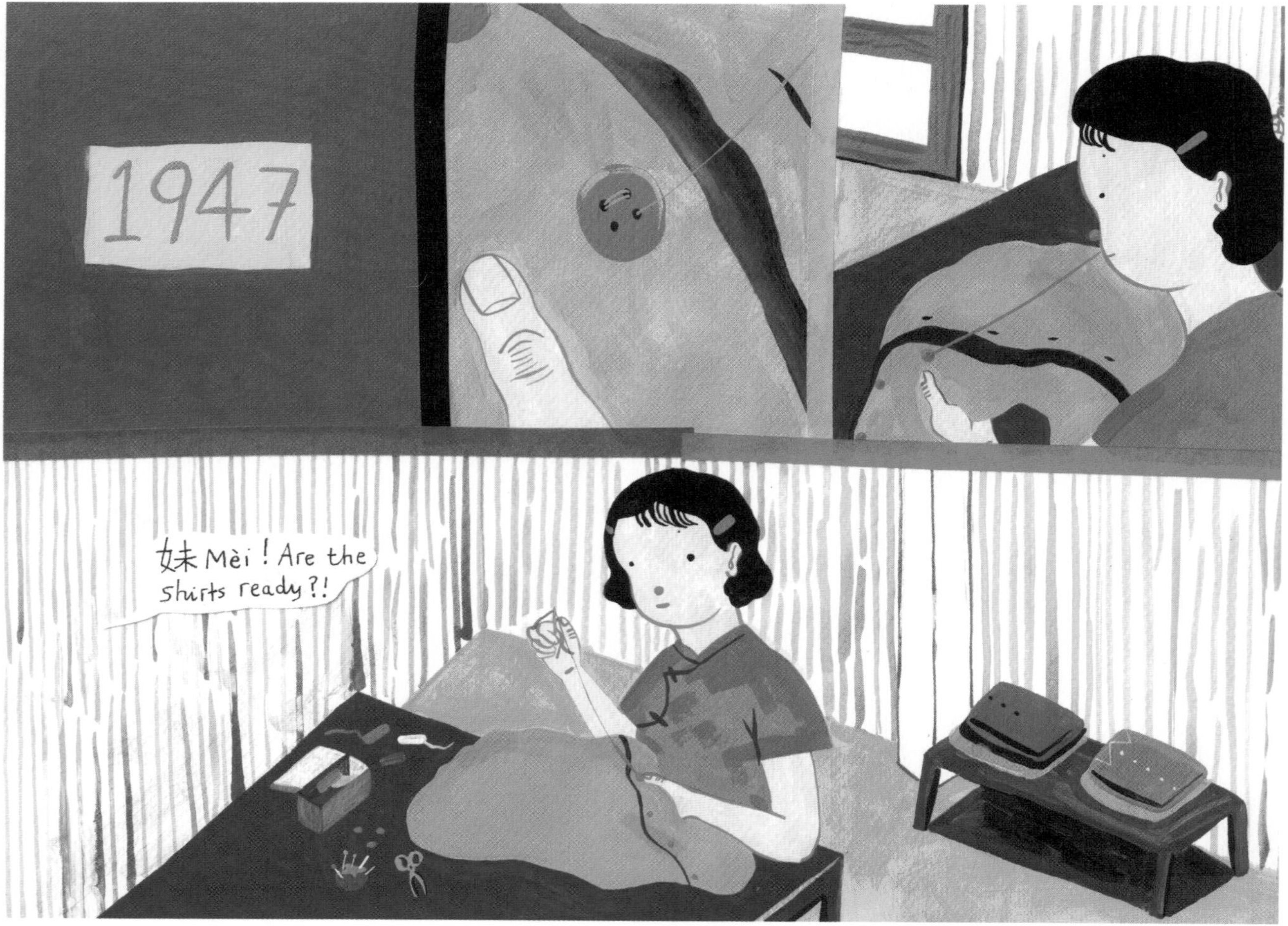
1947
妹 Mèi! Are the shirts ready?!

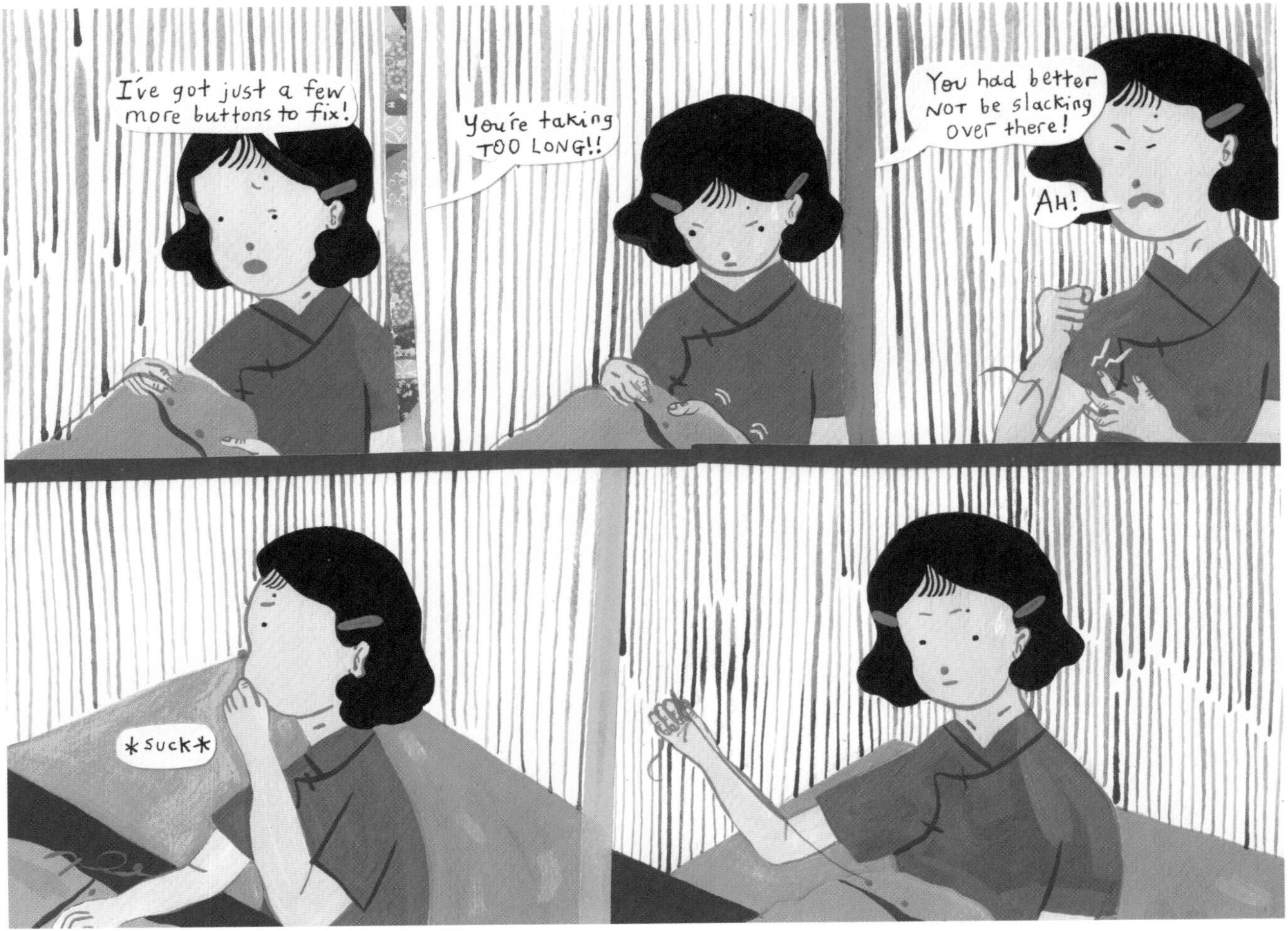
I've got just a few more buttons to fix!
You're taking TOO LONG!!
You had better NOT be slacking over there!
AH!
SUCK

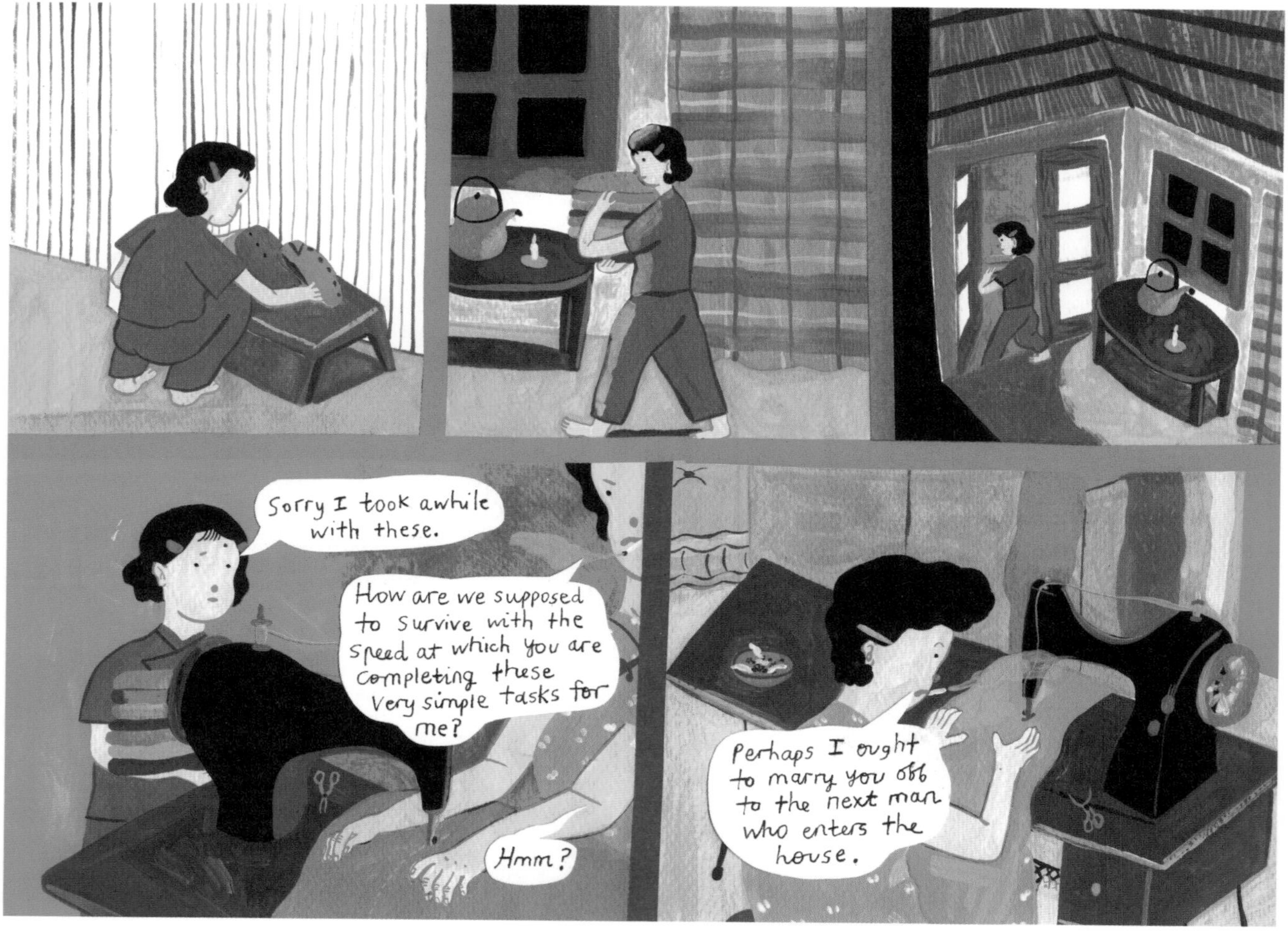
Sorry I took awhile with these.
How are we supposed to survive with the speed at which you are completing these very simple tasks for me?
Hmm?
Perhaps I ought to marry you off to the next man who enters the house.

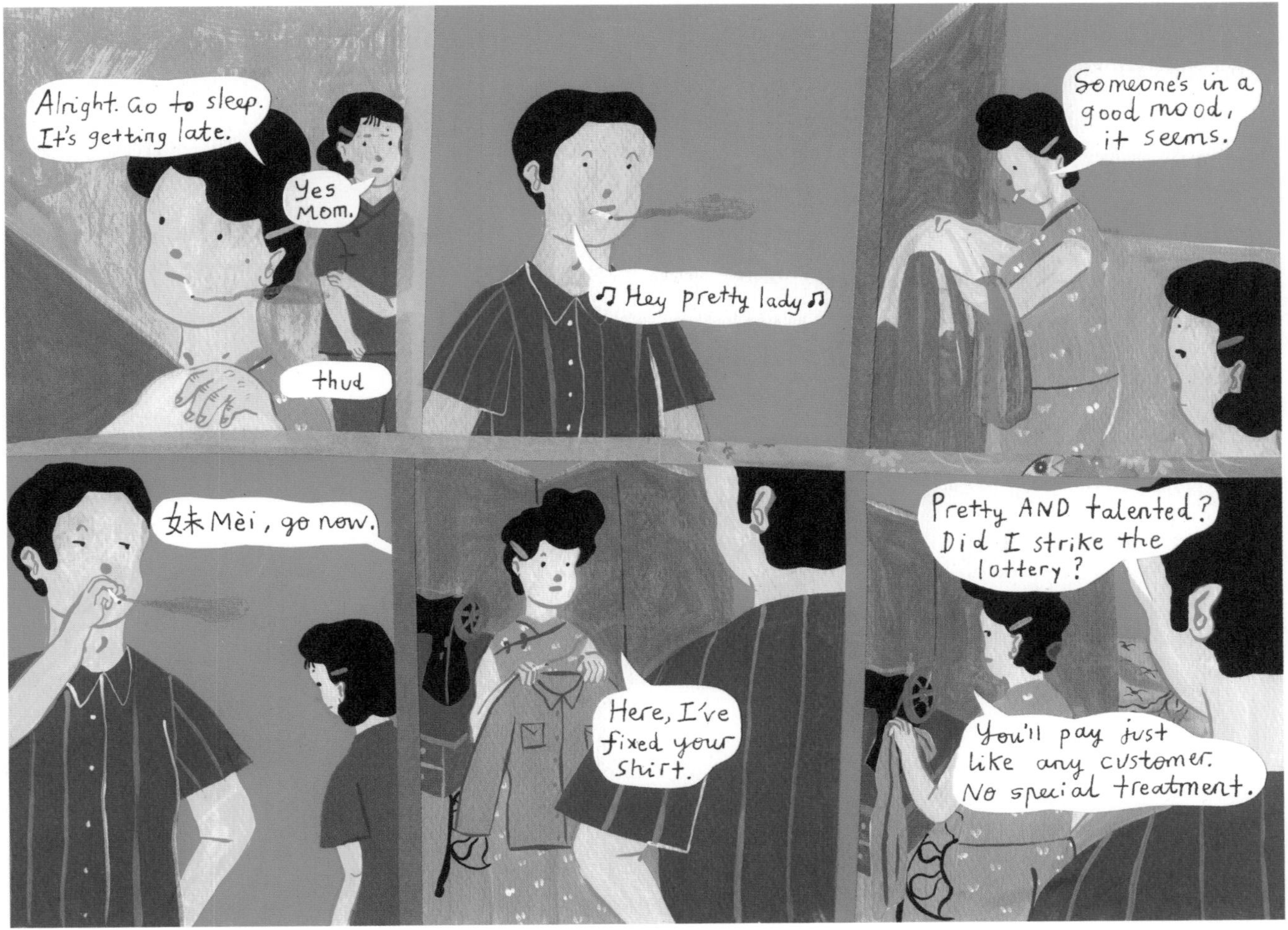
Alright. Go to sleep. It's getting late.
Yes Mom.
thud
♫ Hey pretty lady ♫
Someone's in a good mood, it seems.
妹 Mèi, go now.
Here, I've fixed your shirt.
Pretty AND talented? Did I strike the lottery?
You'll pay just like any customer. No special treatment.

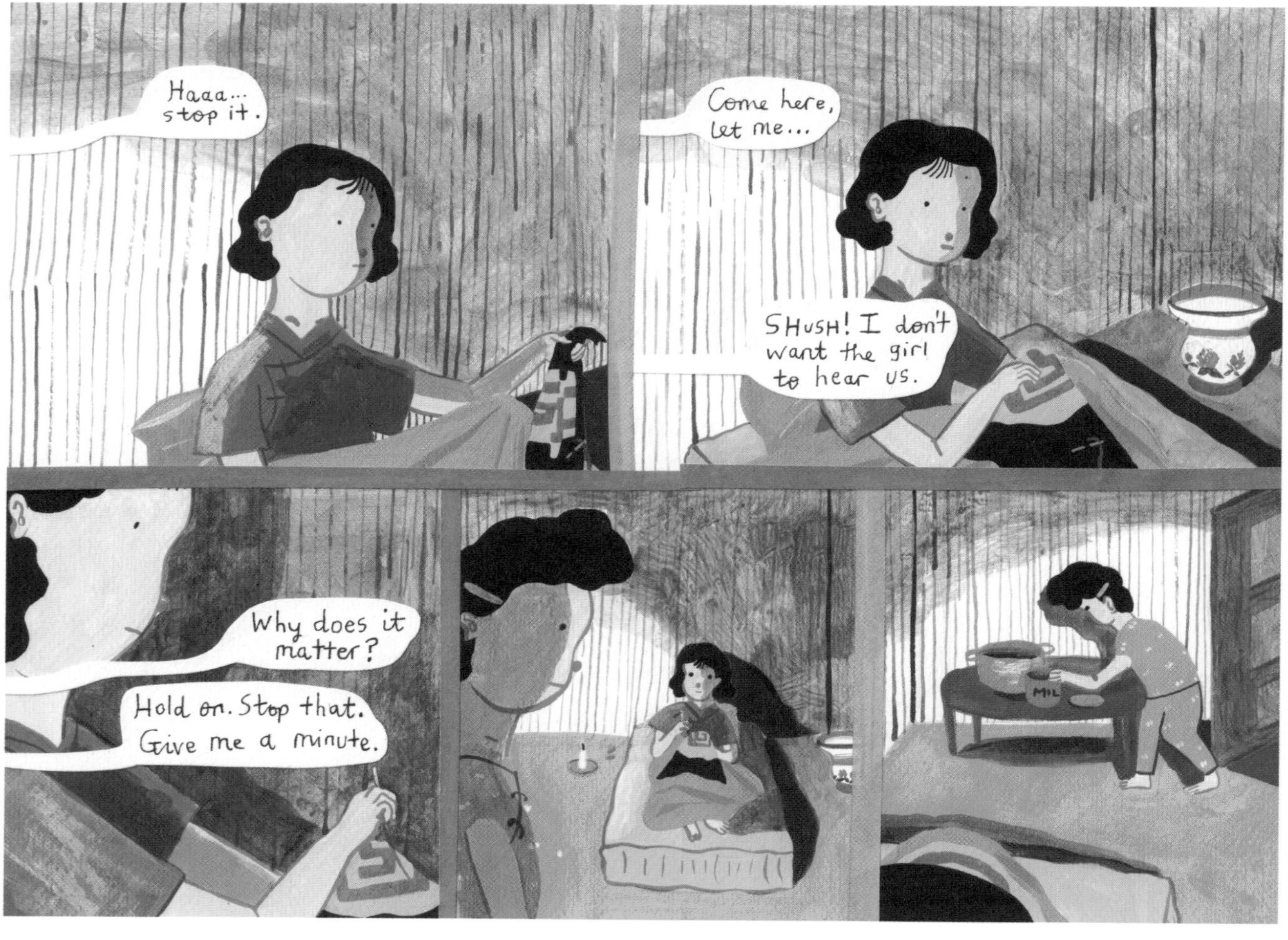
Haaa... stop it.
Come here, let me...
SHUSH! I don't want the girl to hear us.
Why does it matter?
Hold on. Stop that. Give me a minute.
MIL

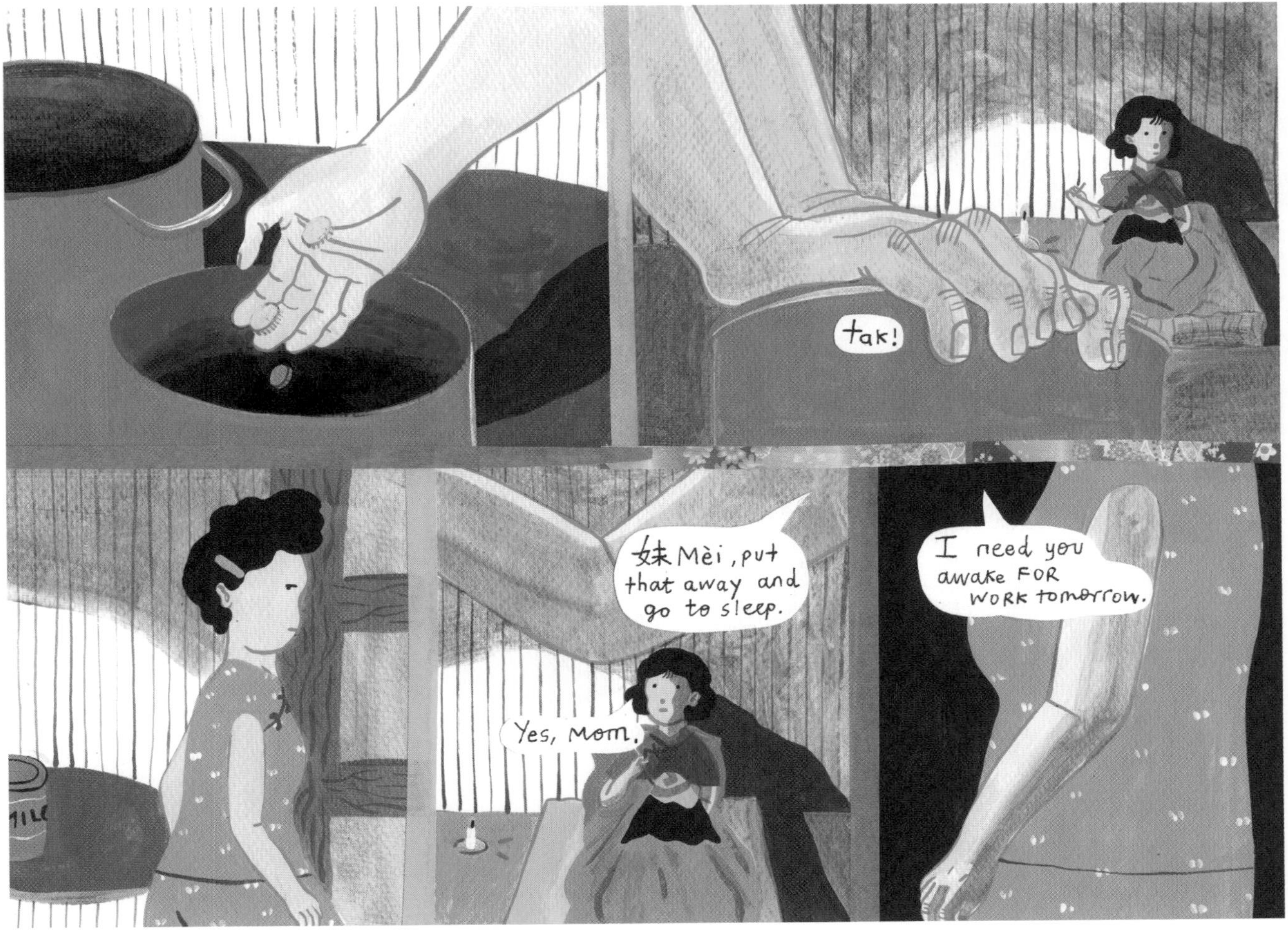
tak!
妹Mèi, put that away and go to sleep.
Yes, Mom.
I need you awake FOR WORK tomorrow.

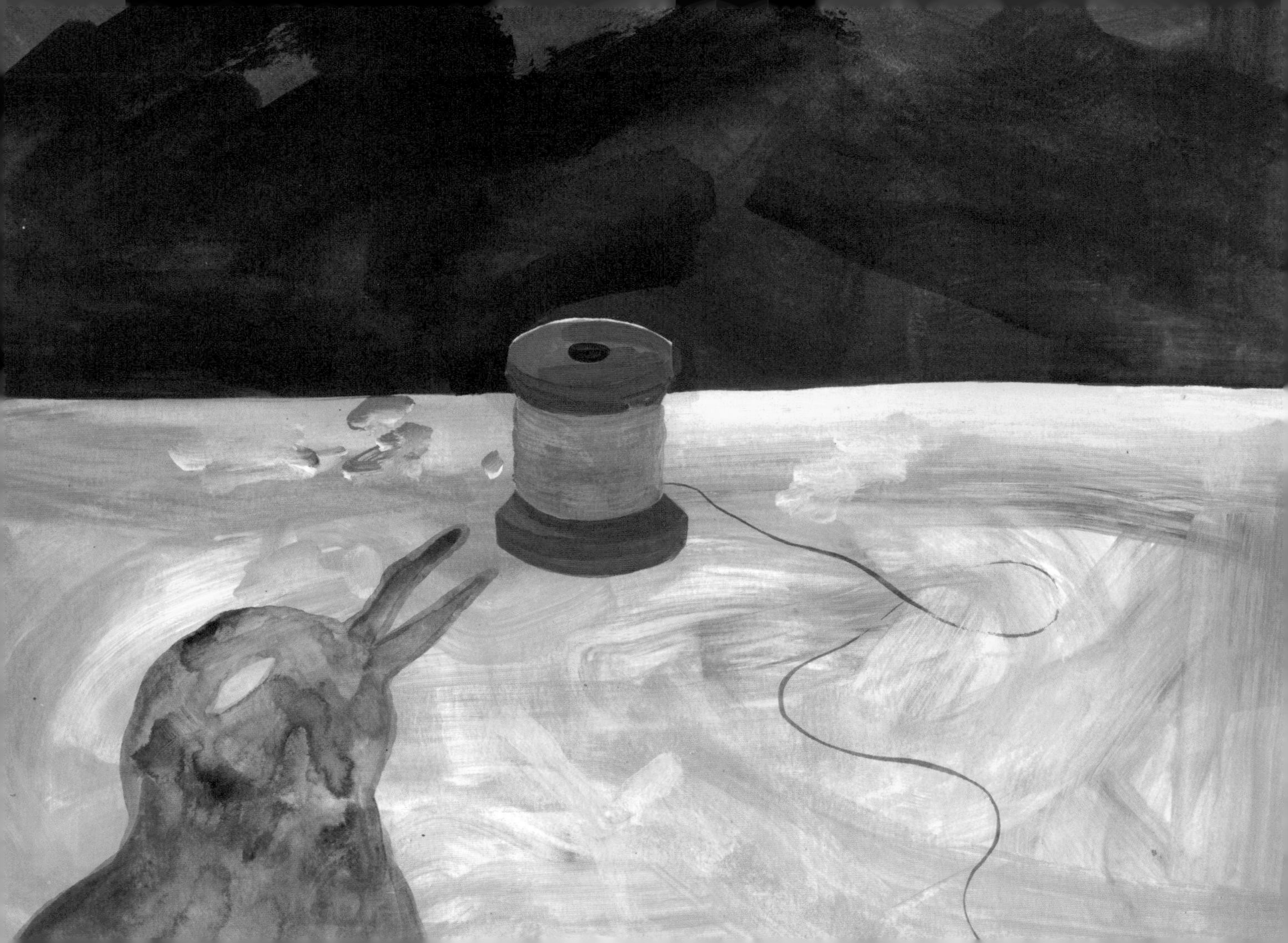

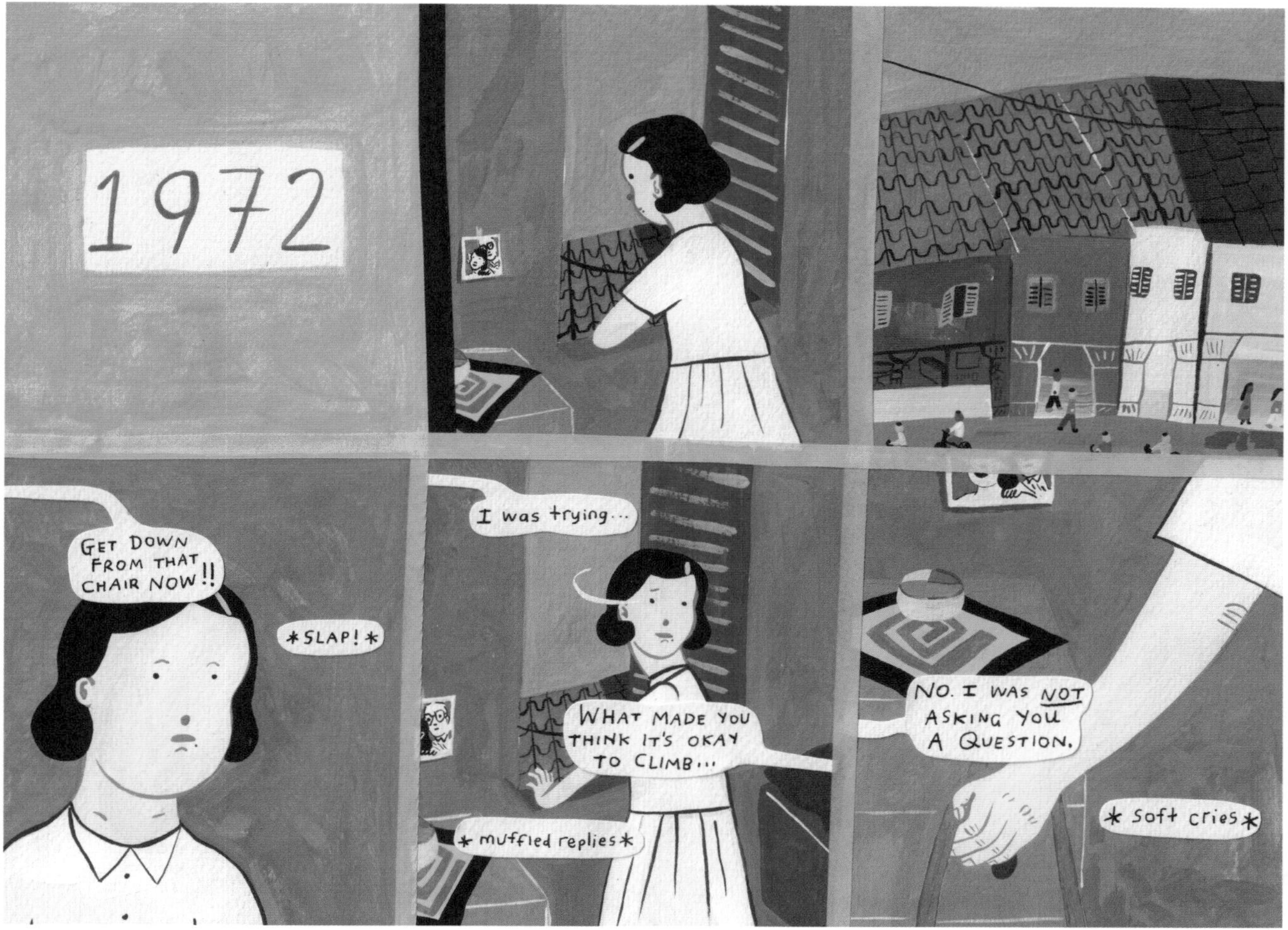
1972
GET DOWN FROM THAT CHAIR NOW!!
SLAP!
I was trying...
WHAT MADE YOU THINK IT'S OKAY TO CLIMB...
* muffled replies*
NO. I WAS NOT ASKING YOU A QUESTION.
* soft cries*

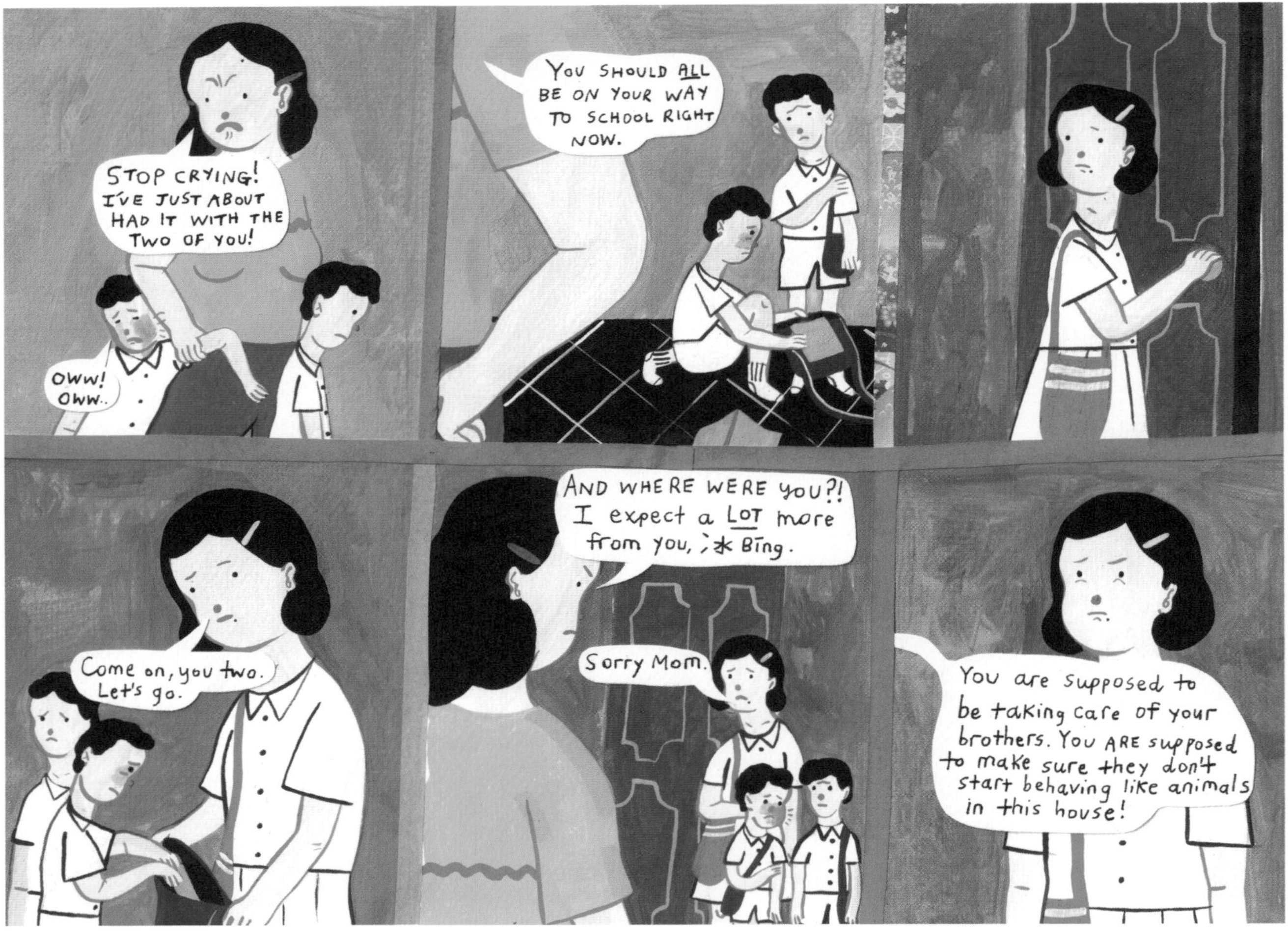
STOP CRYING! I'VE JUST ABOUT HAD IT WITH THE TWO OF YOU!
OWW! OWW..
YOU SHOULD ALL BE ON YOUR WAY TO SCHOOL RIGHT NOW.
AND WHERE WERE YOU?! I expect a LOT more from you, 冰 Bīng.
Come on, you two. Let's go.
Sorry Mom.
You are supposed to be taking care of your brothers. You ARE supposed to make sure they don't start behaving like animals in this house!

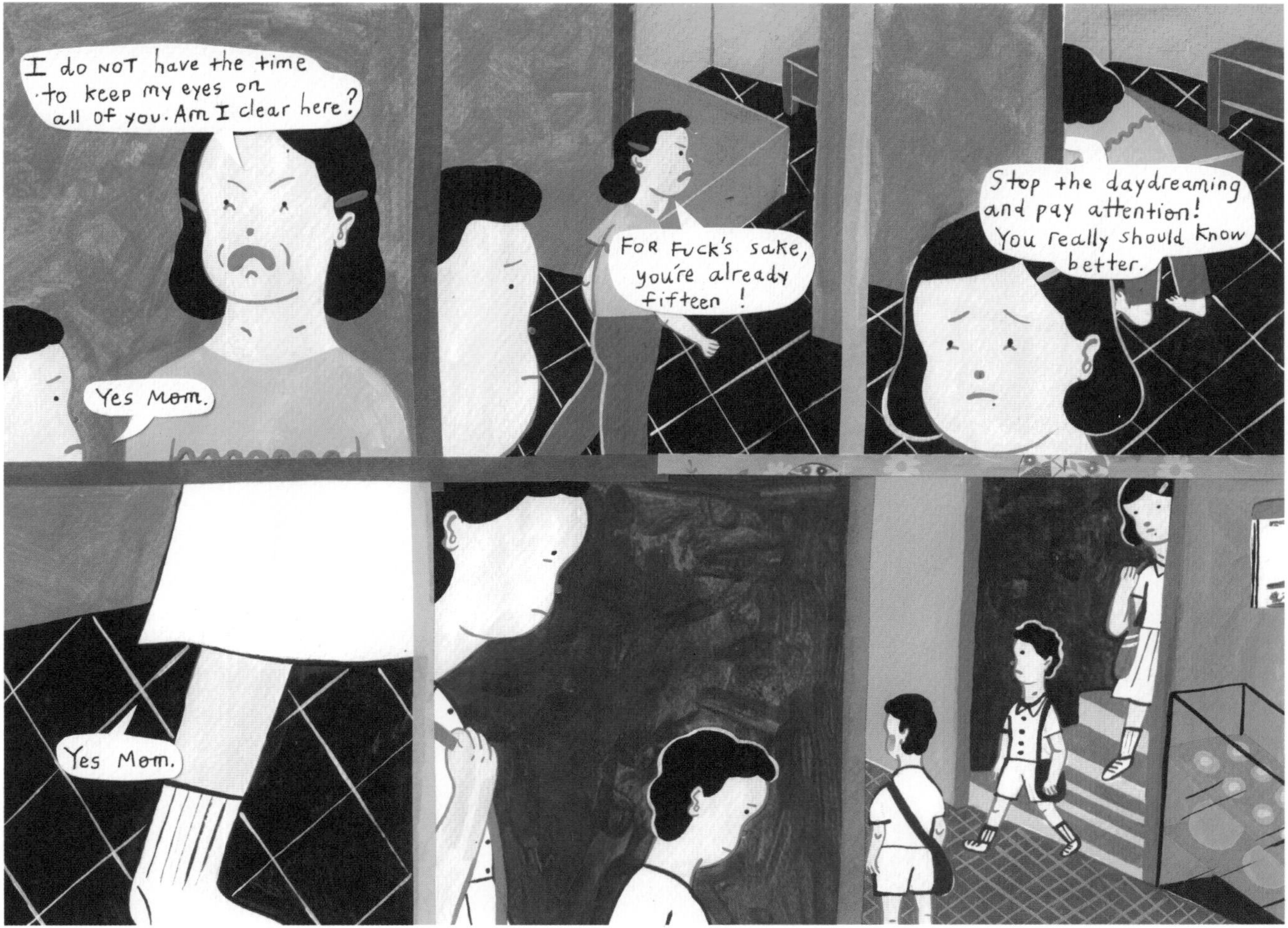
I do NOT have the time to keep my eyes on all of you. Am I clear here?
Yes Mom.
FOR FUCK'S sake, you're already fifteen !
Stop the daydreaming and pay attention! You really should know better.
Yes Mom.

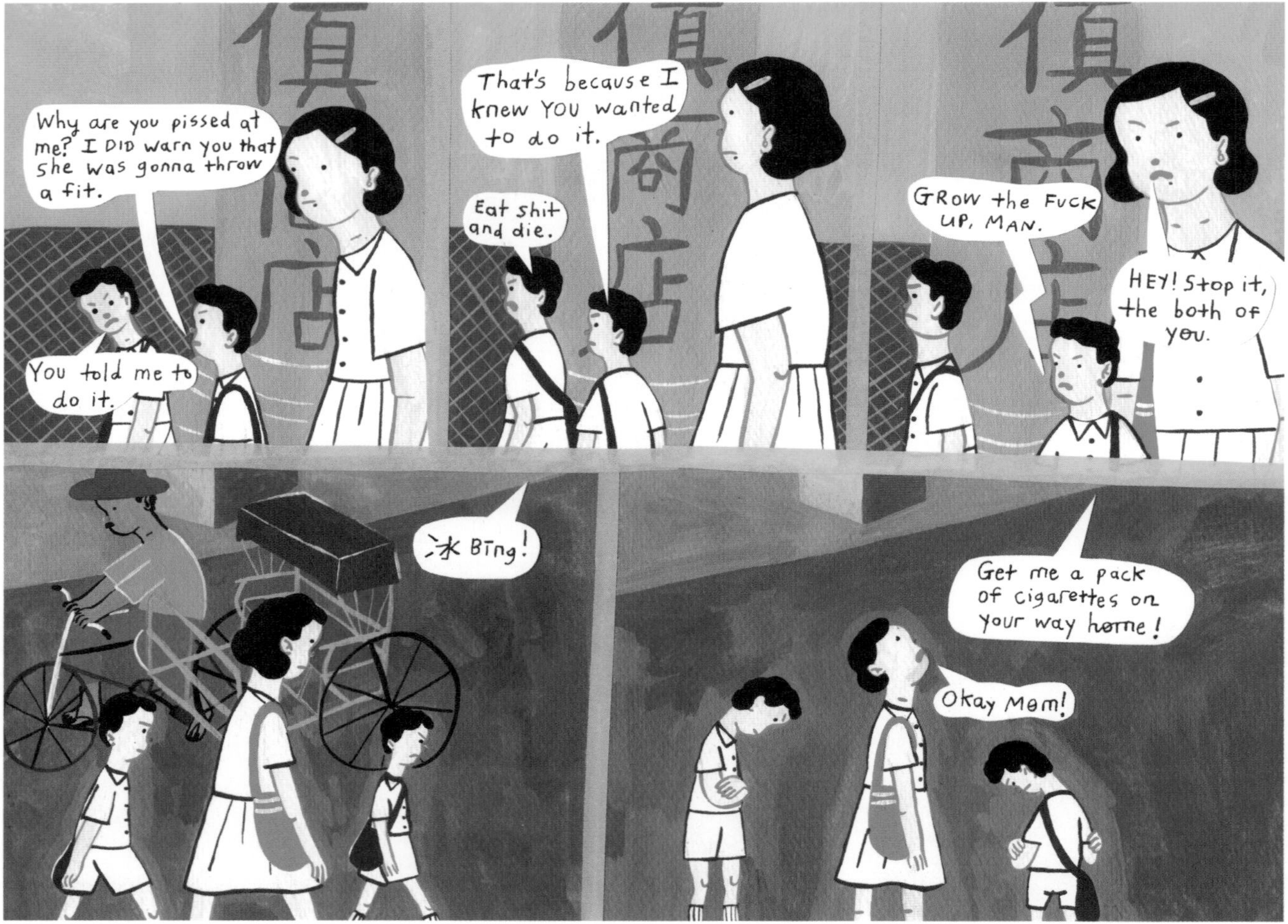
Why are you pissed at me? I DID warn you that she was gonna throw a fit.
You told me to do it.
That's because I knew YOU wanted to do it.
Eat shit and die.
GROW the FUCK UP, MAN.
HEY! Stop it, the both of you.
冰 Bīng!
Get me a pack of cigarettes on your way home!
Okay Mom!

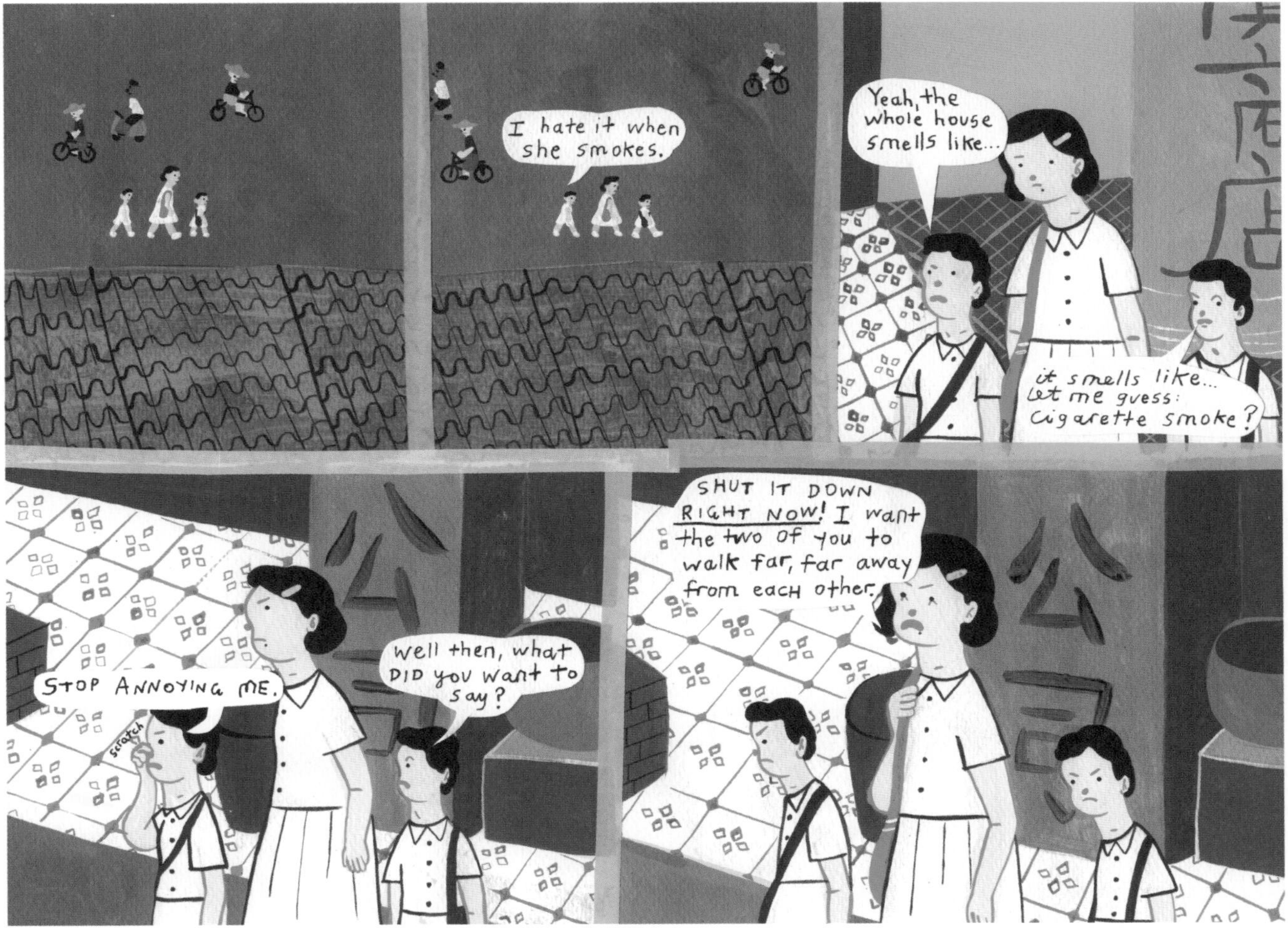
I hate it when she smokes.
Yeah, the whole house smells like...
it smells like... Let me guess: cigarette smoke?
STOP ANNOYING ME.
scratch
Well then, what DID you want to say?
SHUT IT DOWN RIGHT NOW! I want the two of you to walk far, far away from each other.

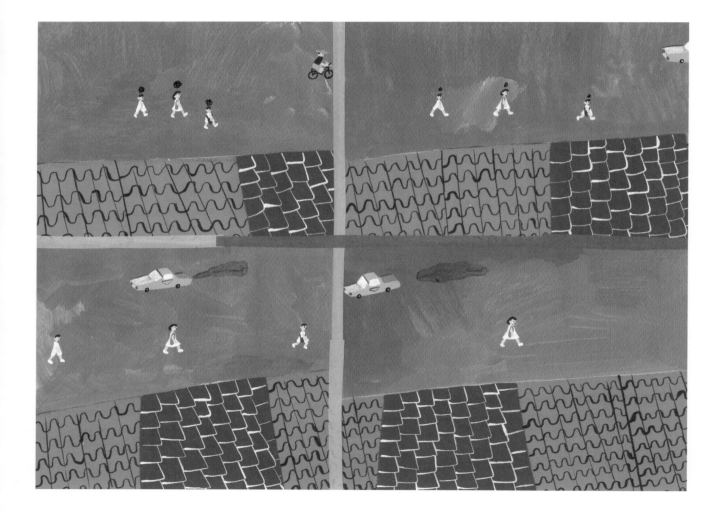

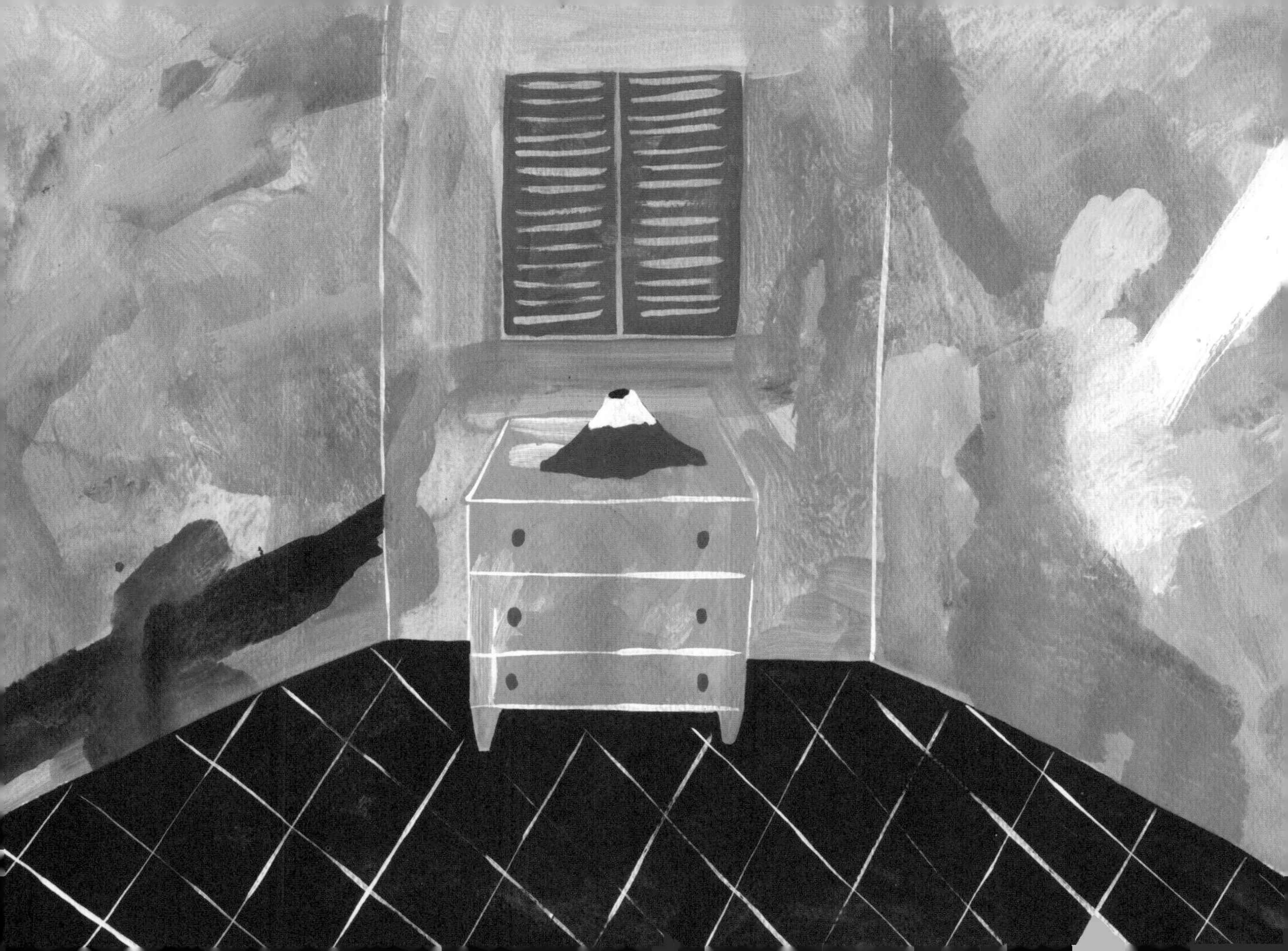

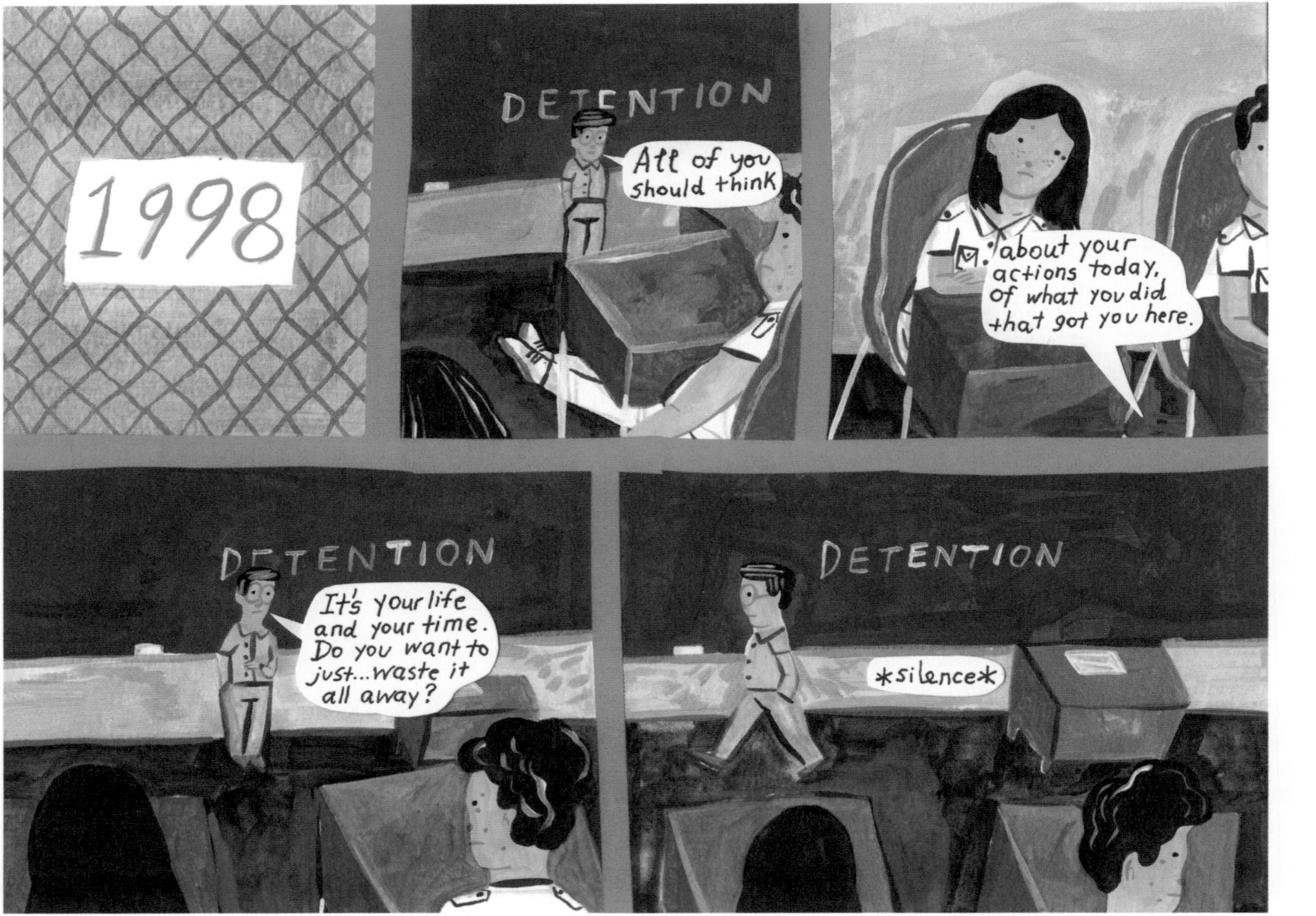
1998
DETENTION
All of you should think
about your actions today, of what you did that got you here.
DETENTION
It's your life and your time. Do you want to just...waste it all away?
DETENTION
silence

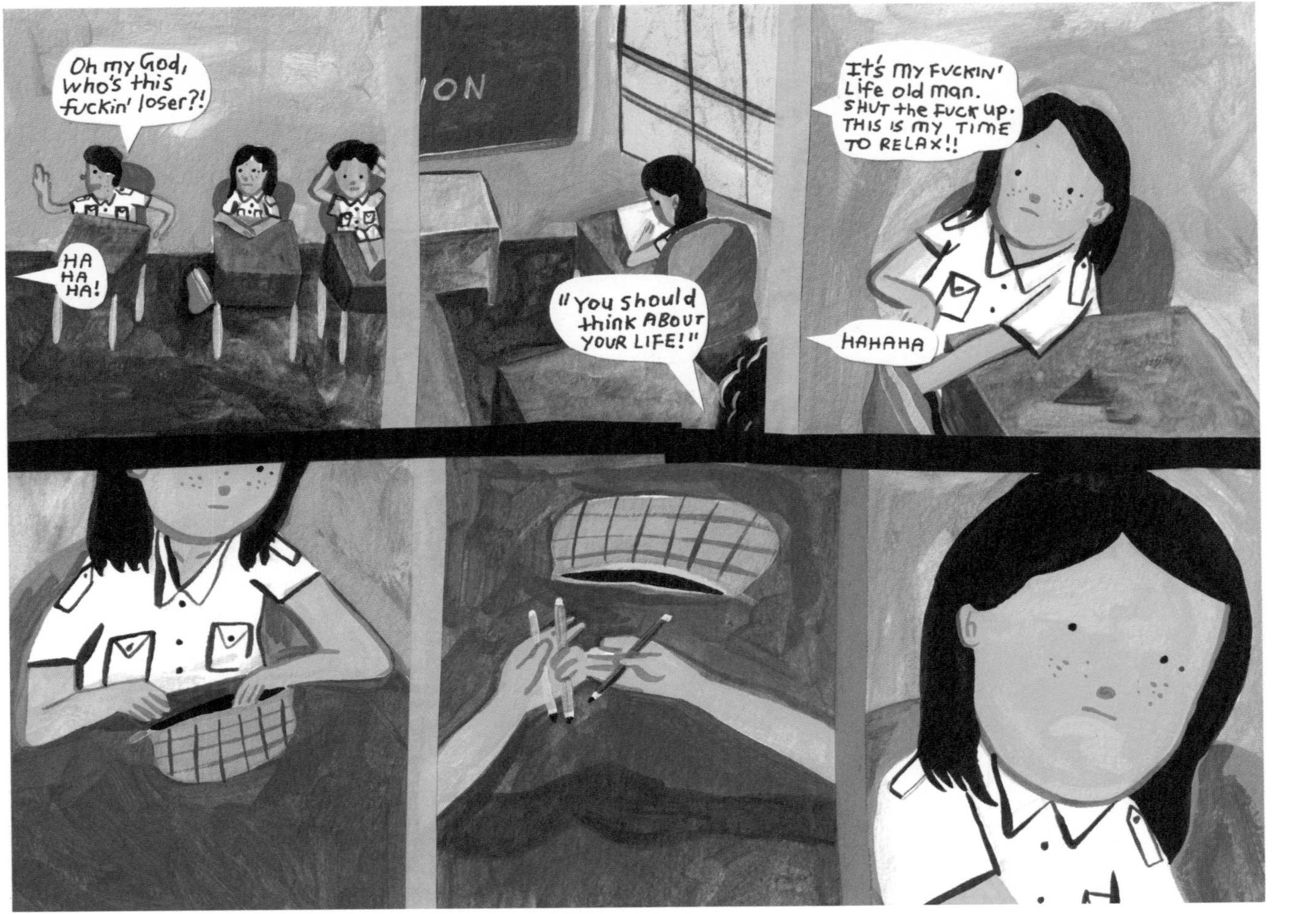

Oh my God, who's this fuckin' loser?!
HA HA HA!
ON
"You should think ABOUT YOUR LIFE!"
It's my FUCKIN' Life old man. SHUT the FUCK up. THIS IS MY TIME TO RELAX!!
HAHAHA

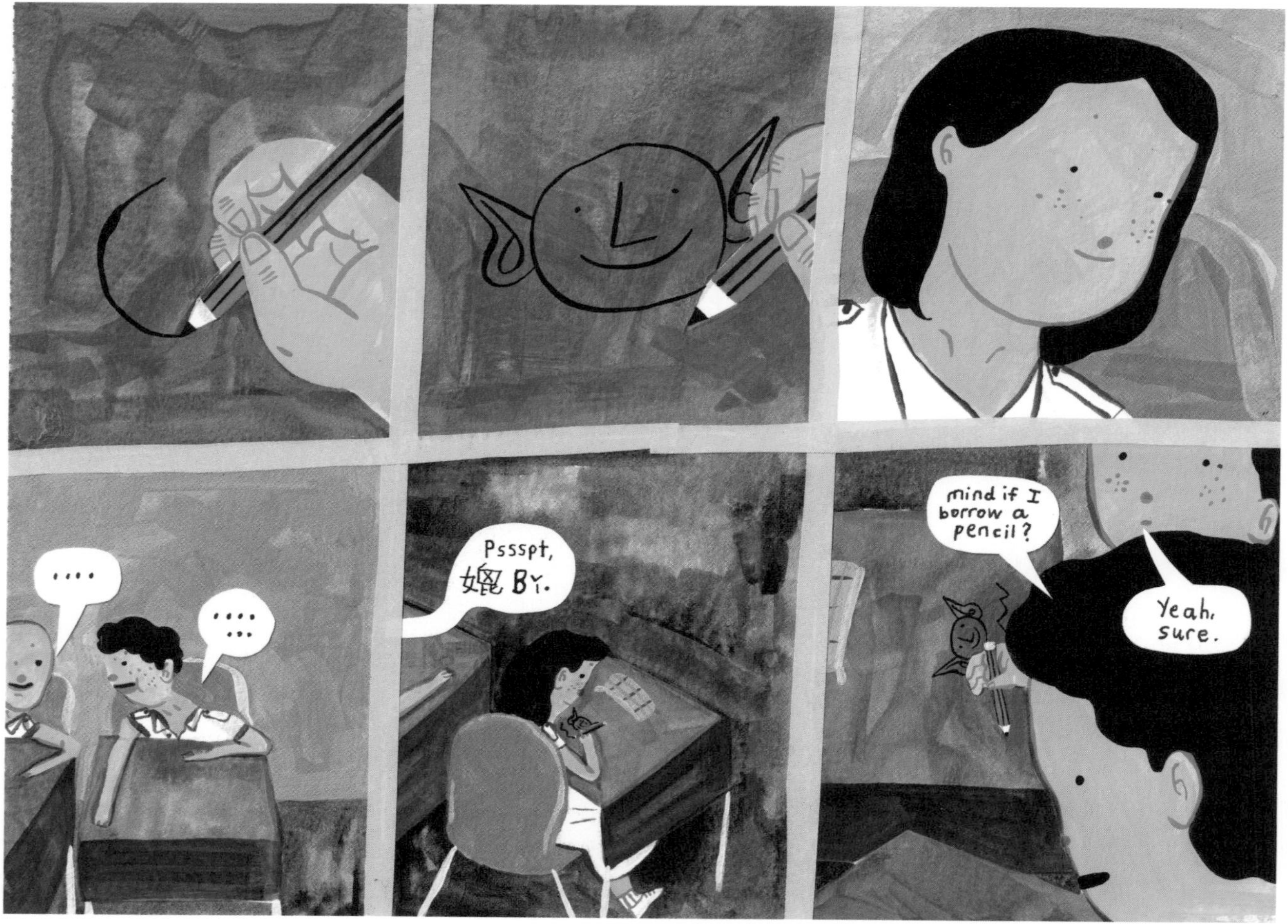
....
.....
Pssspt,
媲 BY.
mind if I borrow a pencil?
Yeah, sure.

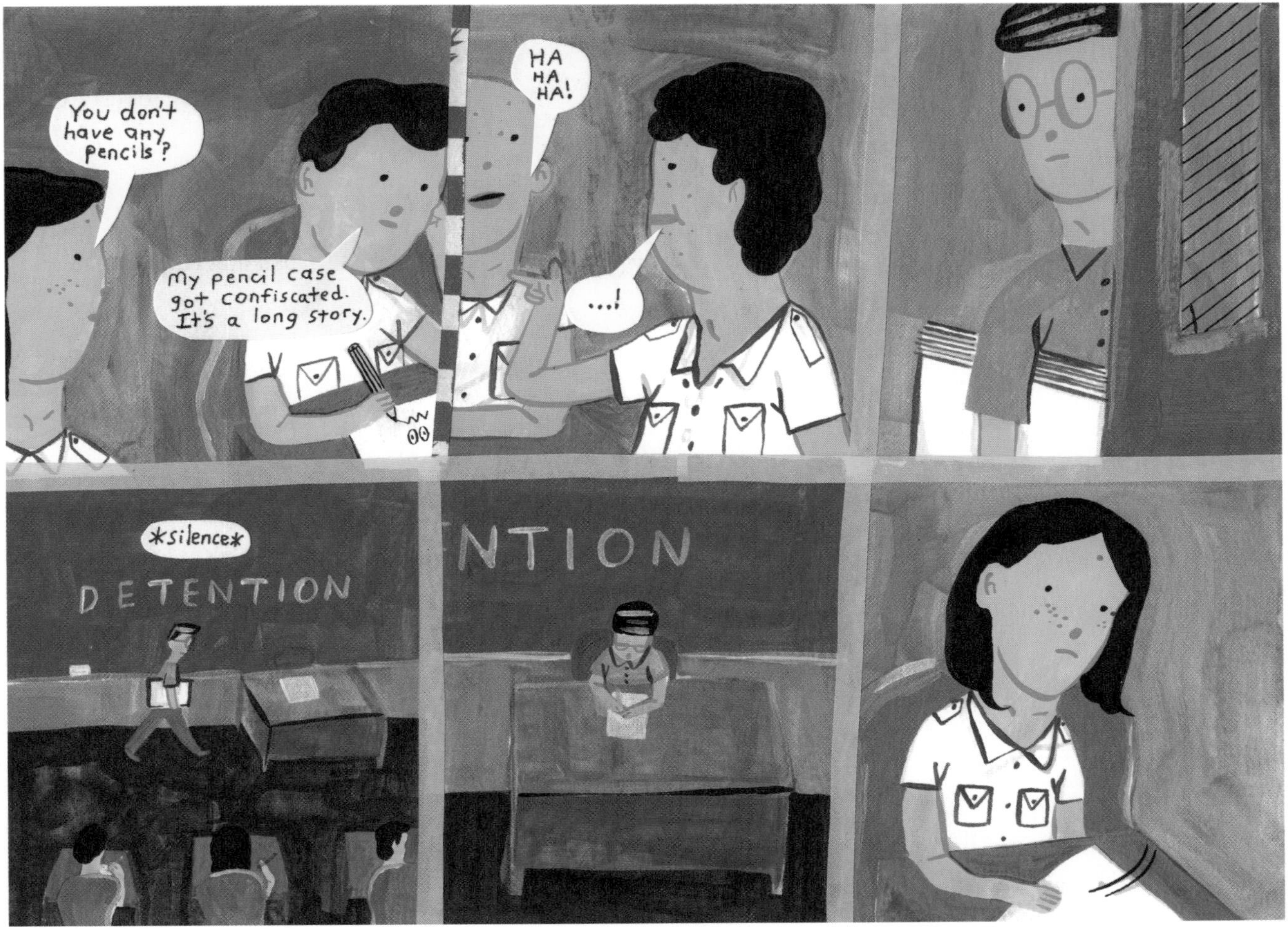
You don't have any pencils?
My pencil case got confiscated. It's a long story.
HA HA HA!
...!
silence
DETENTION
NTION

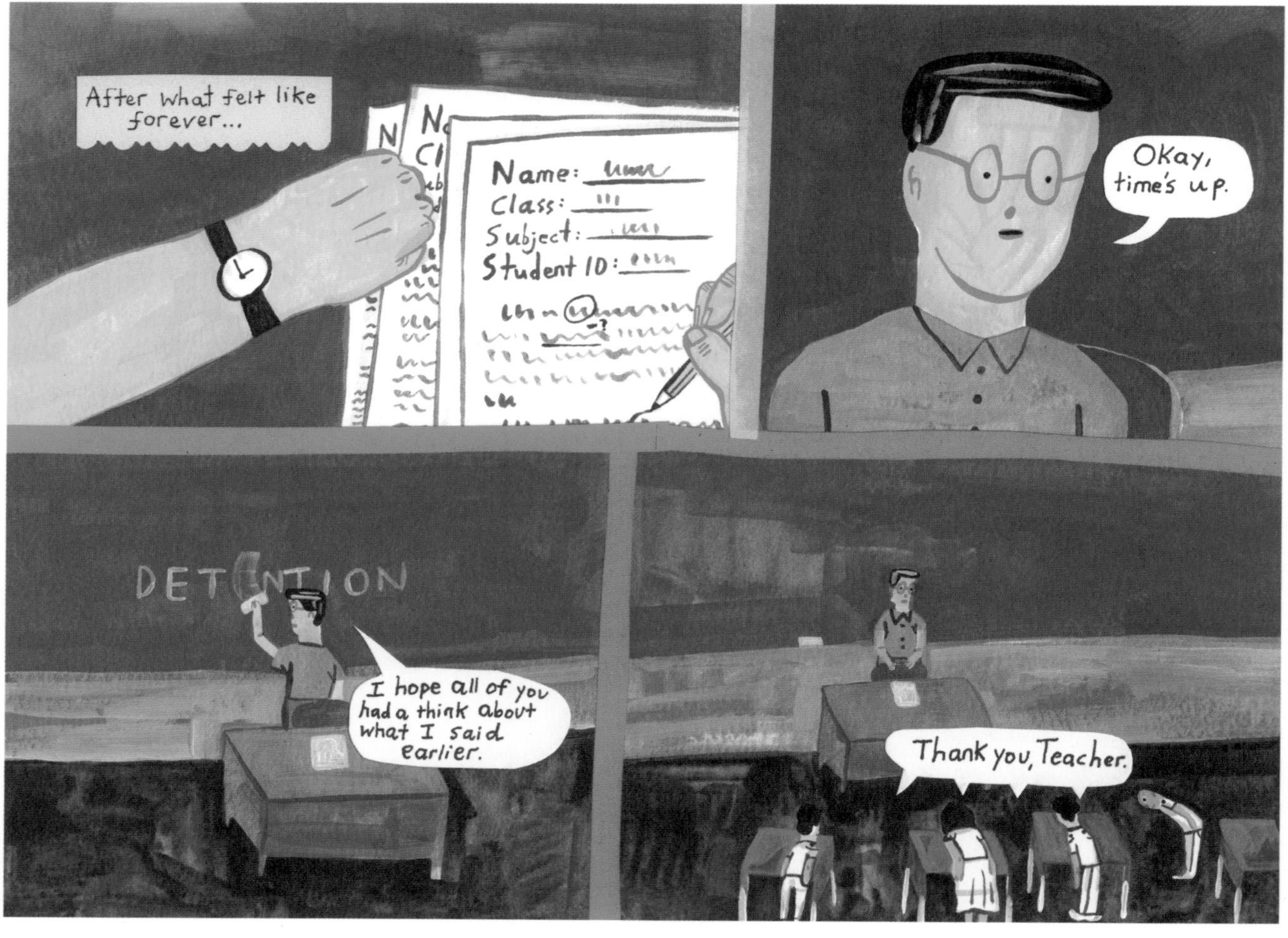
After what felt like forever...
Name:
Class:
Subject:
Student ID:
Okay, time's up.
DETENTION
I hope all of you had a think about what I said earlier.
Thank you, Teacher.

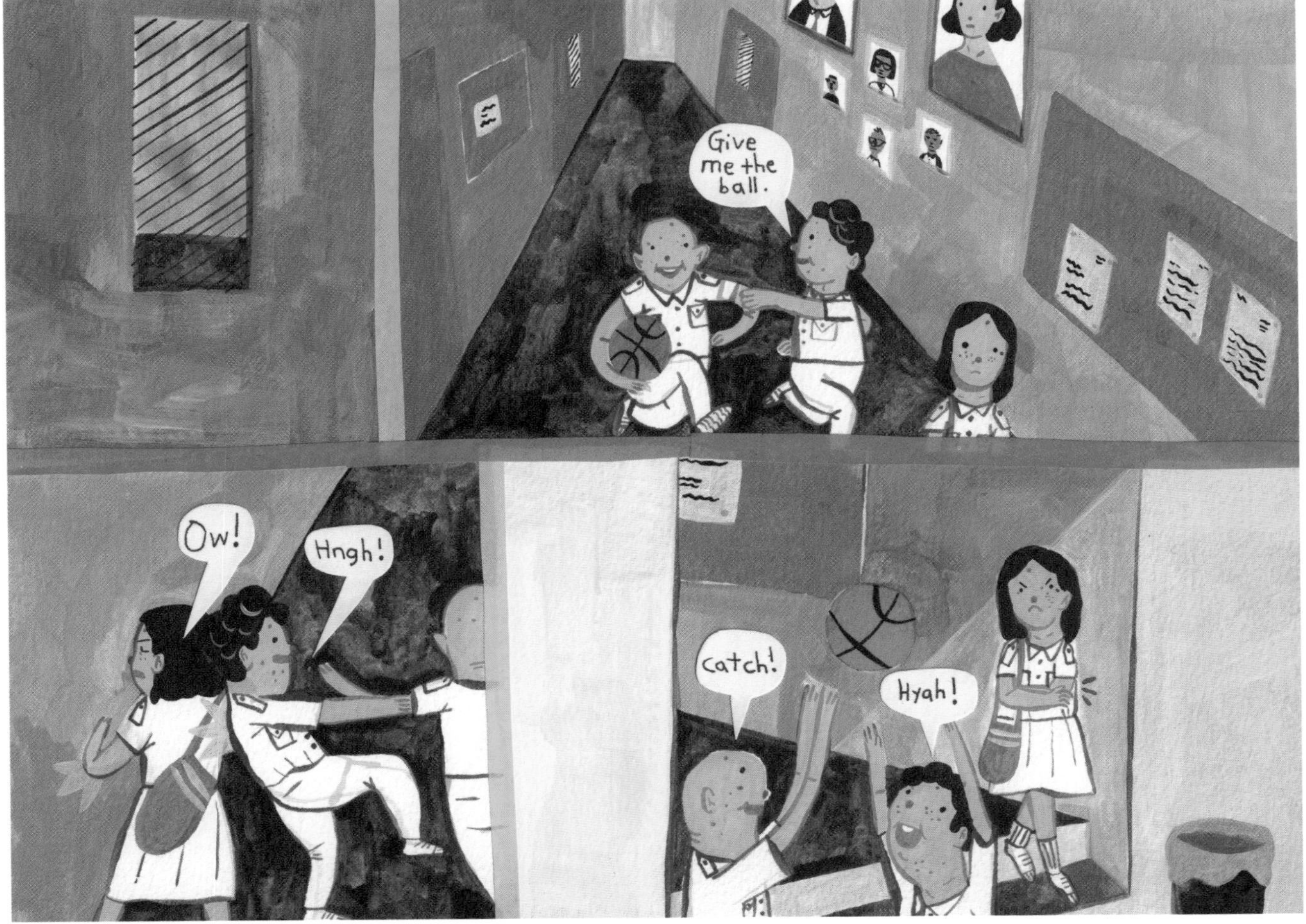
Give me the ball.
Ow!
Hngh!
catch!
Hyah!

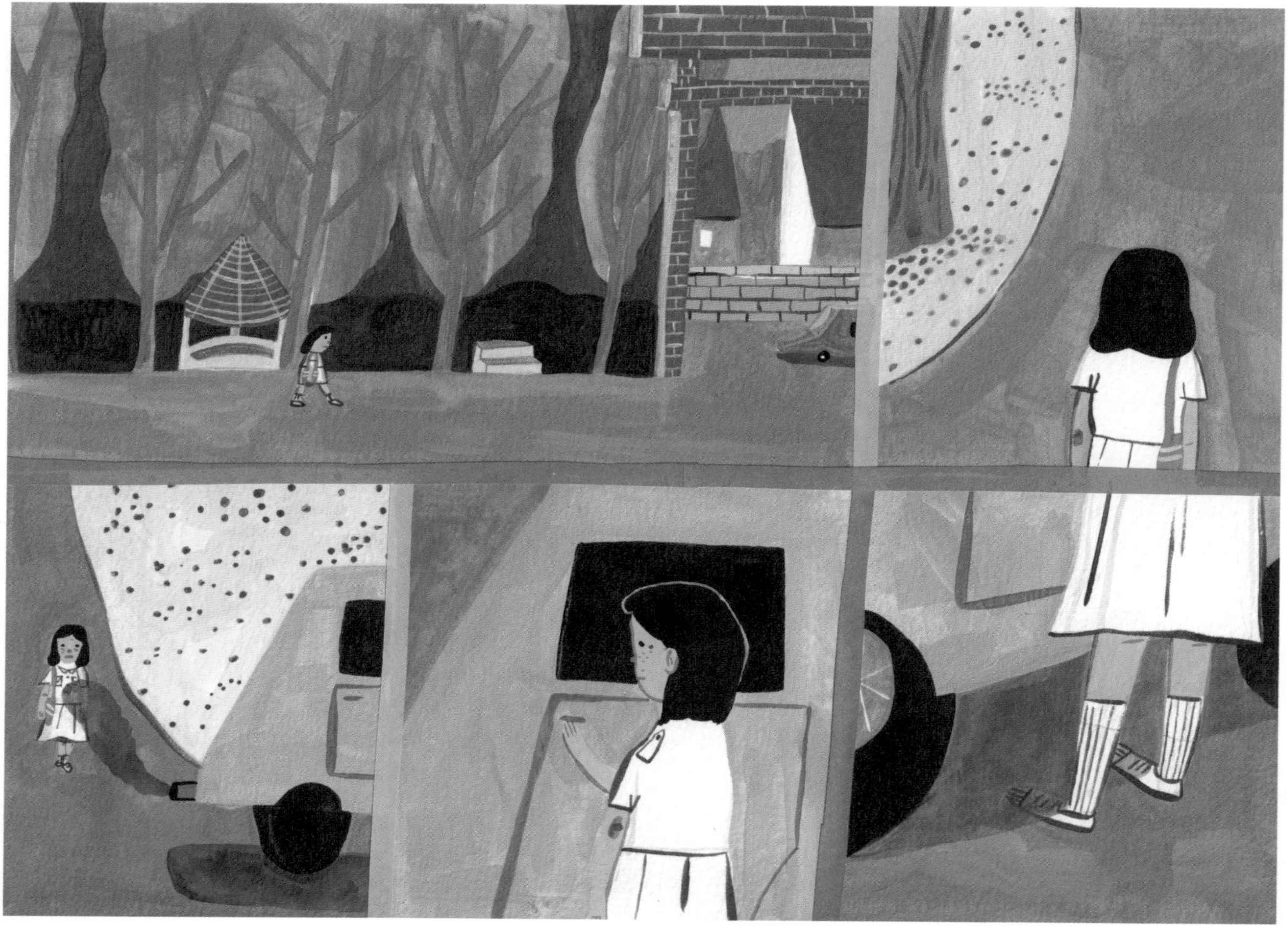

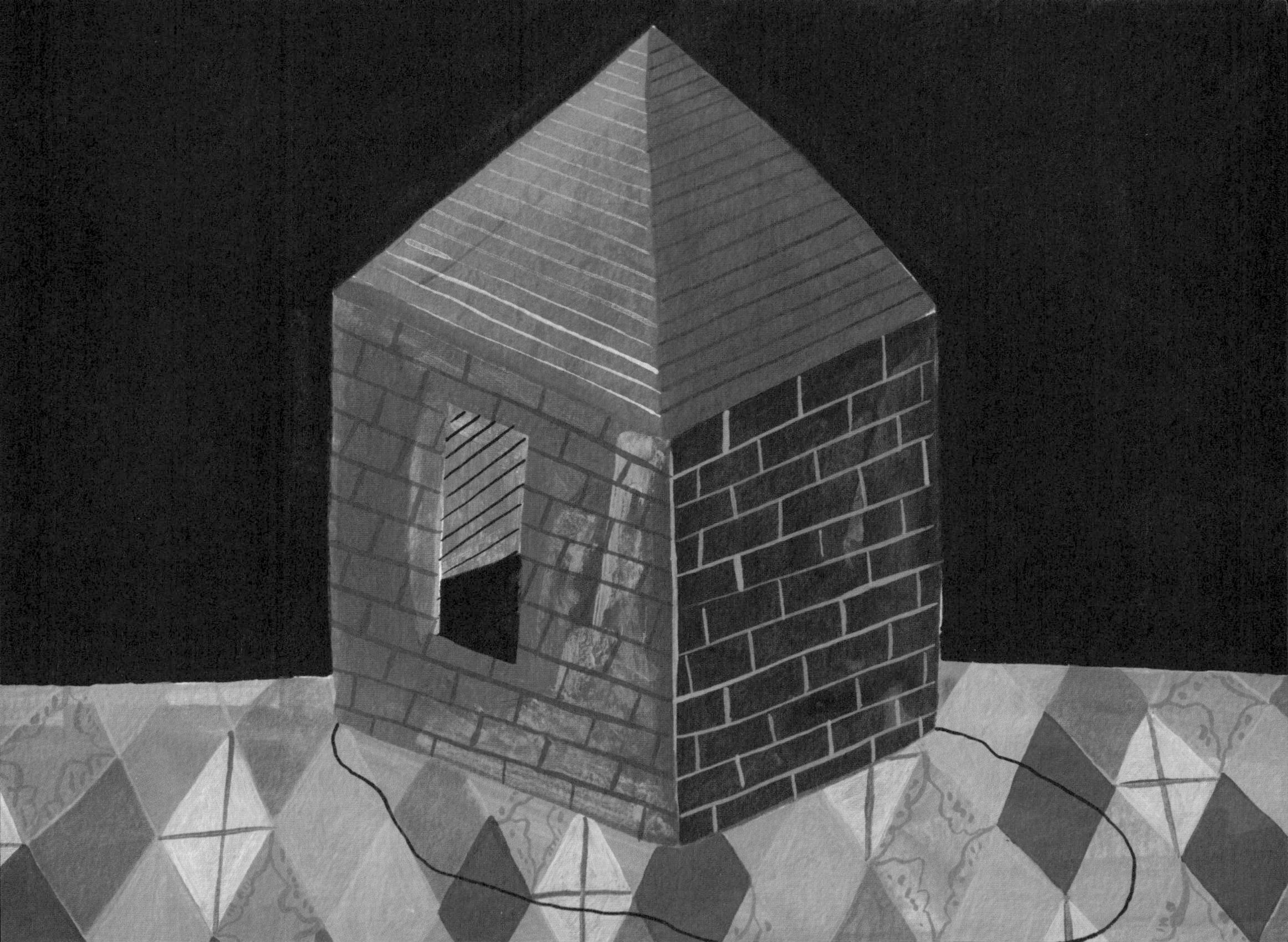

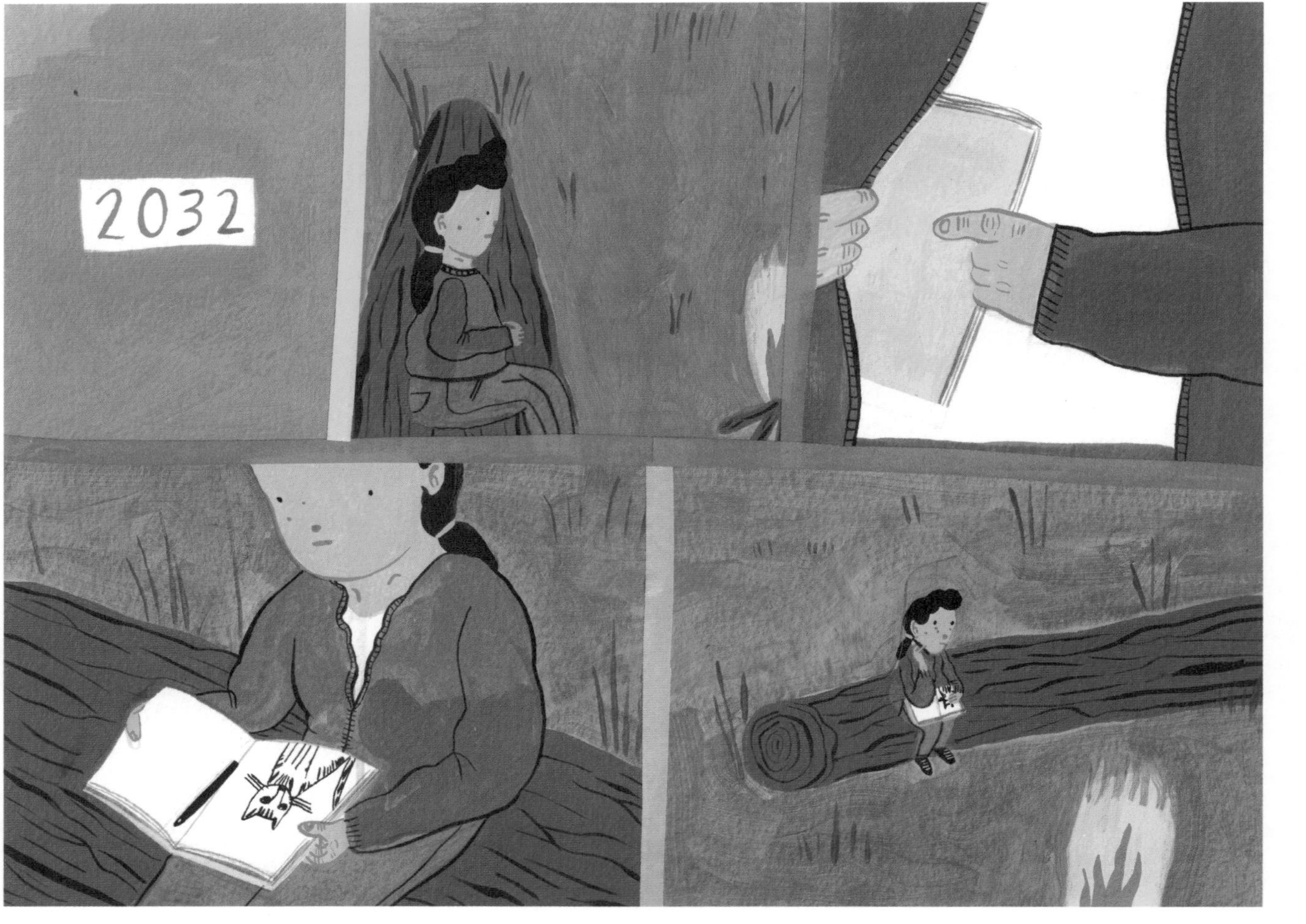
2032

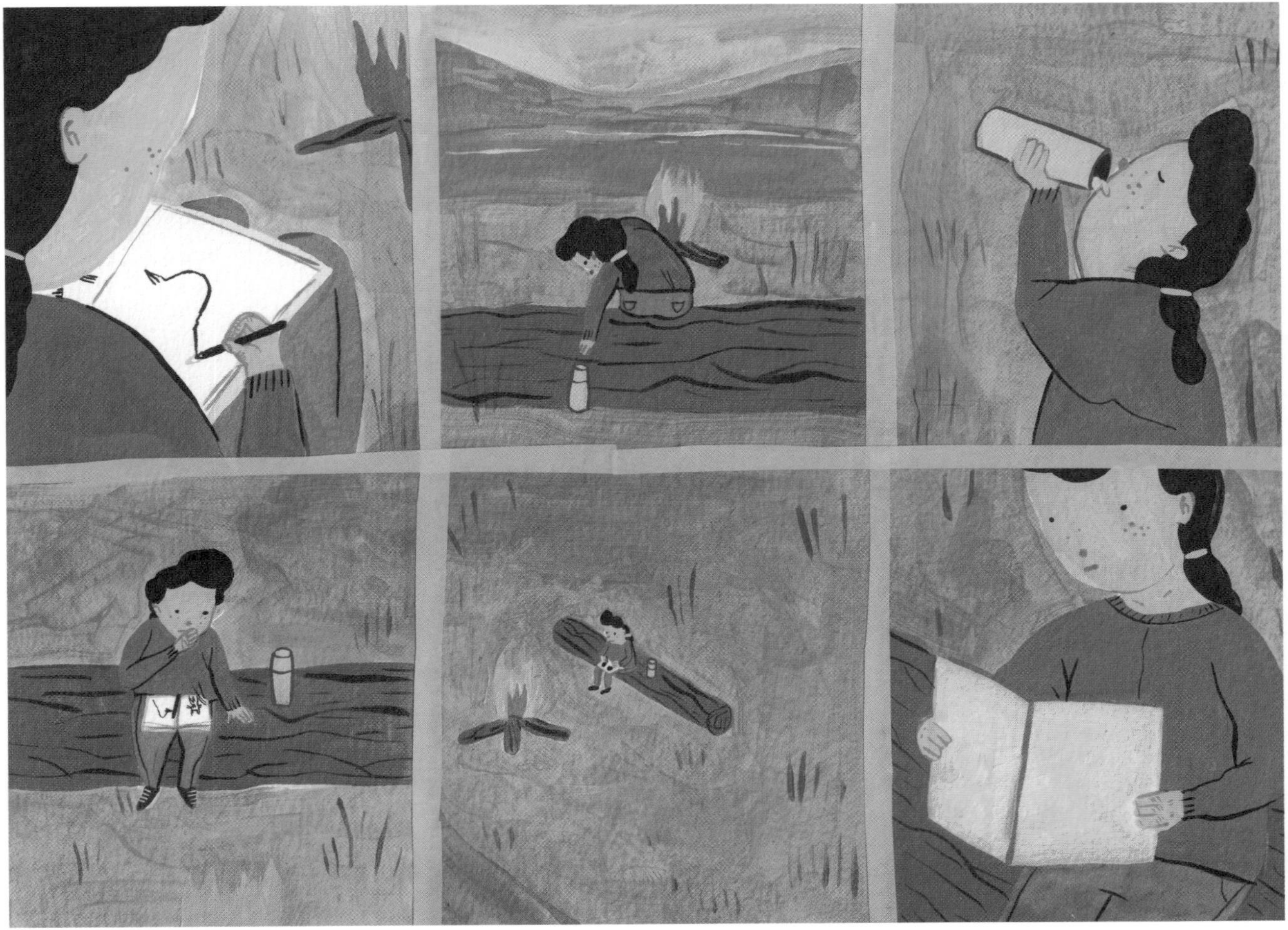

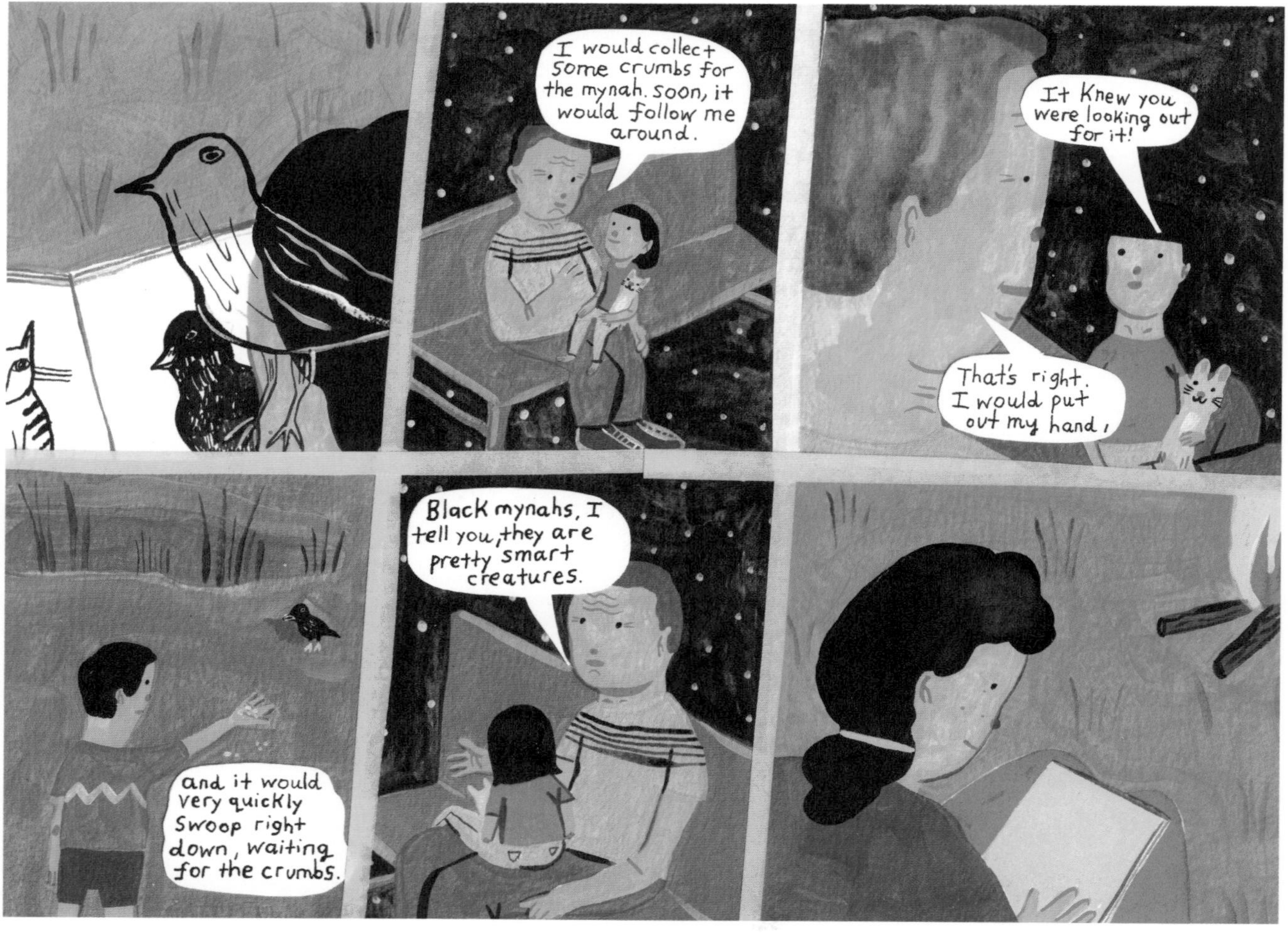
I would collect some crumbs for the mynah. soon, it would follow me around.
It Knew you were looking out for it!
That's right. I would put out my hand,
and it would very quickly swoop right down, waiting for the crumbs.
Black mynahs, I tell you, they are pretty smart creatures.

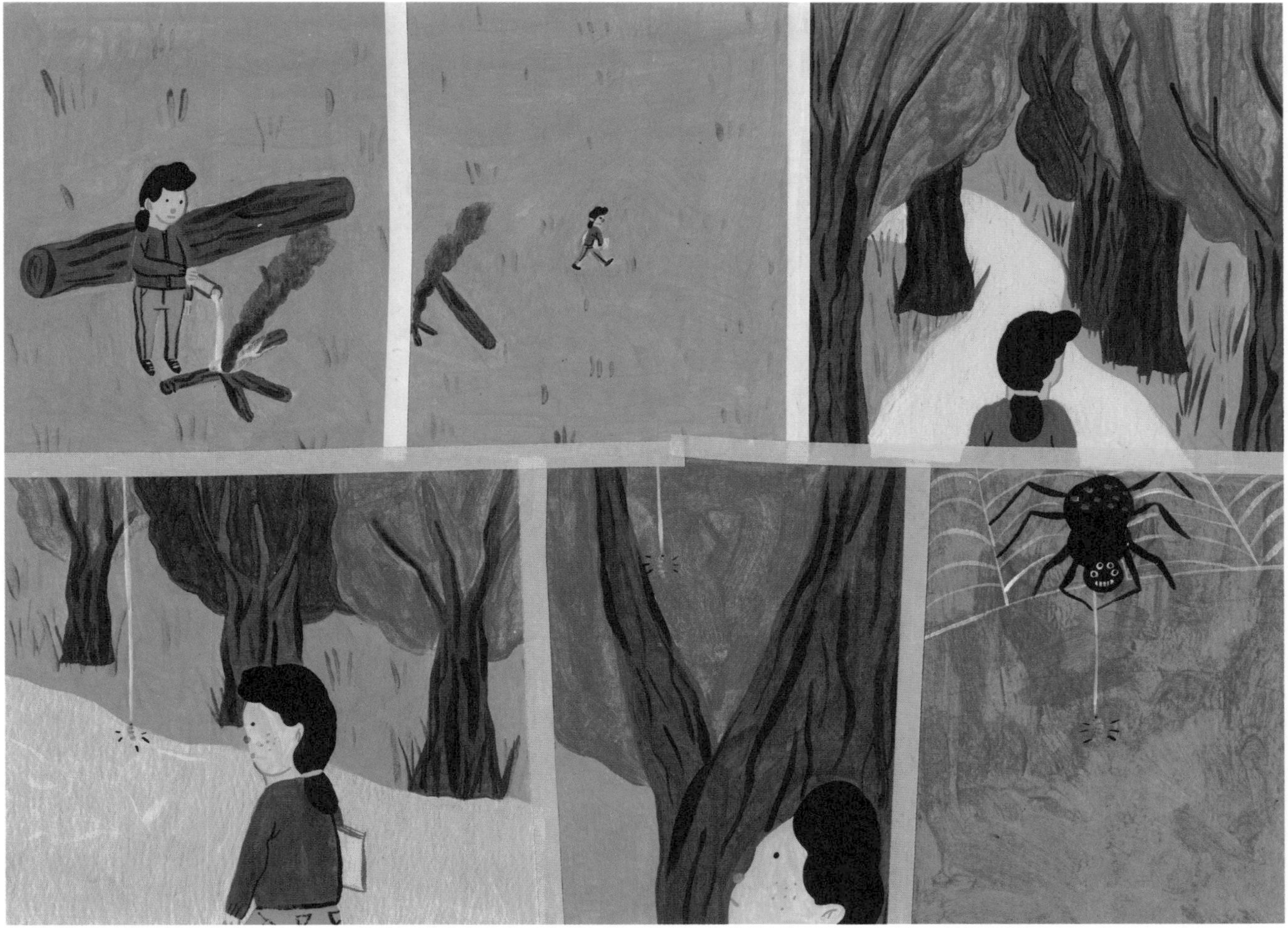

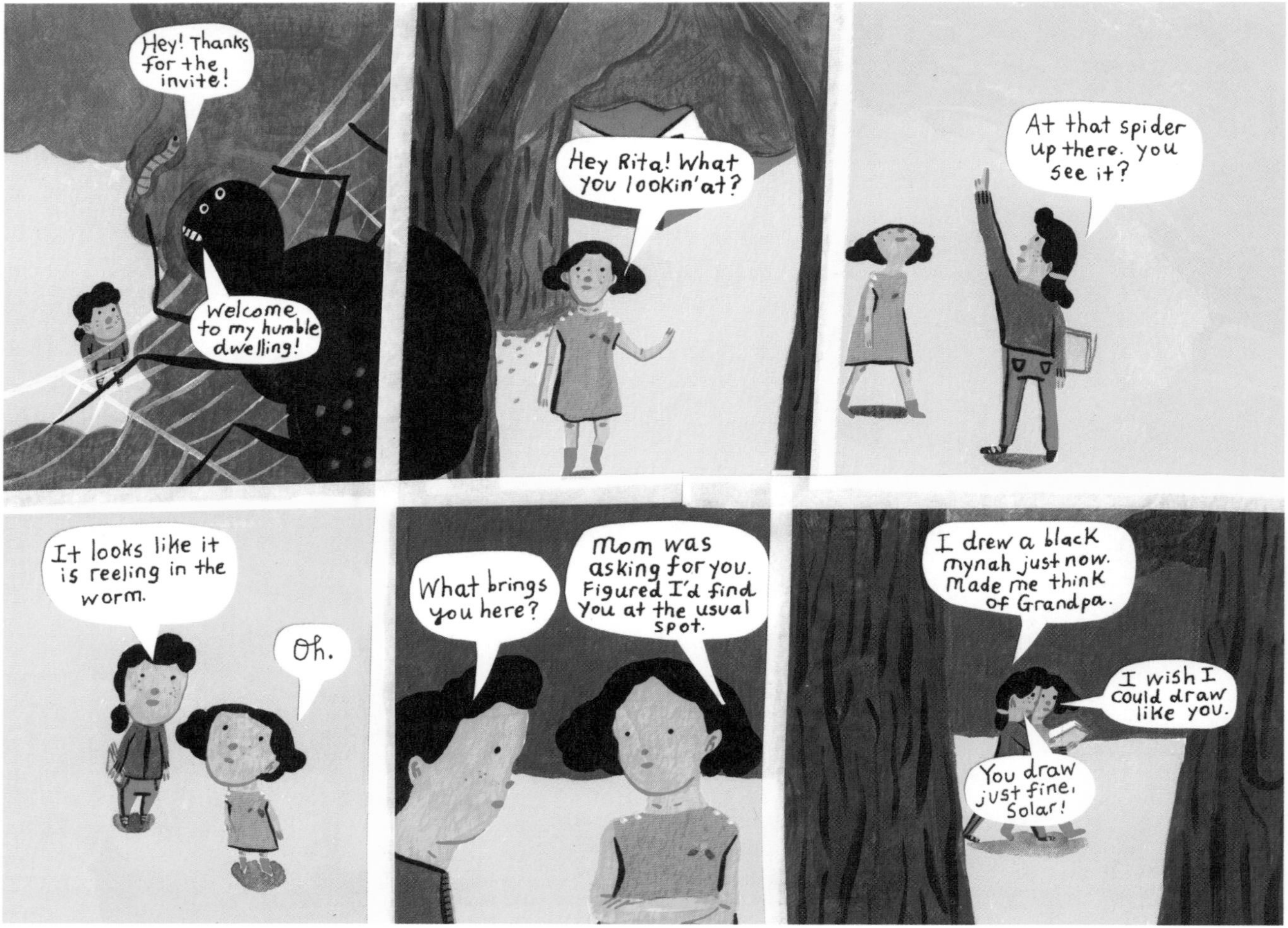
Hey! Thanks for the invite!
Welcome to my humble dwelling!
Hey Rita! What you lookin' at?
At that spider up there. you see it?
It looks like it is reeling in the worm.
Oh.
What brings you here?
Mom was asking for you. Figured I'd find you at the usual spot.
I drew a black mynah just now. Made me think of Grandpa.
I wish I could draw like you.
You draw just fine, Solar!

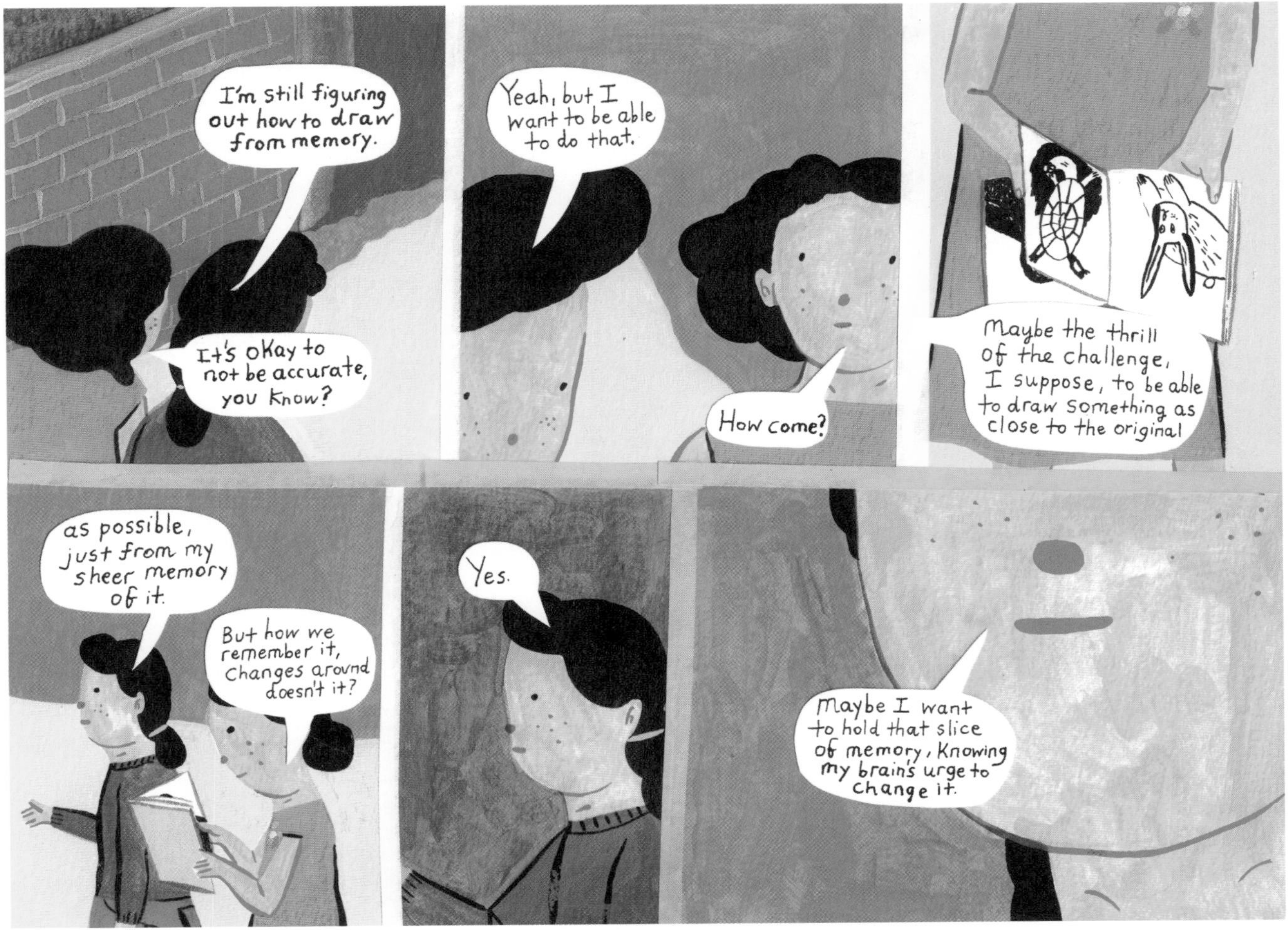
I'm still figuring out how to draw from memory.
It's okay to not be accurate, you know?
Yeah, but I want to be able to do that.
How come?
Maybe the thrill of the challenge, I suppose, to be able to draw something as close to the original
as possible, just from my sheer memory of it.
But how we remember it, changes around doesn't it?
Yes.
Maybe I want to hold that slice of memory, knowing my brain's urge to change it.

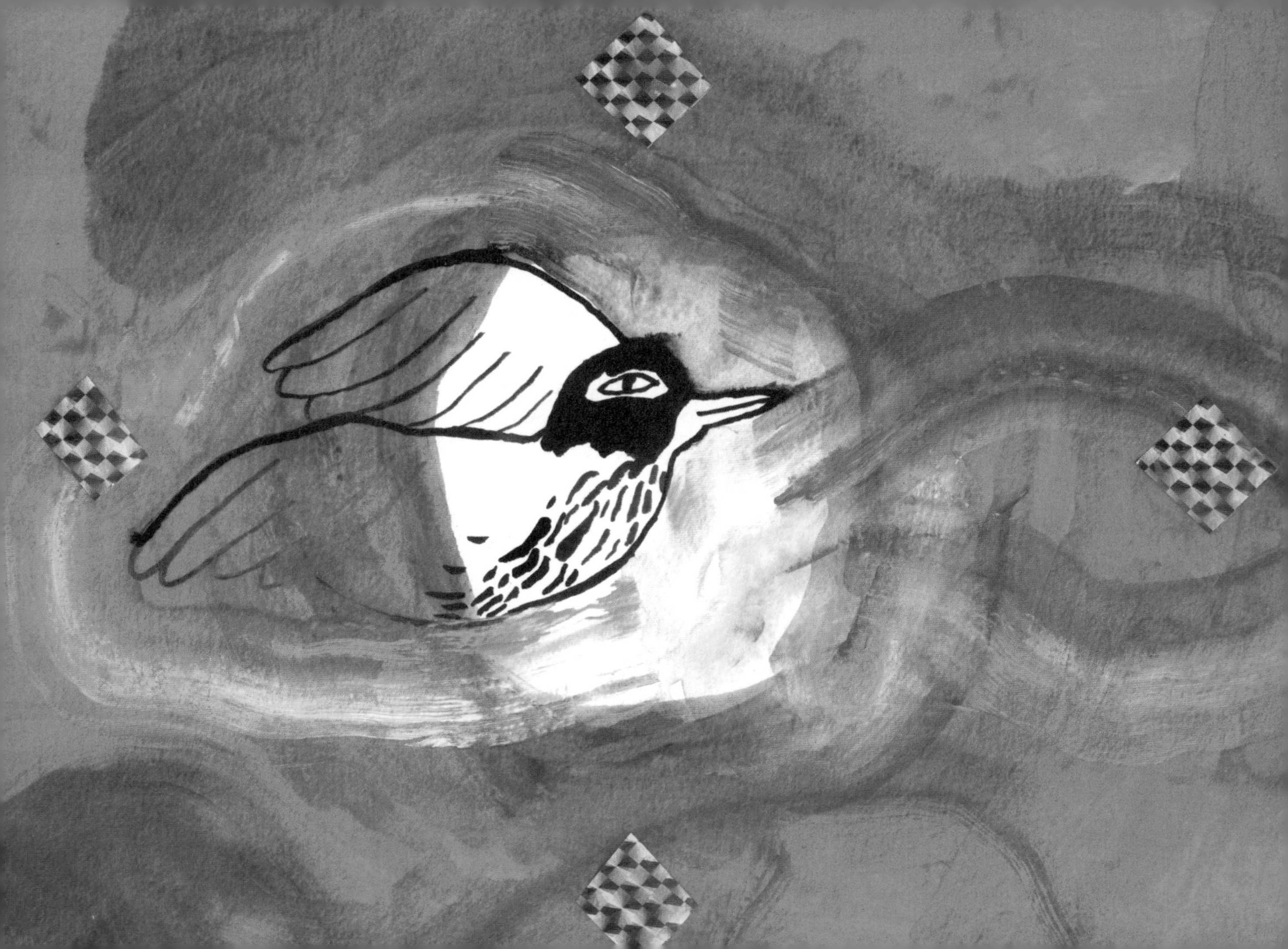

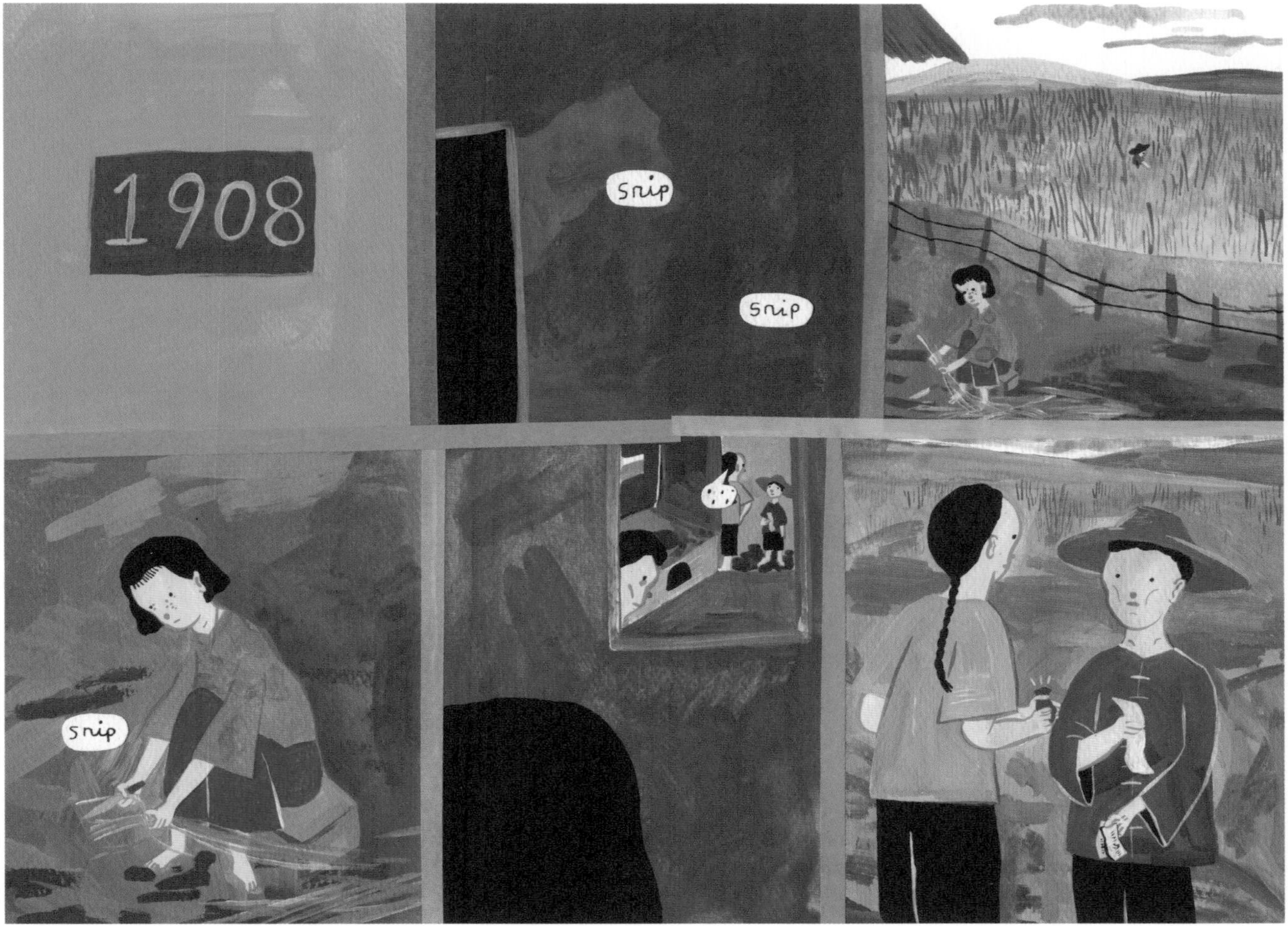
1908
snip
snip
snip

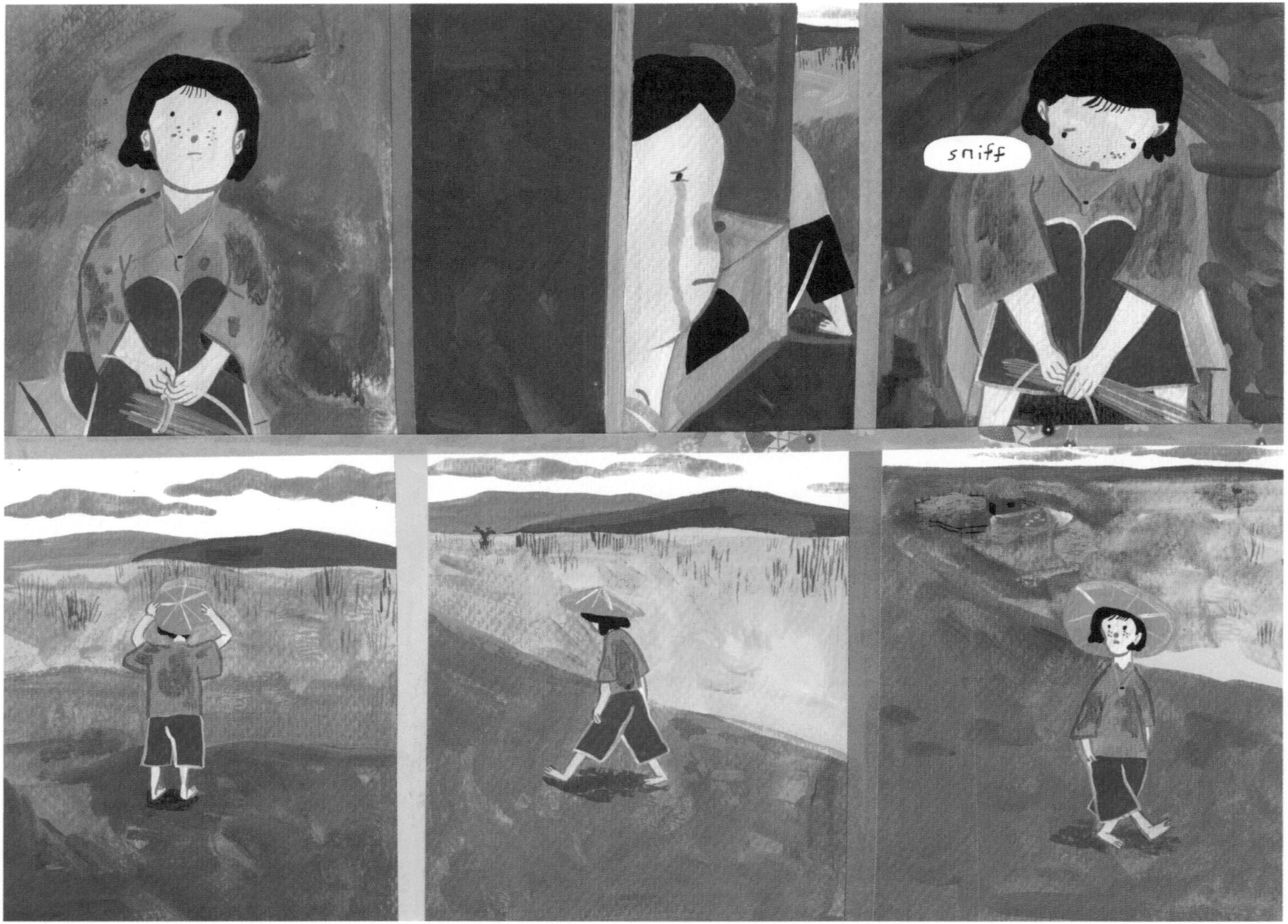
sniff

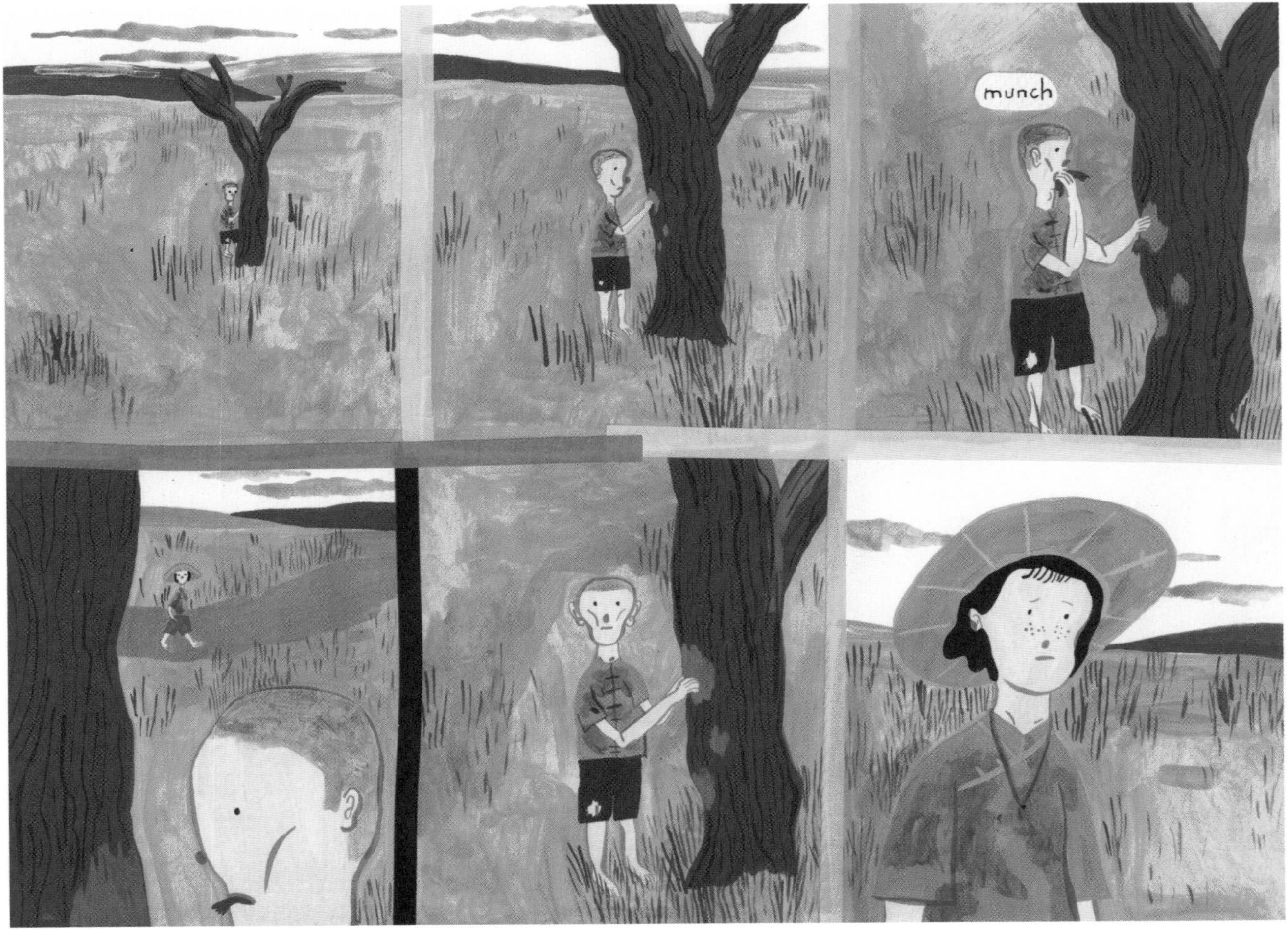
munch

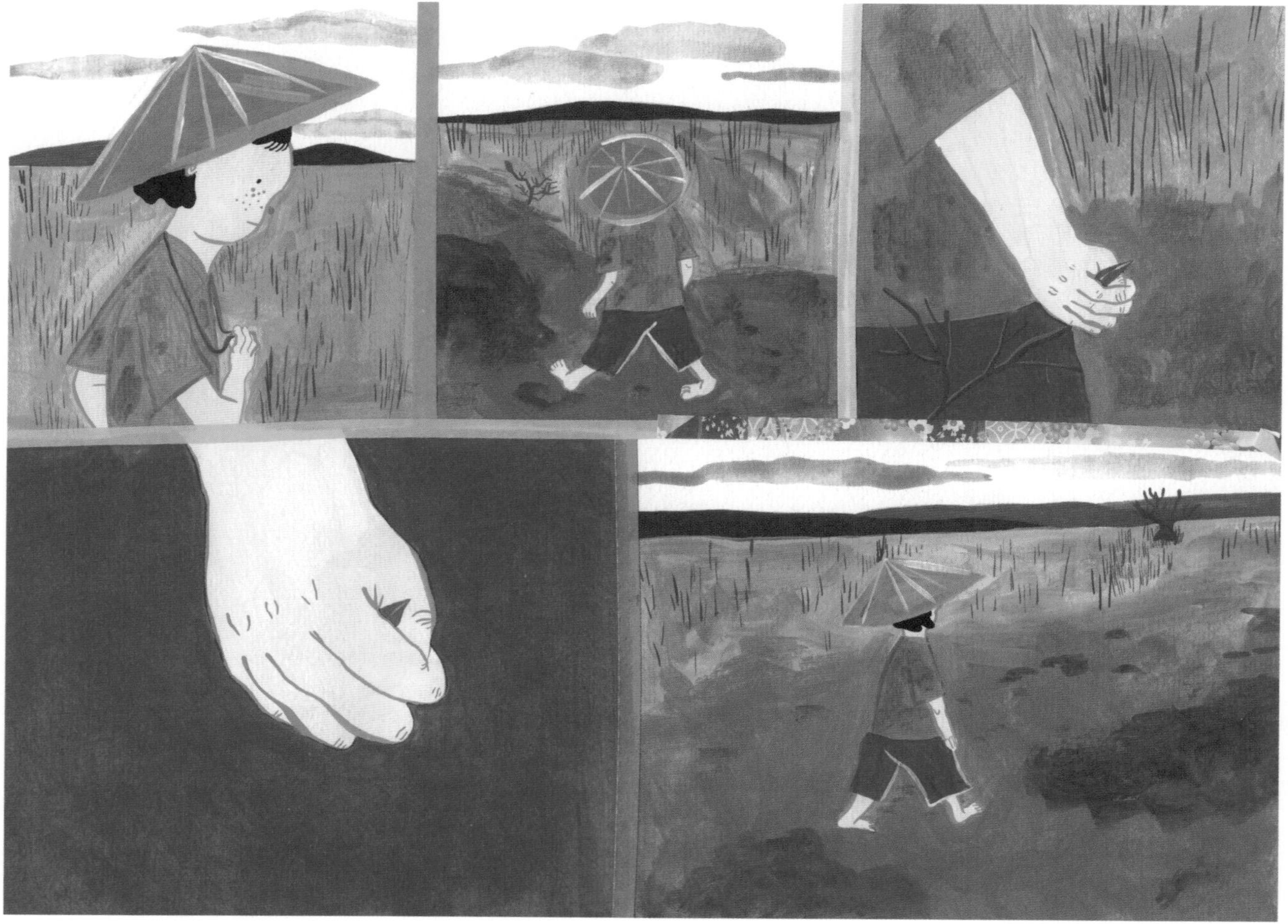

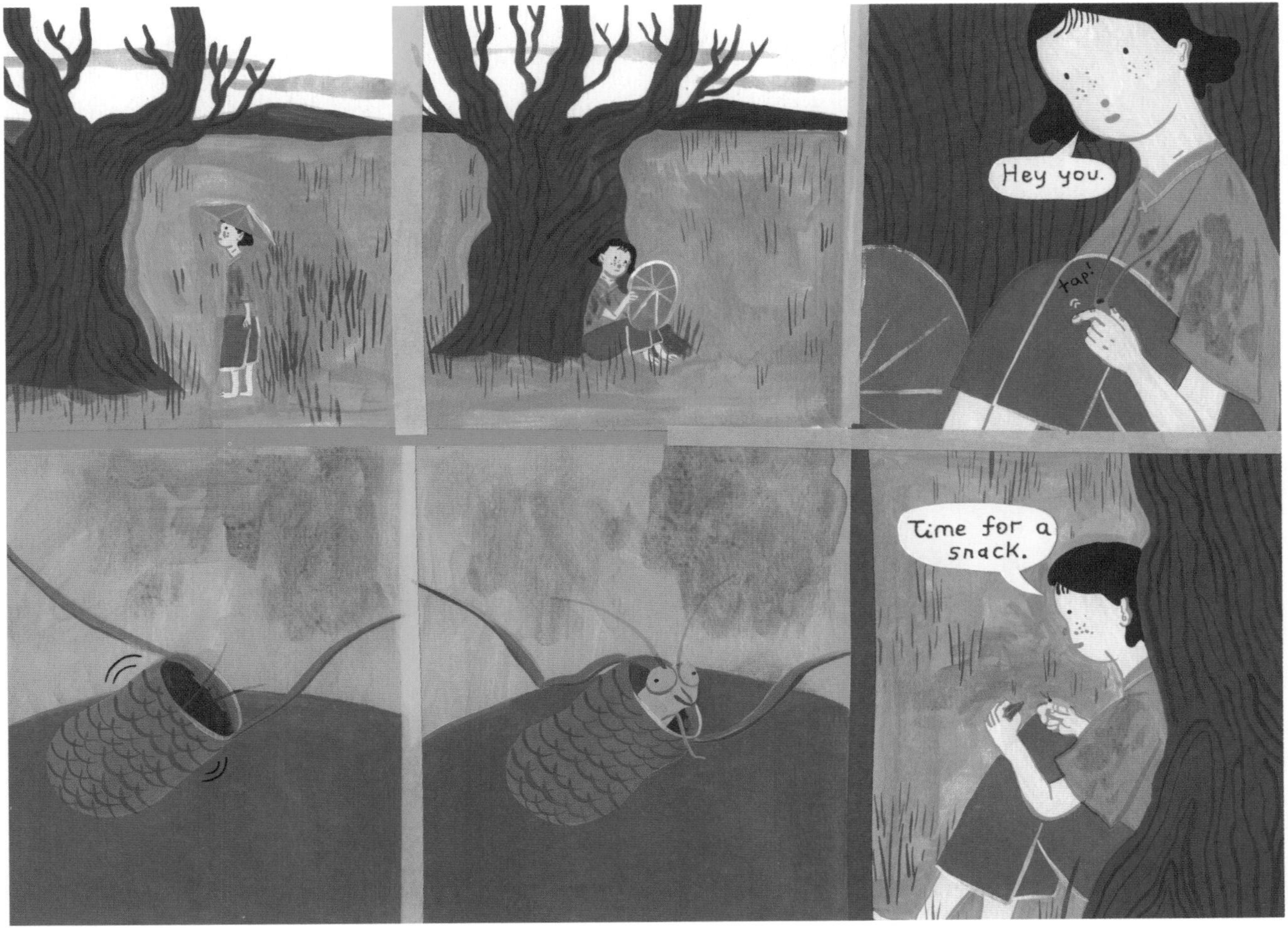
Hey you.
tap!
Time for a snack.

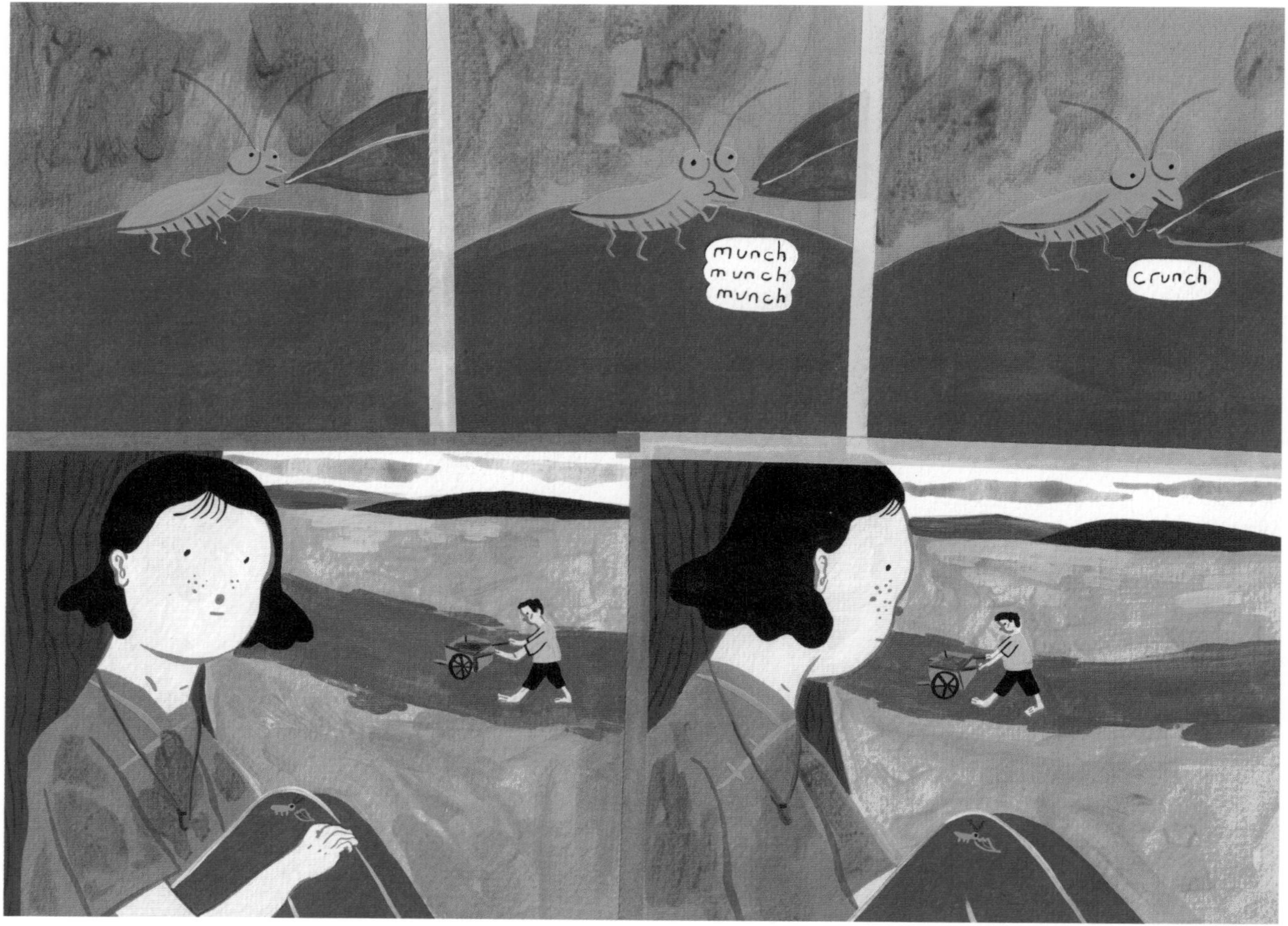
munch
munch
munch
crunch

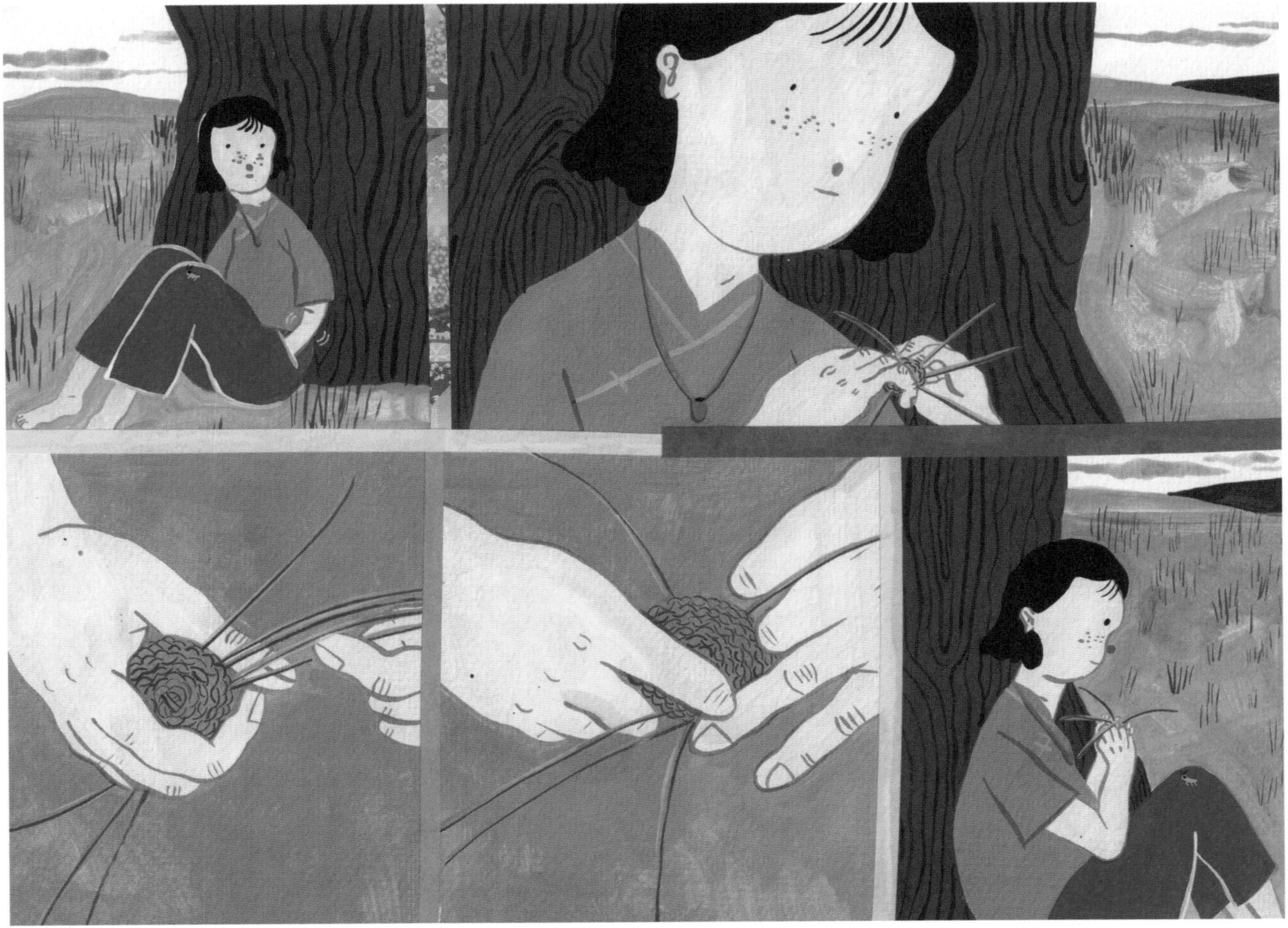

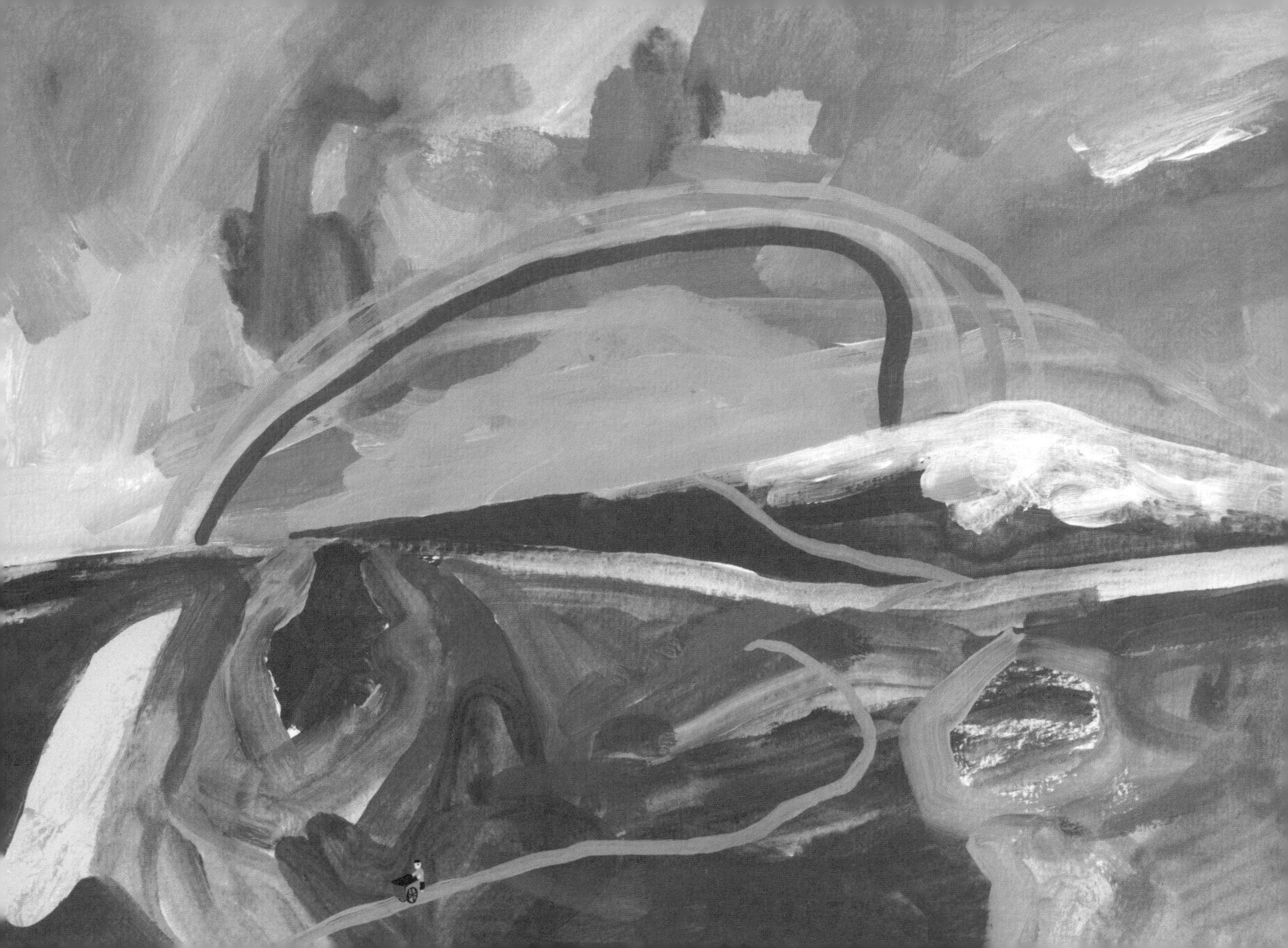

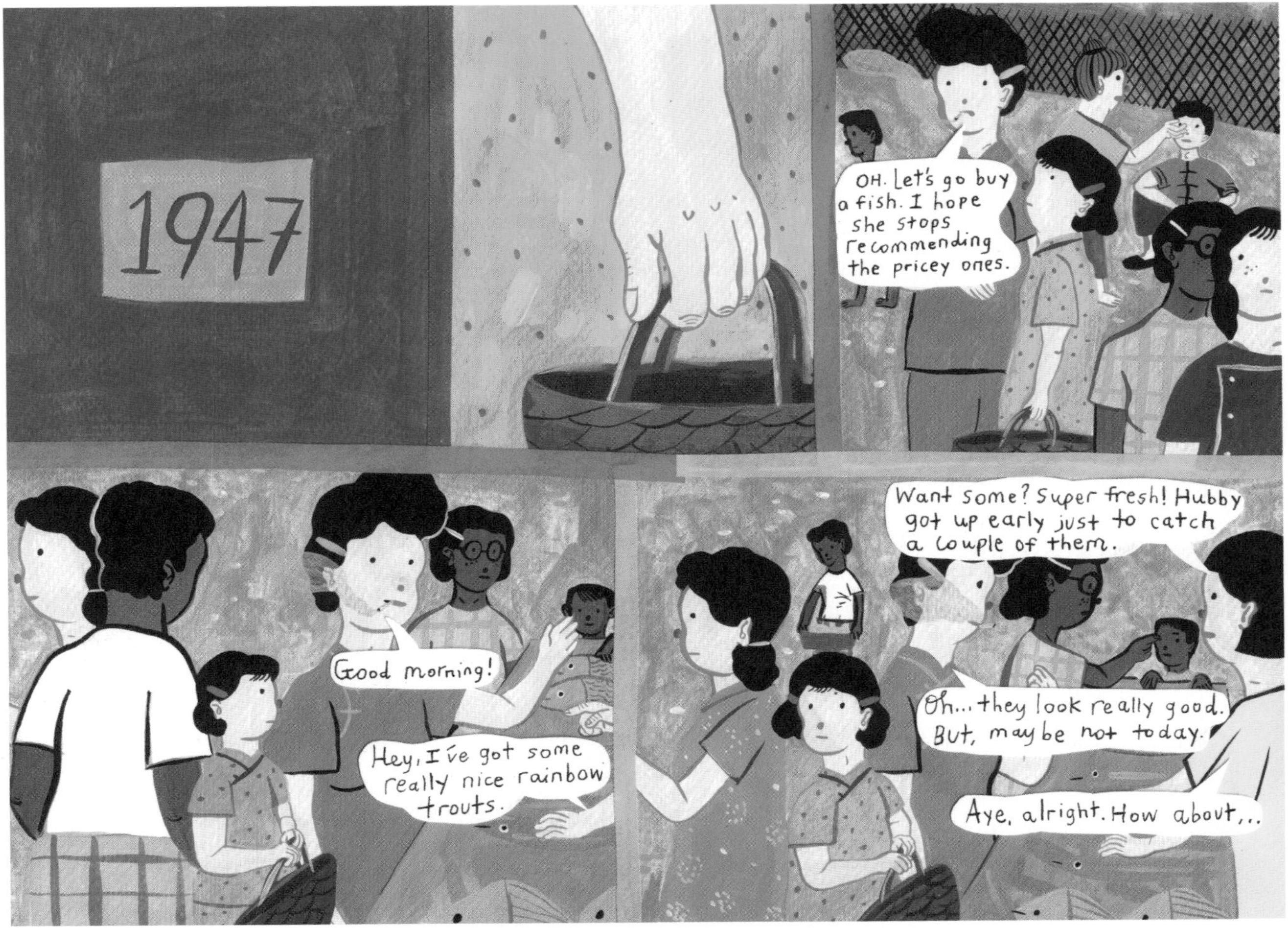
1947
OH. Let's go buy a fish. I hope she stops recommending the pricey ones.
Good morning!
Hey, I've got some really nice rainbow trouts.
Want some? Super fresh! Hubby got up early just to catch a couple of them.
Oh... they look really good. But, maybe not today.
Aye, alright. How about...

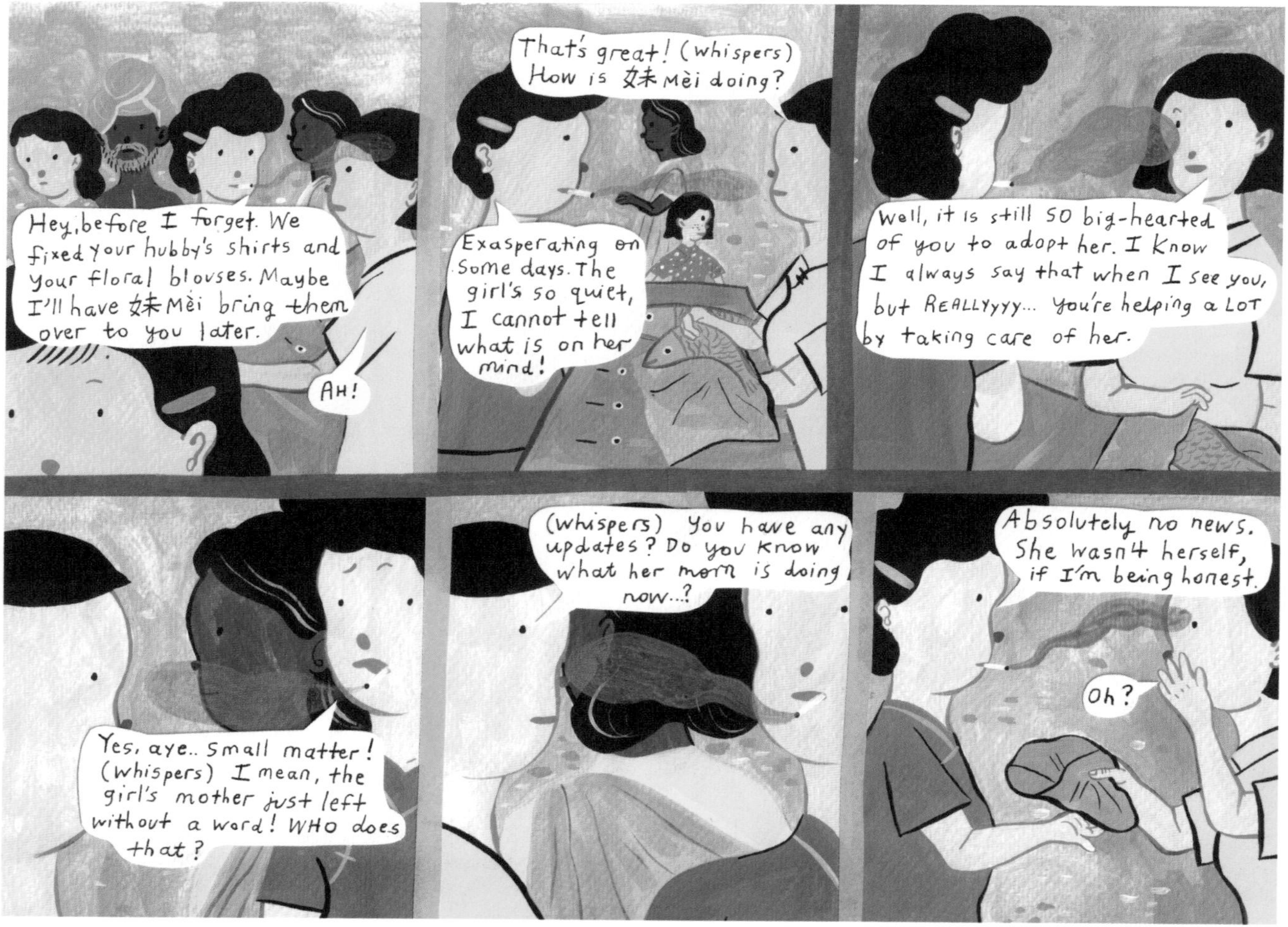
Hey, before I forget. We fixed your hubby's shirts and your floral blouses. Maybe I'll have 妹 Mèi bring them over to you later.
AH!
That's great! (whispers) How is 妹 Mèi doing?
Exasperating on some days. The girl's so quiet, I cannot tell what is on her mind!
Well, it is still SO big-hearted of you to adopt her. I know I always say that when I see you, but REALLYyyy... you're helping a LOT by taking care of her.
Yes, aye.. small matter! (whispers) I mean, the girl's mother just left without a word! WHO does that?
(whispers) You have any updates? Do you know what her mom is doing now...?
Absolutely no news. She wasn't herself, if I'm being honest.
Oh?

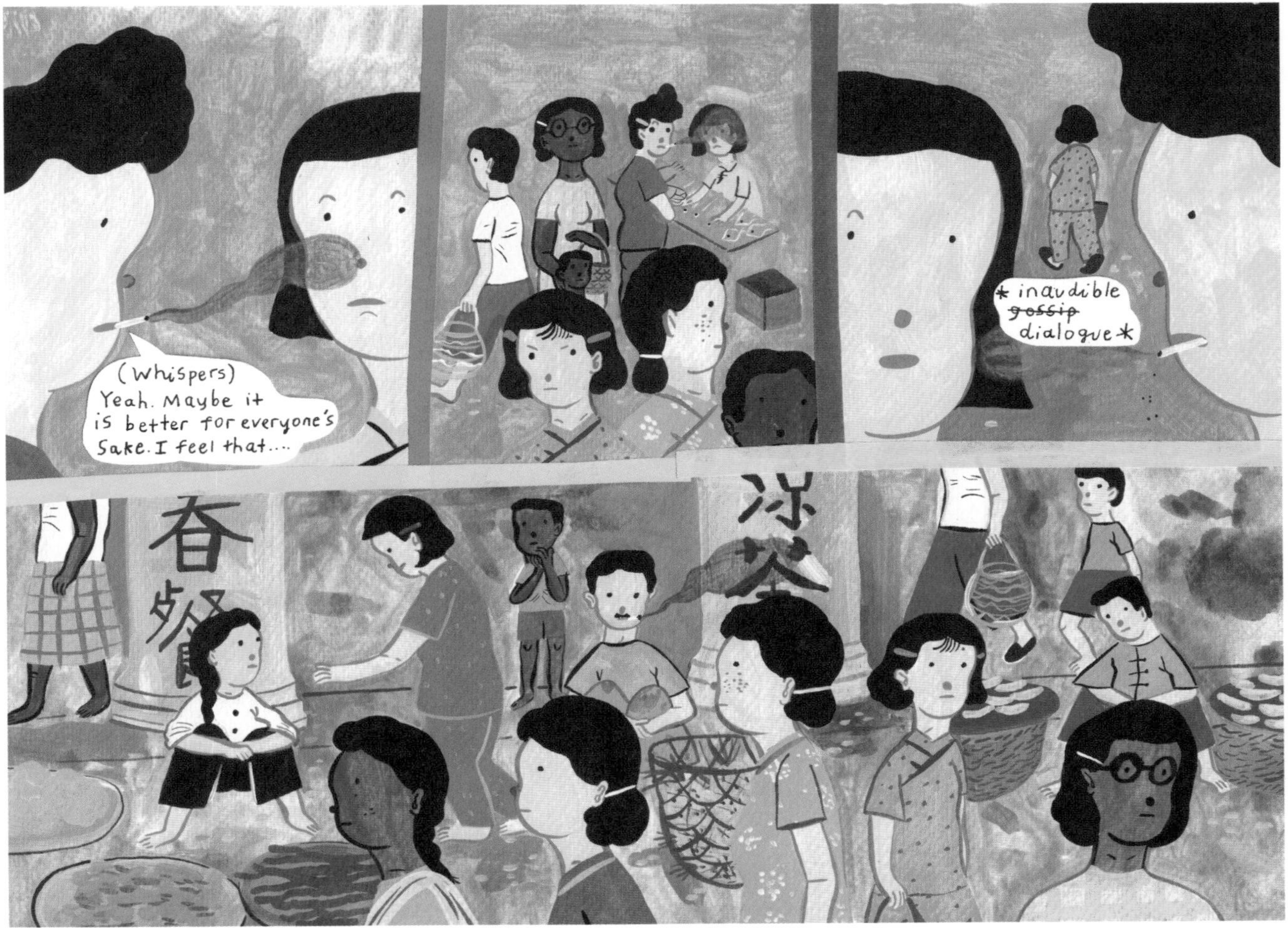
(Whispers) Yeah. Maybe it is better for everyone's sake. I feel that....
* inaudible ~~gossip~~ dialogue *
春

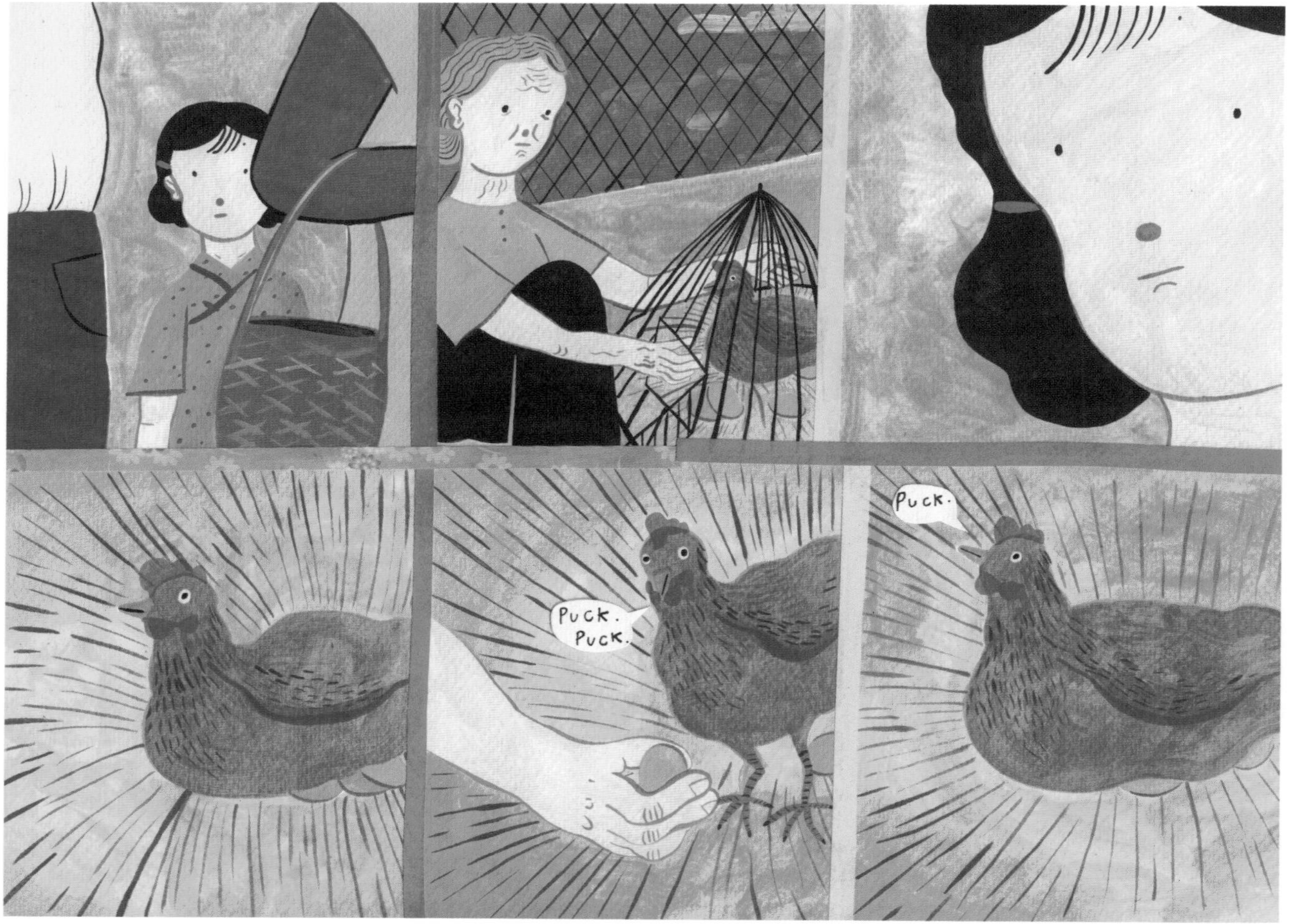
PUCK.
PUCK.
PUCK.

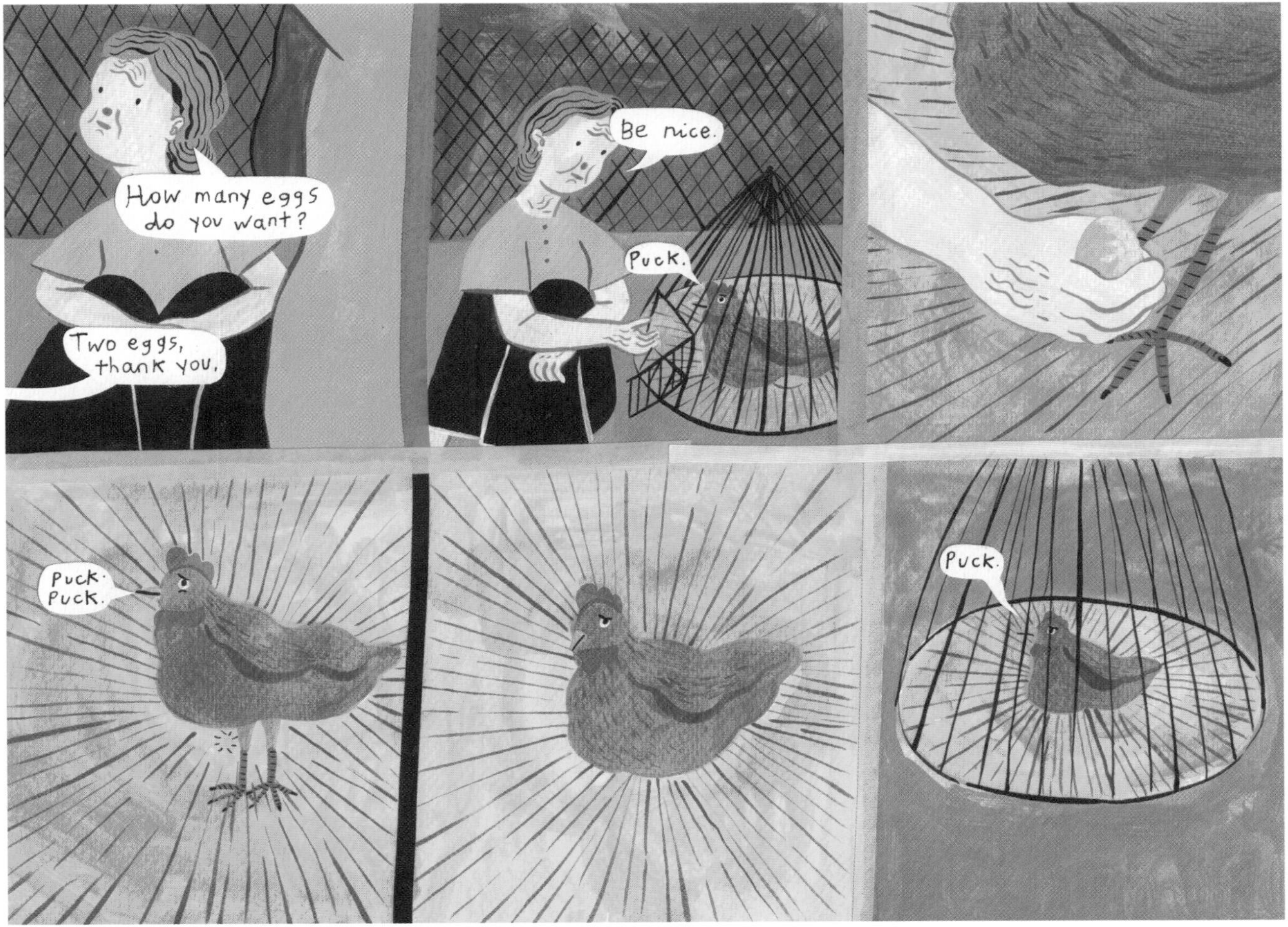
How many eggs do you want?
Two eggs, thank you.
Be nice.
Puck.
Puck. Puck.
Puck.

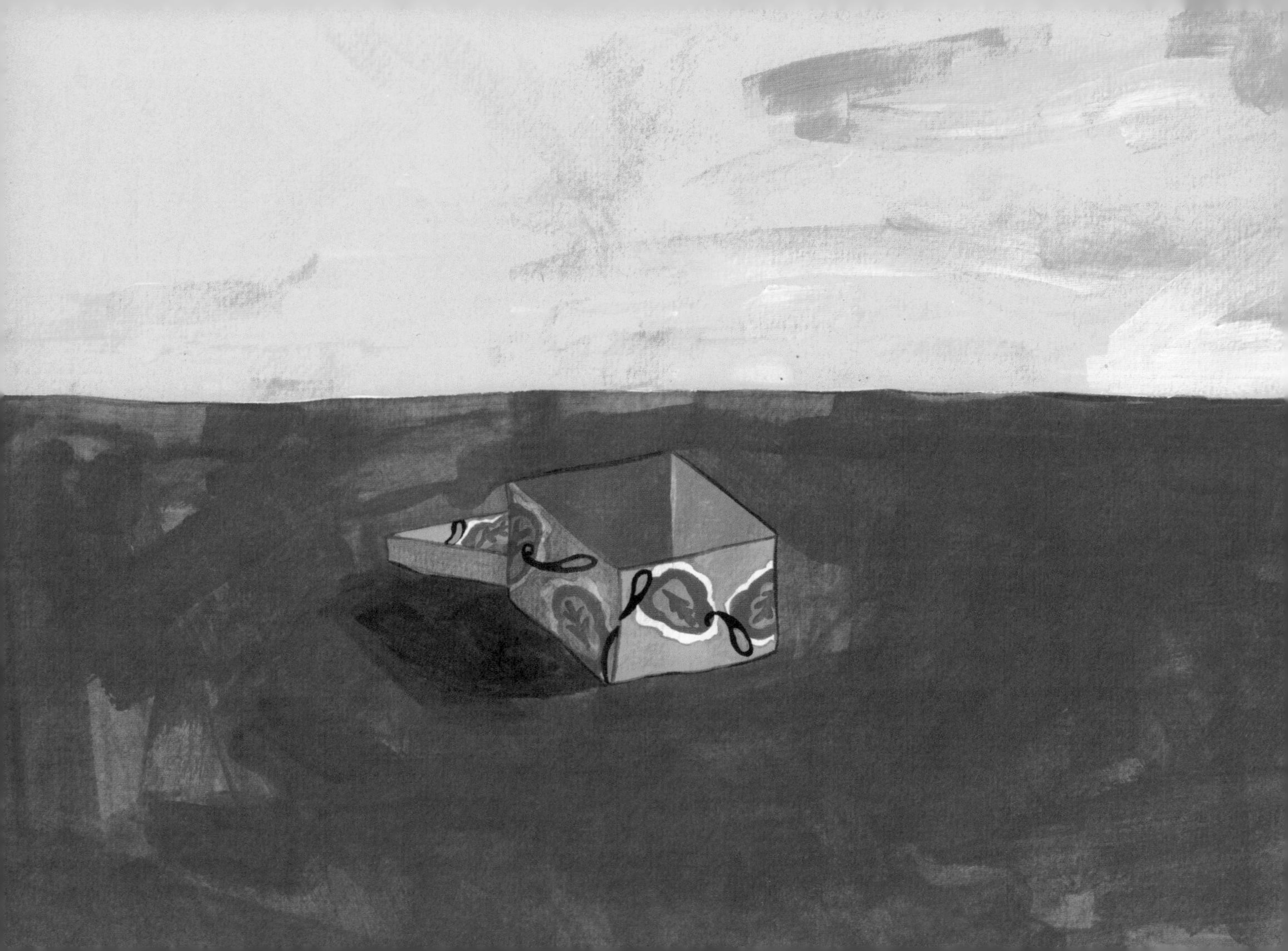

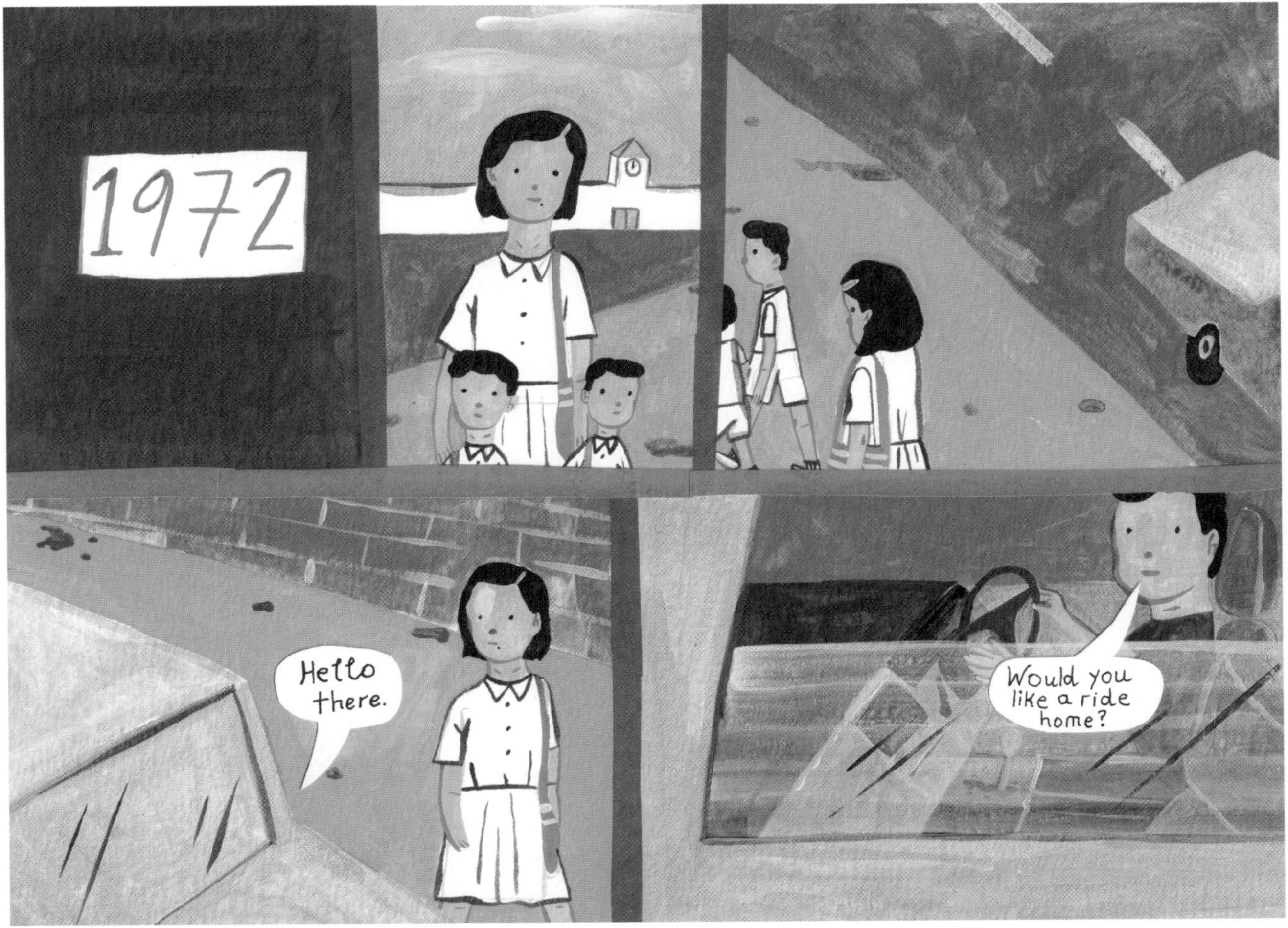
1972
Hello there.
Would you like a ride home?

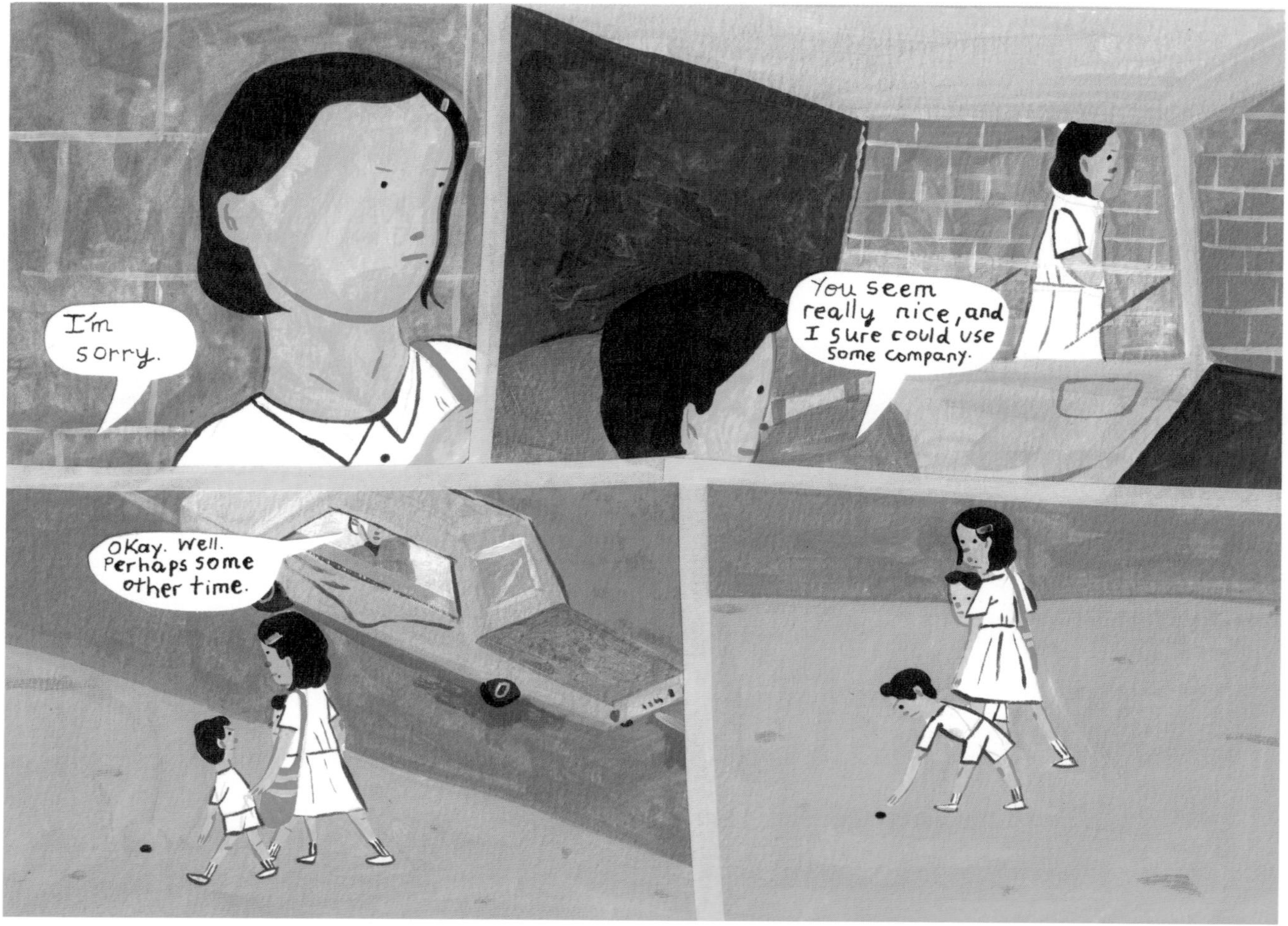
I'm sorry.
You seem really nice, and I sure could use some company.
Okay. Well. Perhaps some other time.

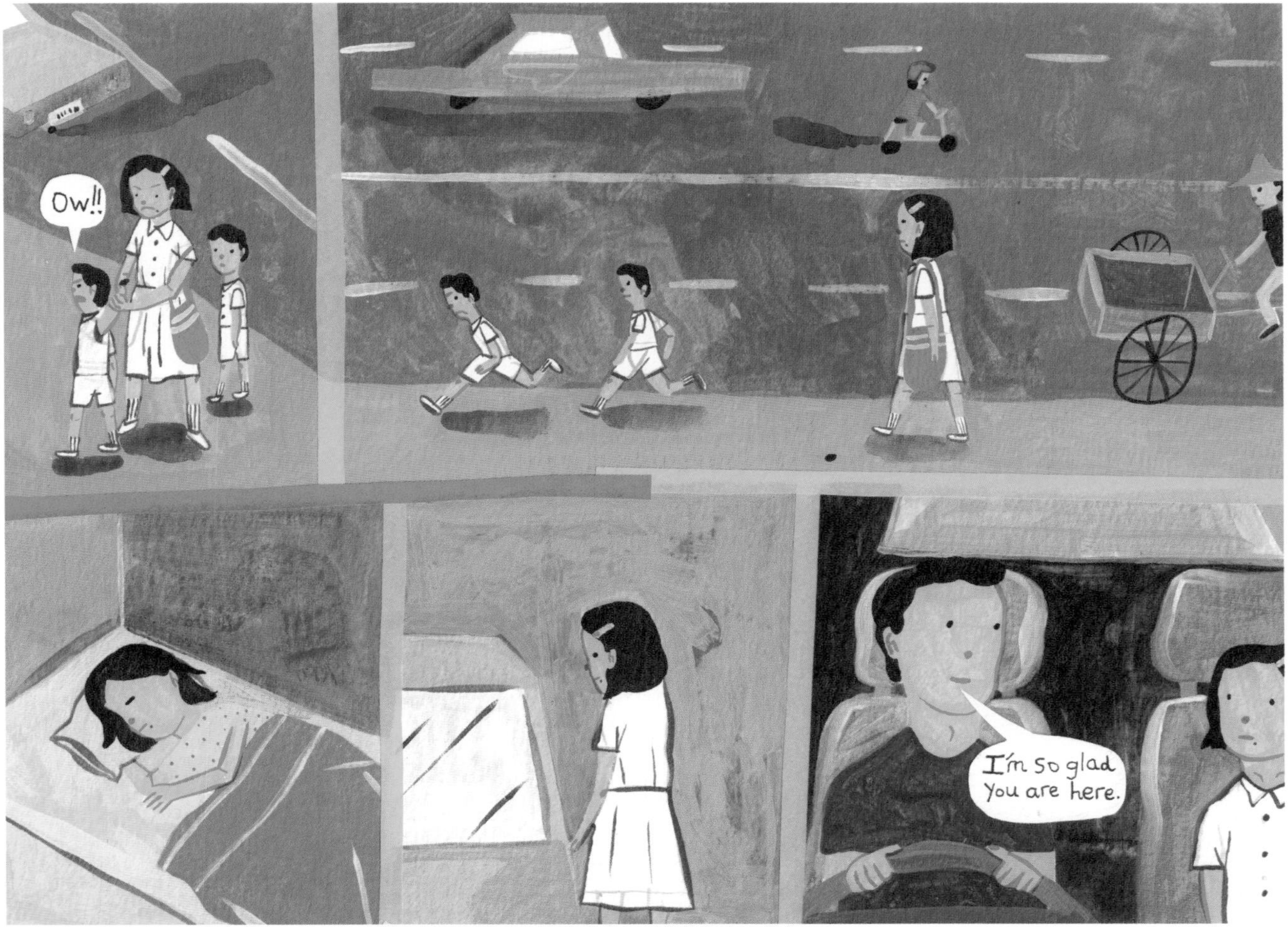
Ow!!
I'm so glad you are here.

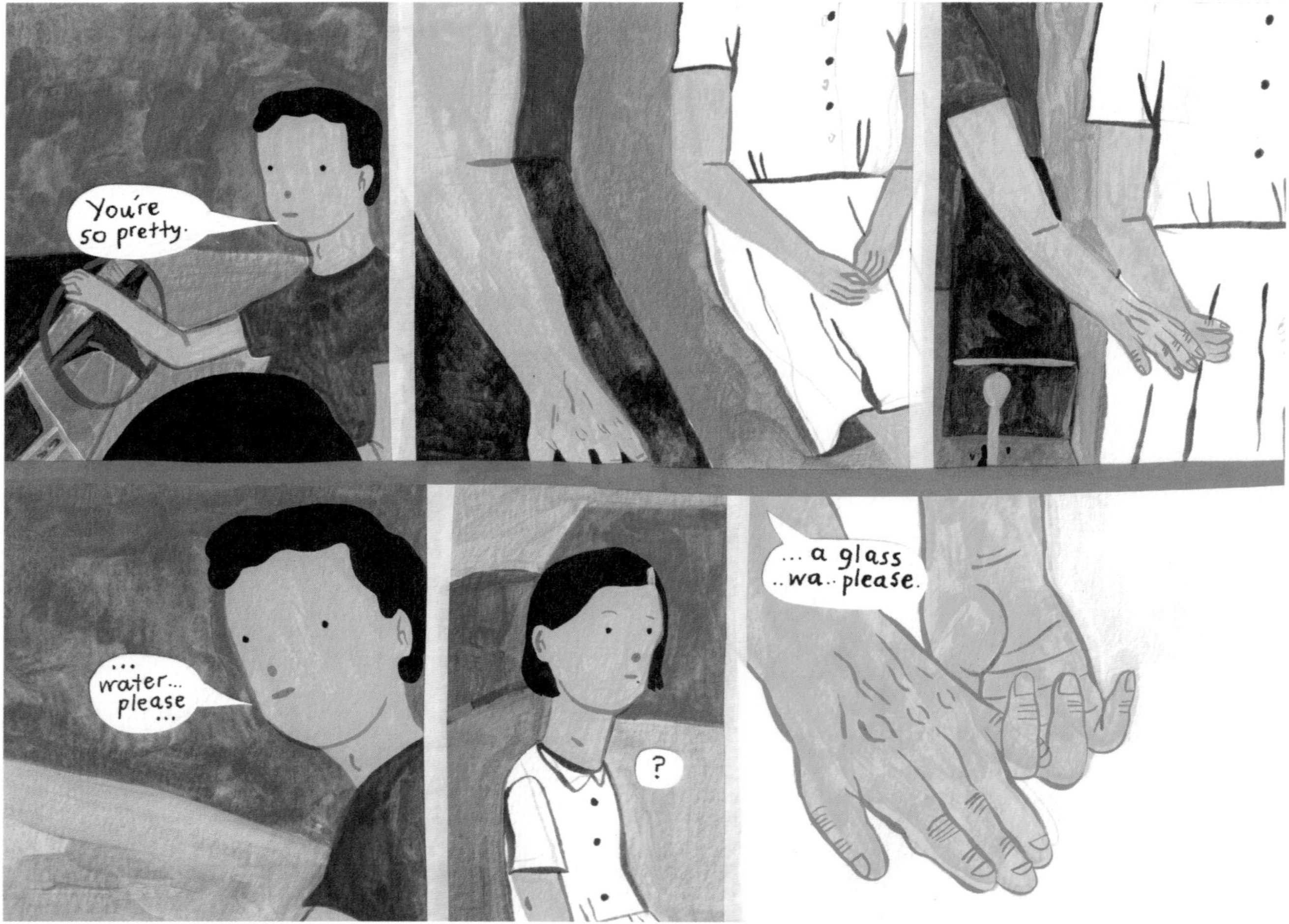

You're so pretty.
... water... please ...
?
... a glass .. wa.. please.

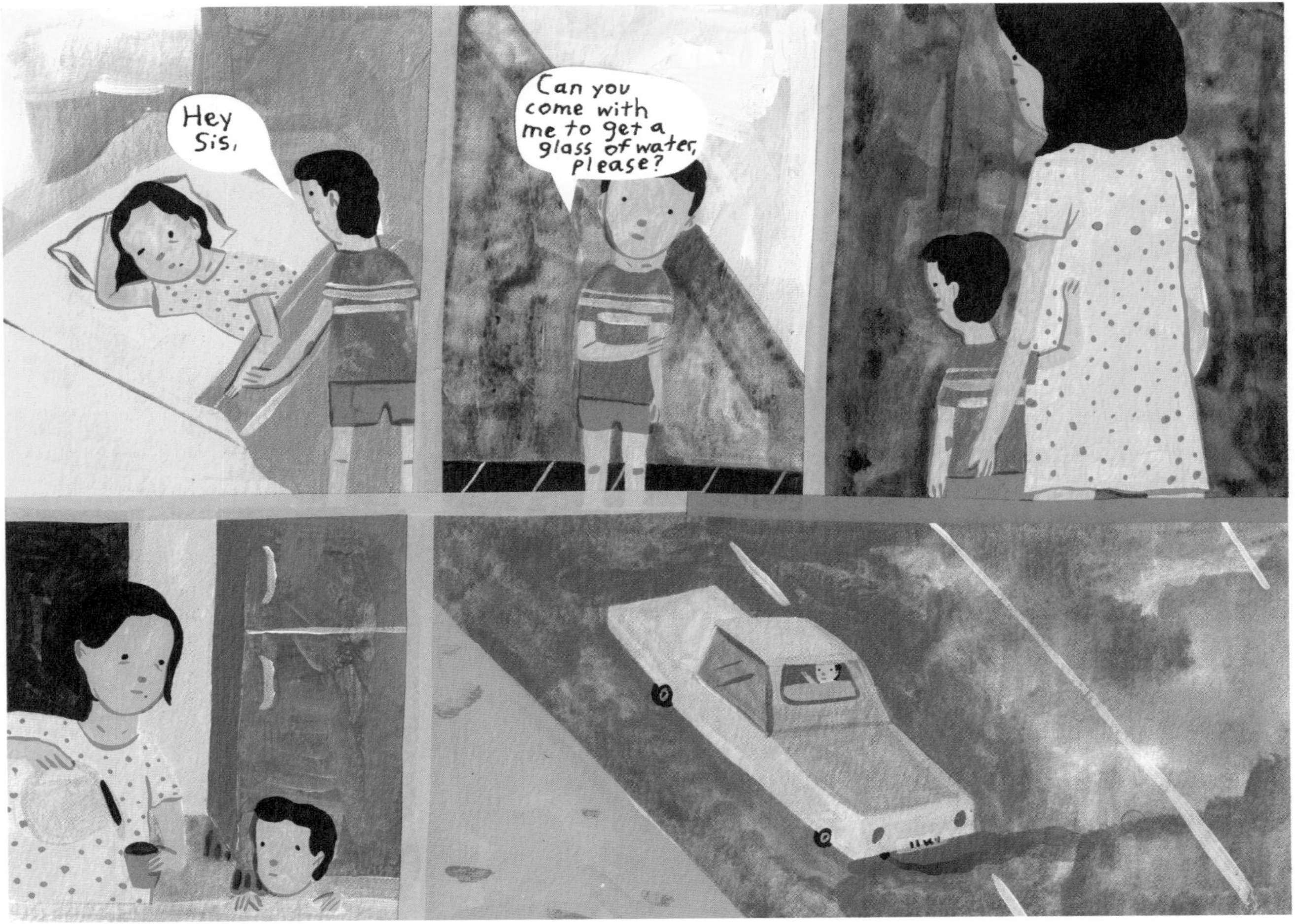
Hey Sis,
Can you come with me to get a glass of water, please?

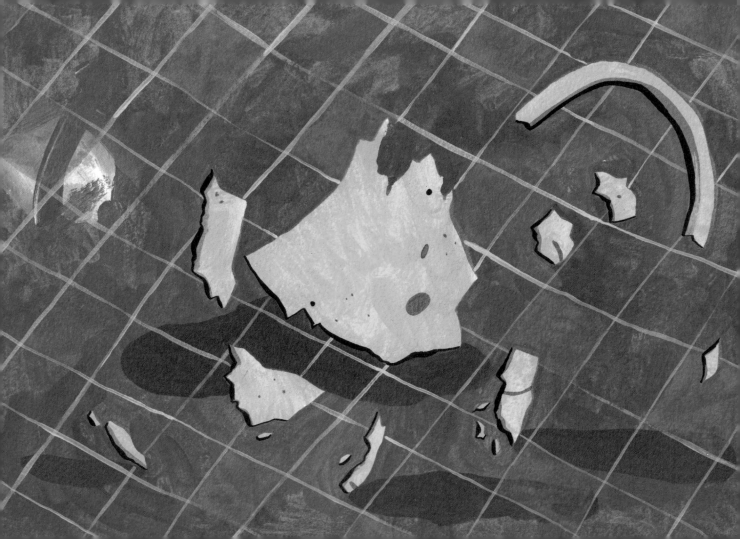

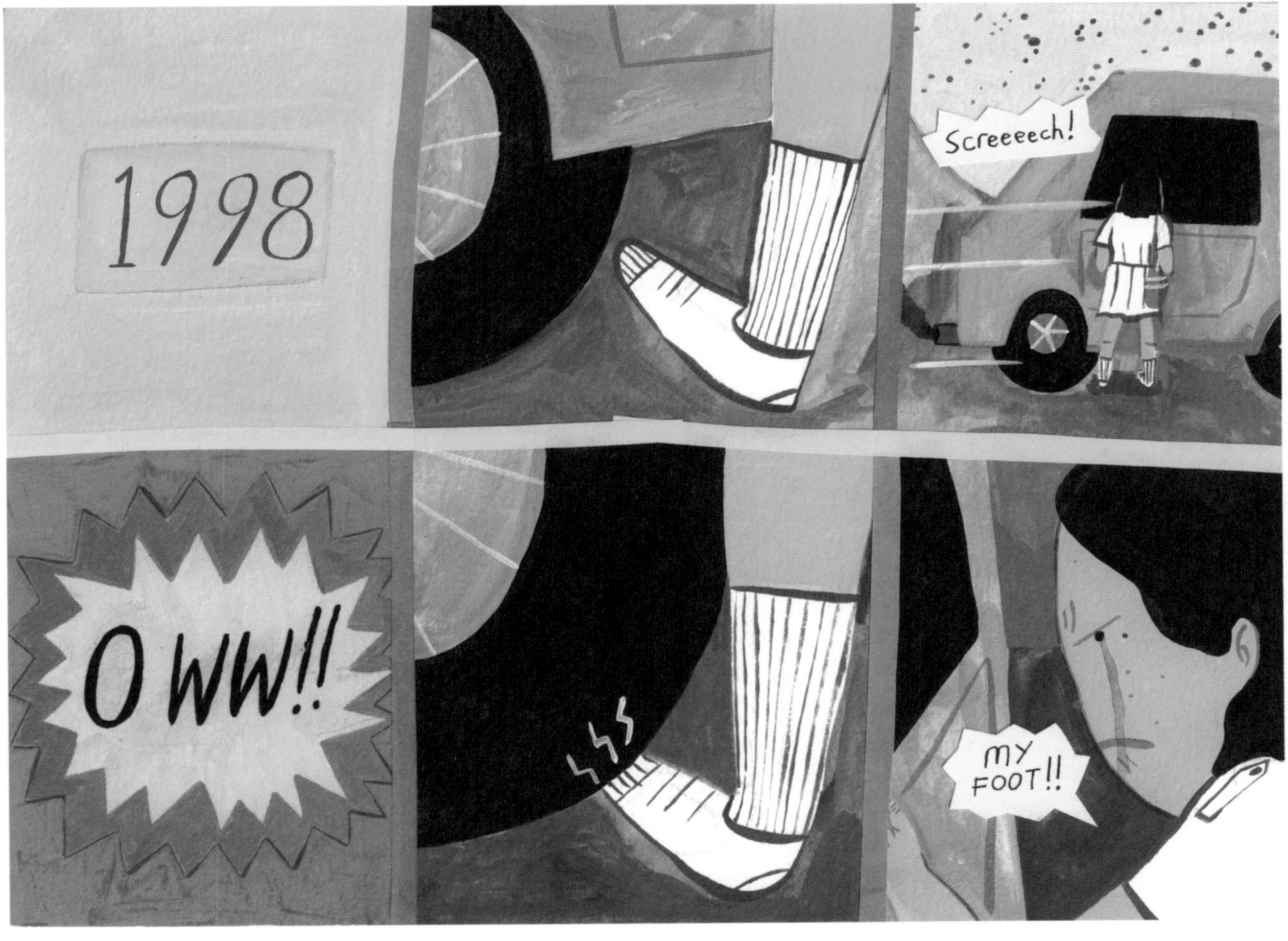
1998
Screeeech!
OWW!!
MY FOOT!!

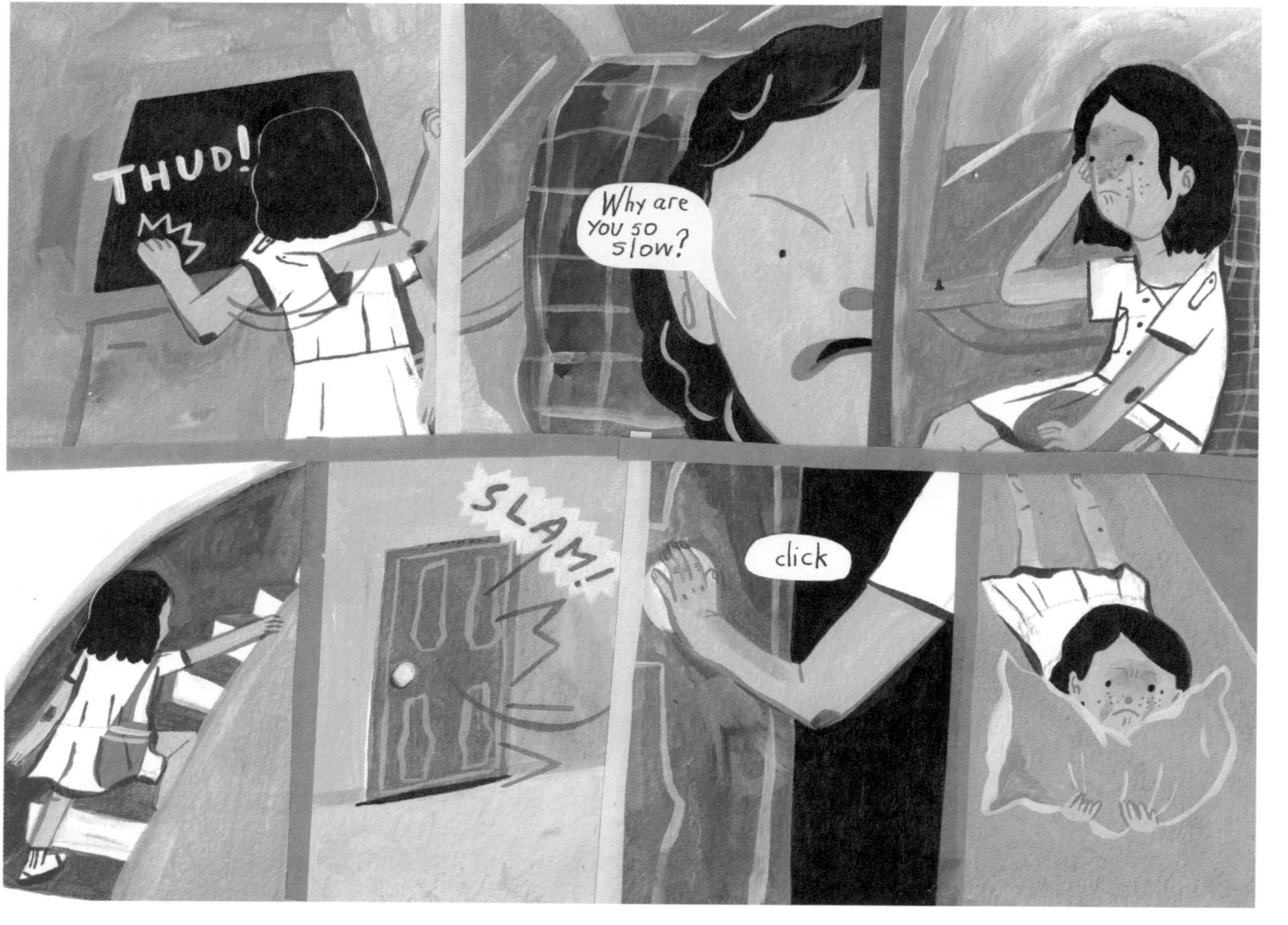
THUD!
Why are you so slow?
SLAM!
click

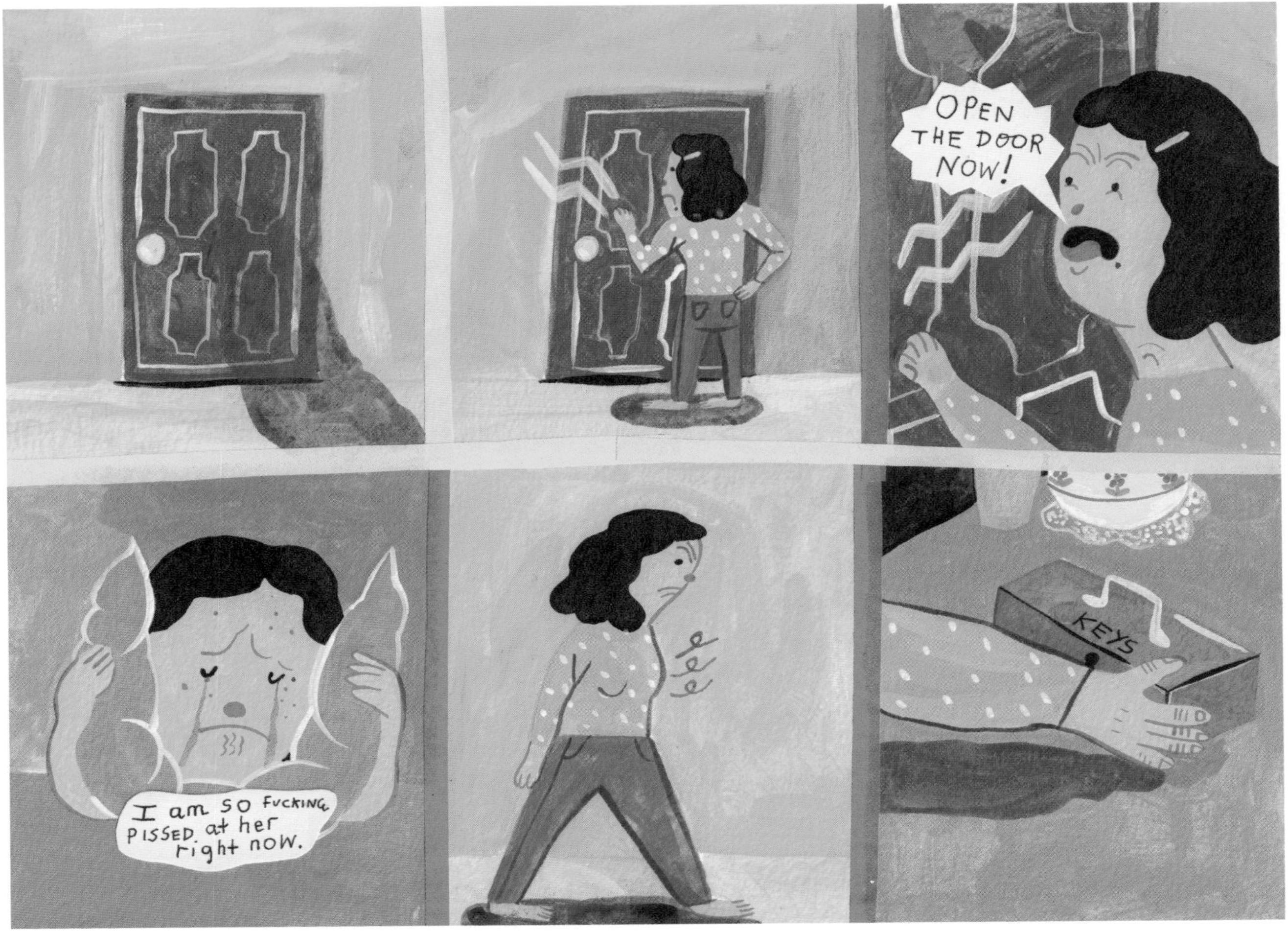
OPEN THE DOOR NOW!
I am SO FUCKING PISSED at her right now.
KEYS

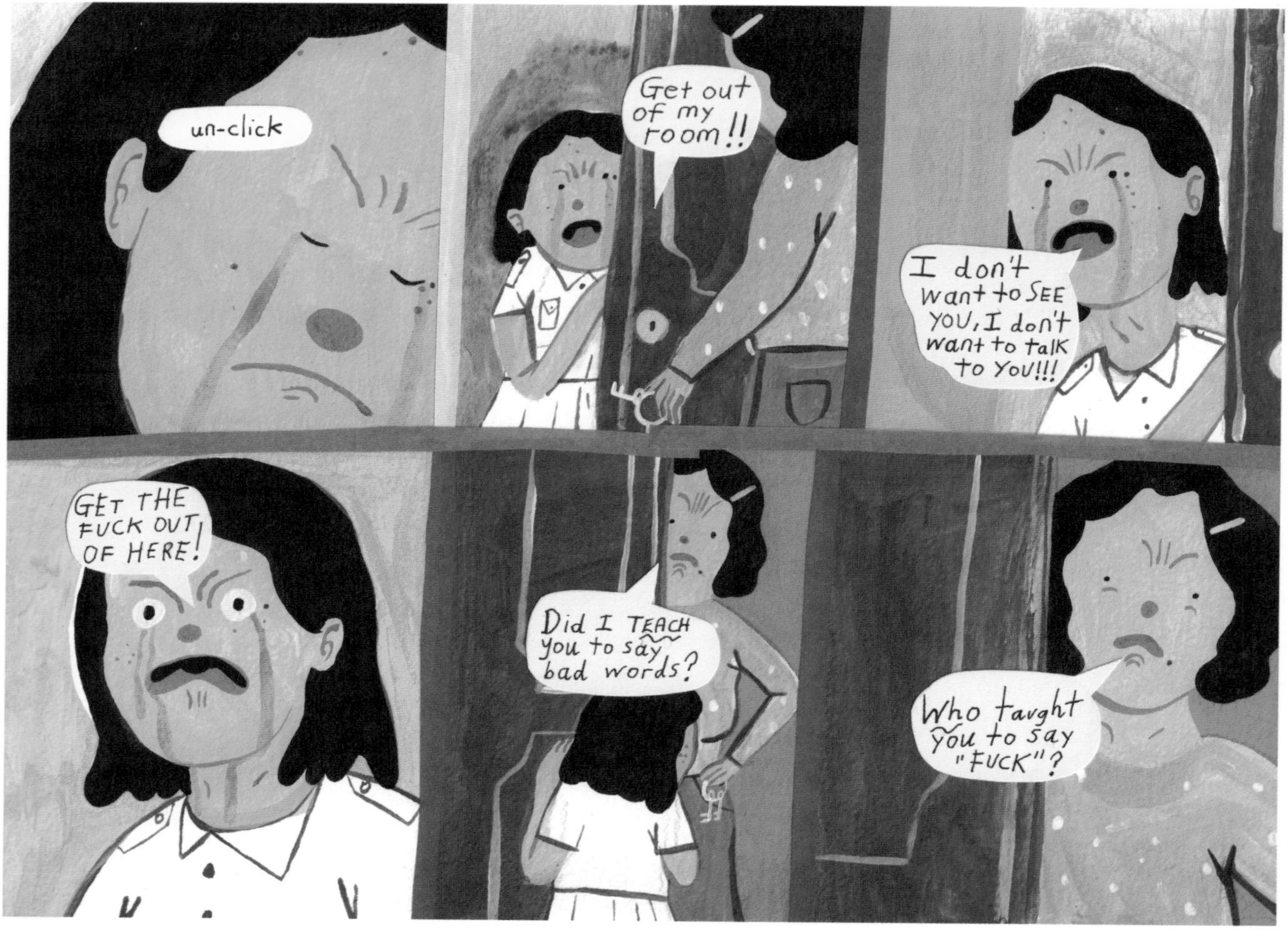
un-click
Get out of my room!!
I don't want to SEE YOU, I don't want to talk to YOU!!!
GET THE FUCK OUT OF HERE!
Did I TEACH you to say bad words?
Who taught you to say "FUCK"?

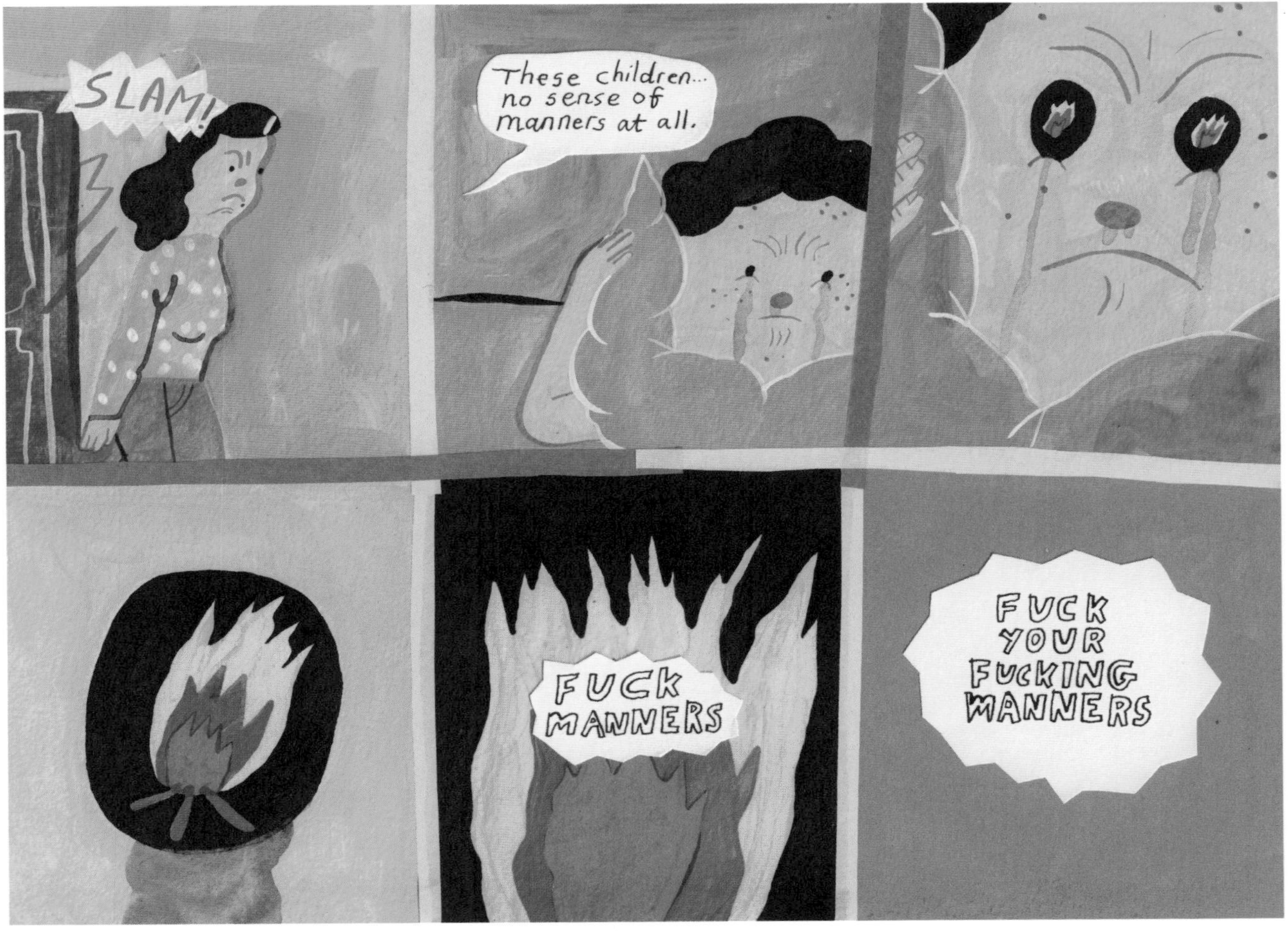
SLAM!
These children... no sense of manners at all.
FUCK MANNERS
FUCK YOUR FUCKING MANNERS

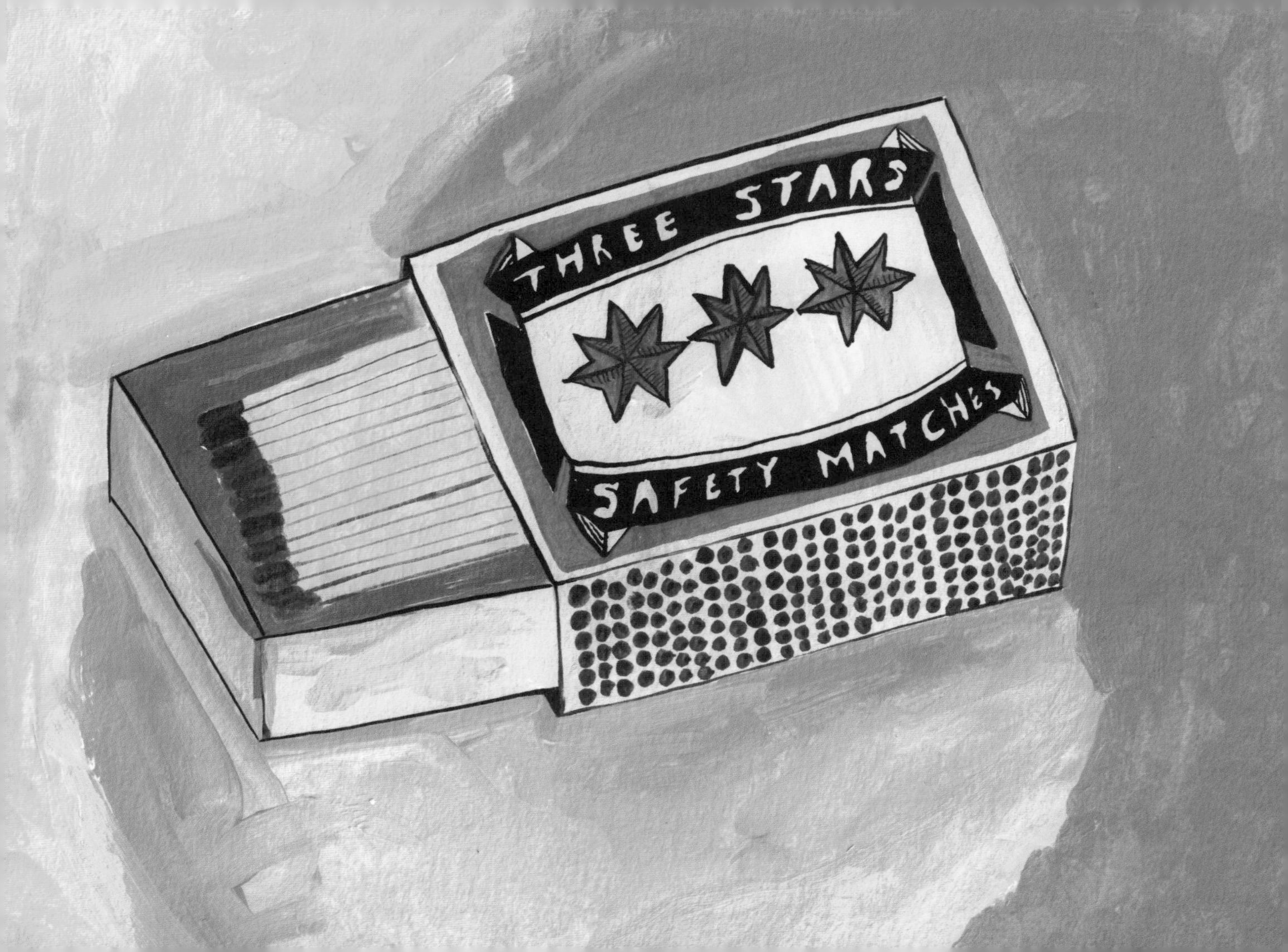
THREE STARS
SAFETY MATCHES

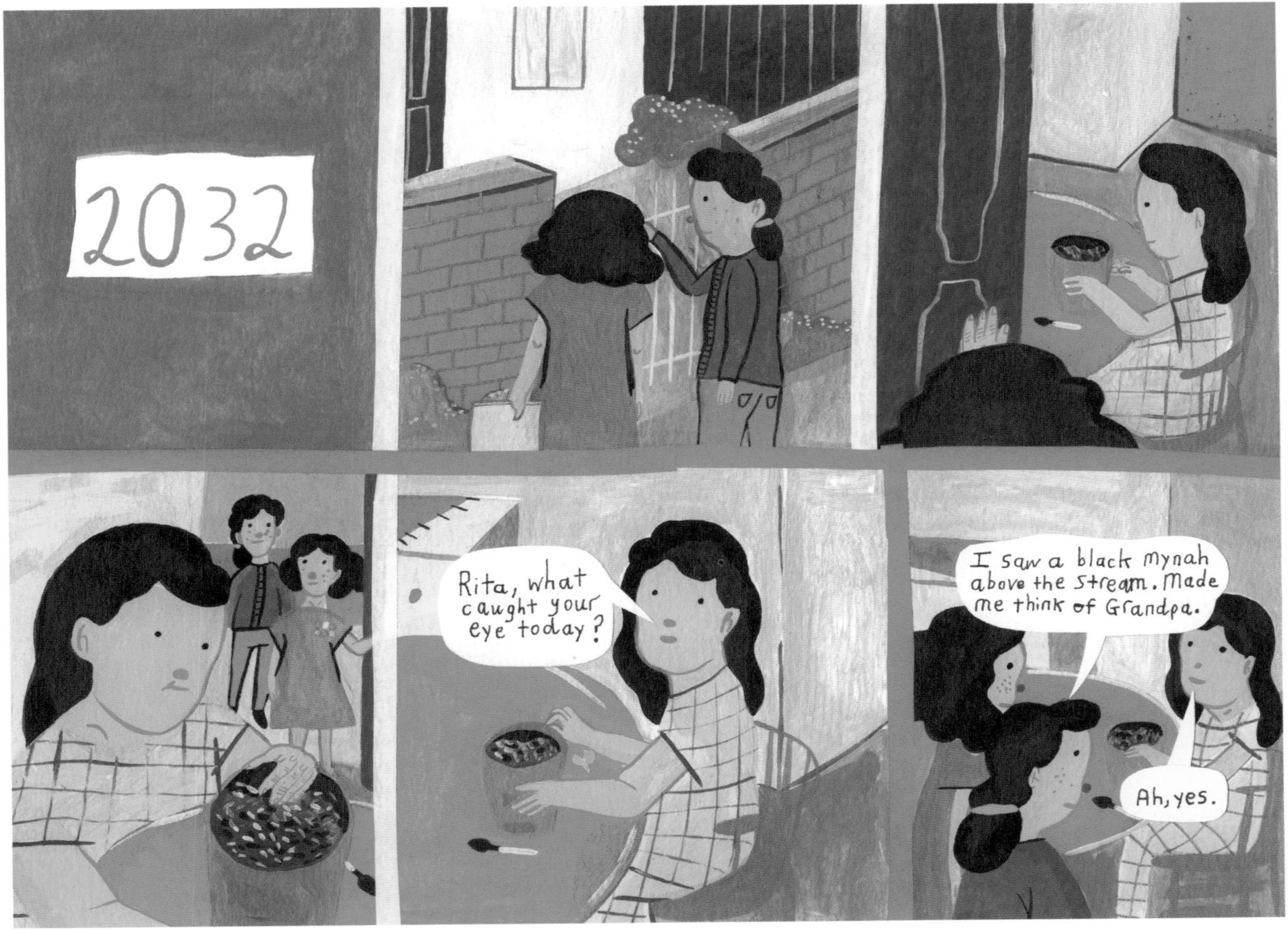
2032
Rita, what caught your eye today?
I saw a black mynah above the stream. Made me think of Grandpa.
Ah, yes.

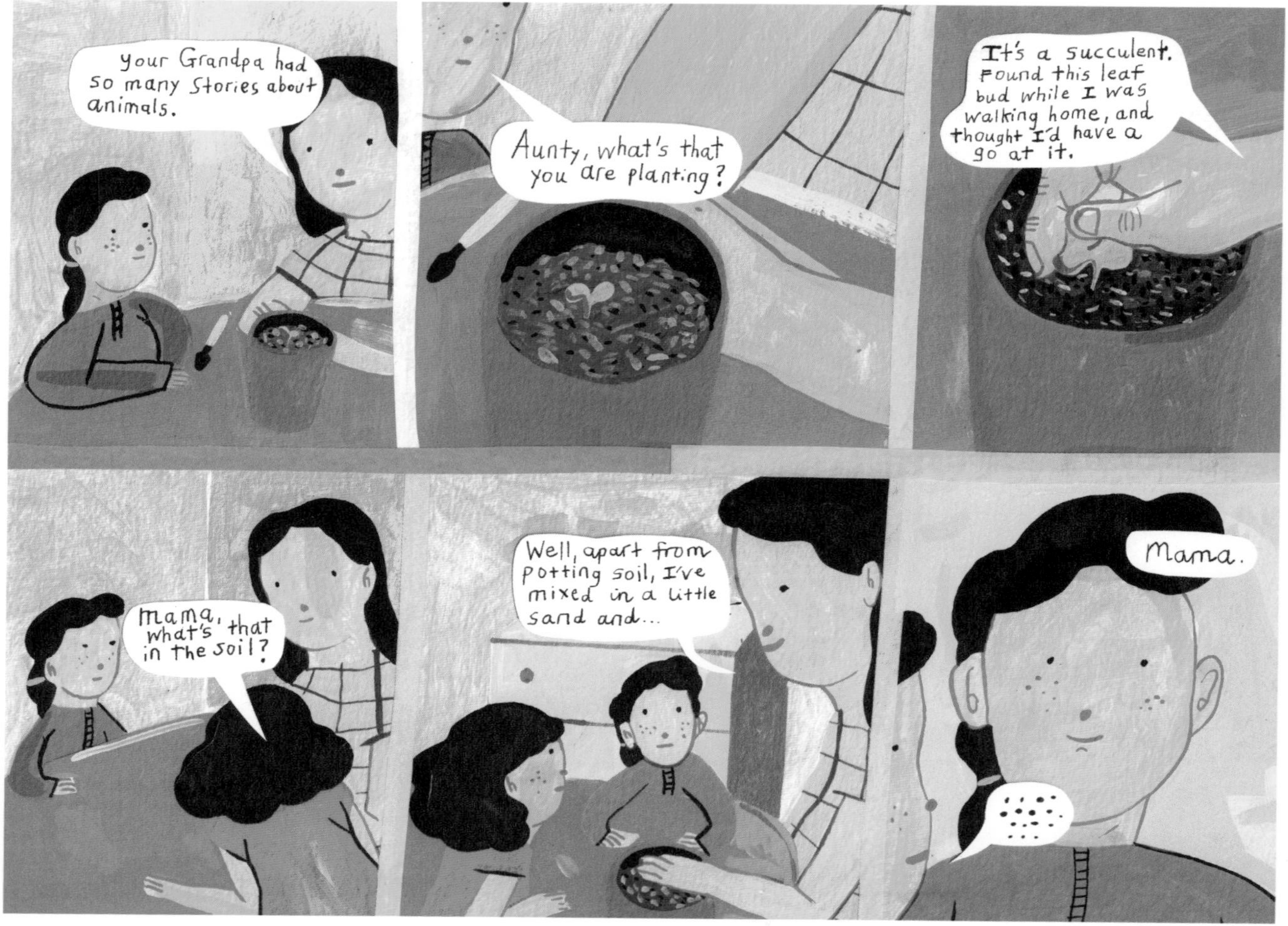
Your Grandpa had so many Stories about animals.
Aunty, what's that you are planting?
It's a succulent. Found this leaf bud while I was walking home, and thought I'd have a go at it.
Mama, what's that in the soil?
Well, apart from potting soil, I've mixed in a little sand and...
Mama.

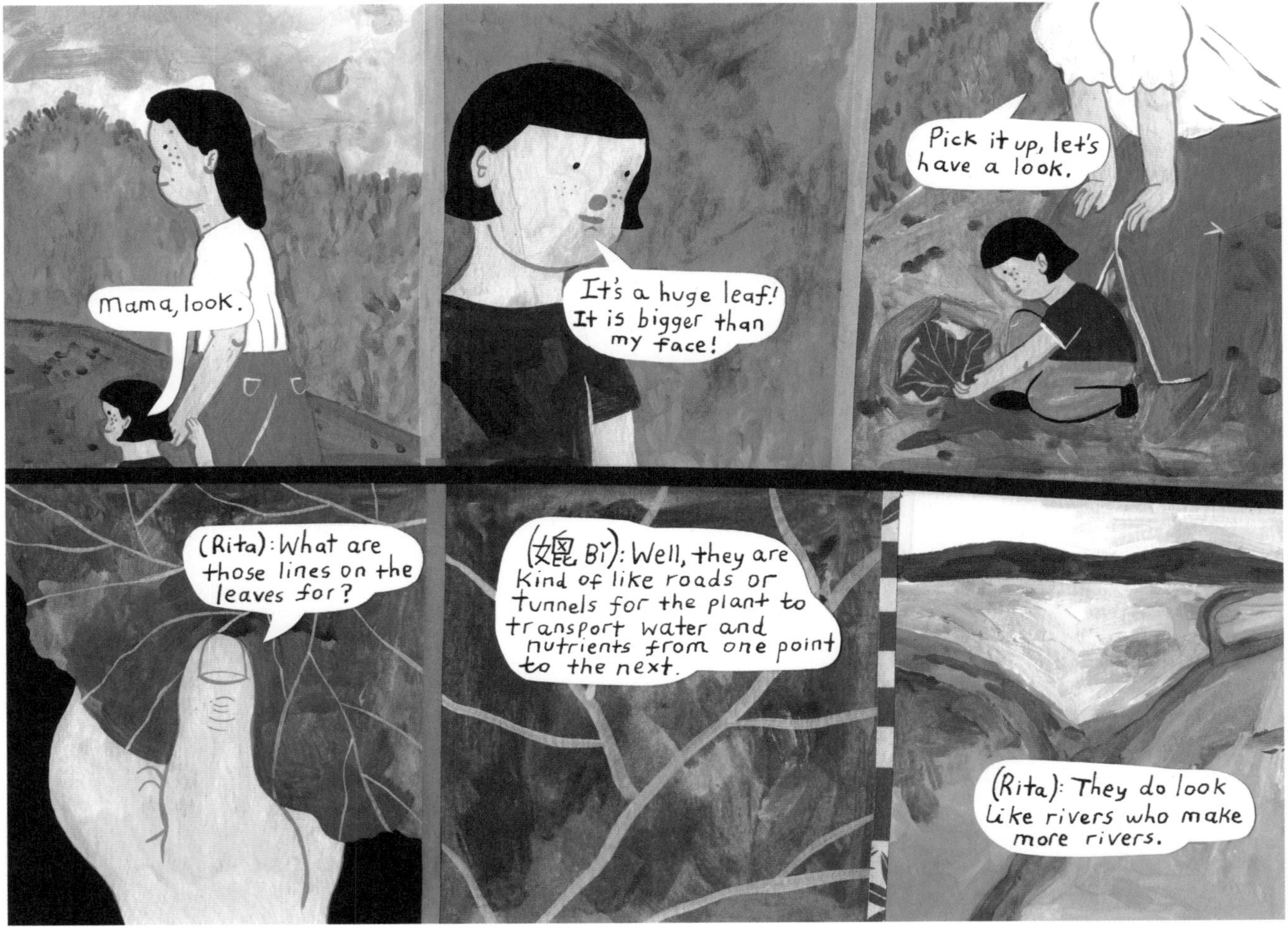

Mama, look.
It's a huge leaf! It is bigger than my face!
Pick it up, let's have a look.
(Rita): What are those lines on the leaves for?
(媲 Bǐ): Well, they are Kind of like roads or tunnels for the plant to transport water and nutrients from one point to the next.
(Rita): They do look like rivers who make more rivers.

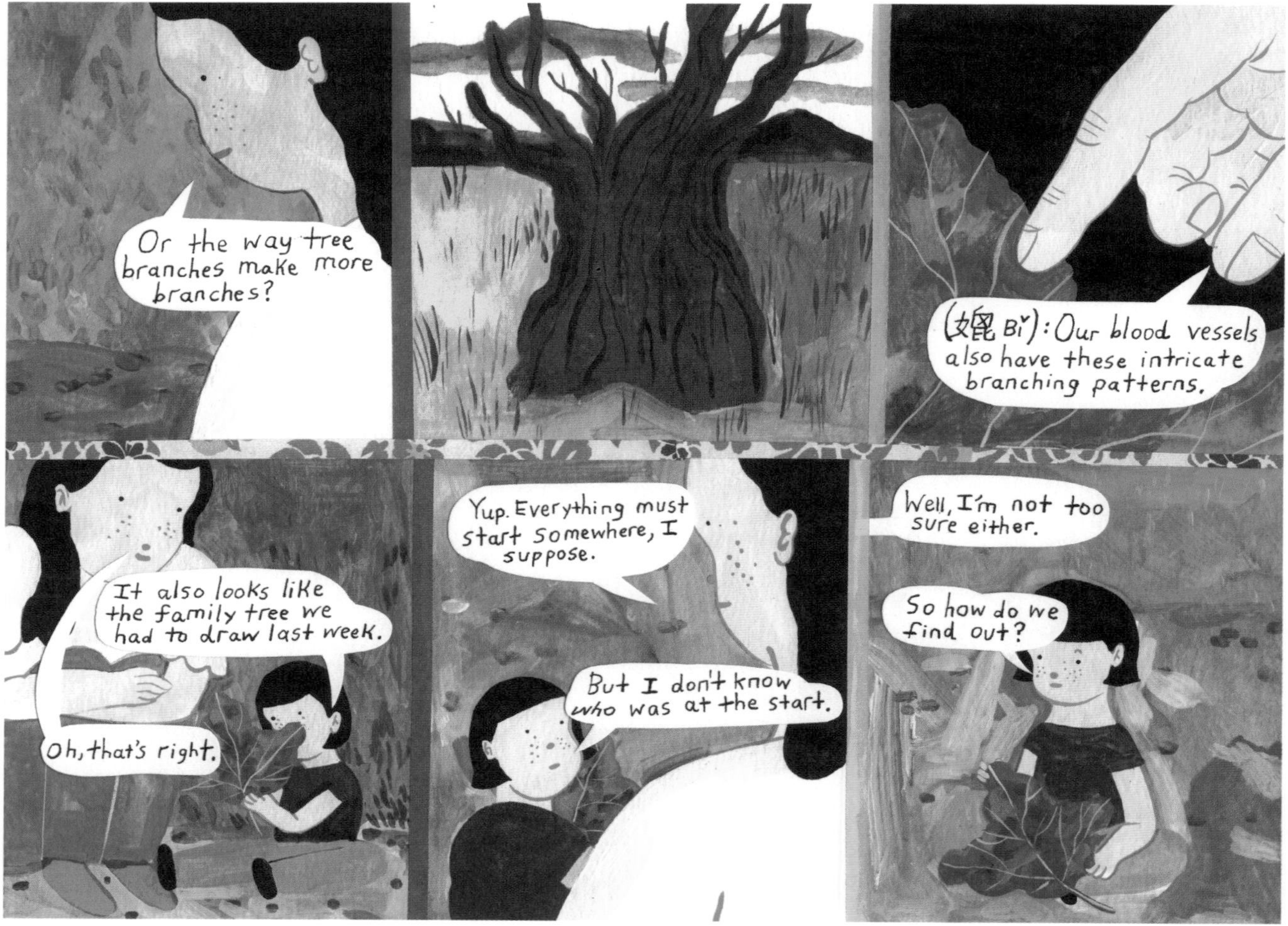

Or the way tree branches make more branches?
(媲 Bǐ): Our blood vessels also have these intricate branching patterns.
It also looks like the family tree we had to draw last week.
Oh, that's right.
Yup. Everything must start somewhere, I suppose.
But I don't know who was at the start.
Well, I'm not too sure either.
So how do we find out?

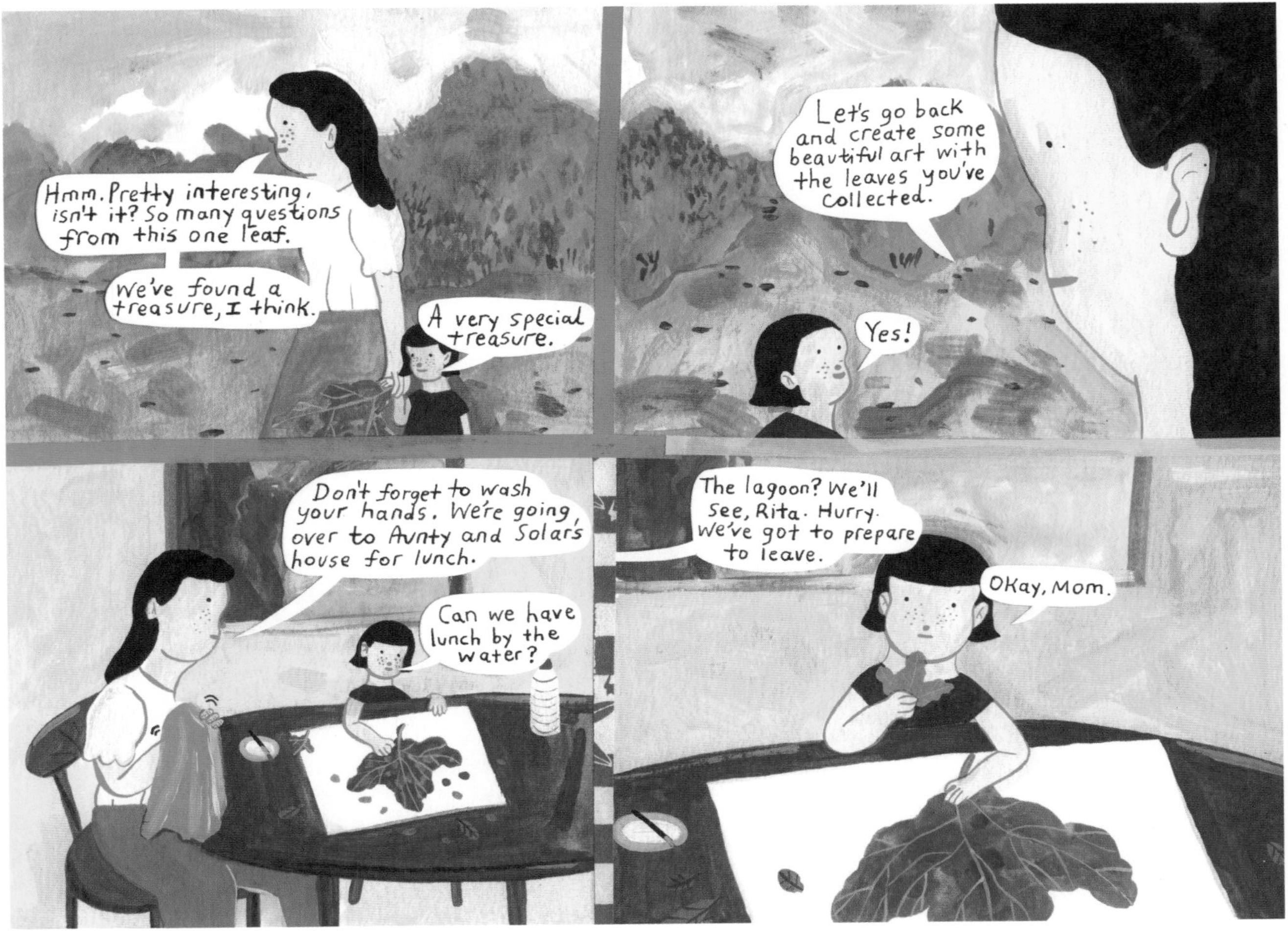
Hmm. Pretty interesting, isn't it? So many questions from this one leaf.
We've found a treasure, I think.
A very special treasure.
Let's go back and create some beautiful art with the leaves you've collected.
Yes!
Don't forget to wash your hands. We're going over to Aunty and Solar's house for lunch.
Can we have lunch by the water?
The lagoon? We'll see, Rita. Hurry. We've got to prepare to leave.
Okay, Mom.

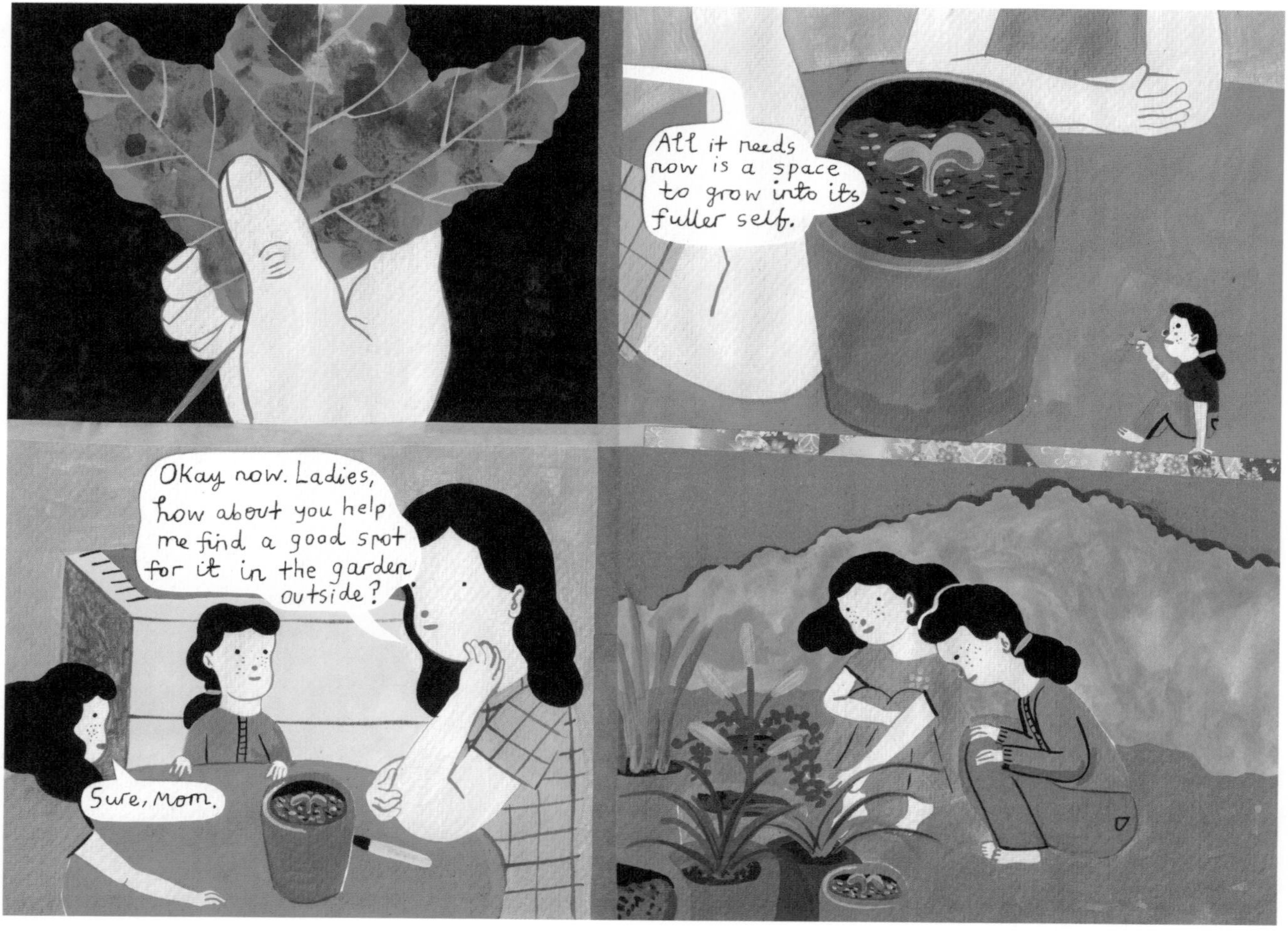
All it needs now is a space to grow into its fuller self.
Okay now. Ladies, how about you help me find a good spot for it in the garden outside?
Sure, Mom.

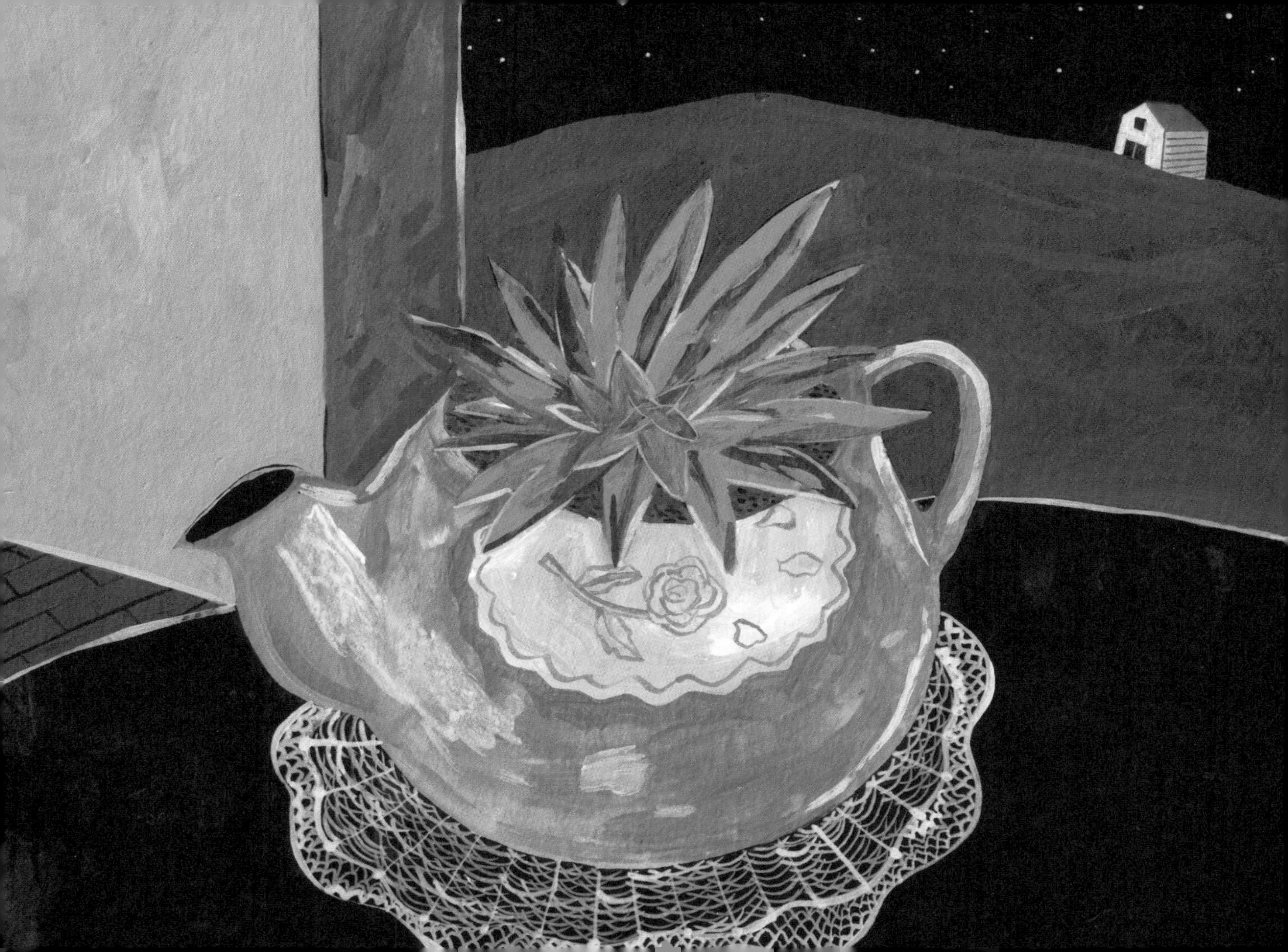

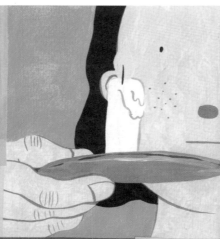

1908

Ready?

Yes, Mom.

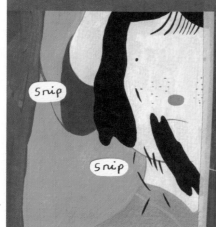

Snip

Snip

Now, put this on.

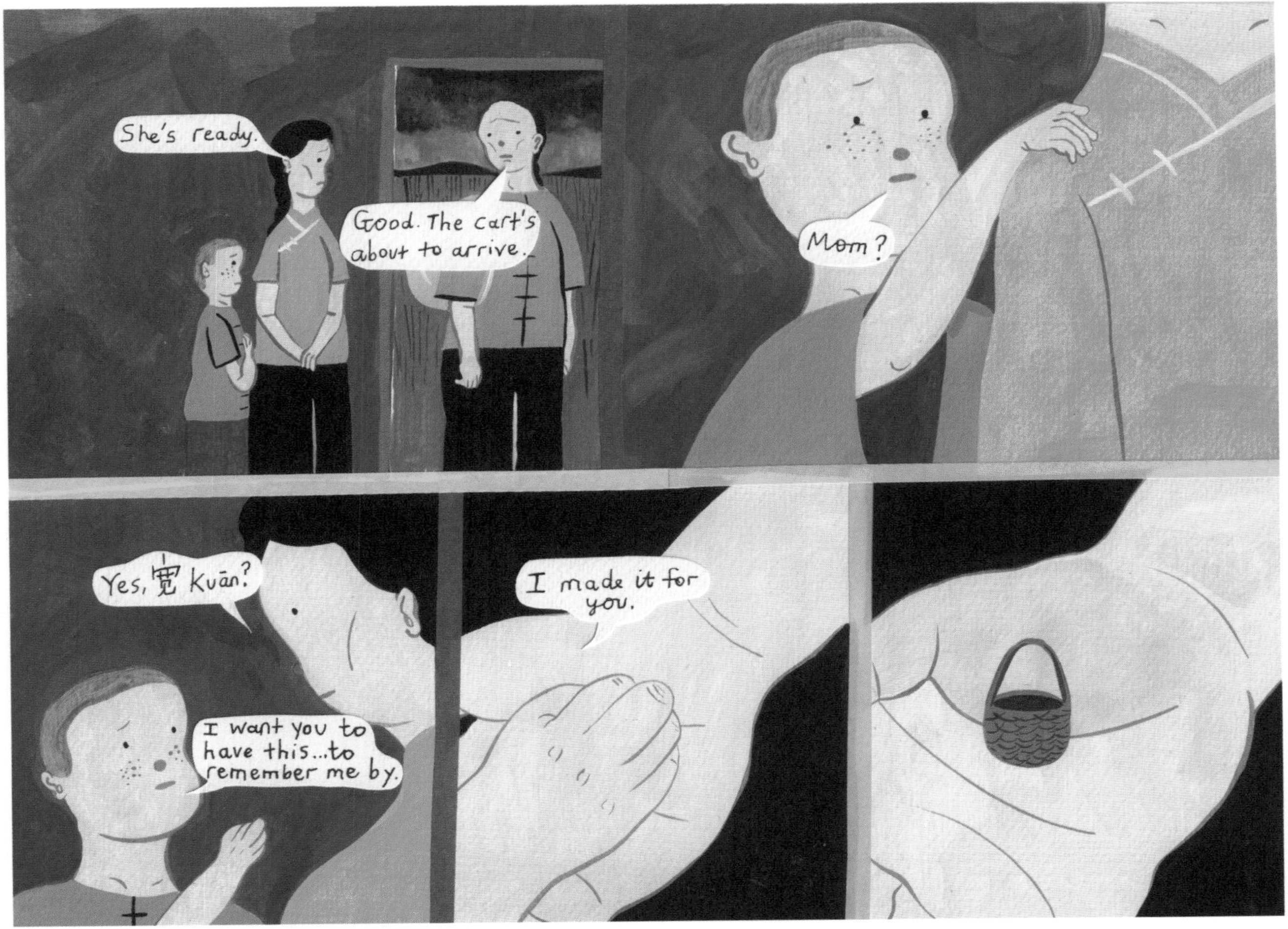
She's ready.
Good. The cart's about to arrive.
Mom?
Yes, 宽 Kuān?
I want you to have this...to remember me by.
I made it for you.

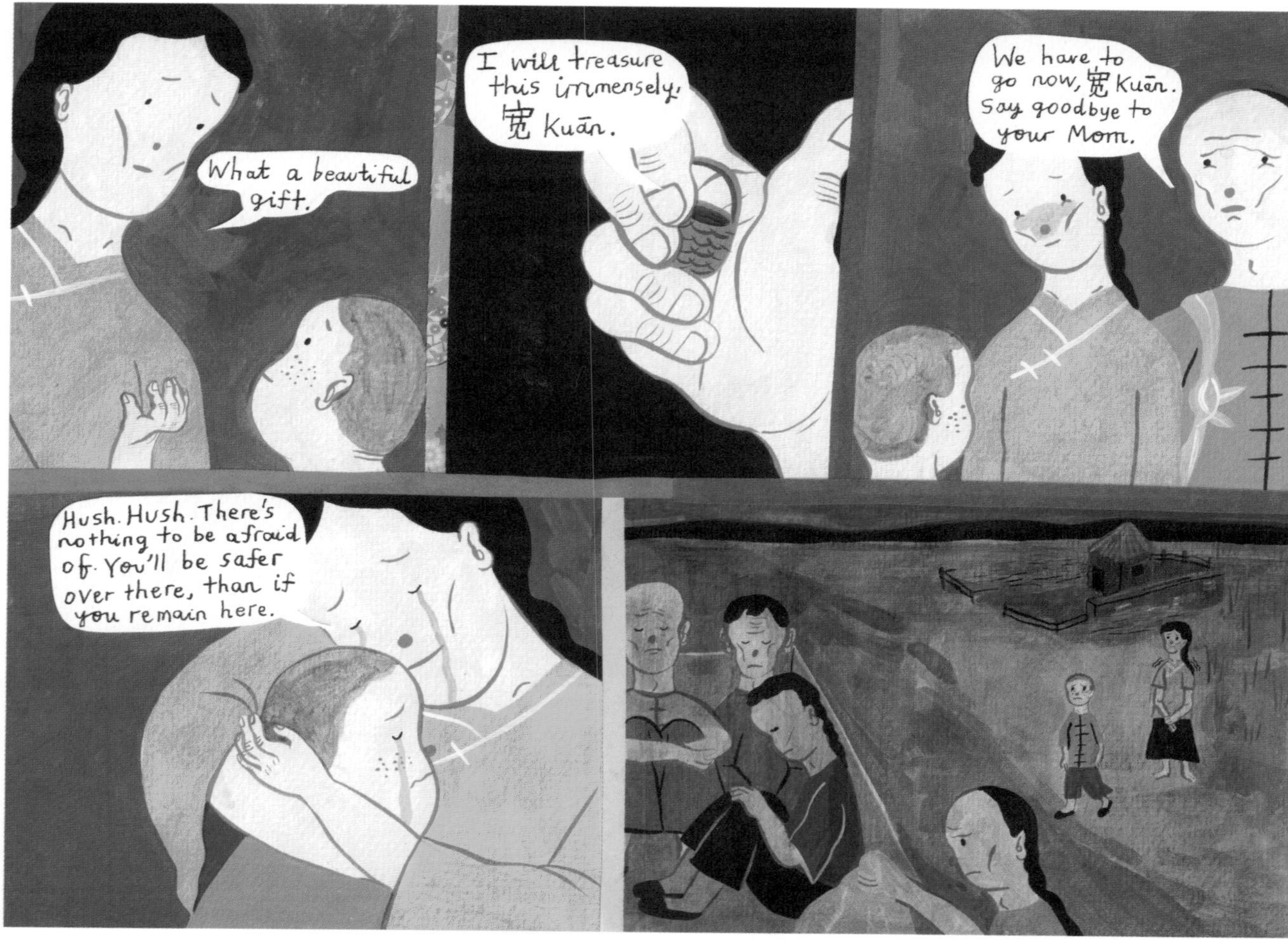
What a beautiful gift.
I will treasure this immensely, 宽 Kuān.
We have to go now, 宽 Kuān. Say goodbye to your Mom.
Hush. Hush. There's nothing to be afraid of. You'll be safer over there, than if you remain here.

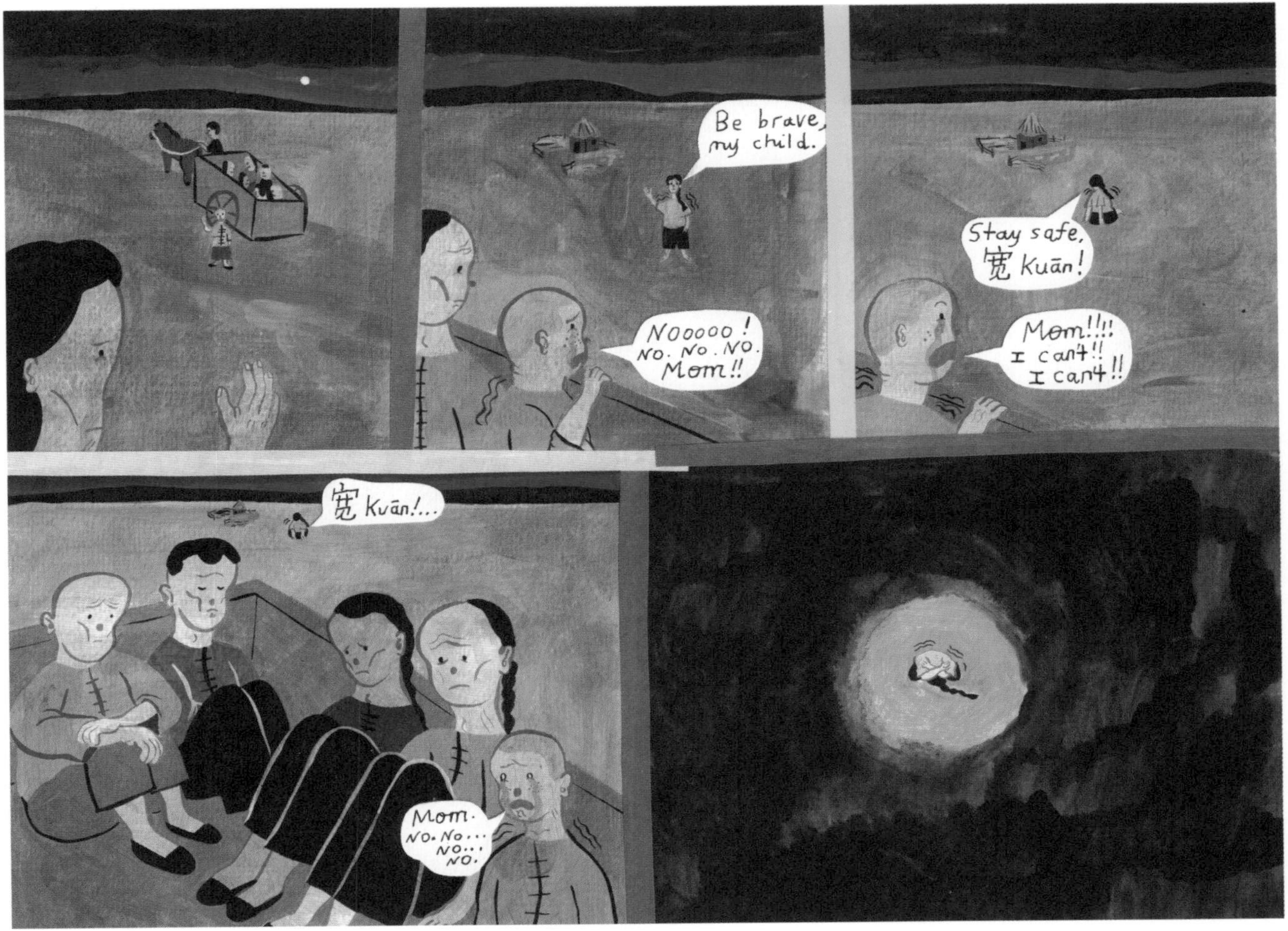
Be brave, my child.
Nooooo! No. No. No. Mom!!
Stay safe, 宽 Kuān!
Mom!!!! I can't!! I can't!!
宽 Kuān!...
Mom. No. No... No... No.

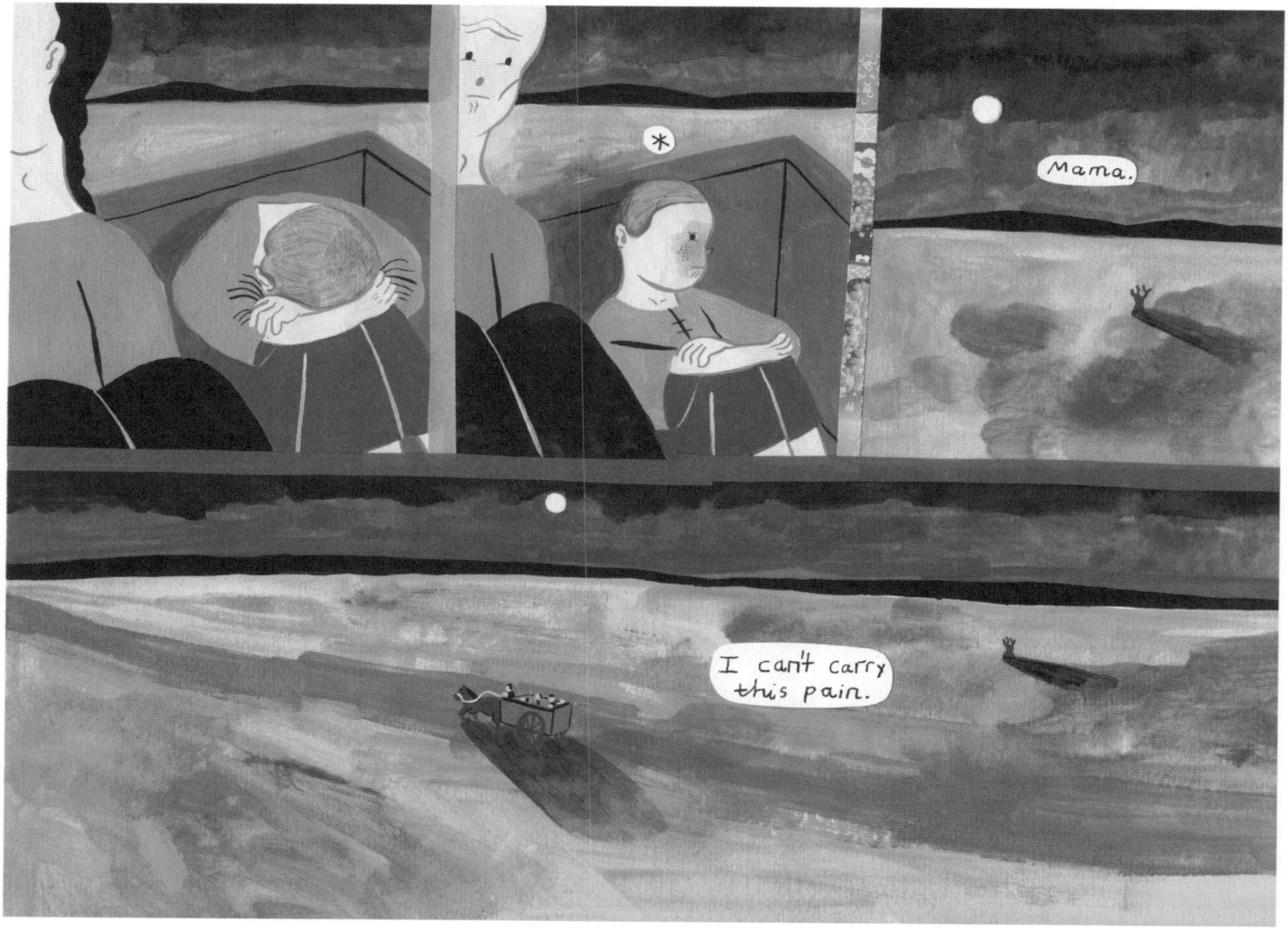
*
Mama.
I can't carry this pain.

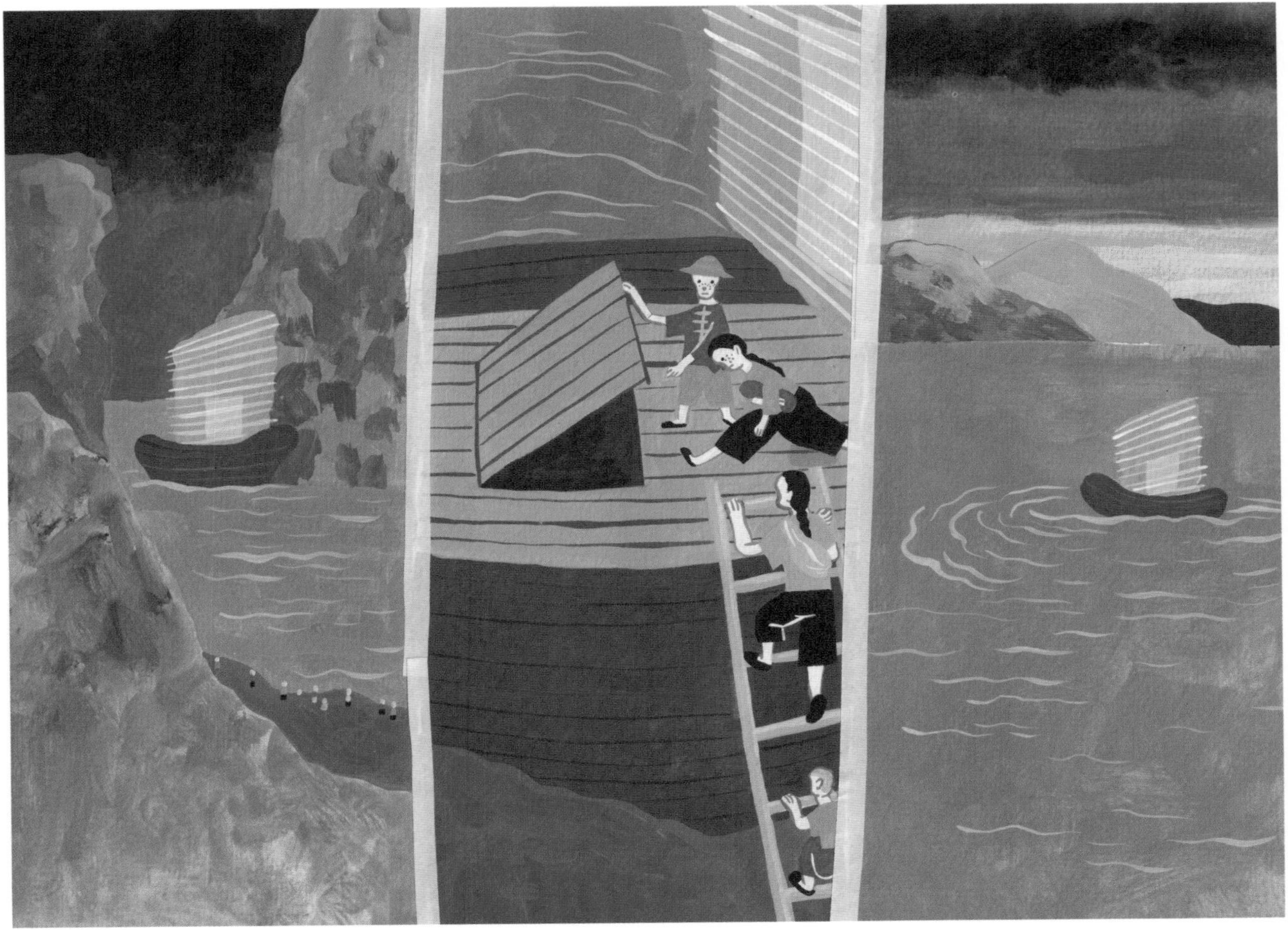

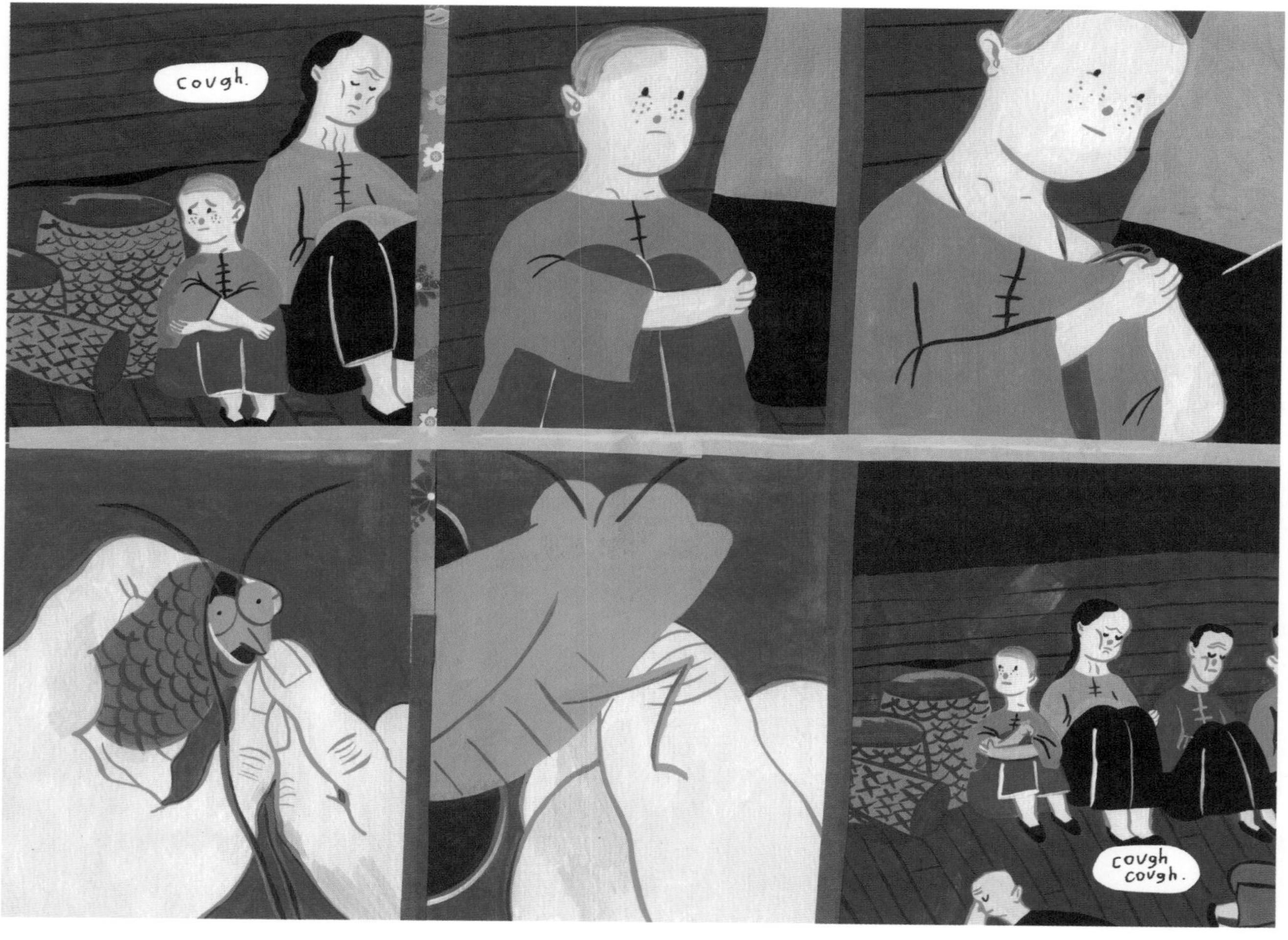
cough.
cough cough.

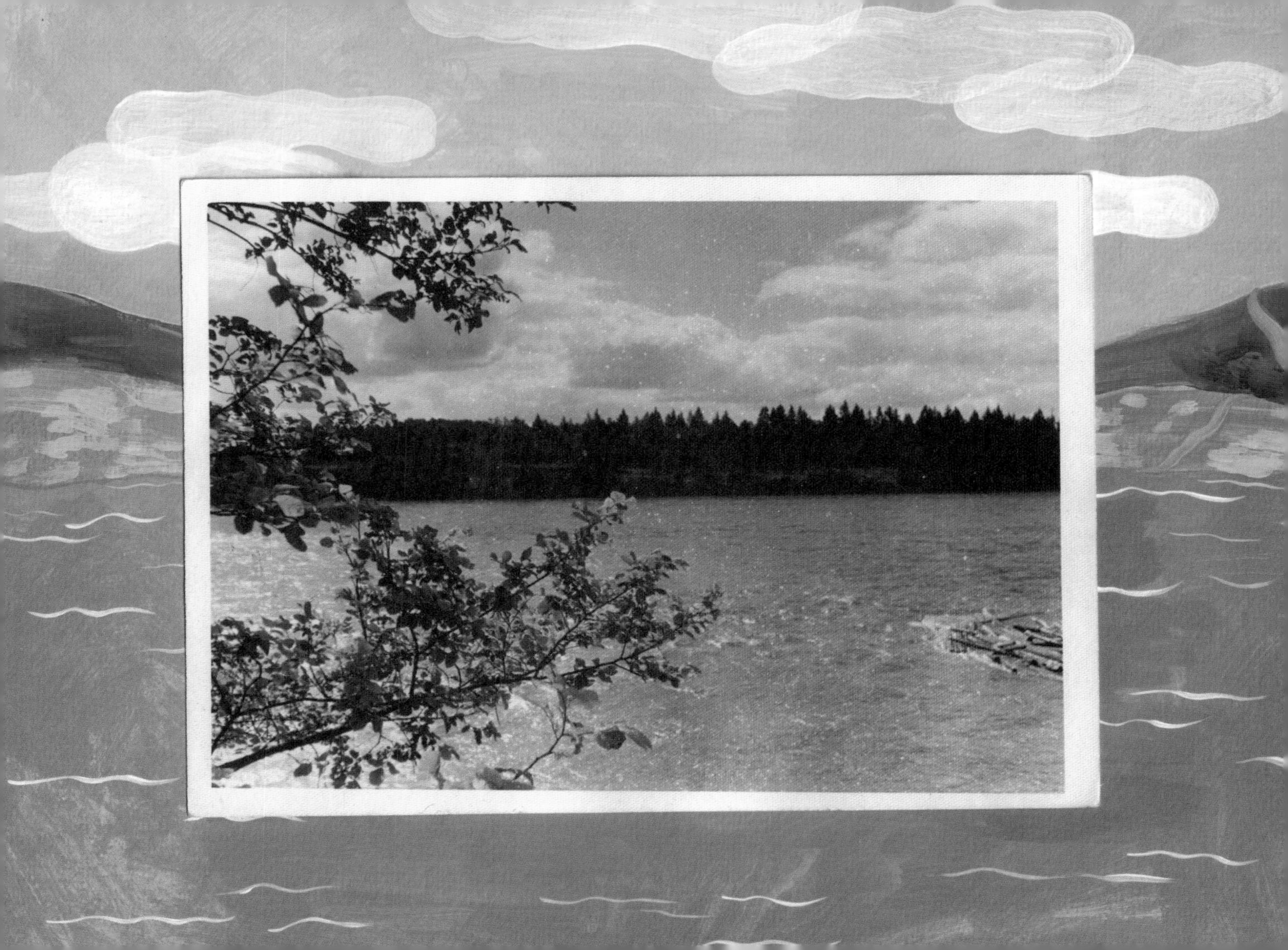

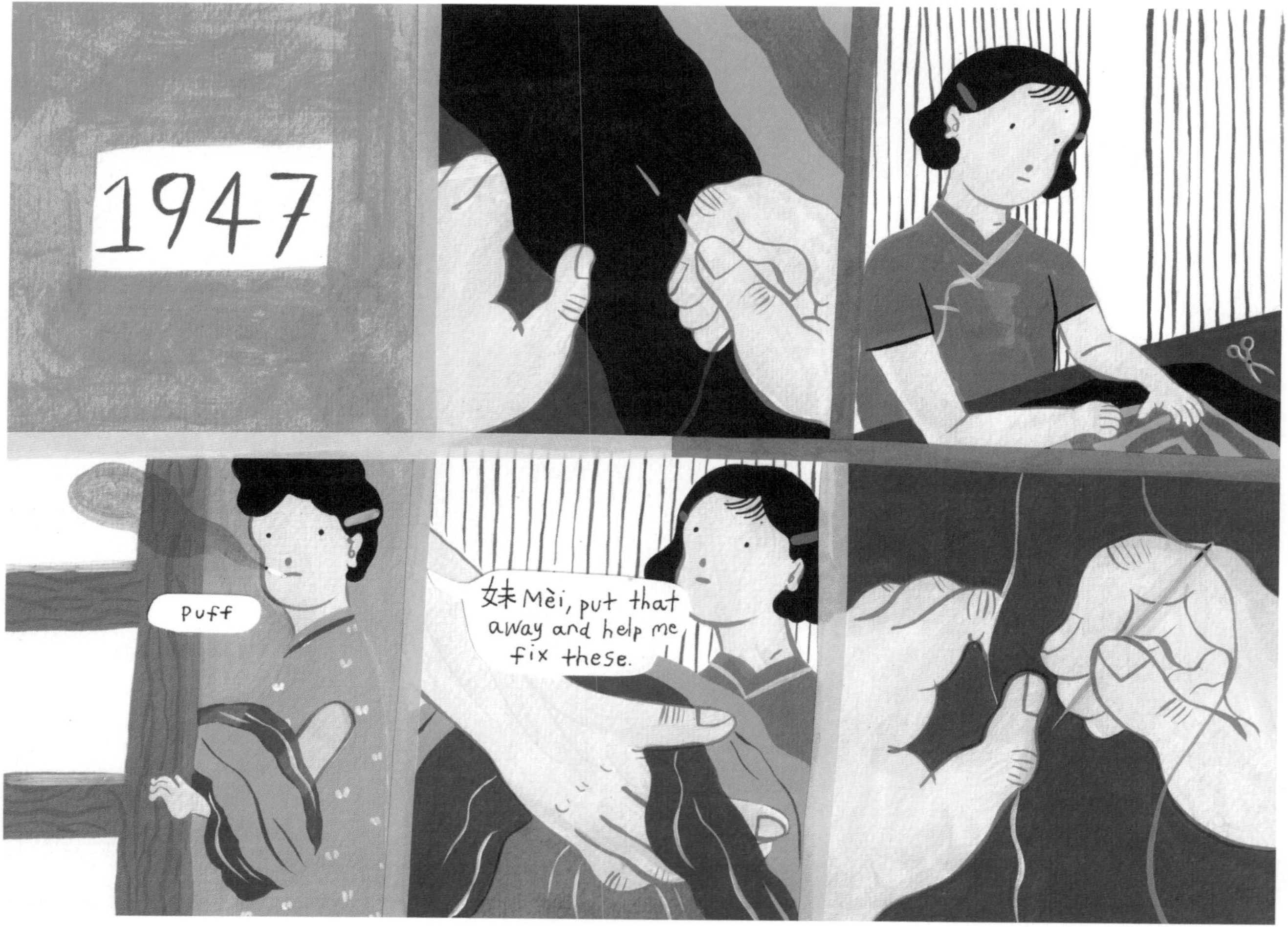
1947
puff
妹 Mèi, put that away and help me fix these.

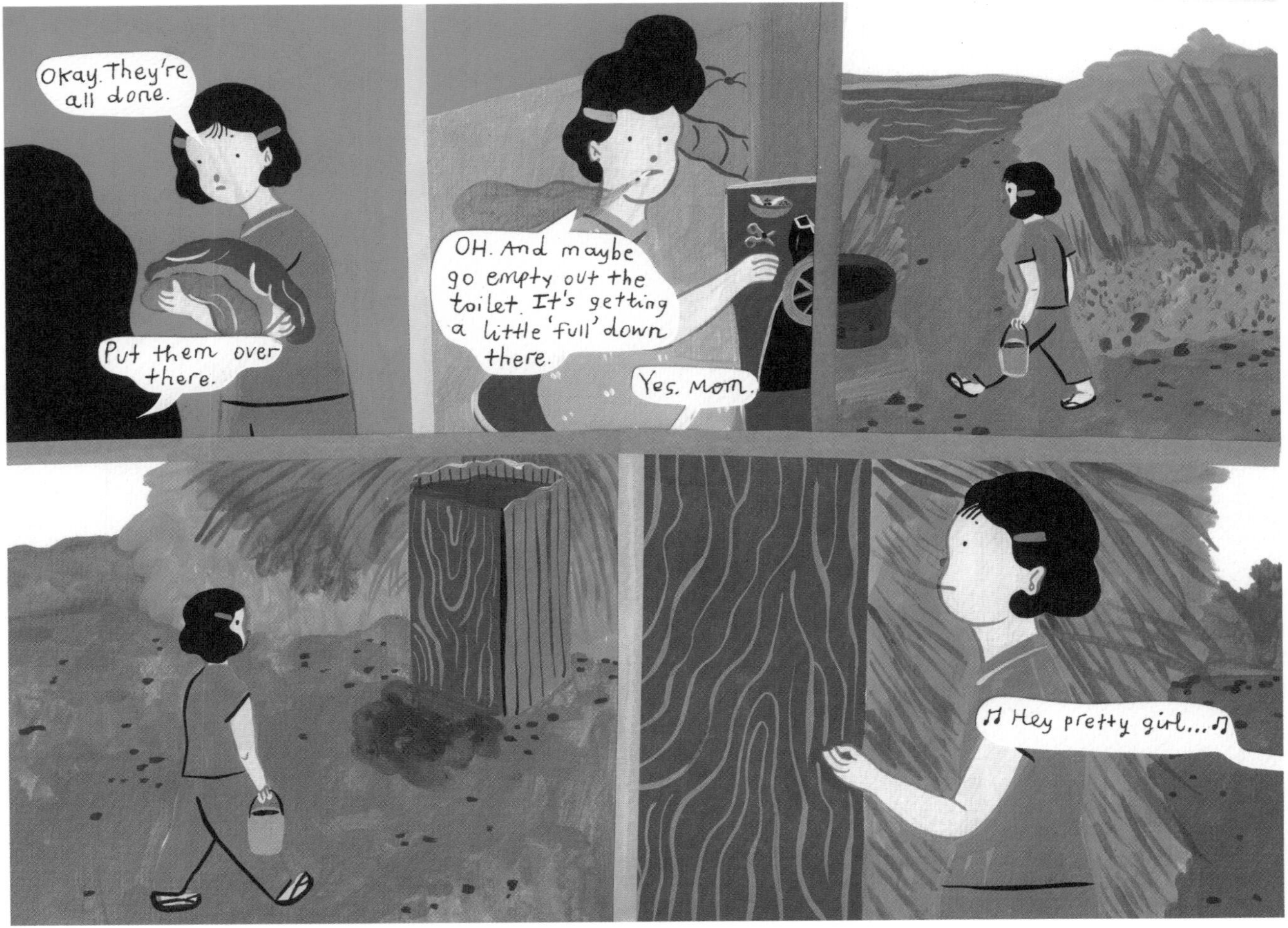
Okay. They're all done.
Put them over there.
OH. And maybe go empty out the toilet. It's getting a little 'full' down there.
Yes, Mom.
♫ Hey pretty girl... ♫

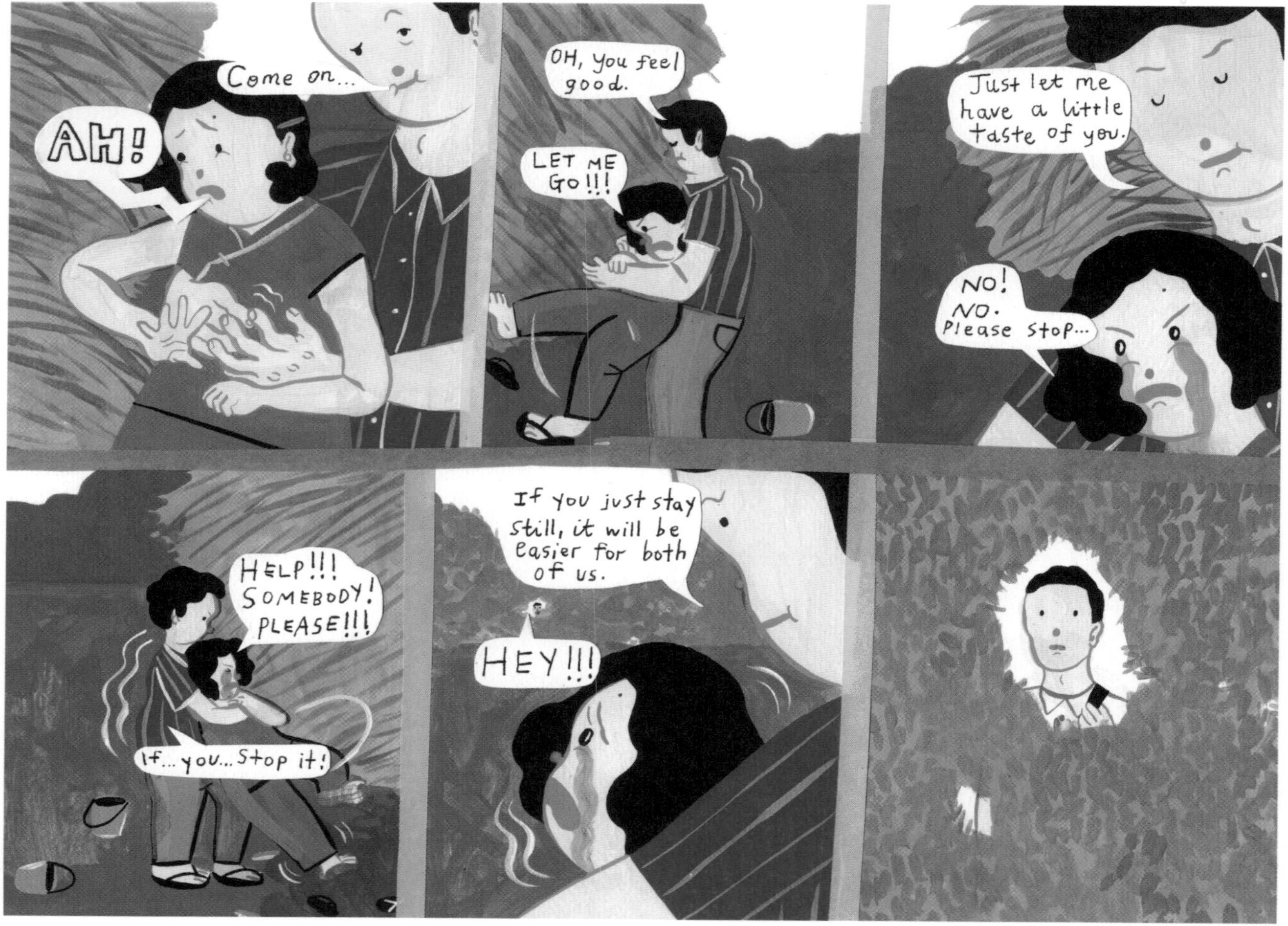
Come on...
AH!
OH, you feel good.
LET ME GO!!!
Just let me have a little taste of you.
NO! NO. Please stop...
HELP!!! SOMEBODY! PLEASE!!!
If... you... Stop it!
If you just stay still, it will be easier for both of us.
HEY!!!

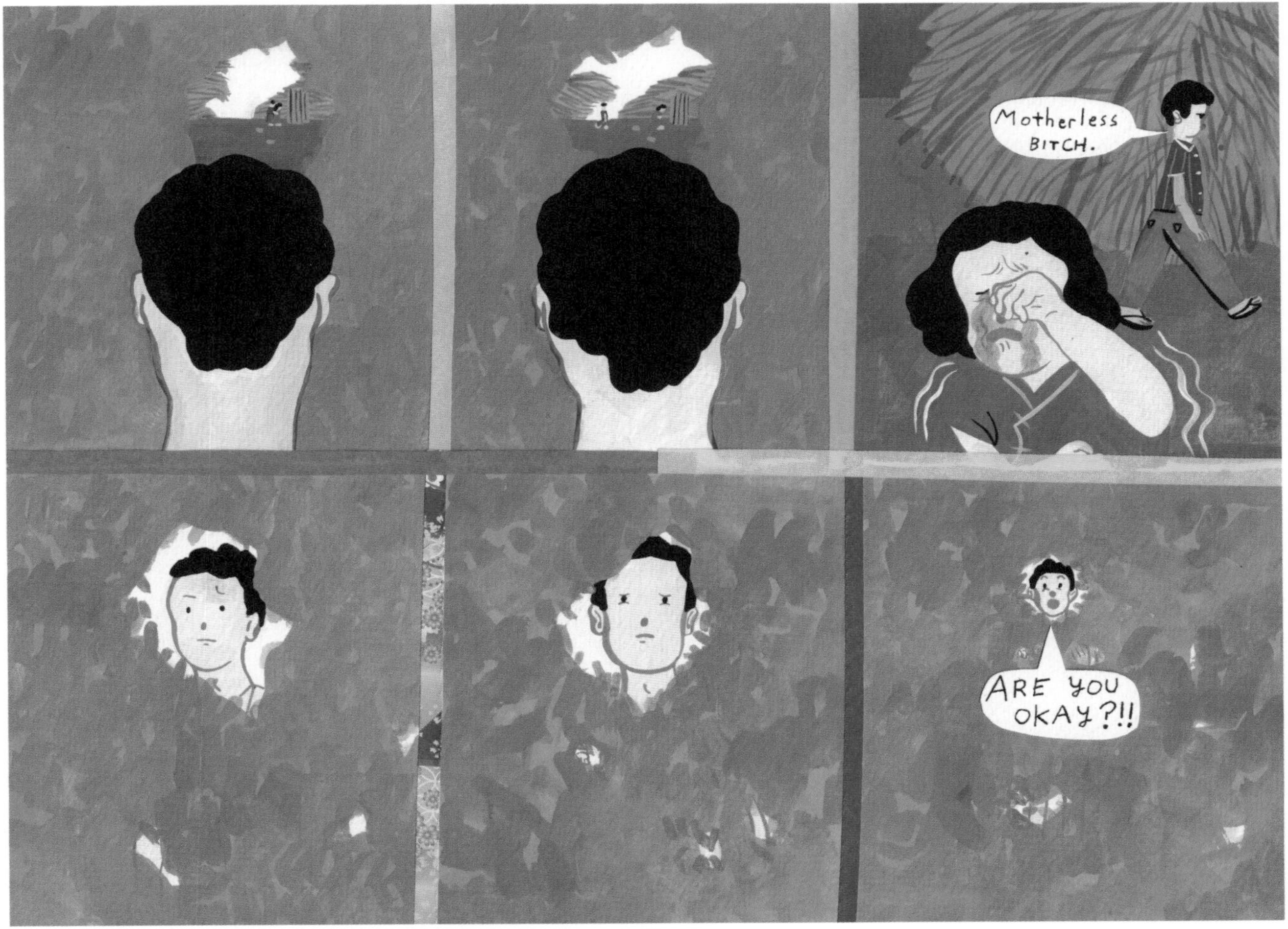
Motherless BITCH.
ARE YOU OKAY?!!

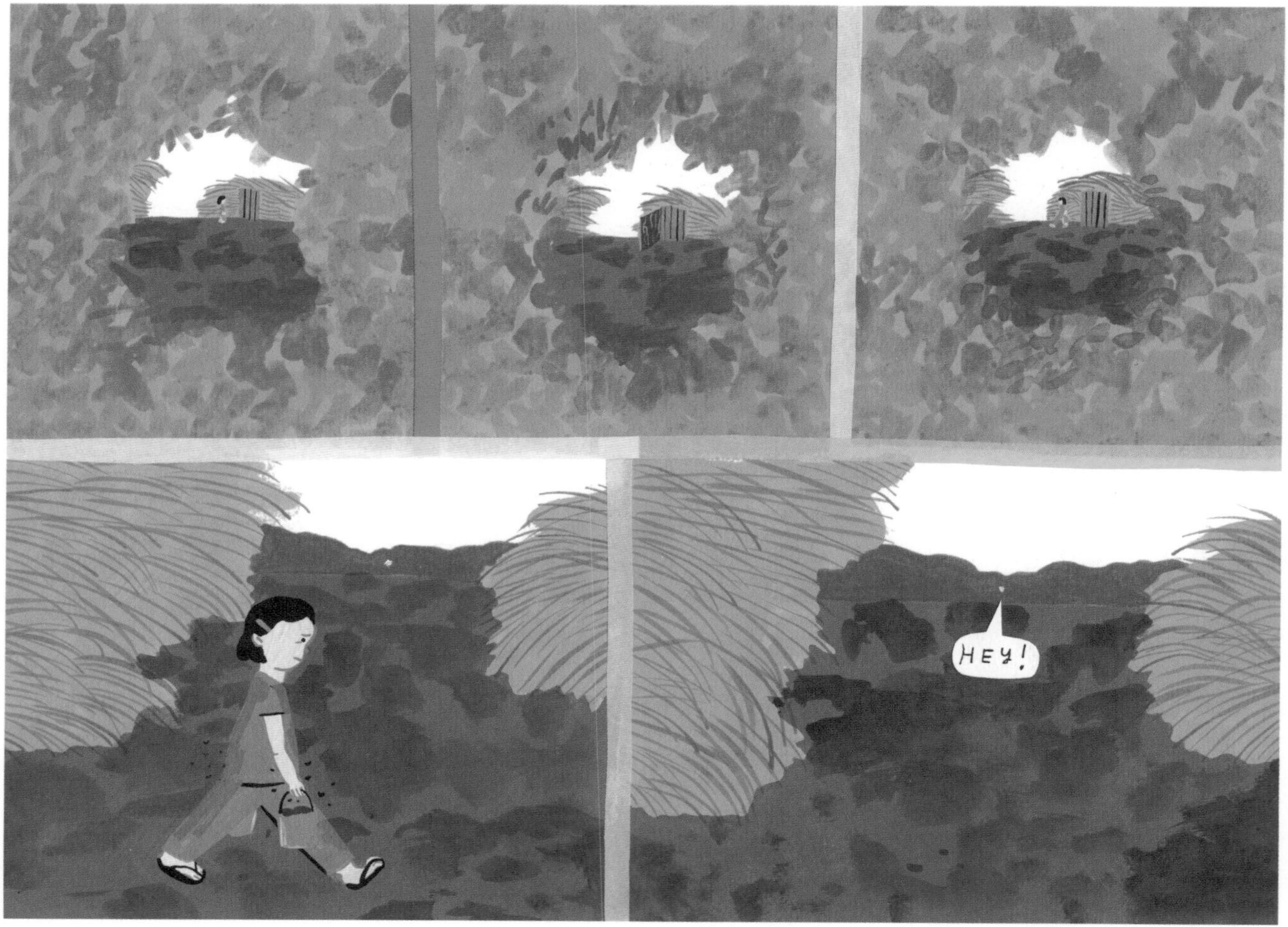
HEY!

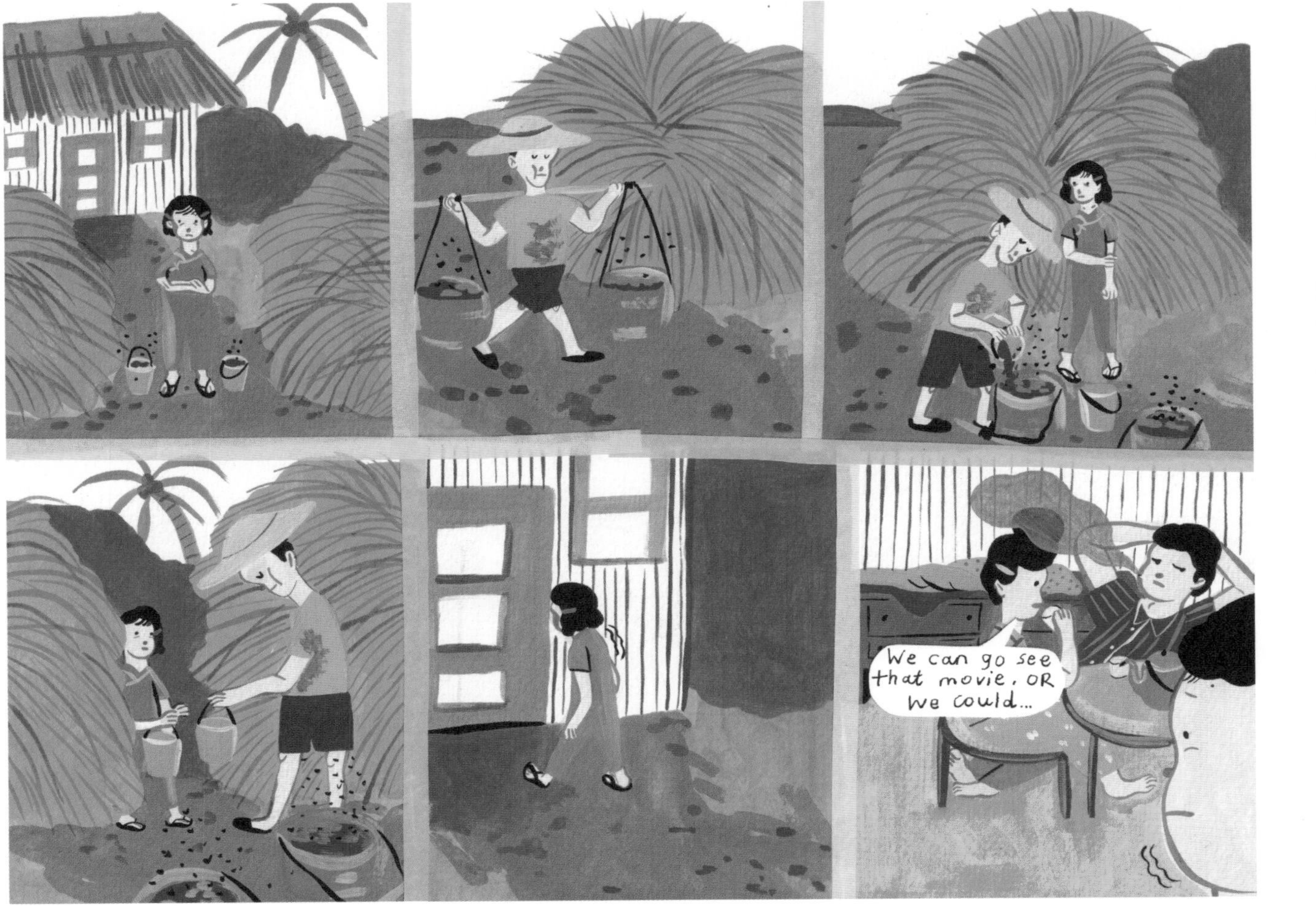
We can go see that movie, OR we could...

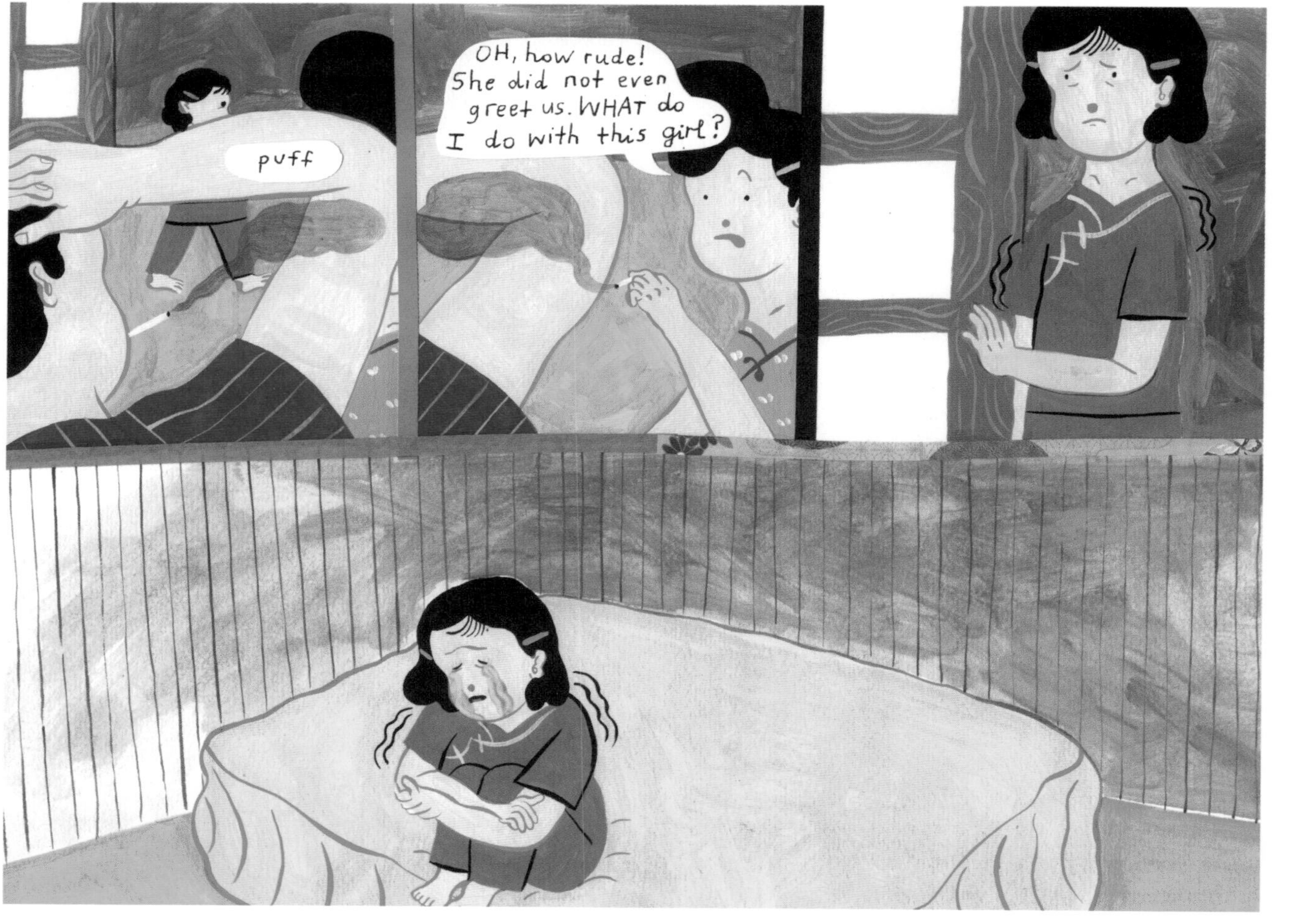
puff
OH, how rude! She did not even greet us. WHAT do I do with this girl?

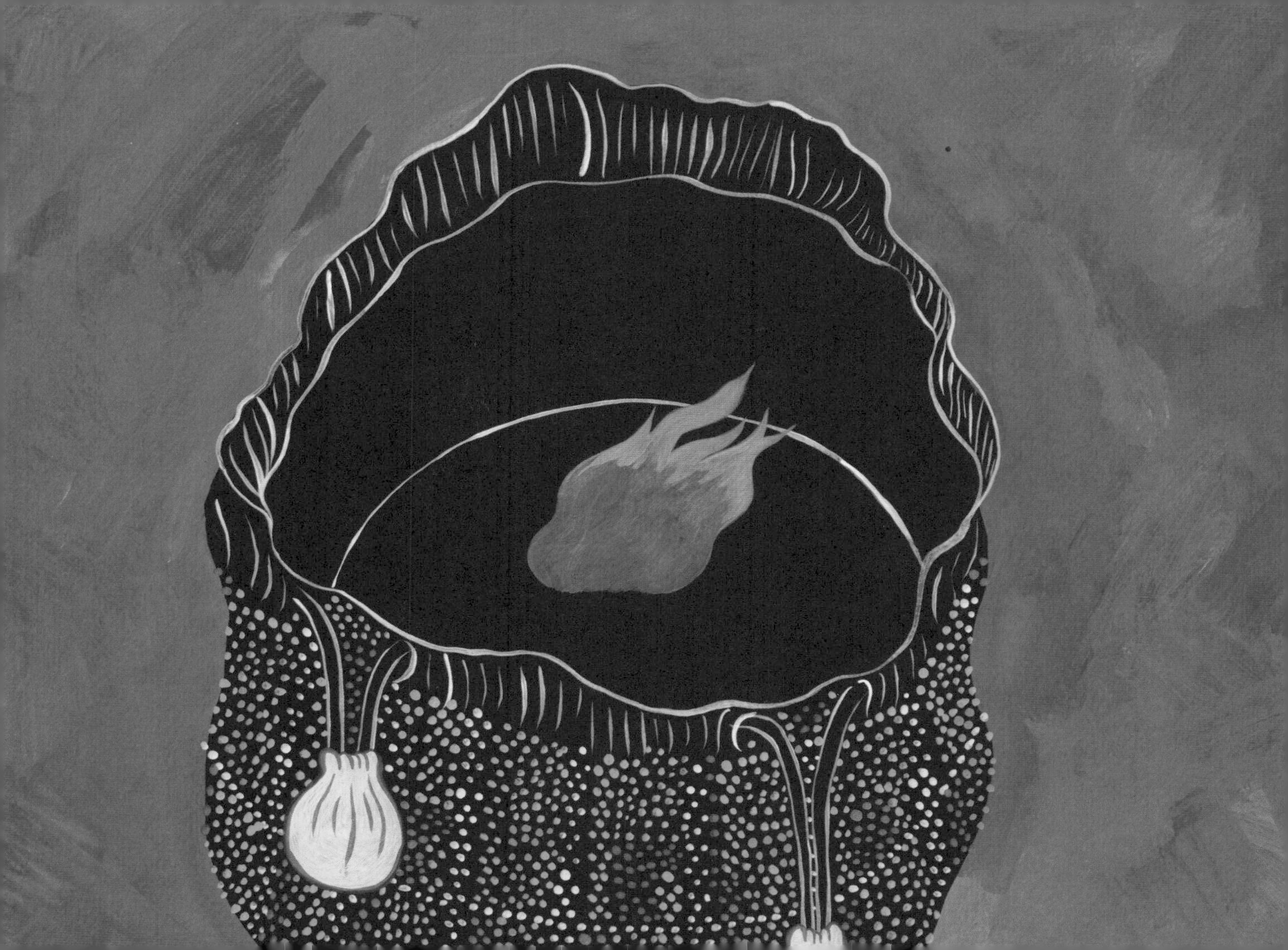

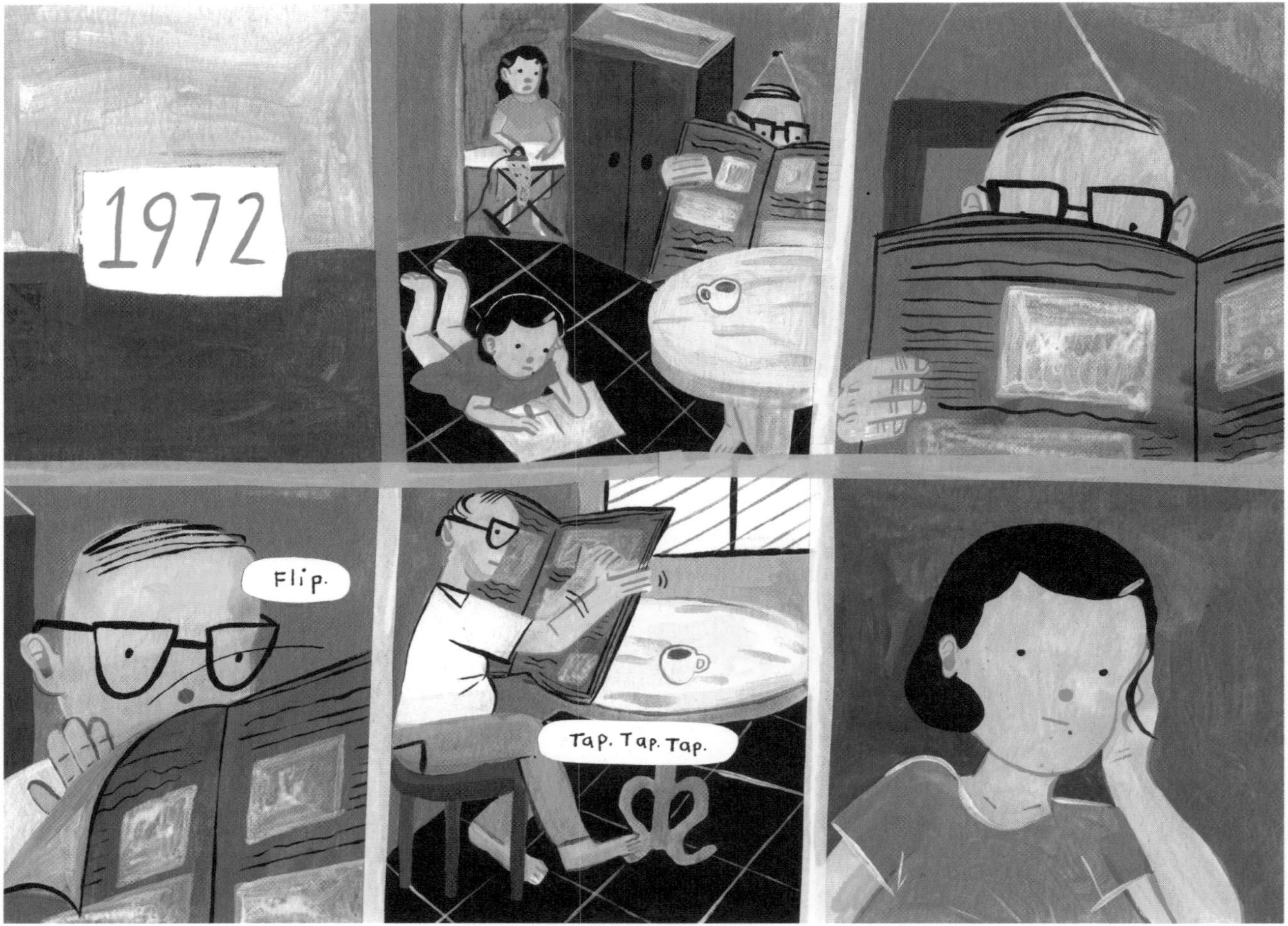
1972
Flip.
Tap. Tap. Tap.

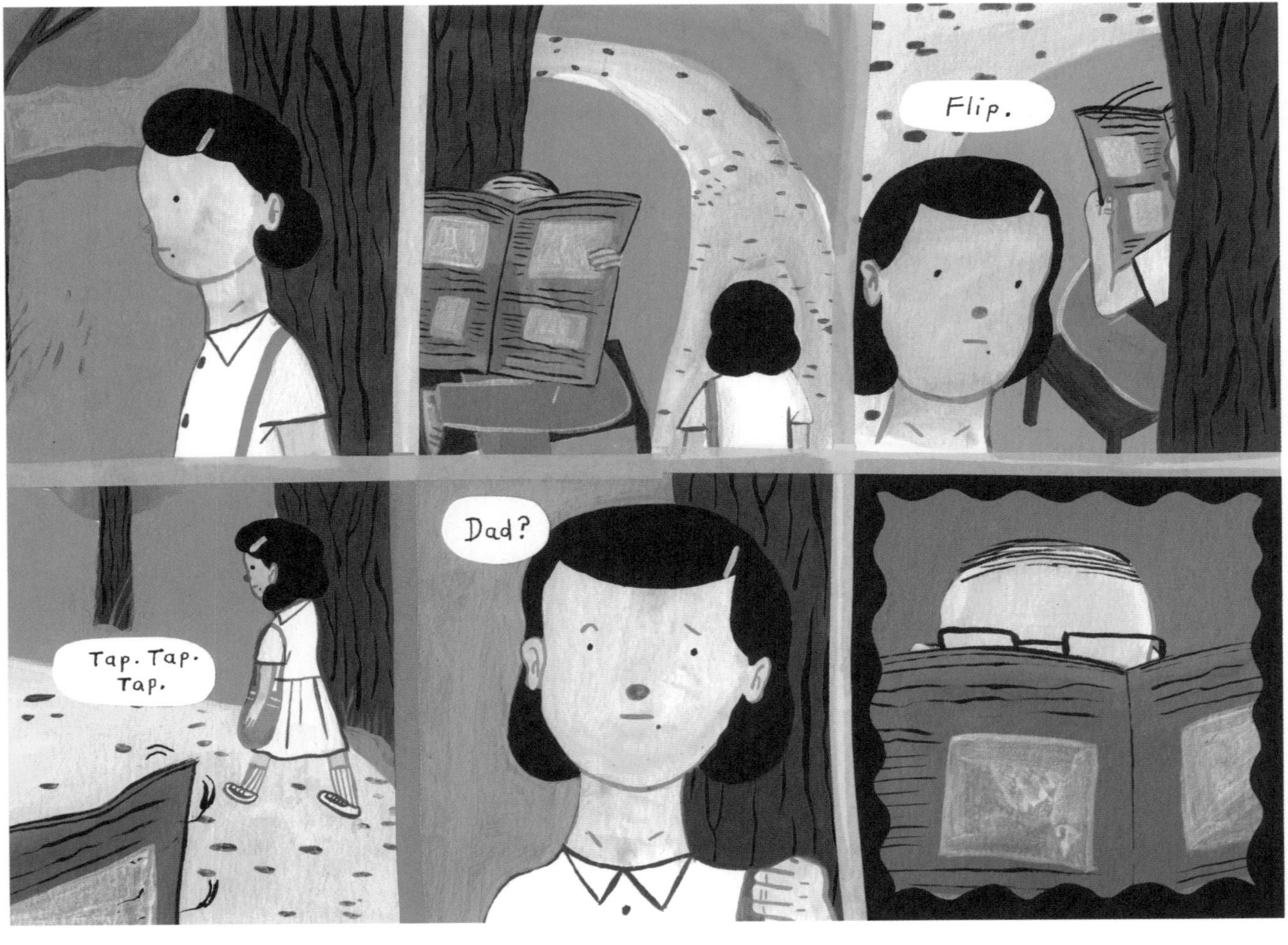
Flip.
Tap. Tap. Tap.
Dad?

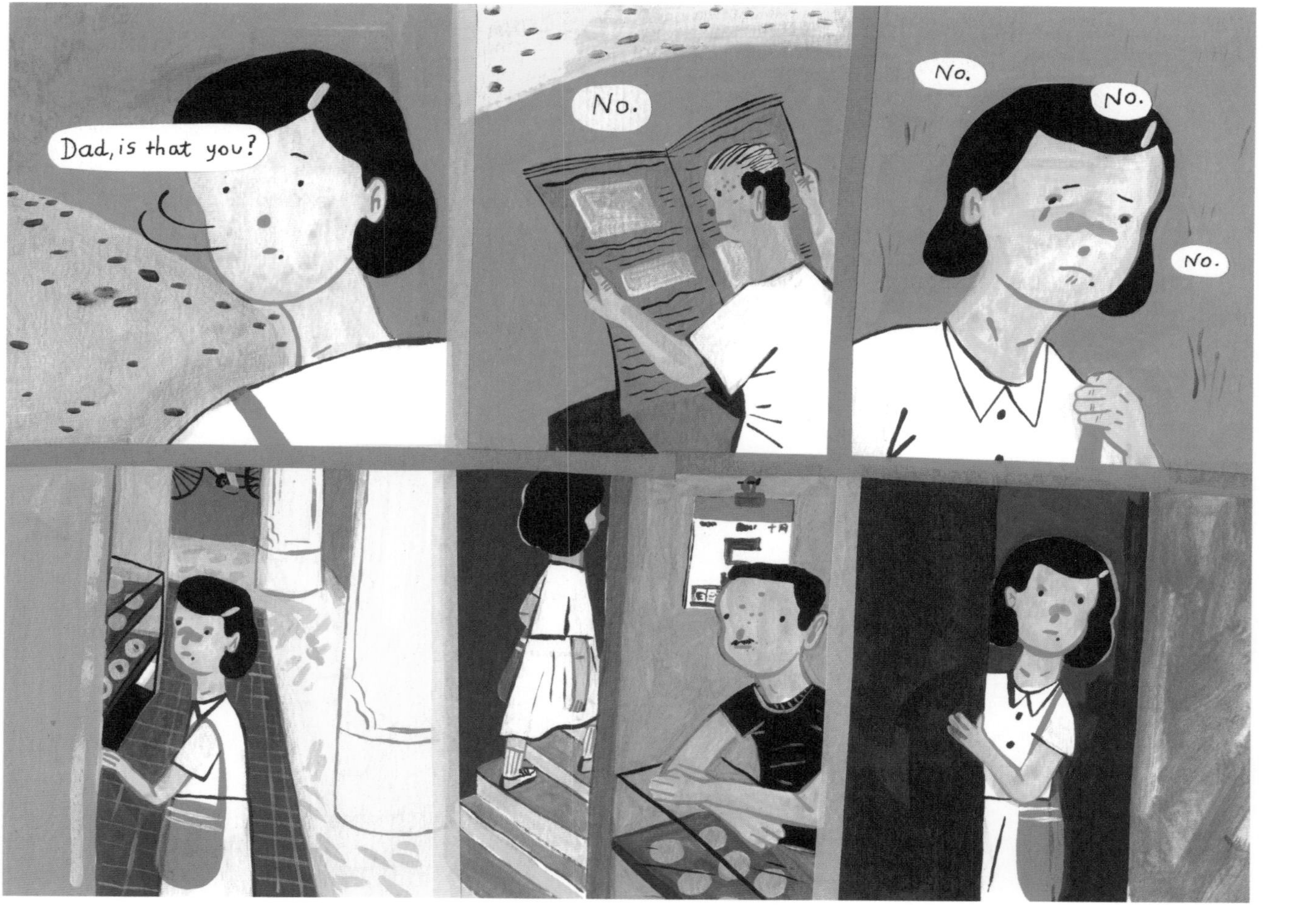
Dad, is that you?
No.
No.
No.
No.

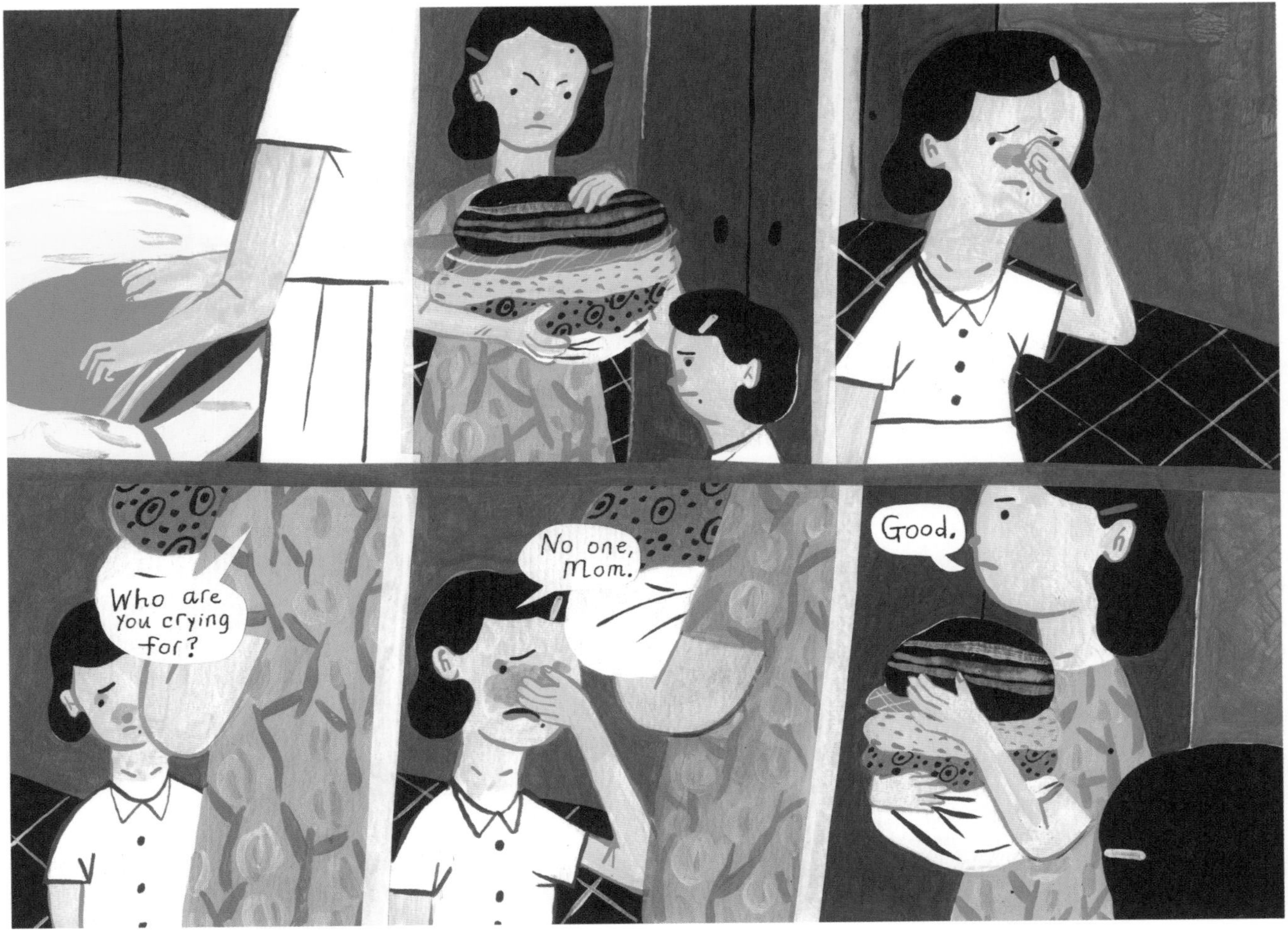
Who are you crying for?
No one, Mom.
Good.

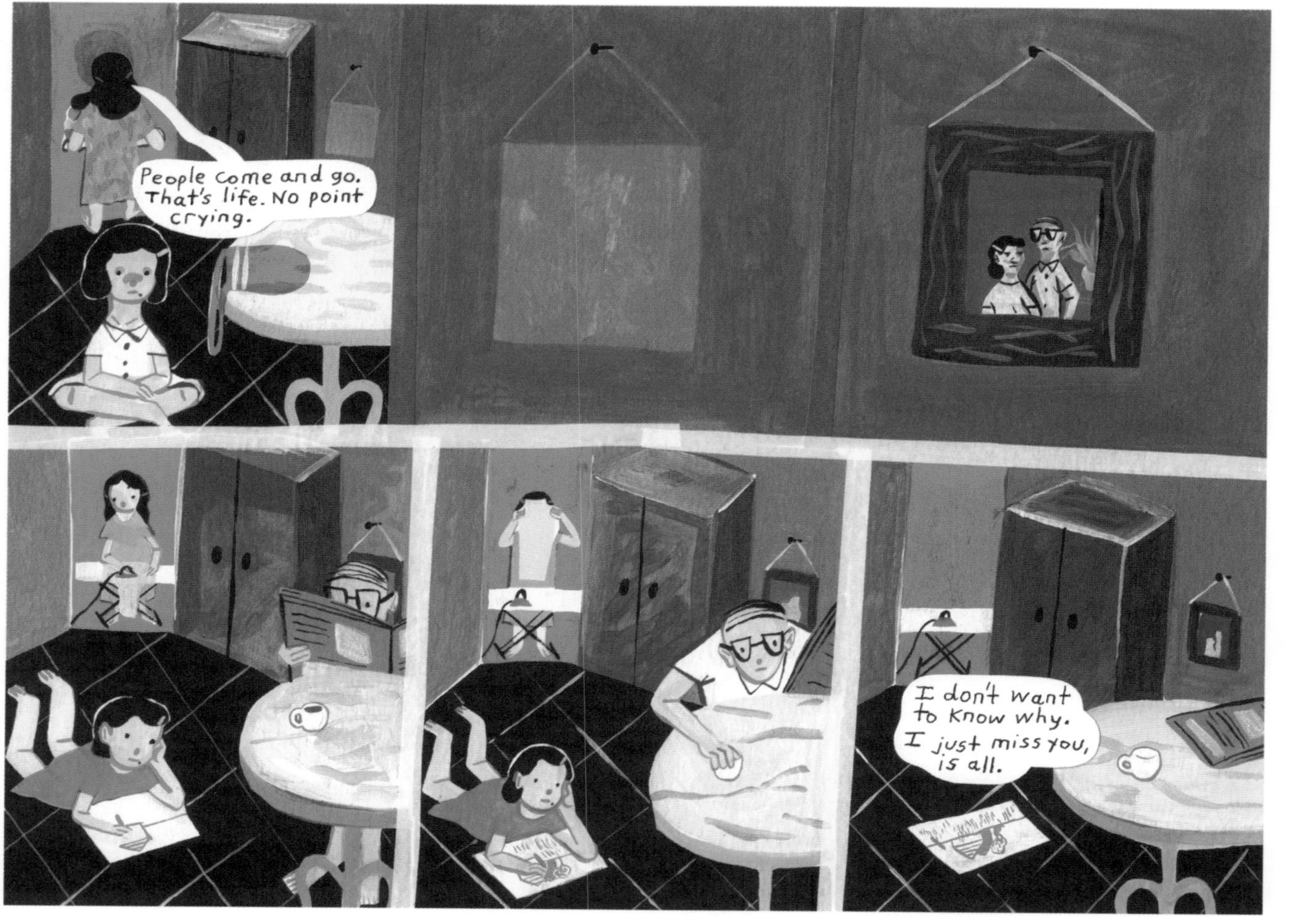
People come and go. That's life. No point crying.
I don't want to know why. I just miss you, is all.

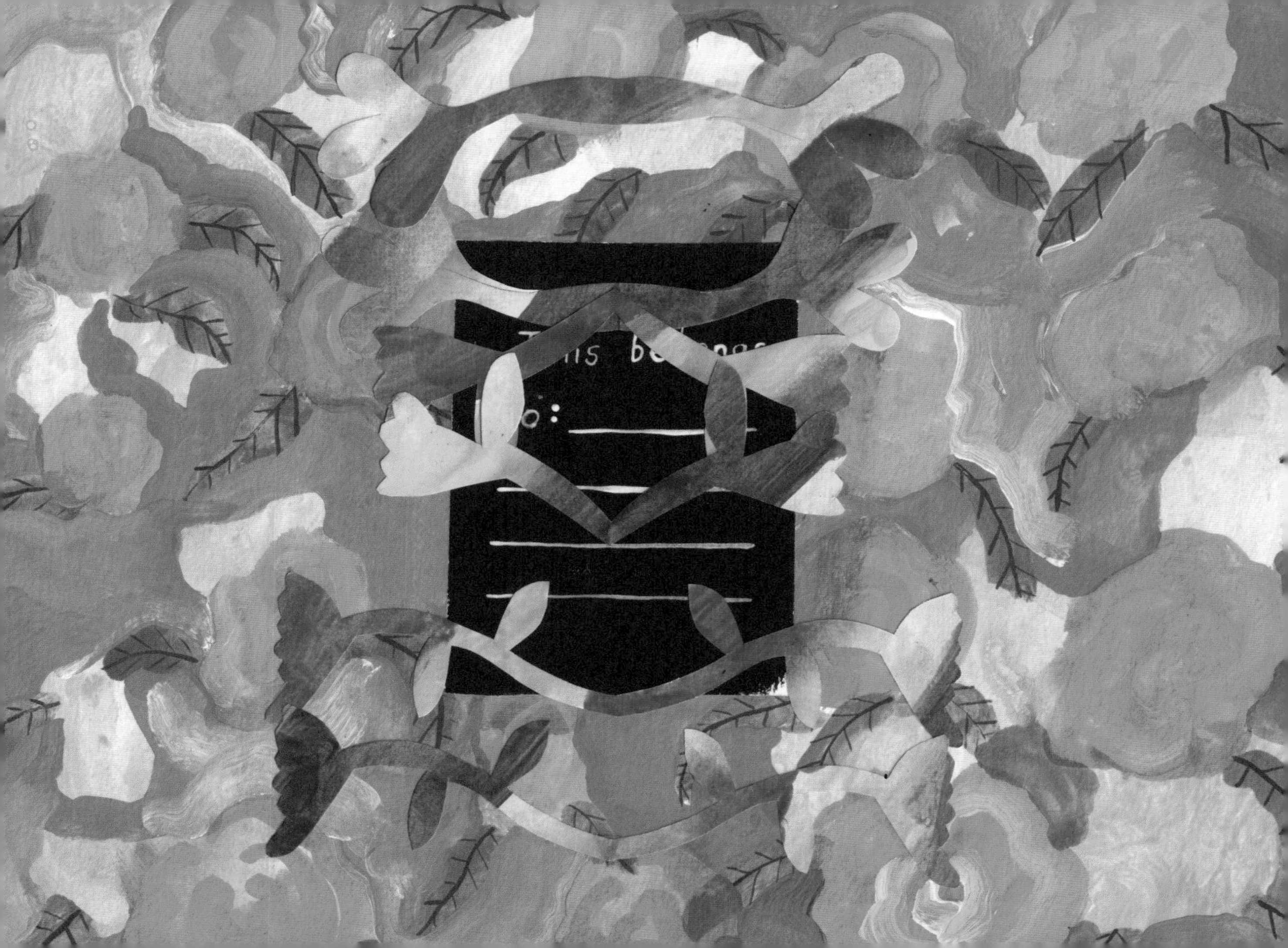

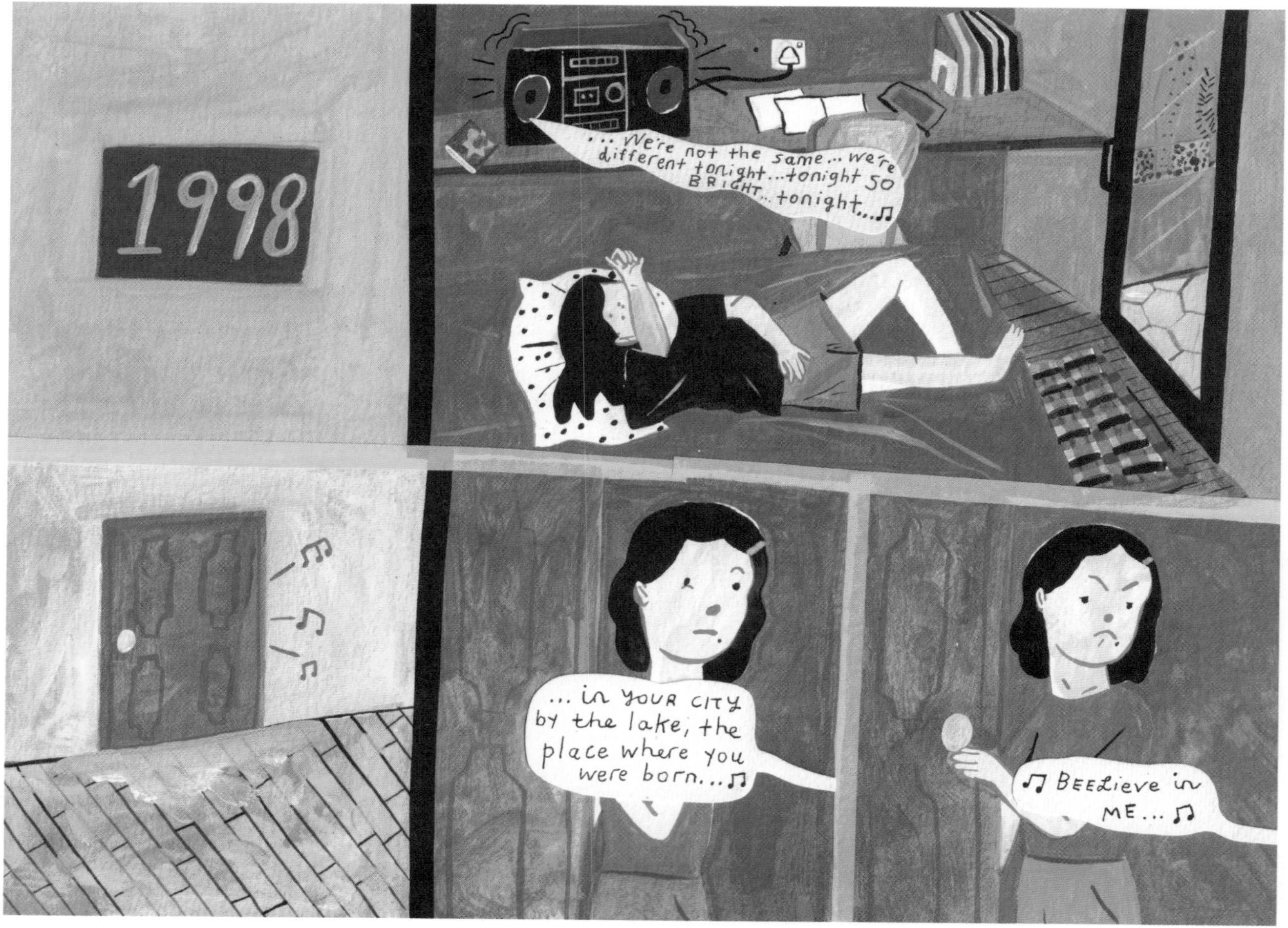
1998
... We're not the same... we're different tonight... tonight so BRIGHT... tonight... ♫
... in YOUR CITY by the lake, the place where you were born... ♫
♫ BEELieve in ME... ♫

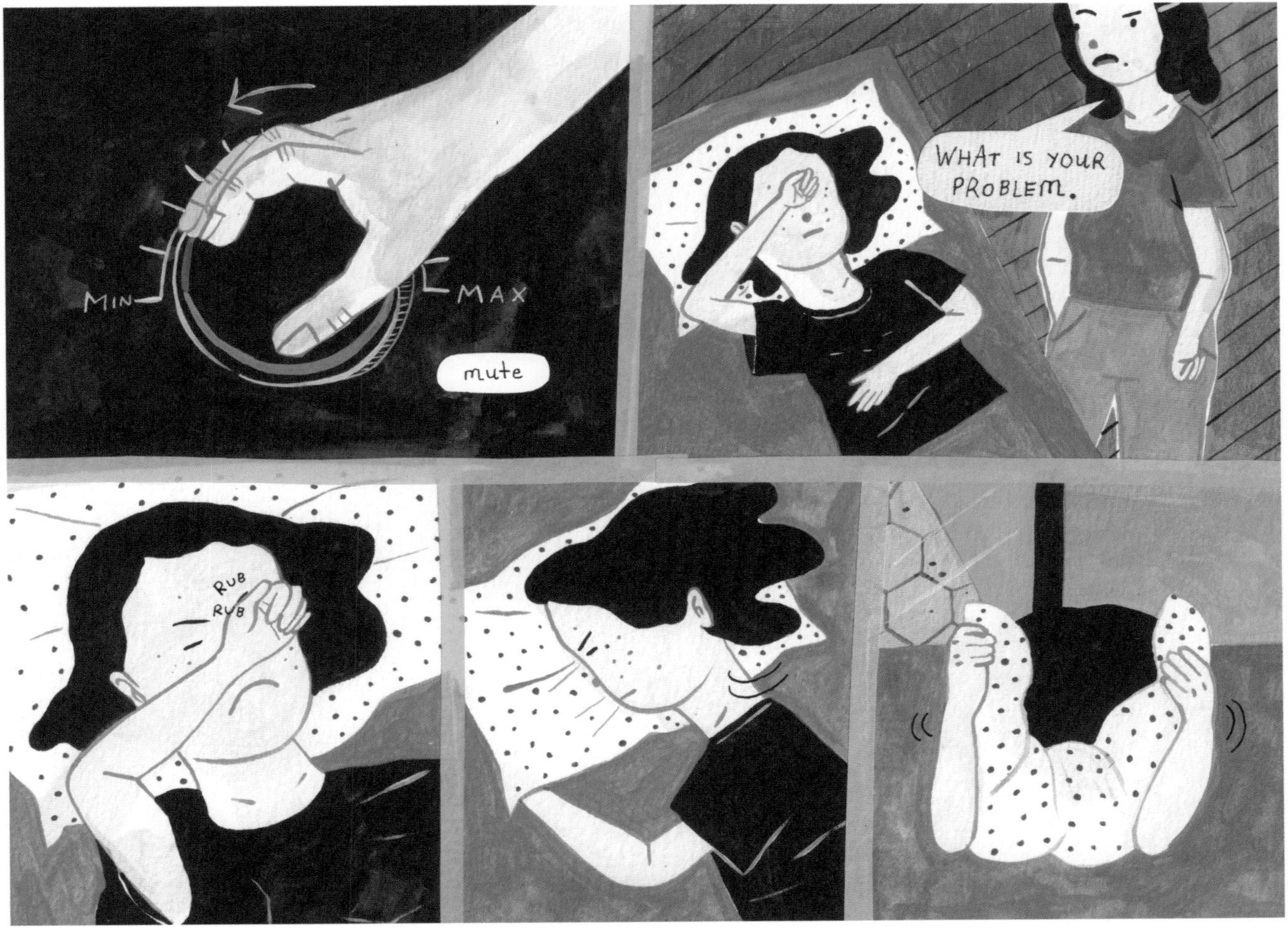
MIN
MAX
mute
WHAT IS YOUR PROBLEM.
RUB RUB

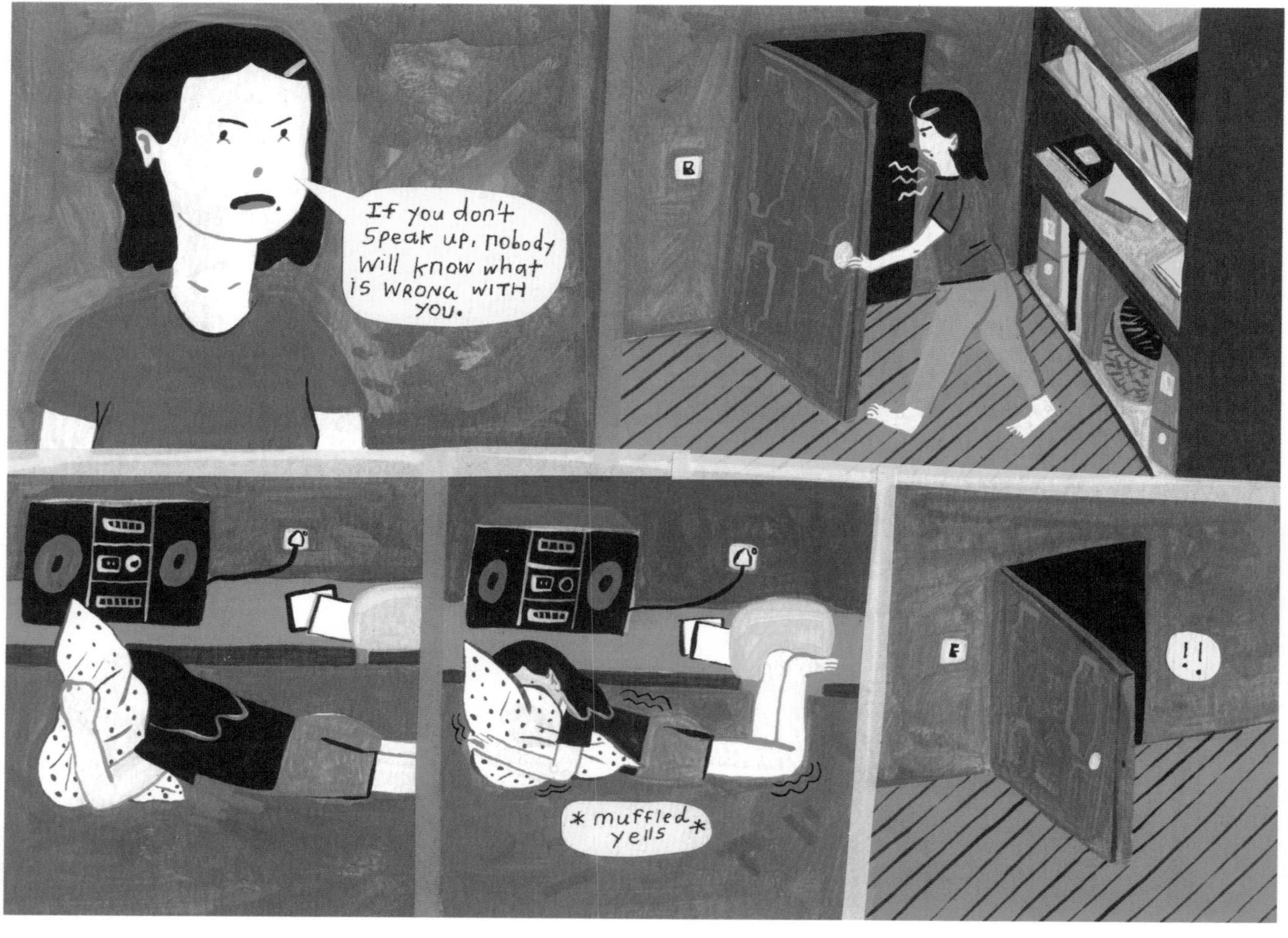
If you don't Speak up, nobody will know what is WRONG WITH YOU.
B
muffled yells
E
!!

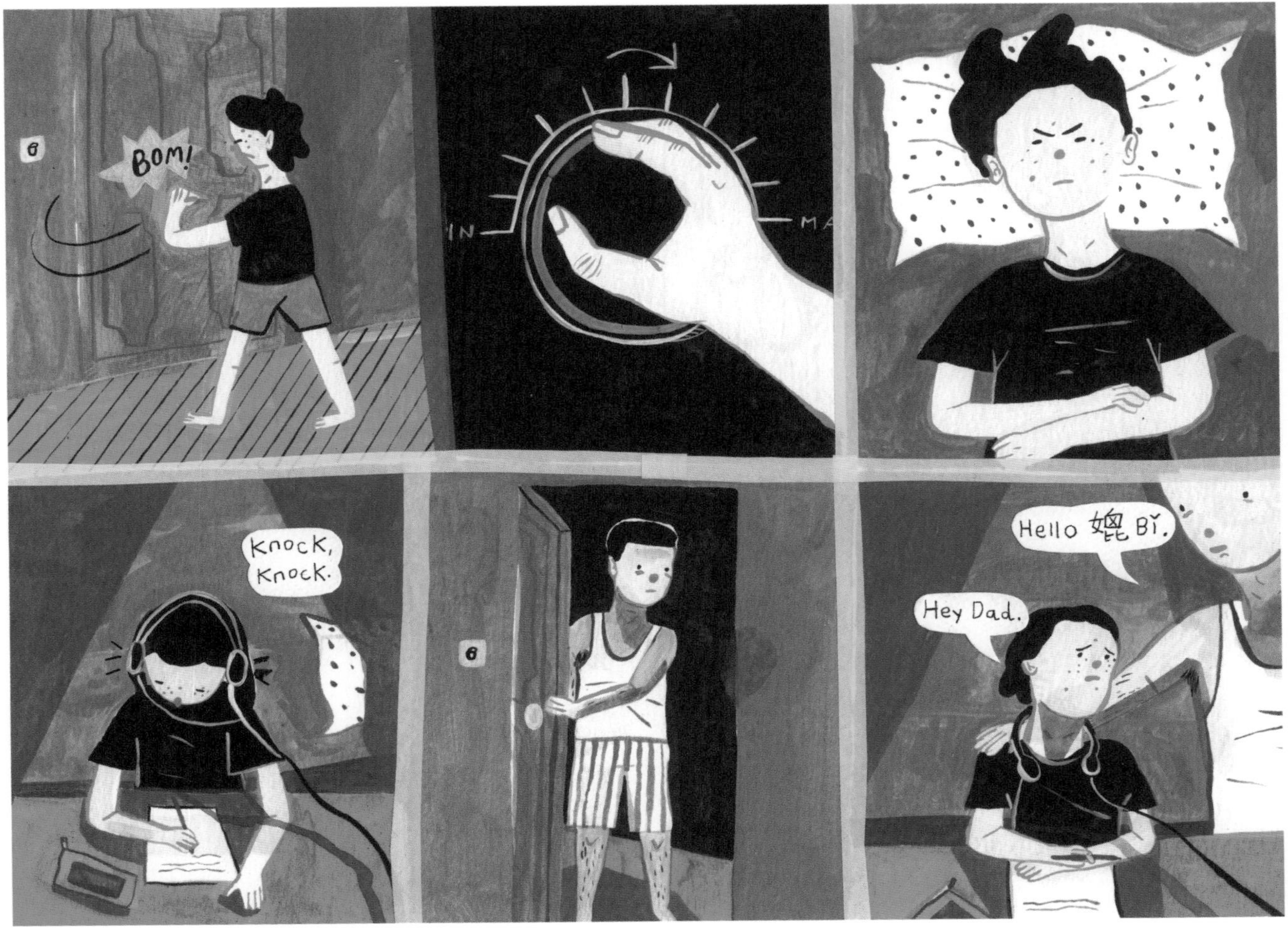
BOM!
Knock, knock.
Hello 媲 BǏ.
Hey Dad.

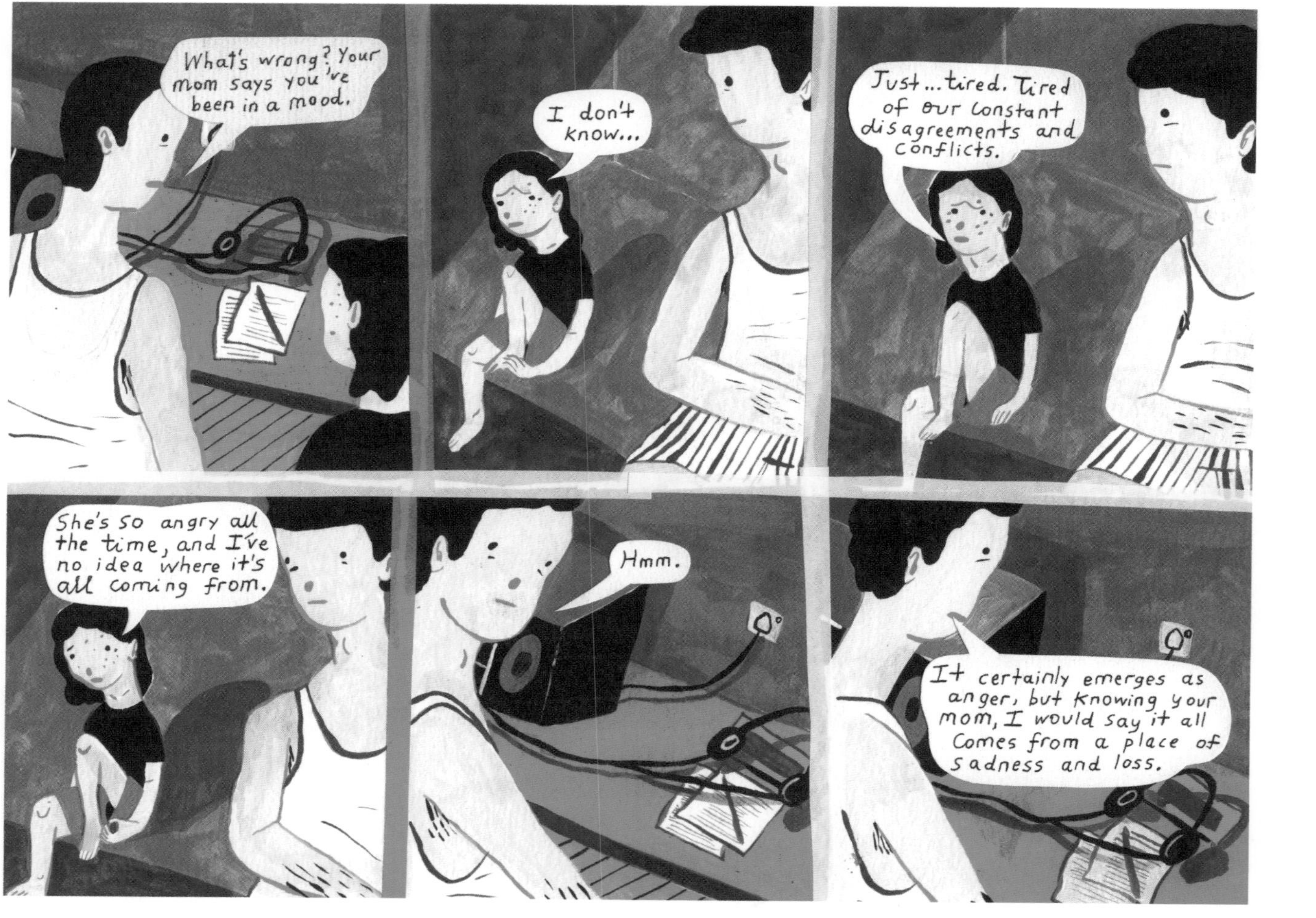
What's wrong? Your mom says you've been in a mood.
I don't know...
Just... tired. Tired of our constant disagreements and conflicts.
She's so angry all the time, and I've no idea where it's all coming from.
Hmm.
It certainly emerges as anger, but knowing your mom, I would say it all comes from a place of sadness and loss.

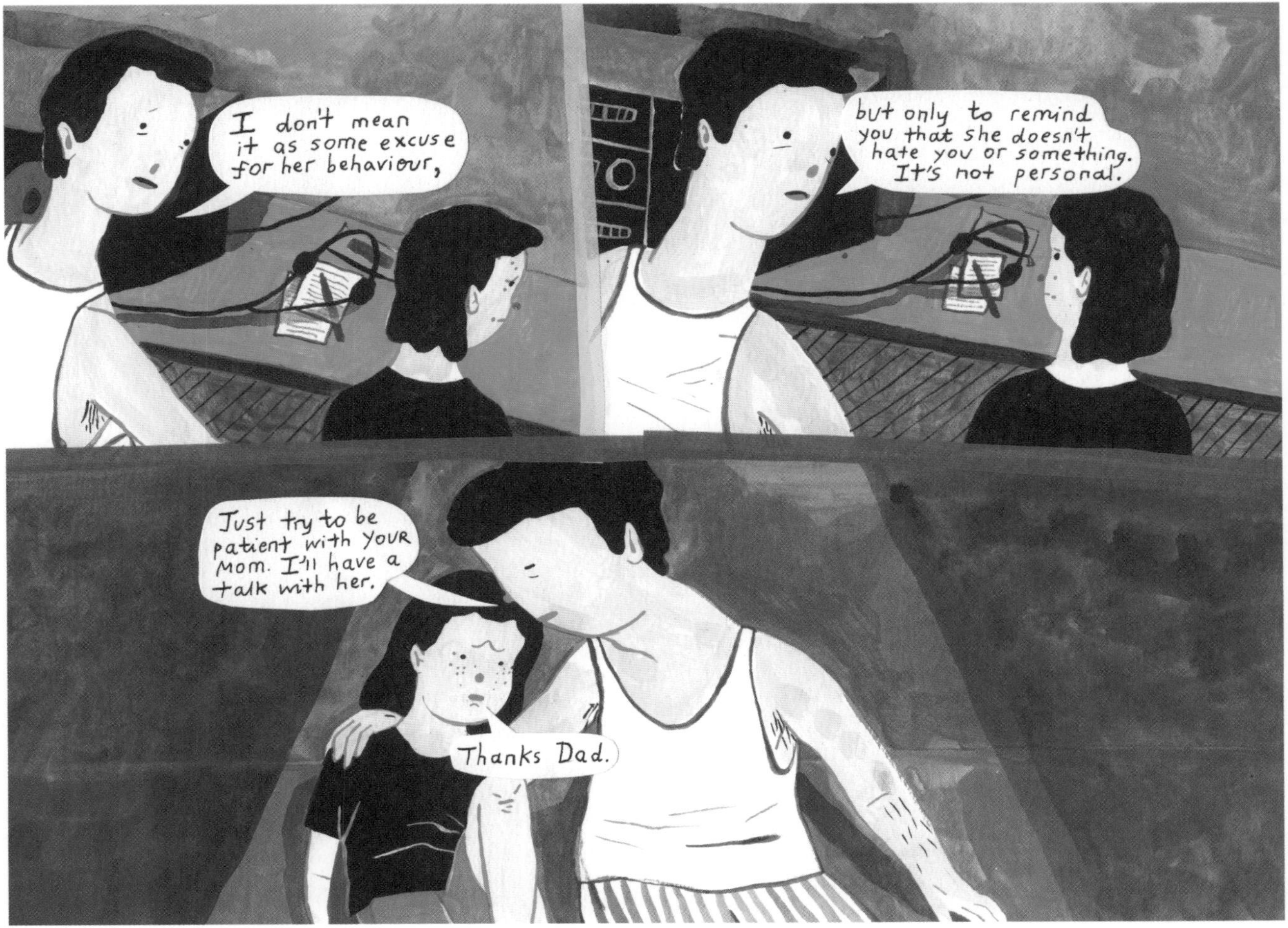
I don't mean it as some excuse for her behaviour,
but only to remind you that she doesn't hate you or something. It's not personal.
Just try to be patient with YOUR Mom. I'll have a talk with her.
Thanks Dad.

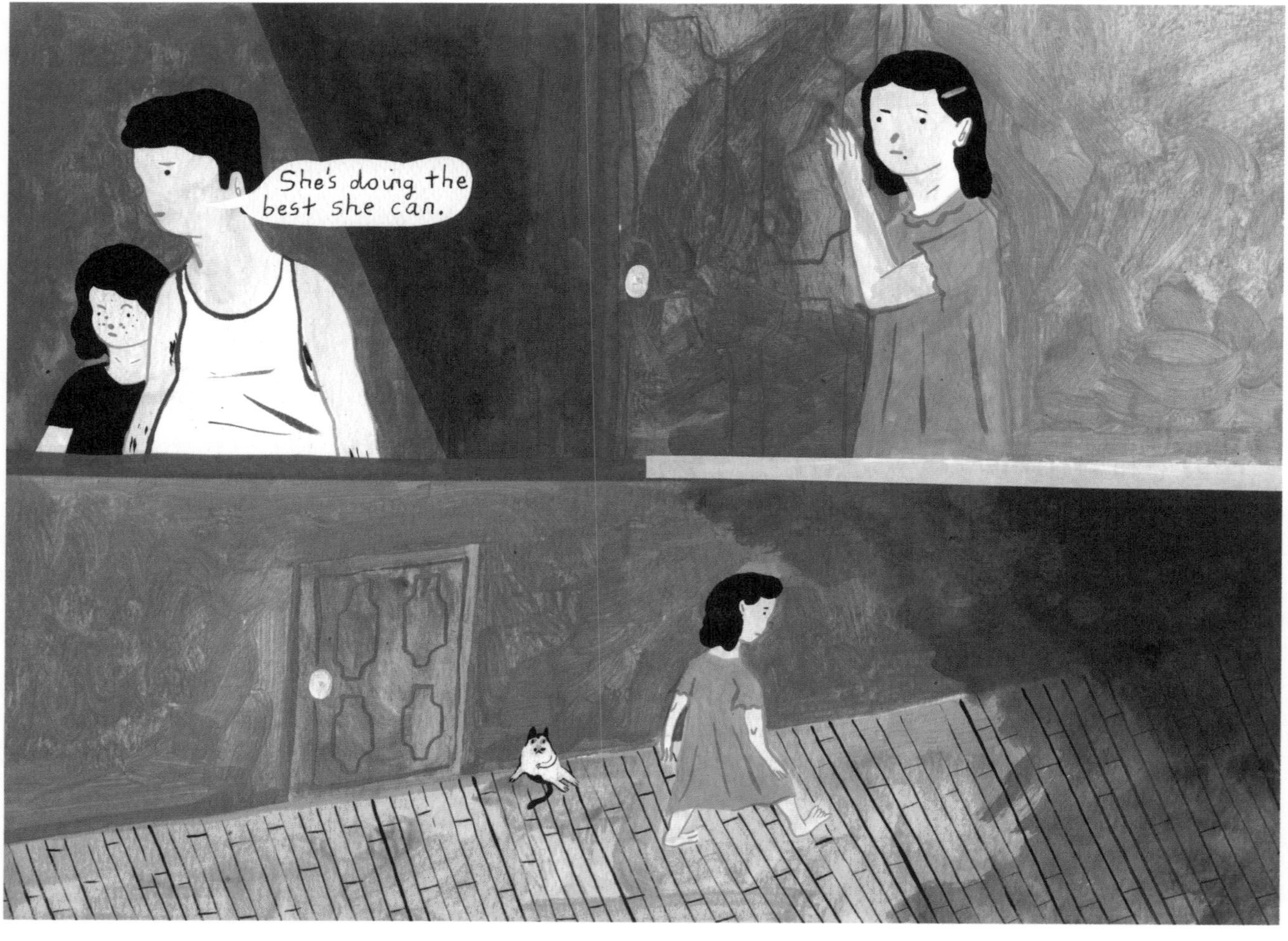
She's doing the best she can.

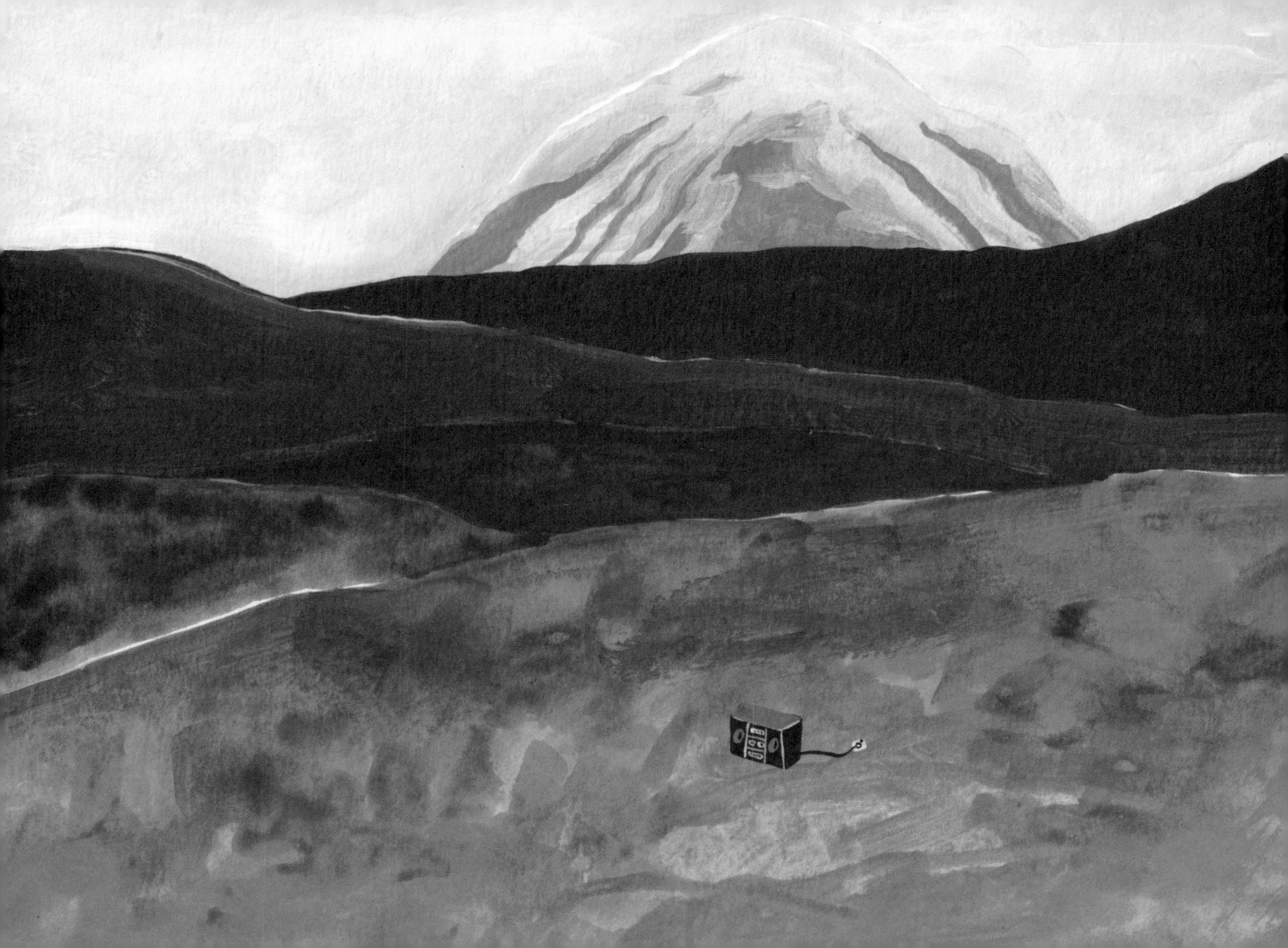

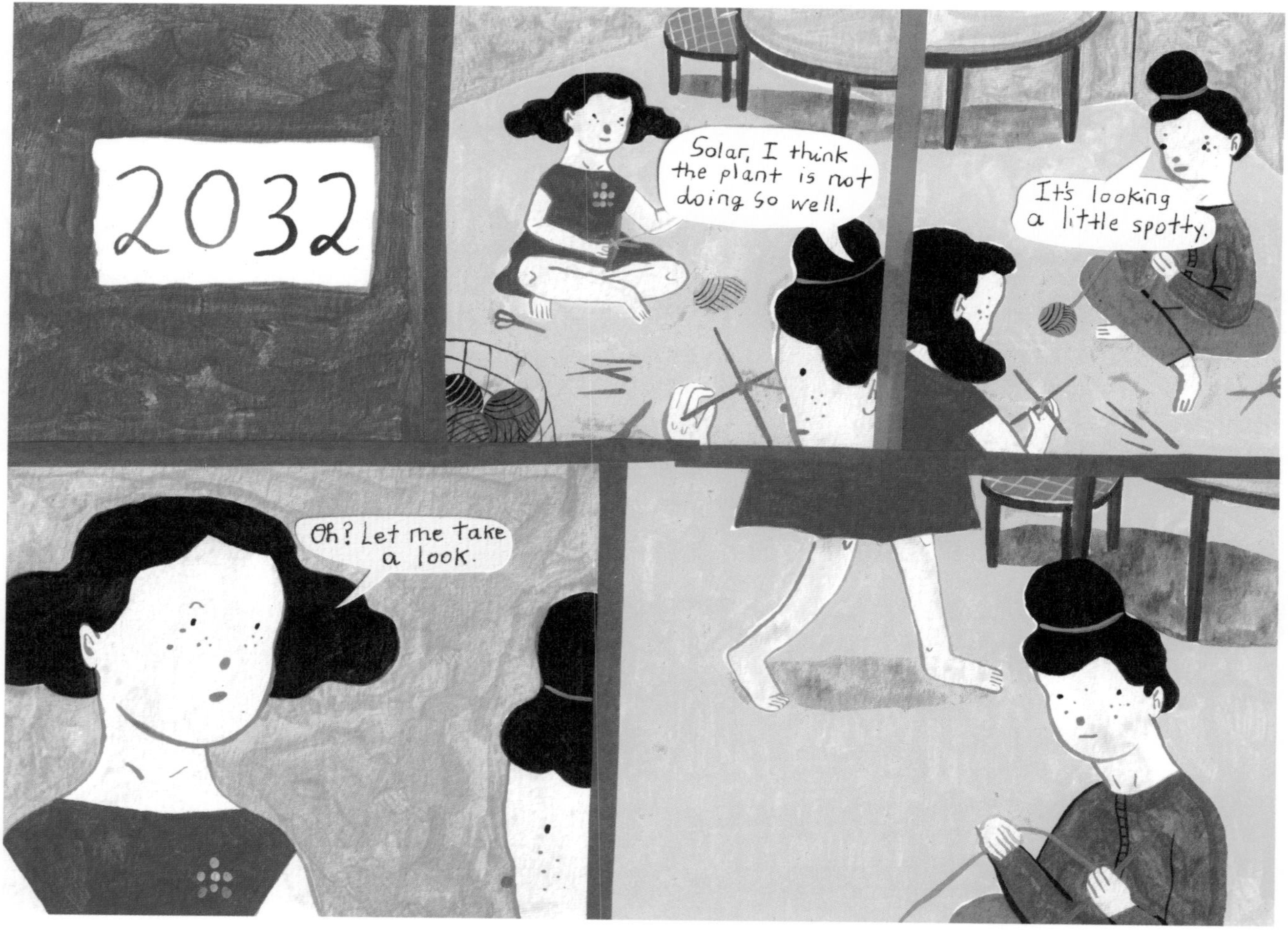
2032
Solar, I think the plant is not doing so well.
It's looking a little spotty.
Oh? Let me take a look.

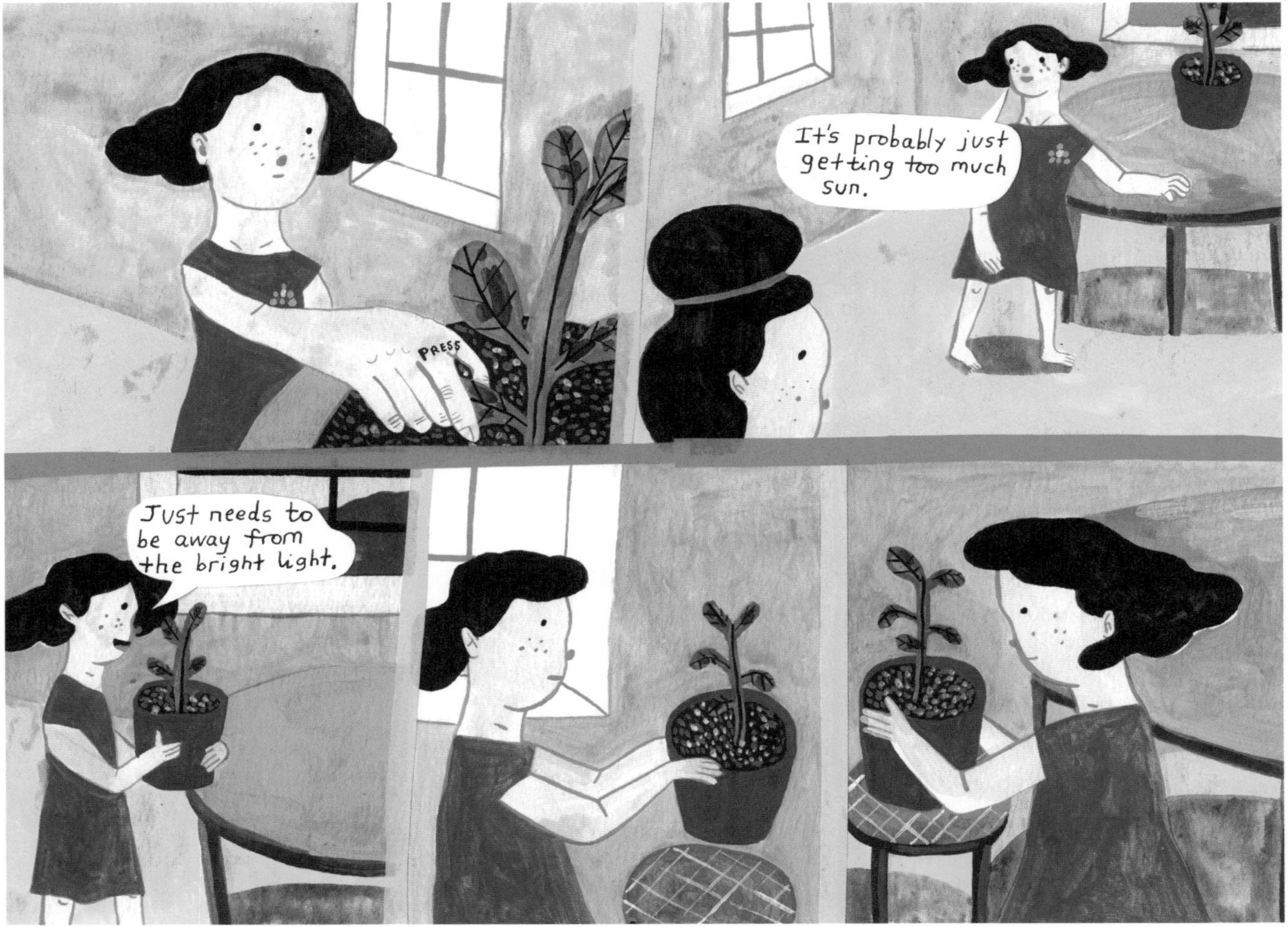
PRESS
It's probably just getting too much sun.
Just needs to be away from the bright light.

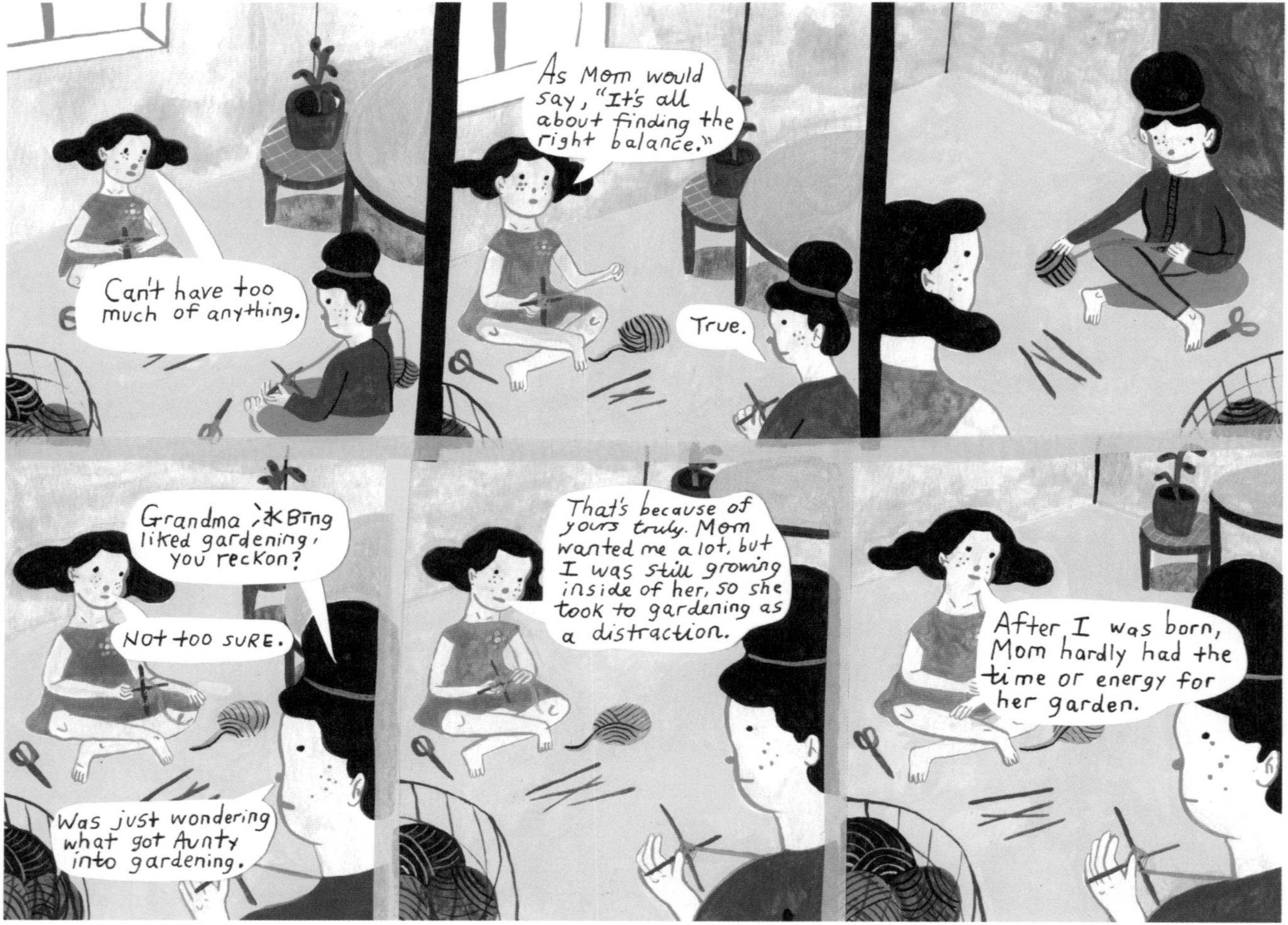
Can't have too much of anything.
As Mom would say, "It's all about finding the right balance."
True.
Grandma 冰Bīng liked gardening, you reckon?
Not too sure.
Was just wondering what got Aunty into gardening.
That's because of yours truly. Mom wanted me a lot, but I was still growing inside of her, so she took to gardening as a distraction.
After I was born, Mom hardly had the time or energy for her garden.

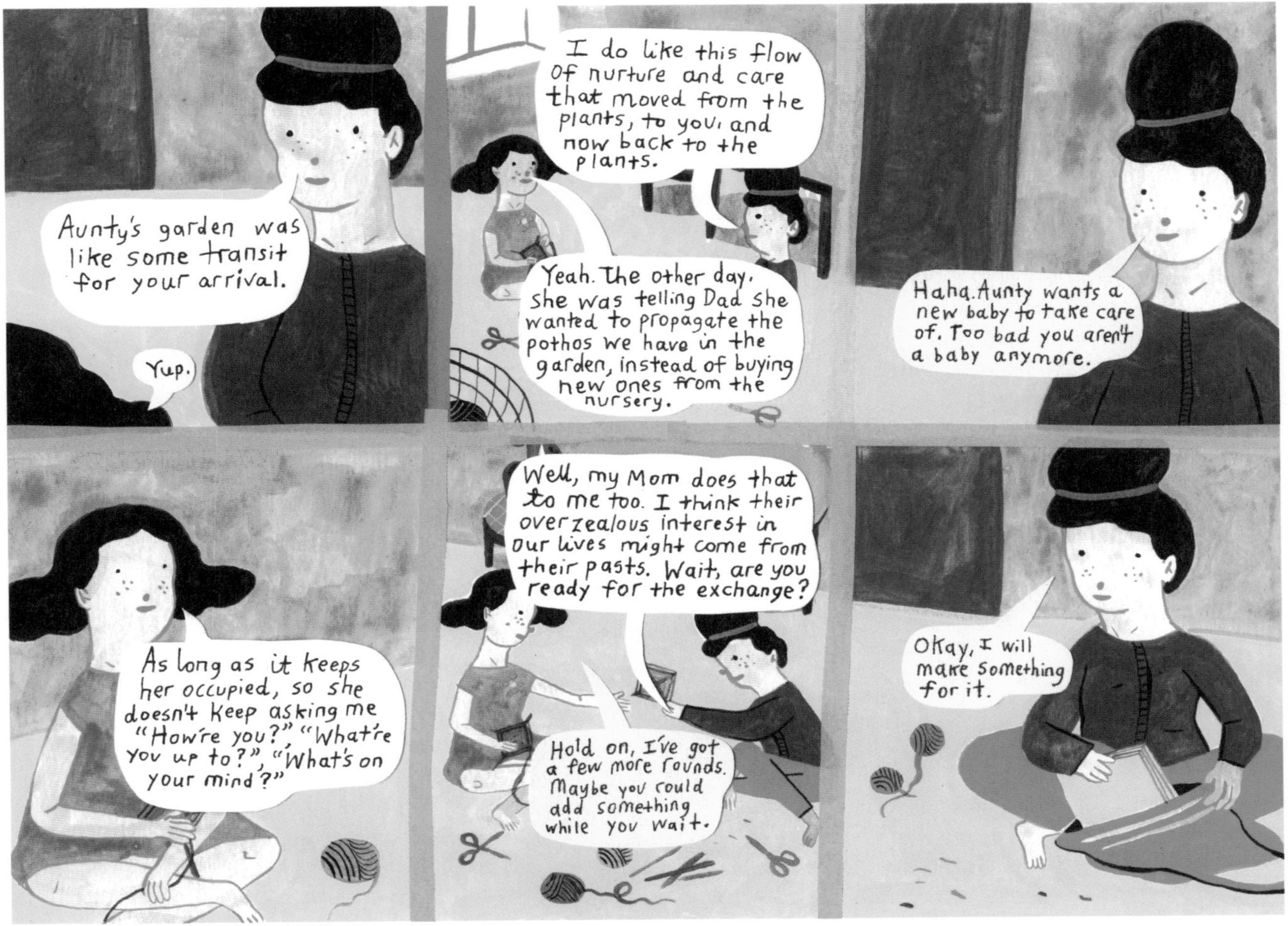
Aunty's garden was like some transit for your arrival.
Yup.
I do like this flow of nurture and care that moved from the plants, to you, and now back to the plants.
Yeah. The other day, she was telling Dad she wanted to propagate the pothos we have in the garden, instead of buying new ones from the nursery.
Haha. Aunty wants a new baby to take care of. Too bad you aren't a baby anymore.
As long as it keeps her occupied, so she doesn't keep asking me "How're you?", "What're you up to?", "What's on your mind?"
Well, my Mom does that to me too. I think their overzealous interest in our lives might come from their pasts. Wait, are you ready for the exchange?
Hold on, I've got a few more rounds. Maybe you could add something while you wait.
Okay, I will make something for it.

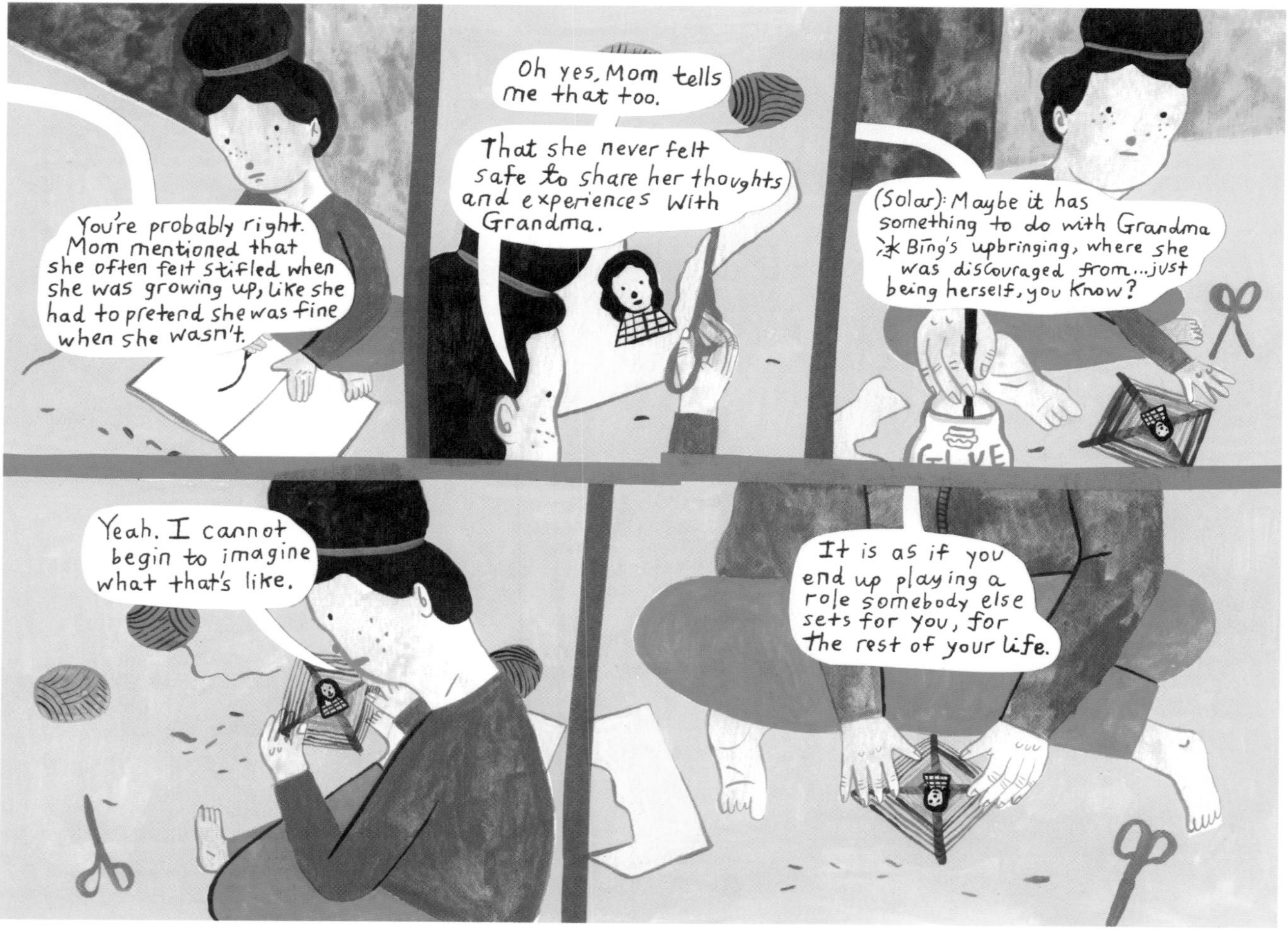
You're probably right. Mom mentioned that she often felt stifled when she was growing up, like she had to pretend she was fine when she wasn't.
Oh yes, Mom tells me that too.
That she never felt safe to share her thoughts and experiences with Grandma.
(Solar): Maybe it has something to do with Grandma 冰 Bing's upbringing, where she was discouraged from... just being herself, you know?
Yeah. I cannot begin to imagine what that's like.
It is as if you end up playing a role somebody else sets for you, for the rest of your life.

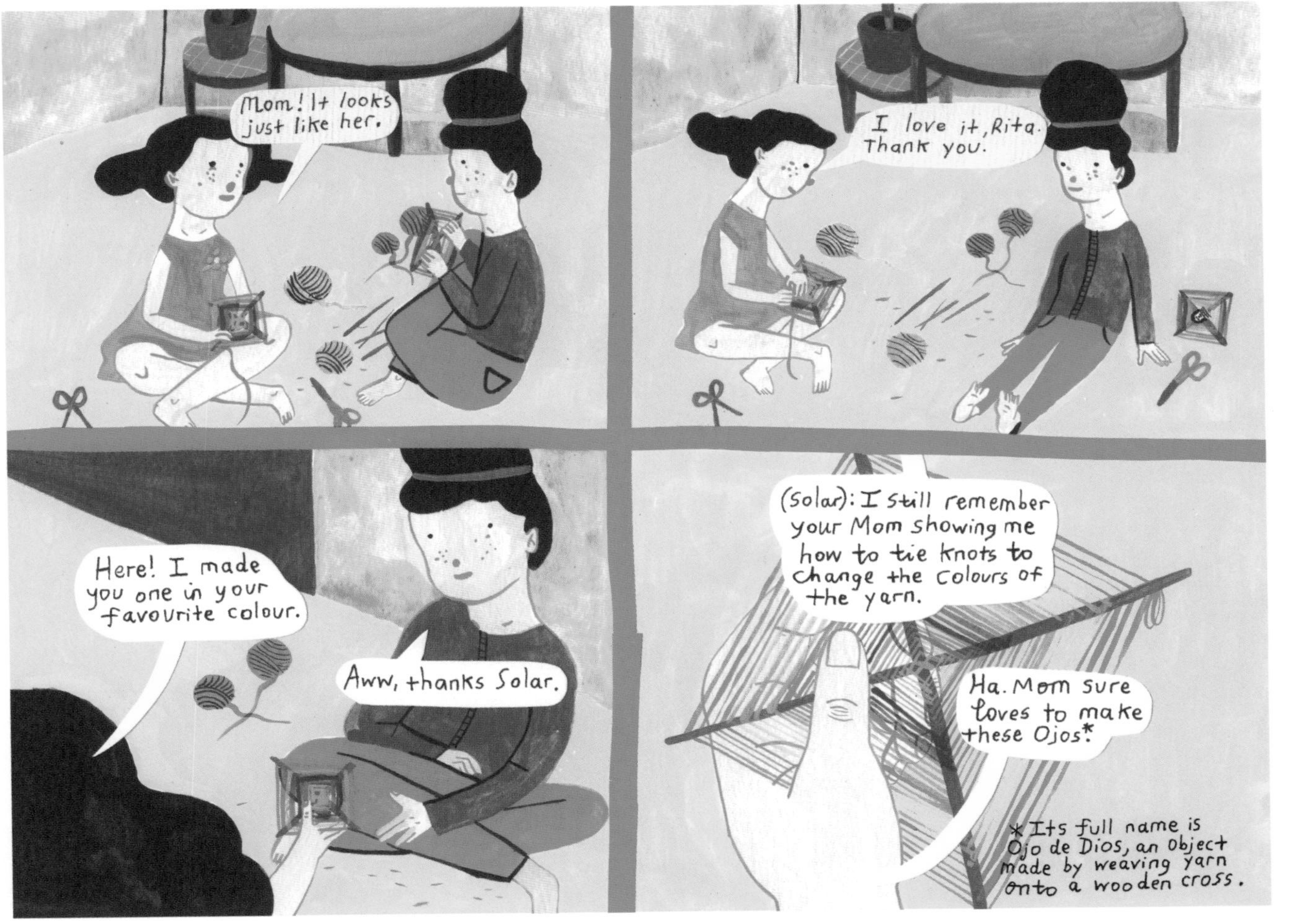
Mom! It looks just like her.
I love it, Rita. Thank you.
Here! I made you one in your favourite colour.
Aww, thanks Solar.
(Solar): I still remember your Mom showing me how to tie knots to change the colours of the yarn.
Ha. Mom sure loves to make these Ojos*.
* Its full name is Ojo de Dios, an object made by weaving yarn onto a wooden cross.

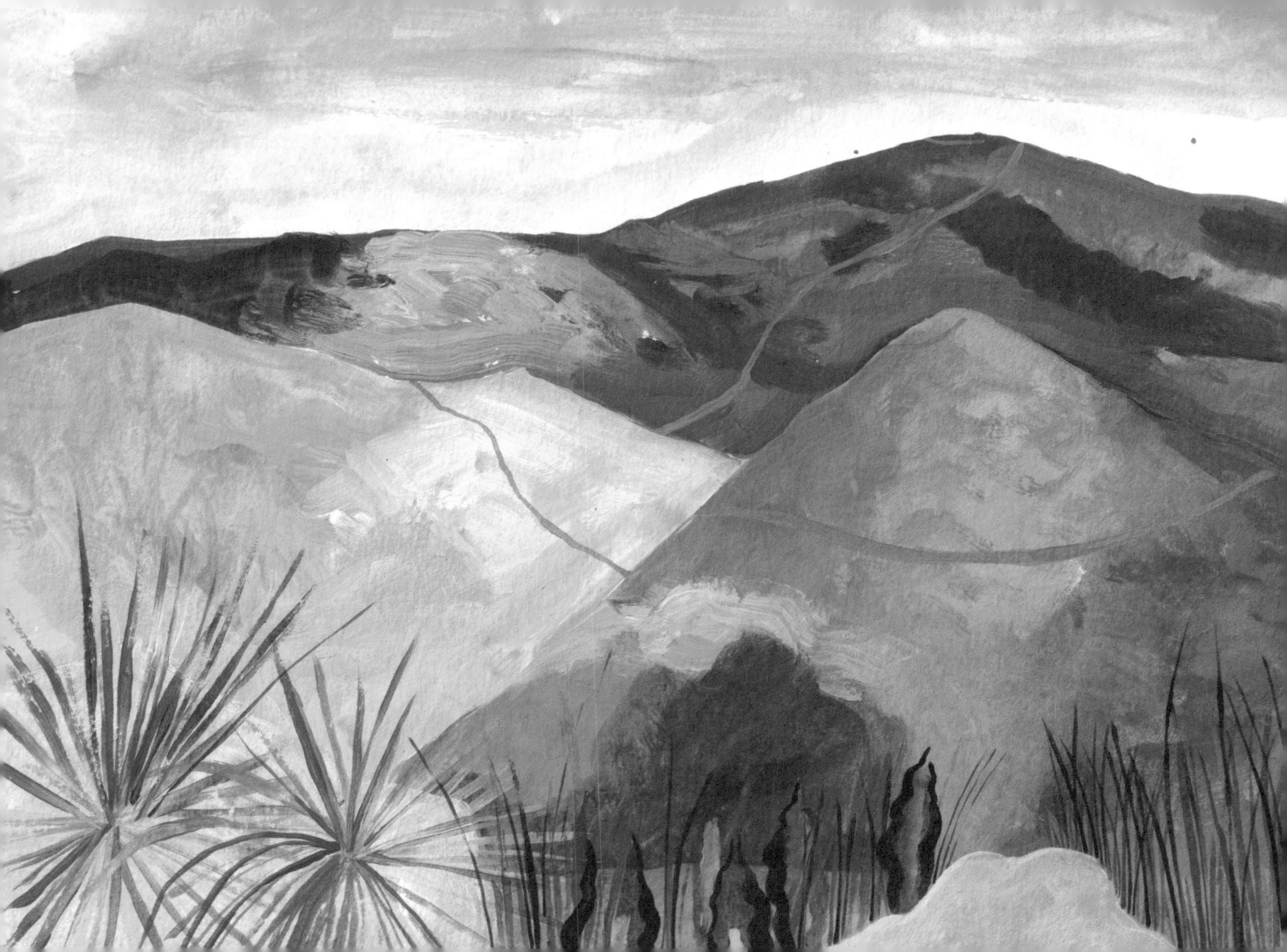

1908
SNORE
snortt+
pfft!

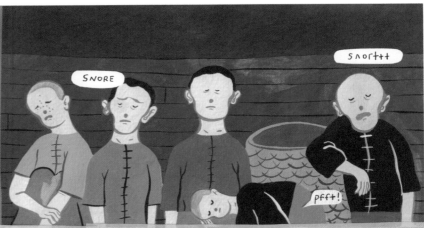

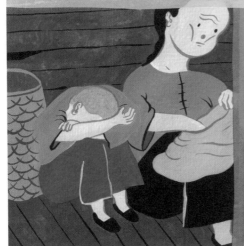

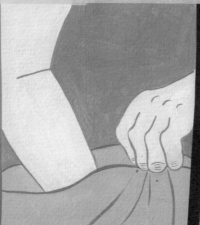

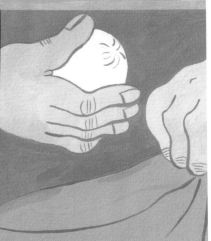

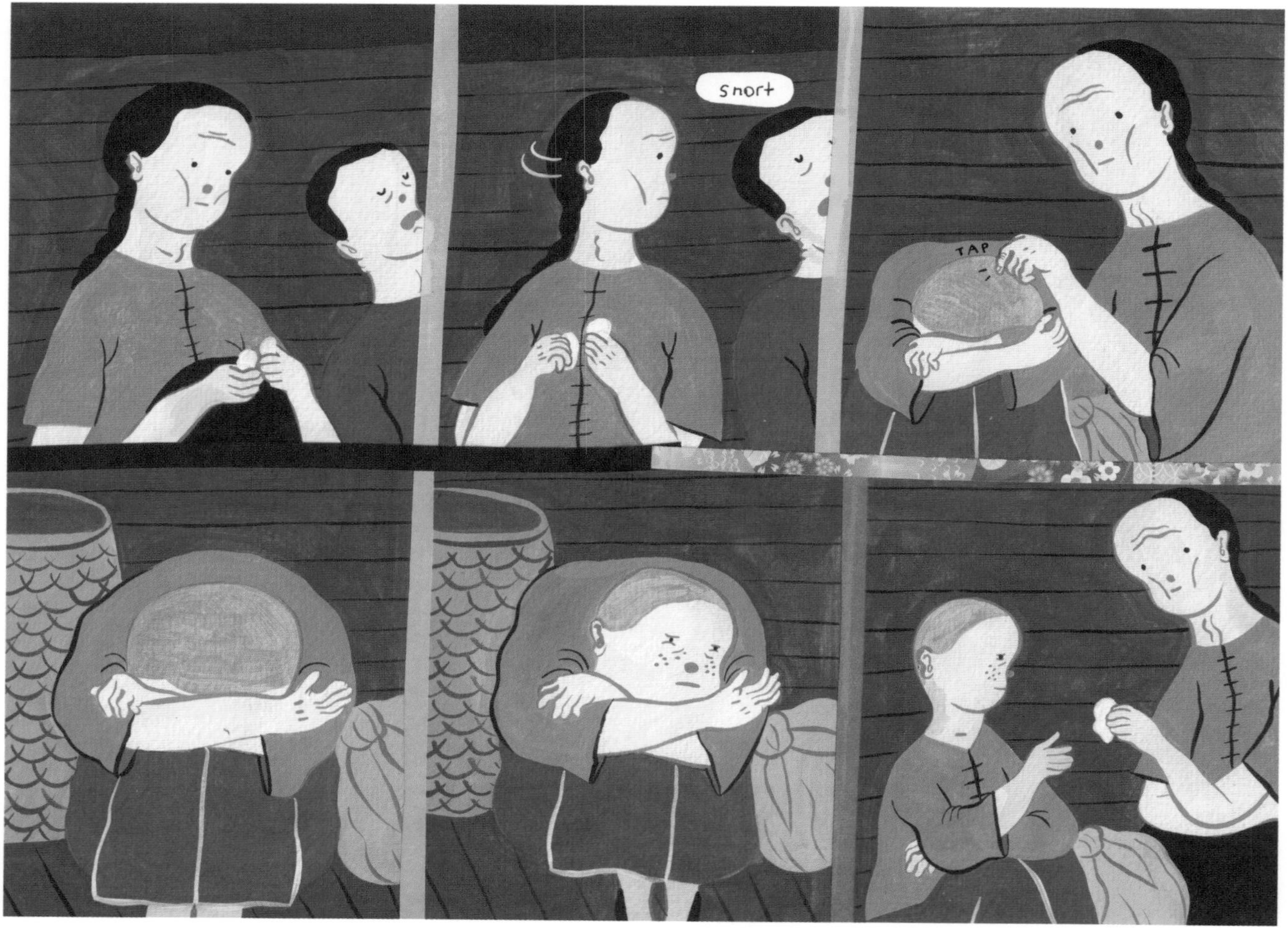
snort
TAP

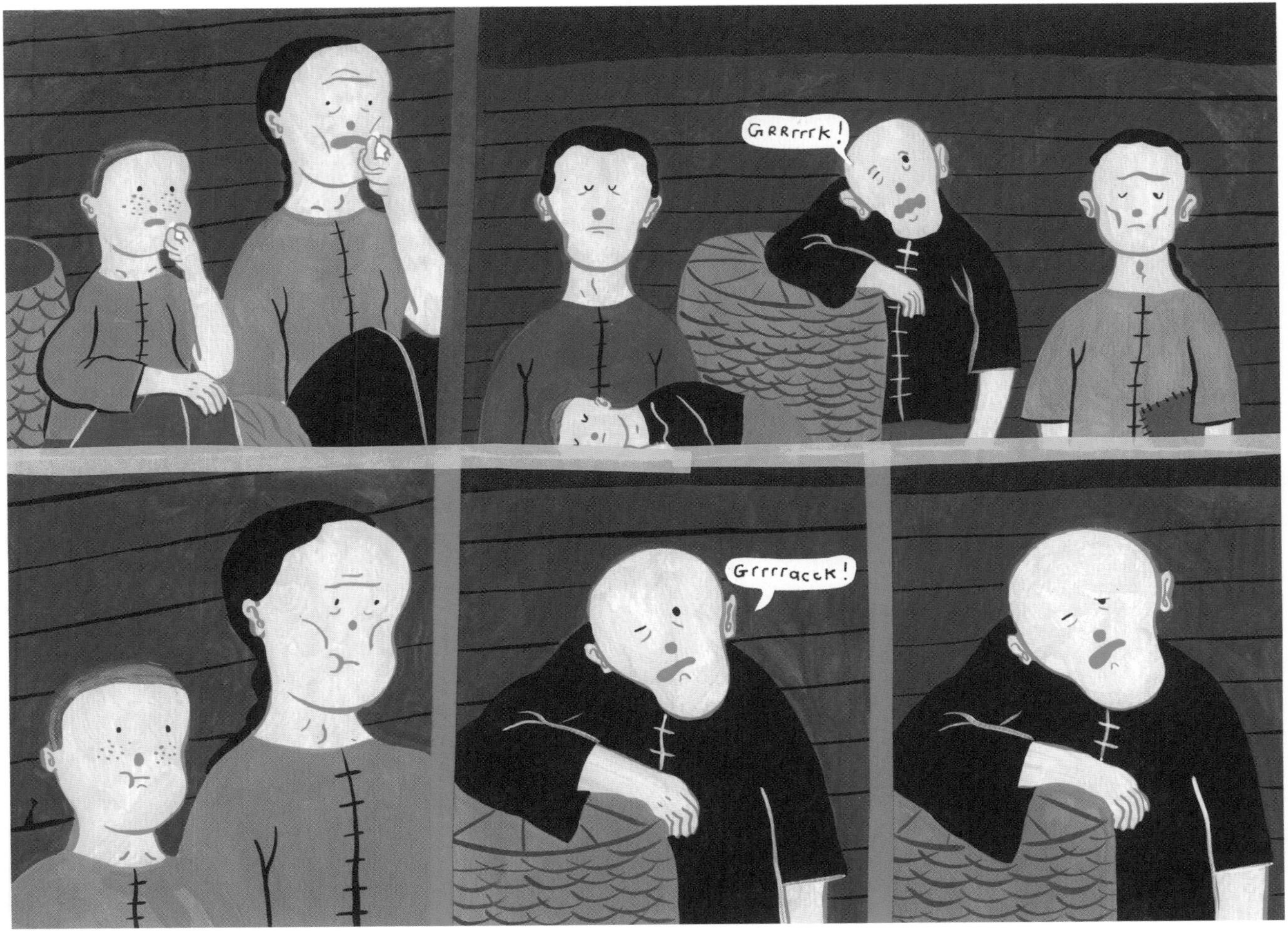
Grrrrrk!
Grrrracck!

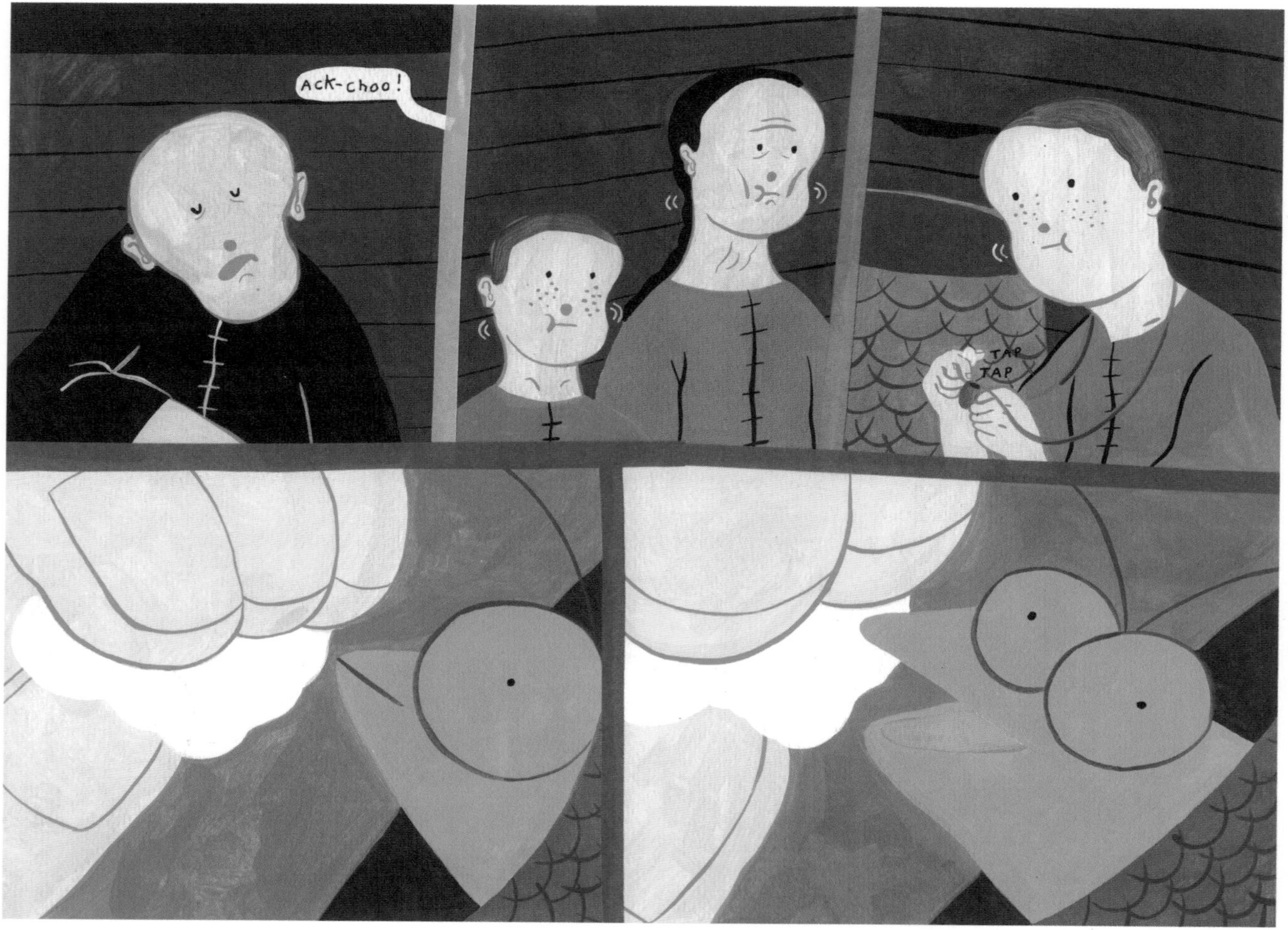
ACK-CHOO!
TAP TAP

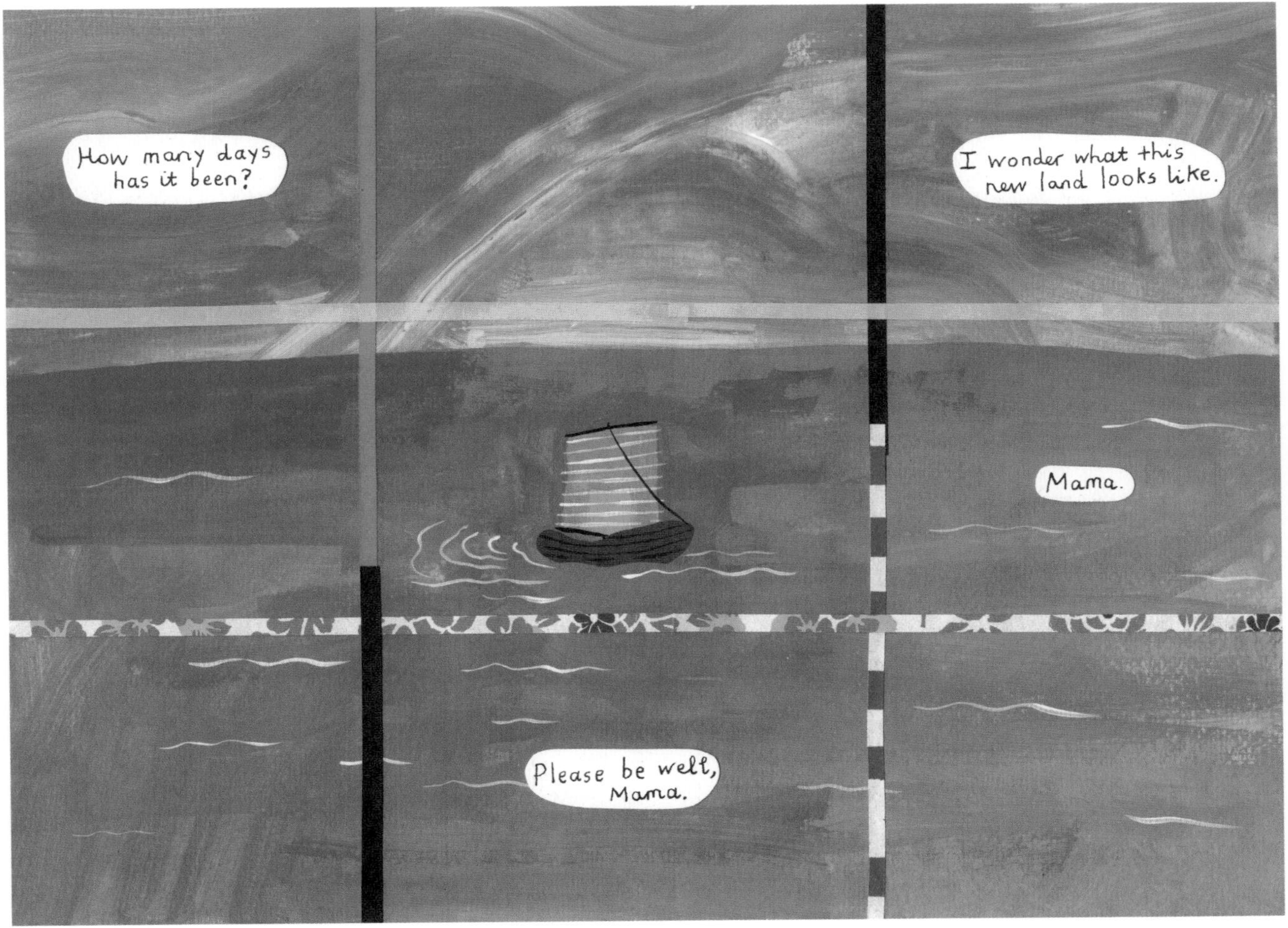
How many days has it been?
I wonder what this new land looks like.
Mama.
Please be well, Mama.

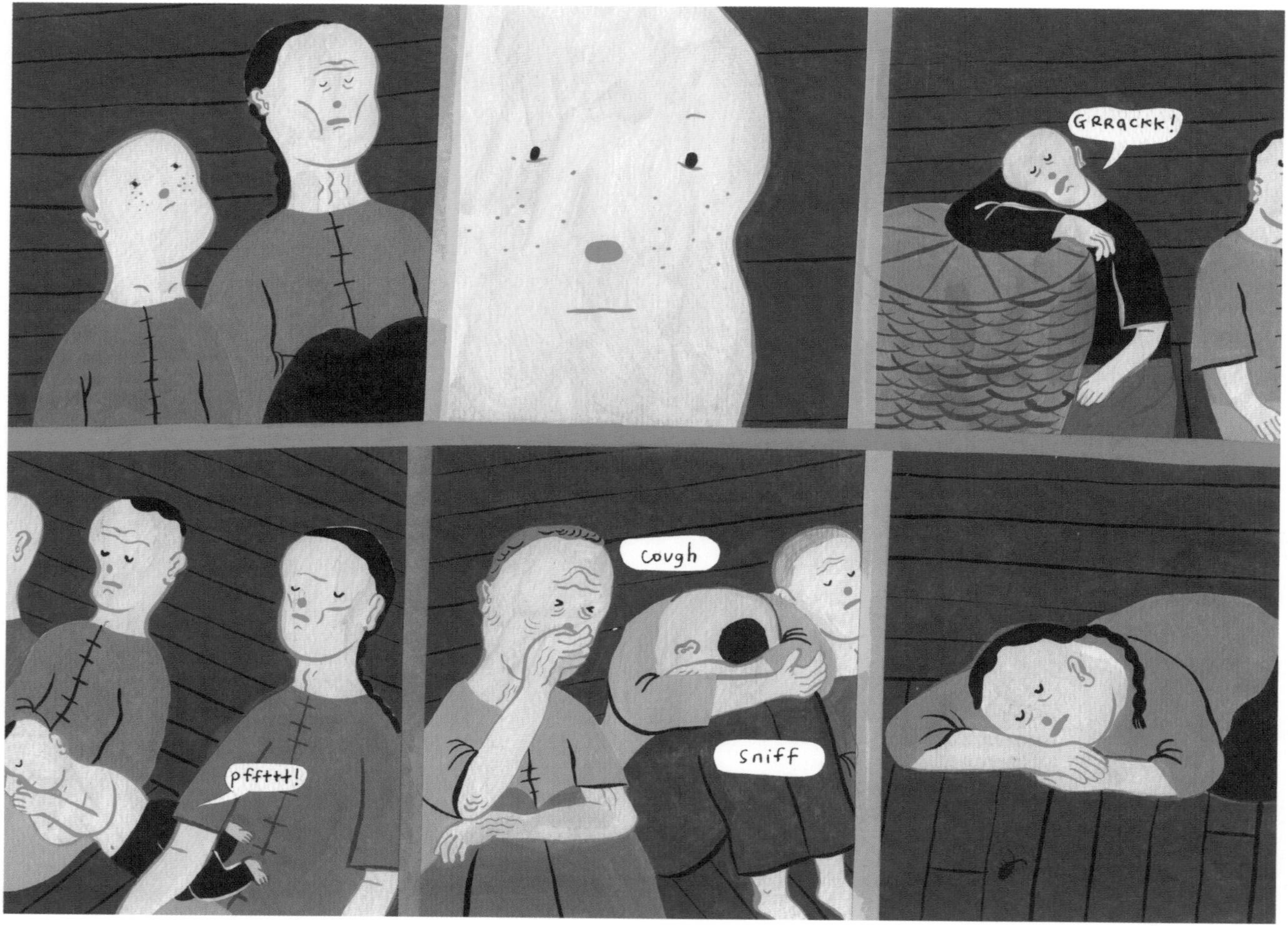
GRRACKK!
pfftttt!
cough
sniff

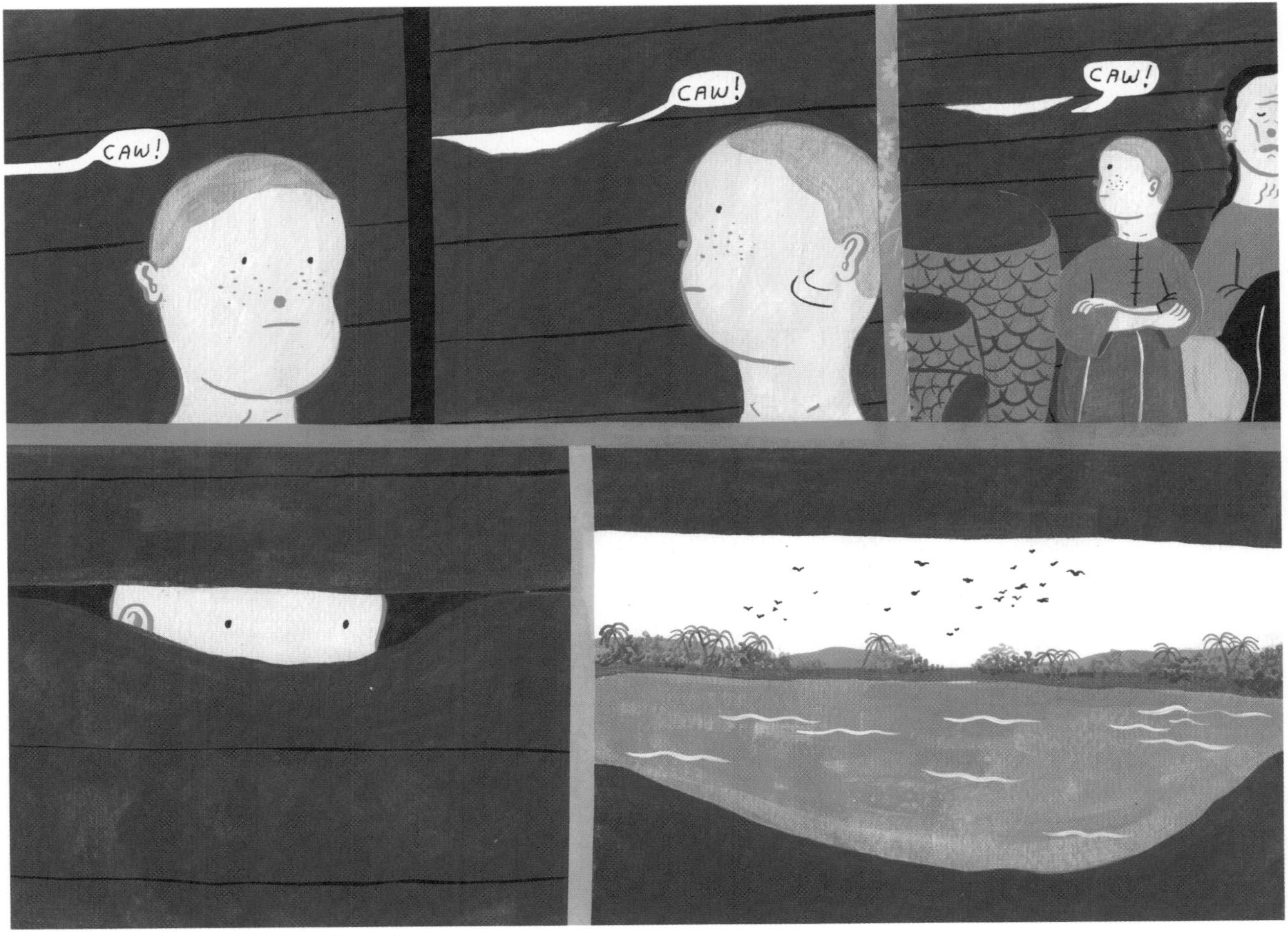
CAW!
CAW!
CAW!

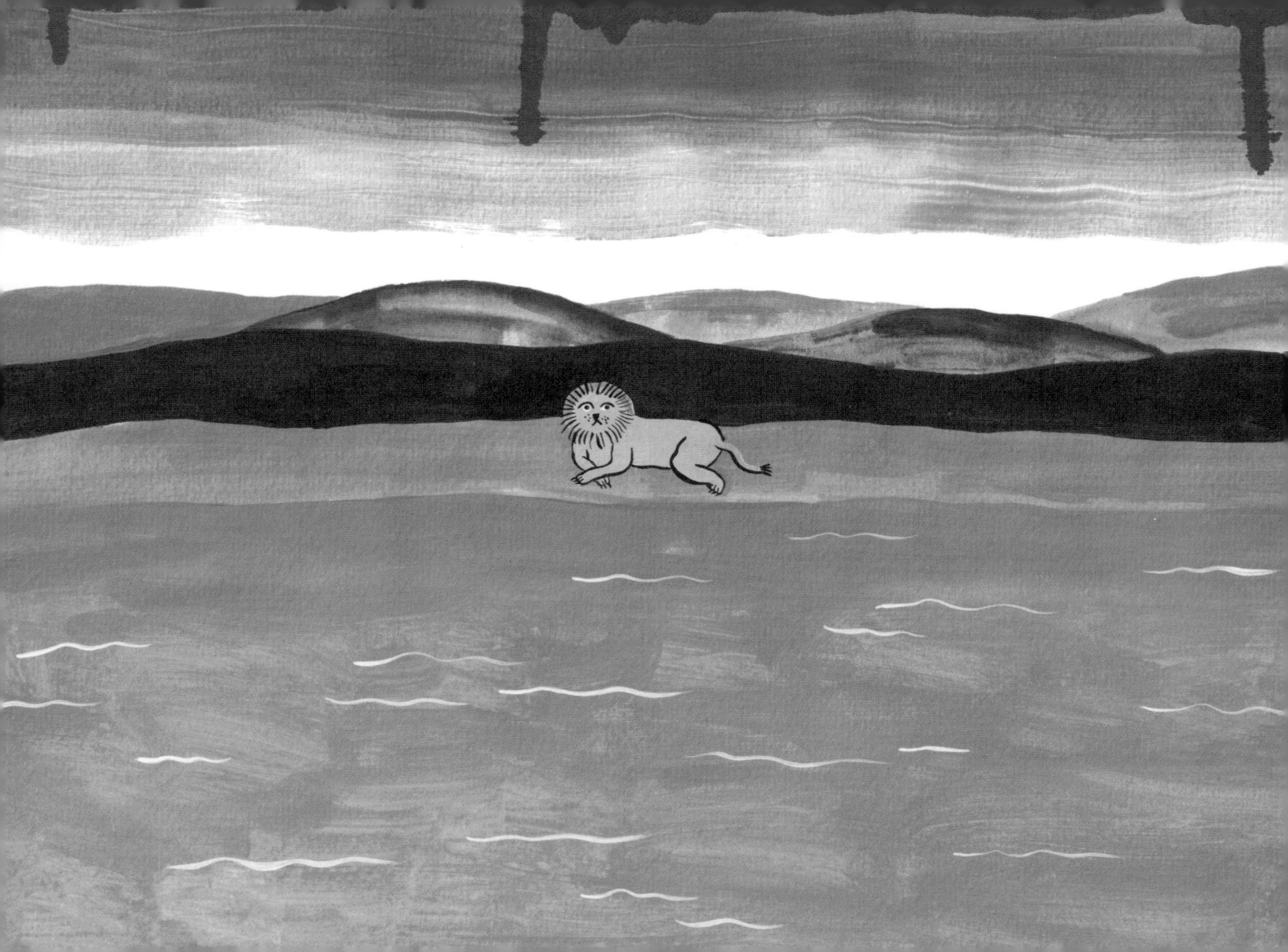

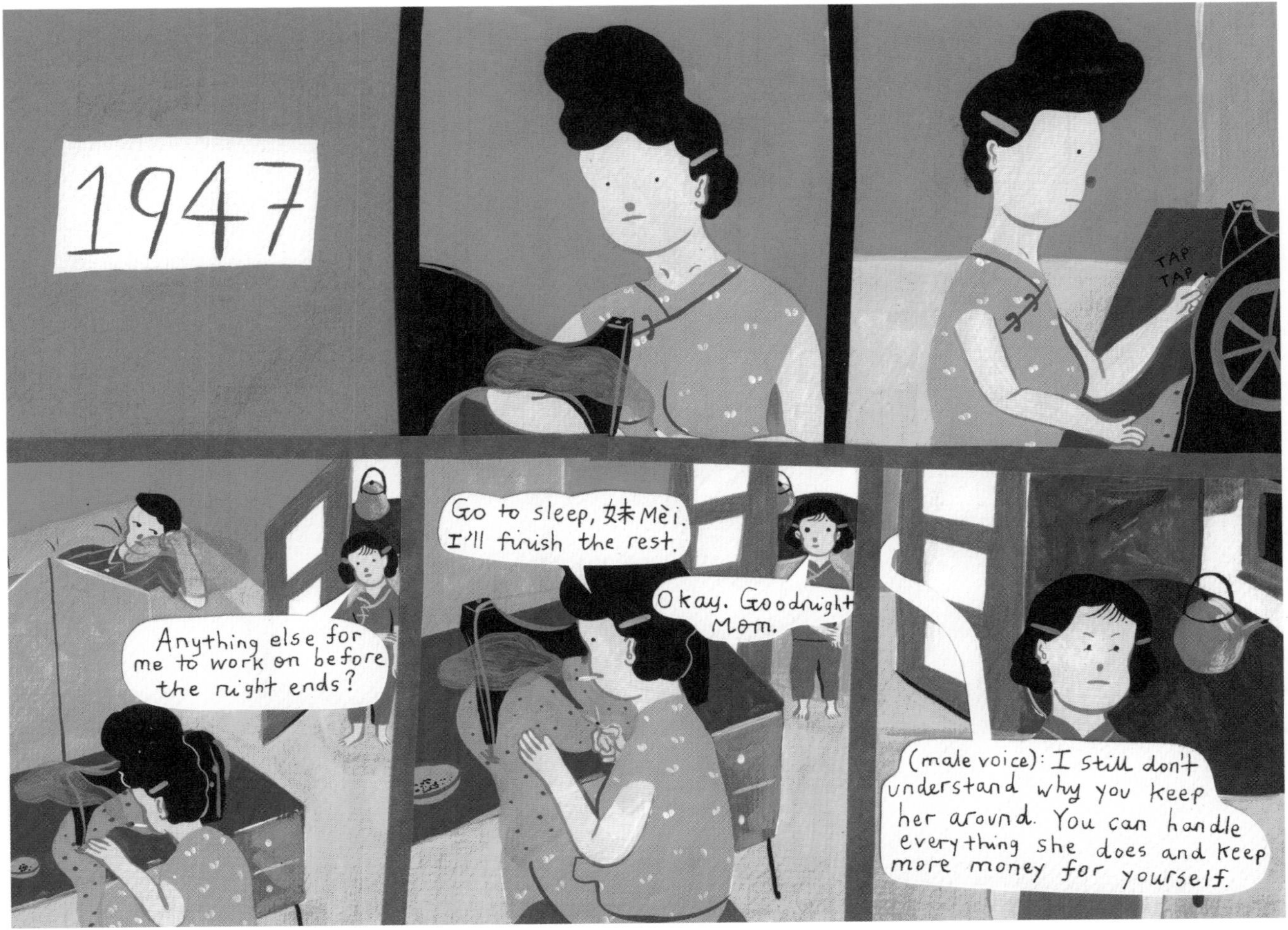
1947
TAP TAP
Anything else for me to work on before the night ends?
Go to sleep, 妹 Mèi. I'll finish the rest.
Okay. Goodnight Mom.
(male voice): I still don't understand why you keep her around. You can handle everything she does and keep more money for yourself.

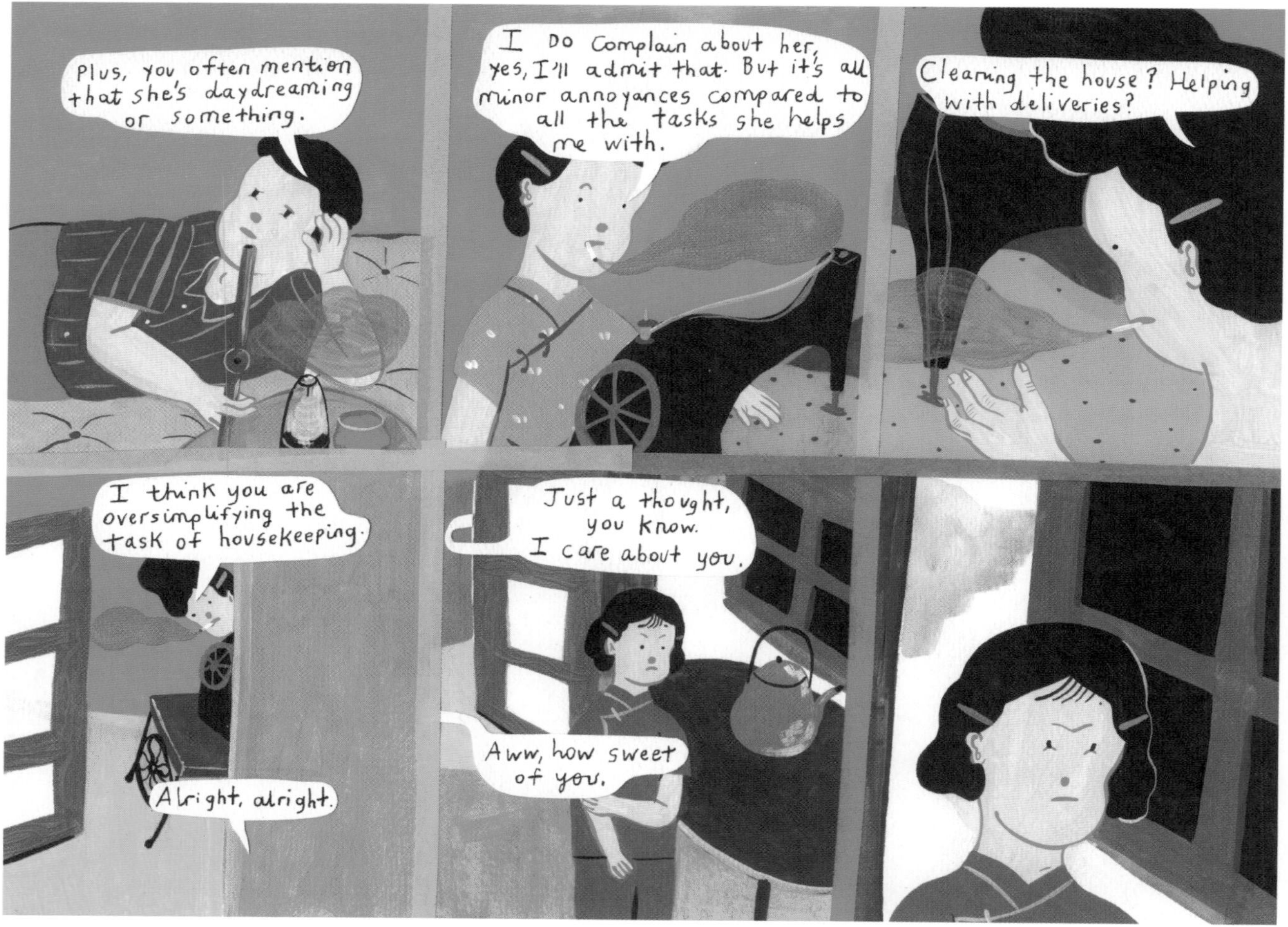
Plus, you often mention that she's daydreaming or something.
I do complain about her, yes, I'll admit that. But it's all minor annoyances compared to all the tasks she helps me with.
Clearing the house? Helping with deliveries?
I think you are oversimplifying the task of housekeeping.
Alright, alright.
Just a thought, you know. I care about you.
Aww, how sweet of you.

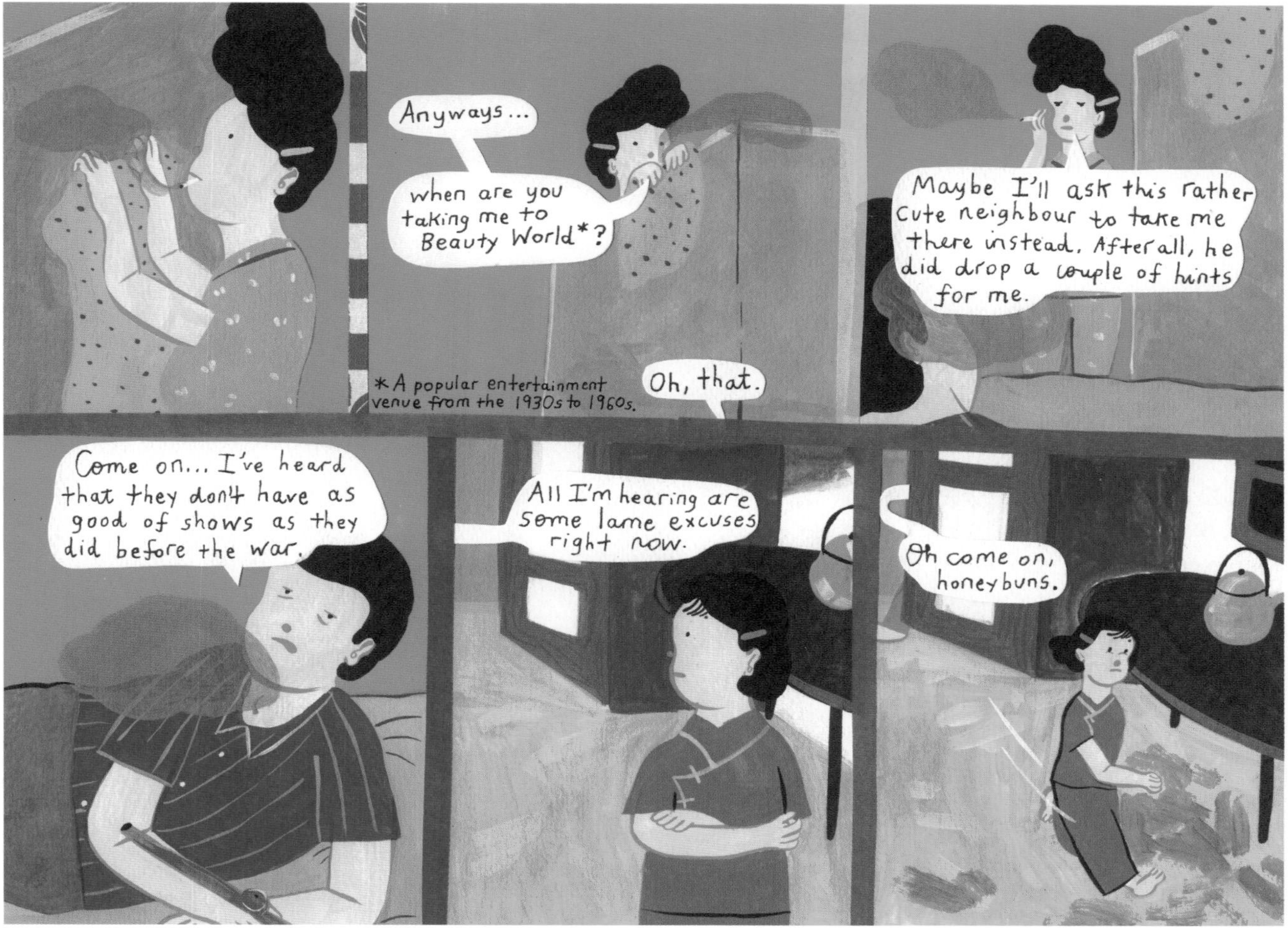
Anyways...
when are you taking me to Beauty World*?
*A popular entertainment venue from the 1930s to 1960s.
Oh, that.
Maybe I'll ask this rather cute neighbour to take me there instead. After all, he did drop a couple of hints for me.
Come on... I've heard that they don't have as good of shows as they did before the war.
All I'm hearing are some lame excuses right now.
Oh come on, honeybuns.

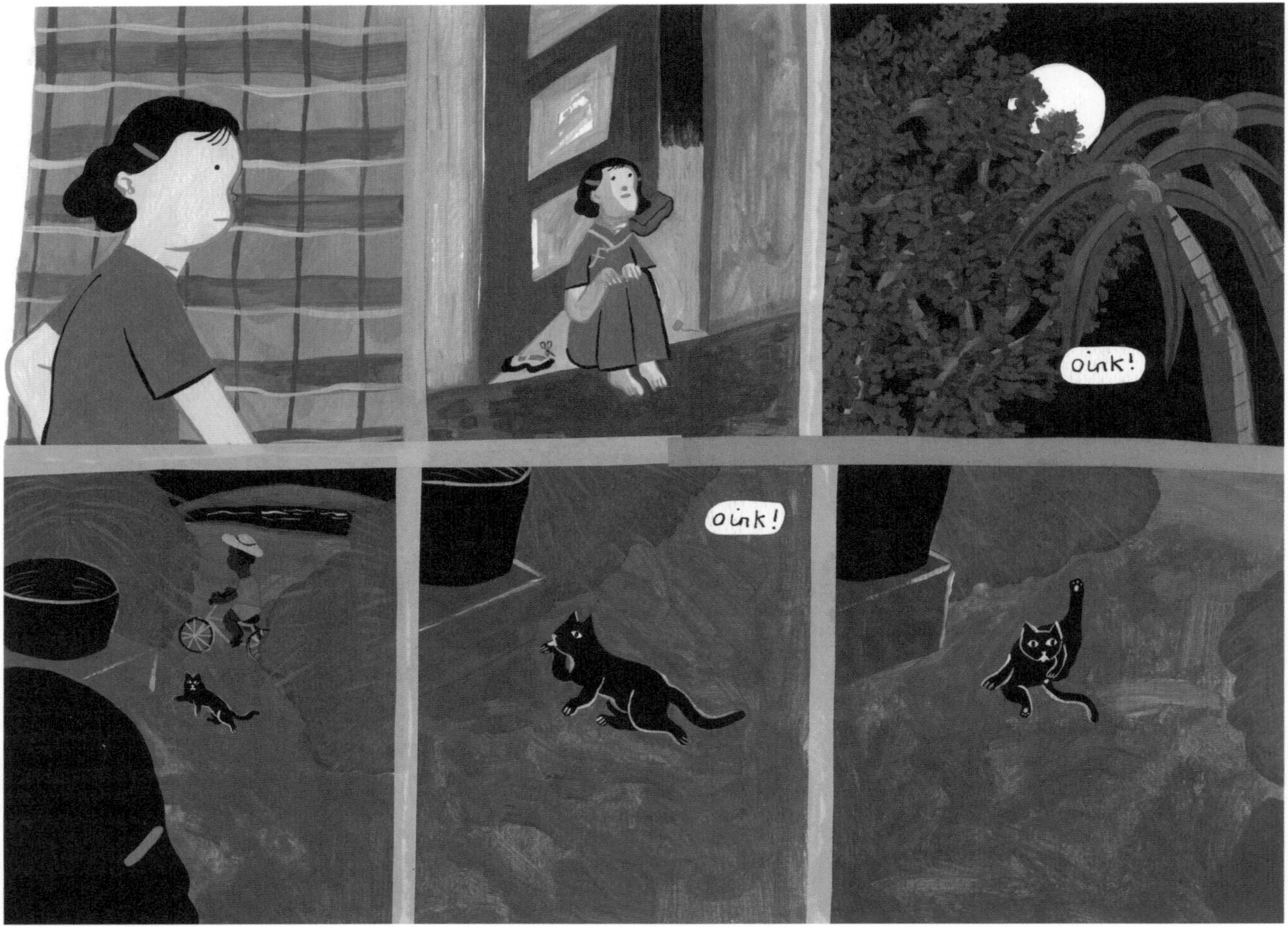
oink!
oink!

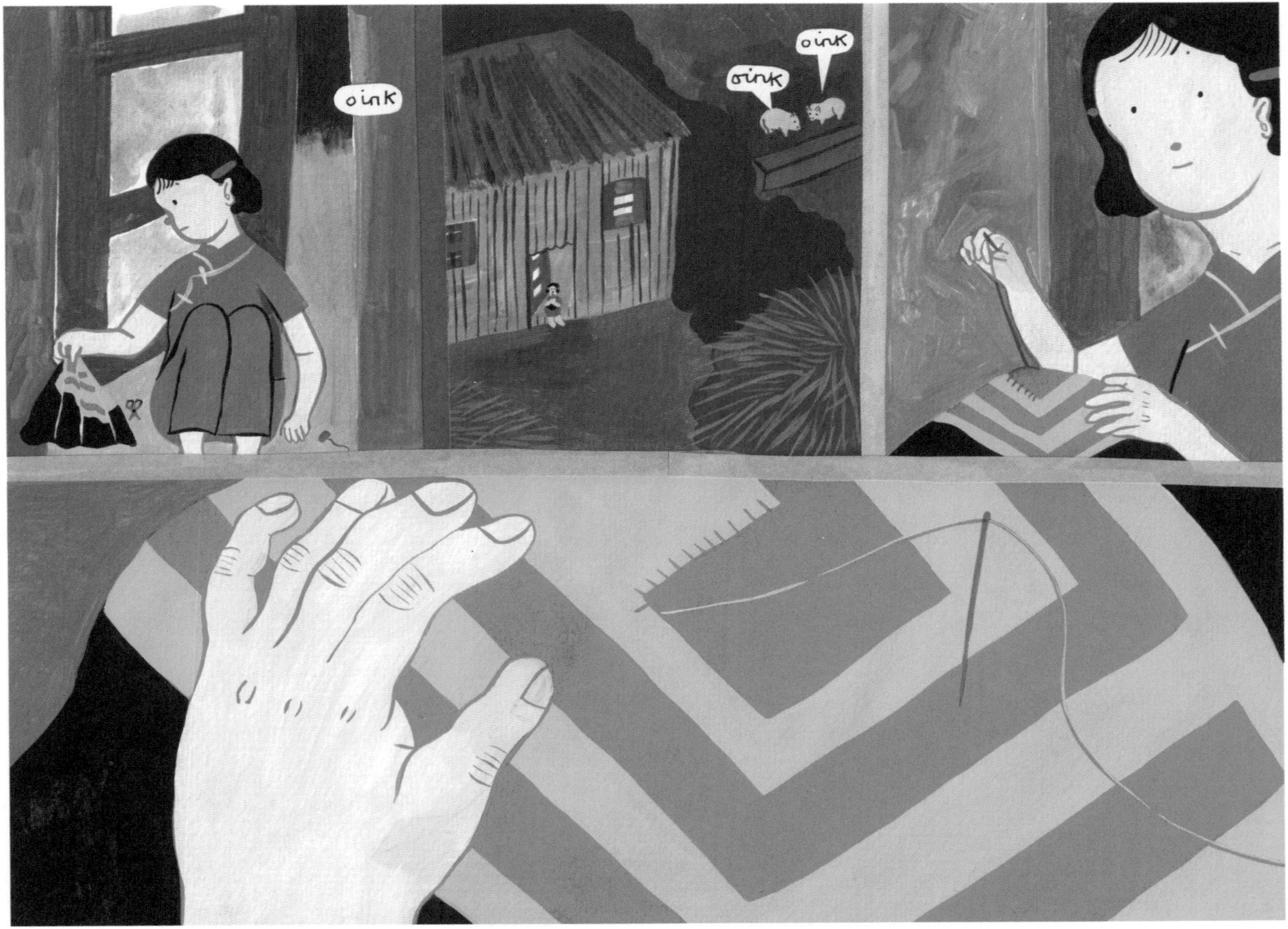
oink
oink
oink

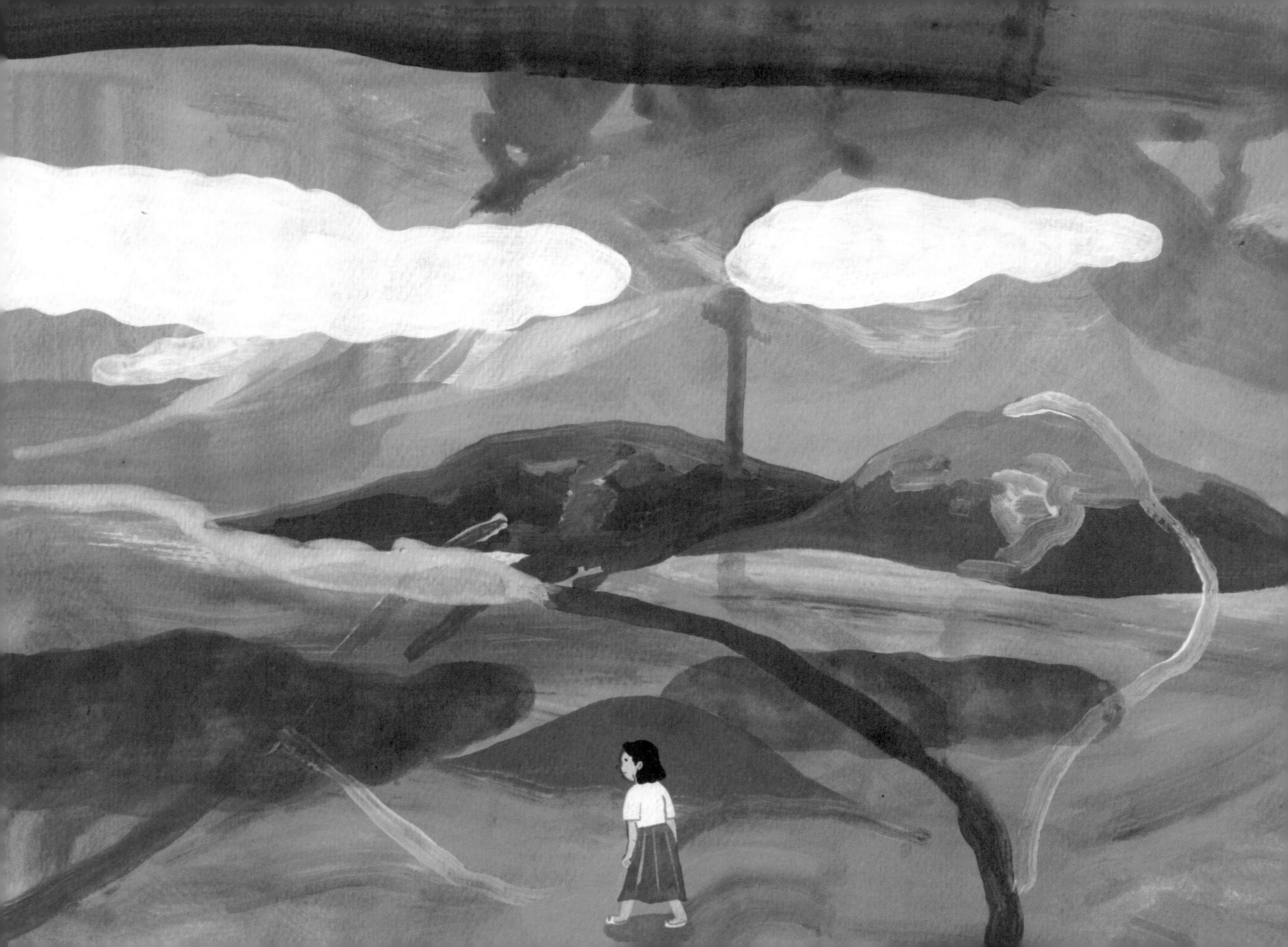

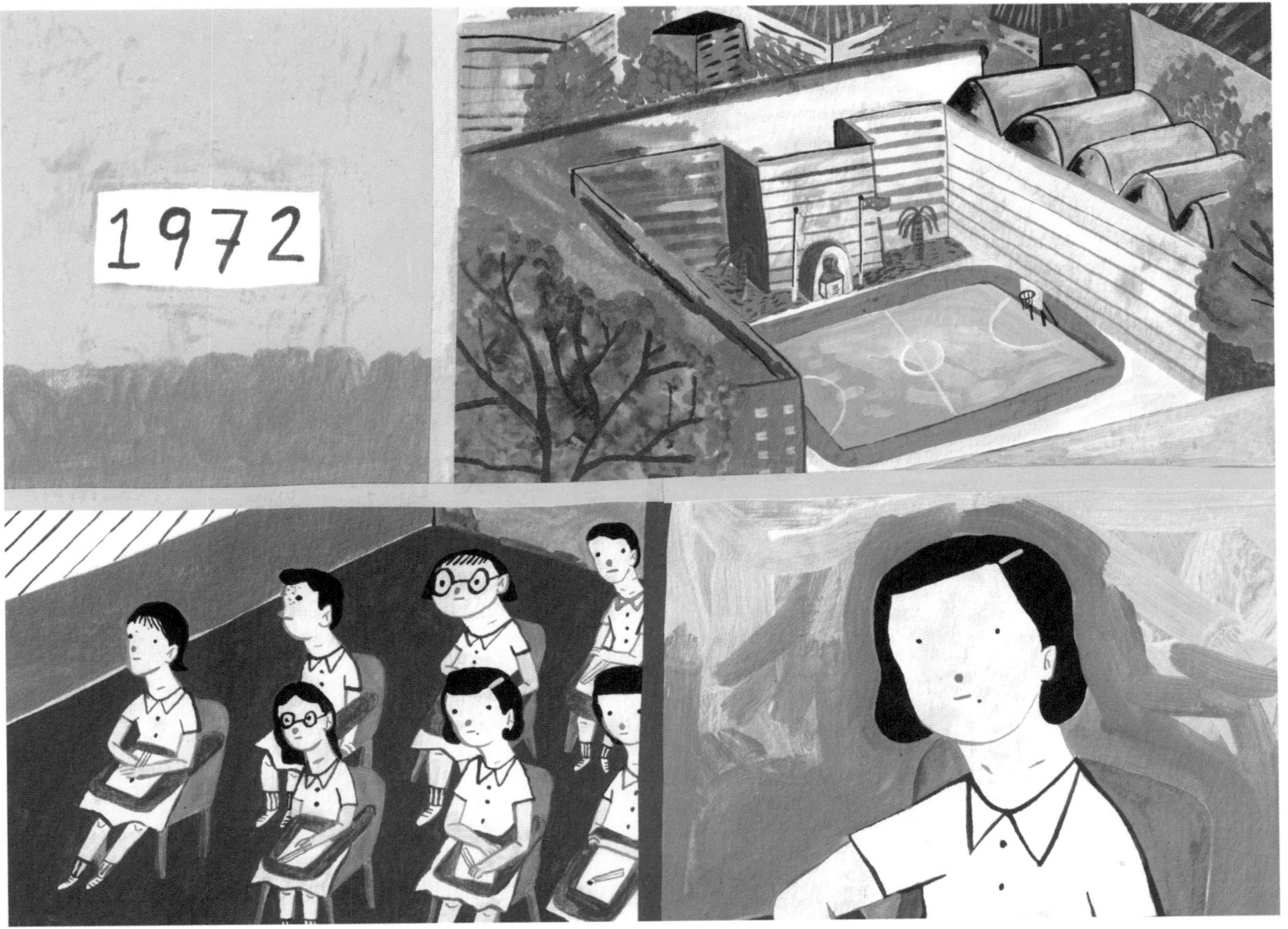
1972

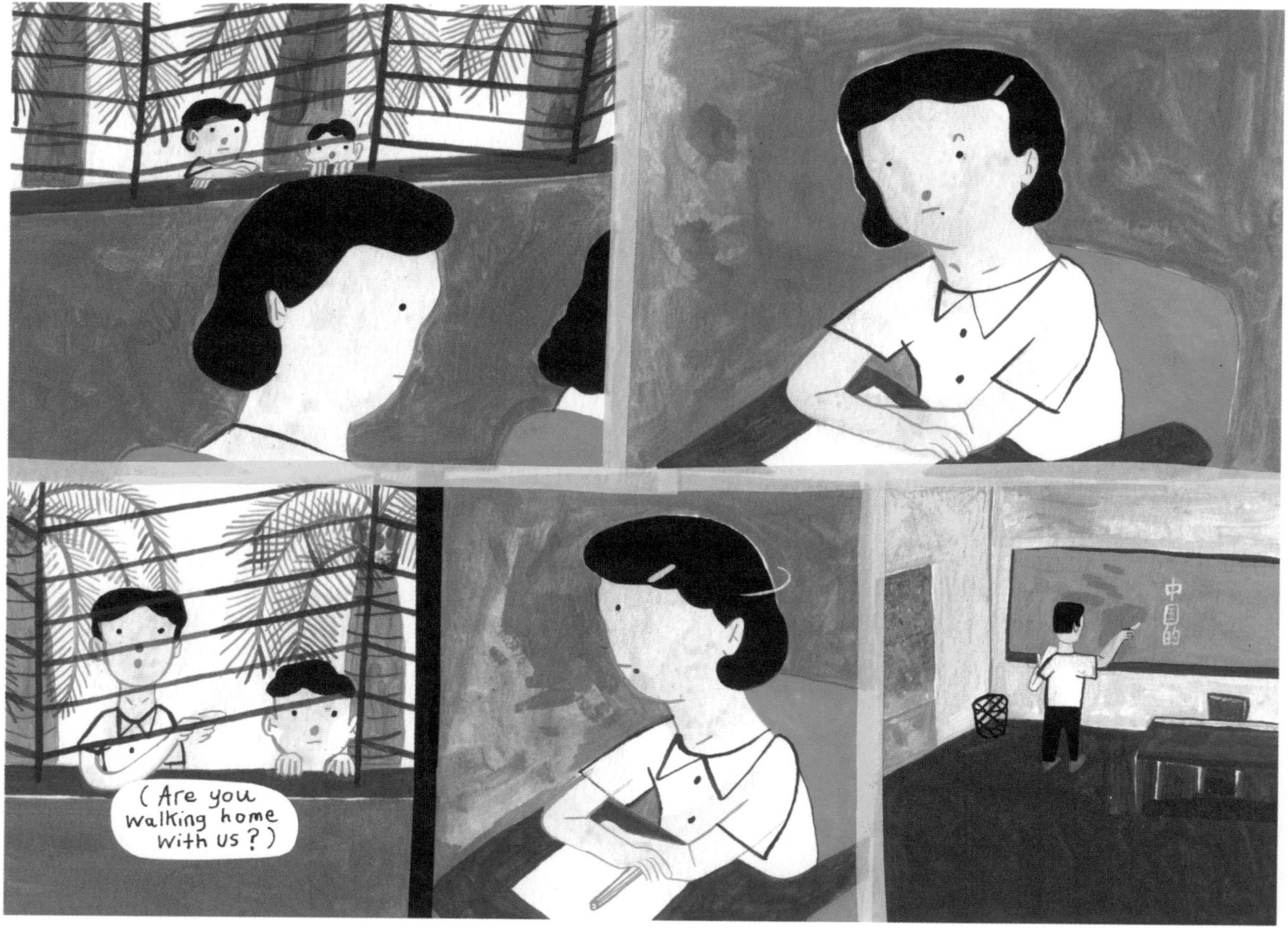
(Are you walking home with us?)
中国的

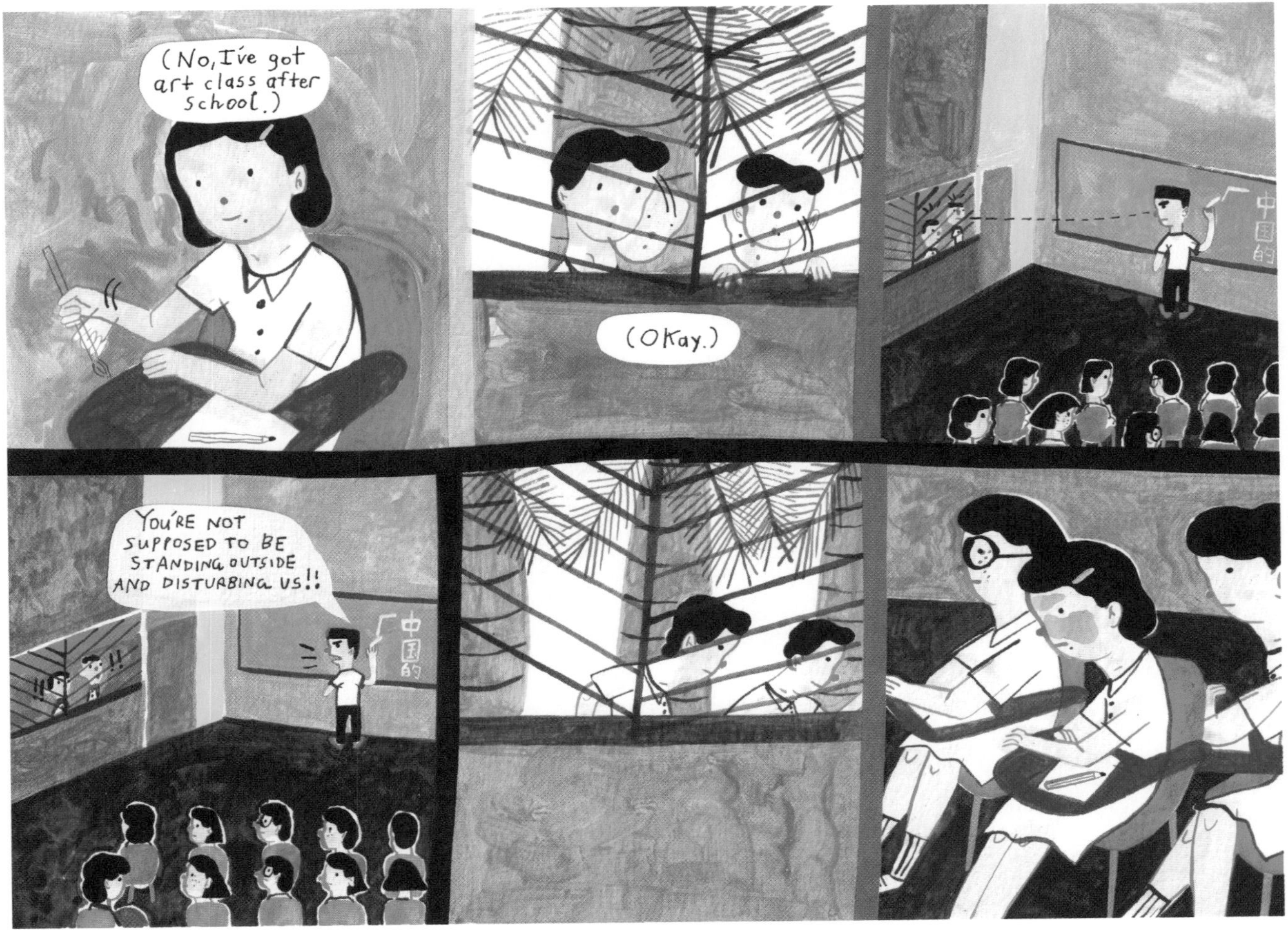
(No, I've got art class after school.)
(Okay.)
中国的
YOU'RE NOT SUPPOSED TO BE STANDING OUTSIDE AND DISTURBING US!!
中国的

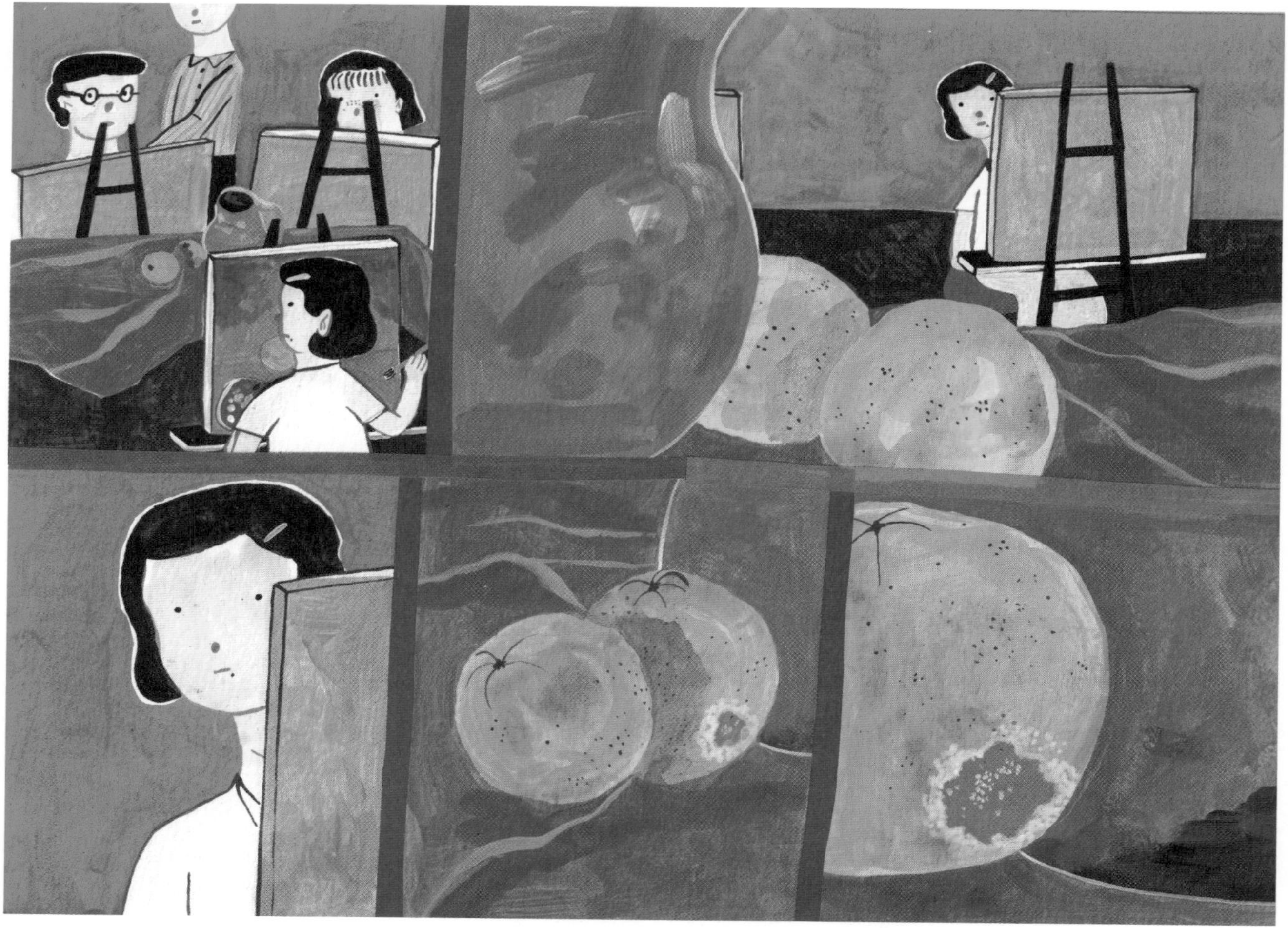

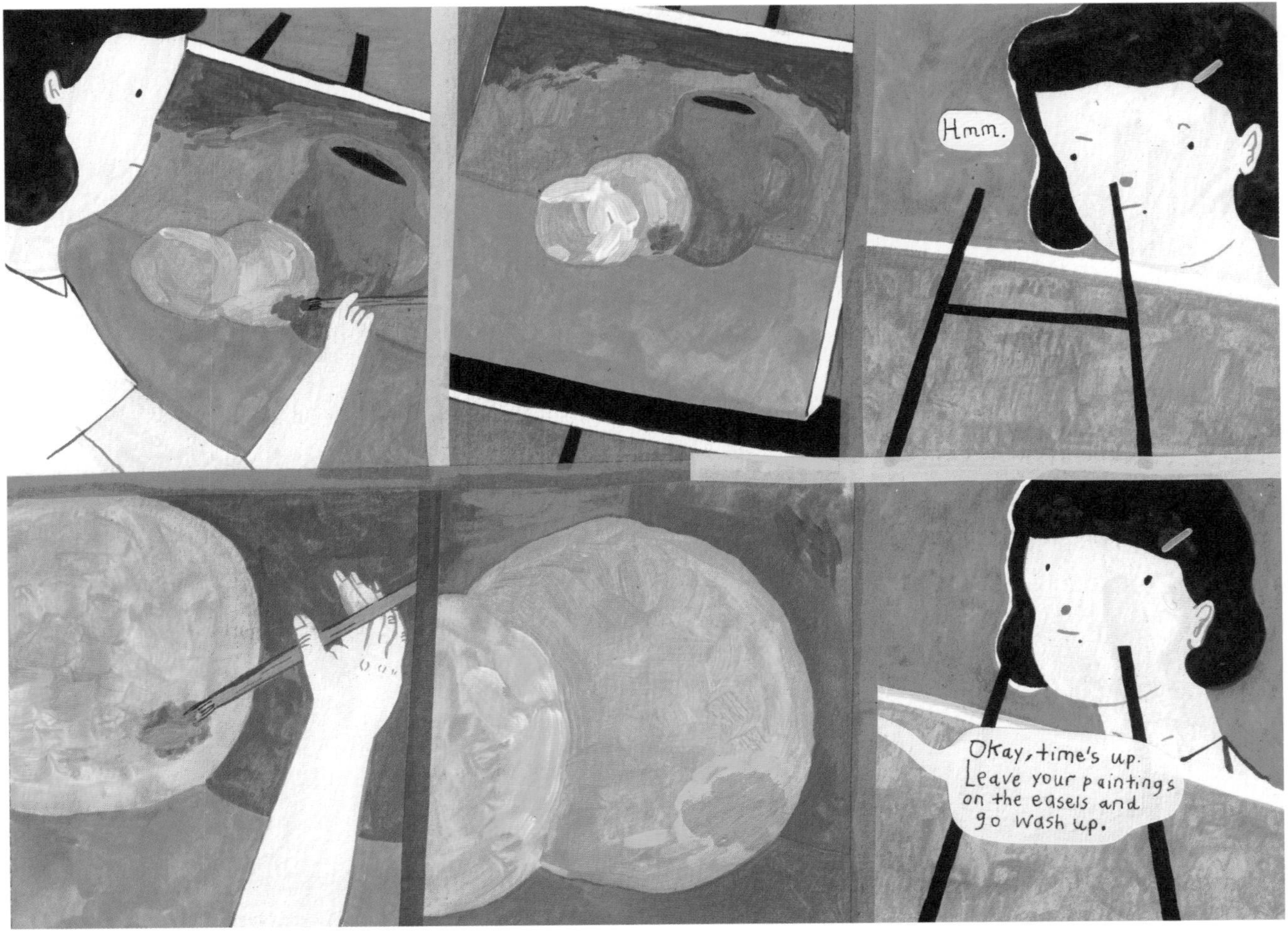
Hmm.
Okay, time's up. Leave your paintings on the easels and go wash up.

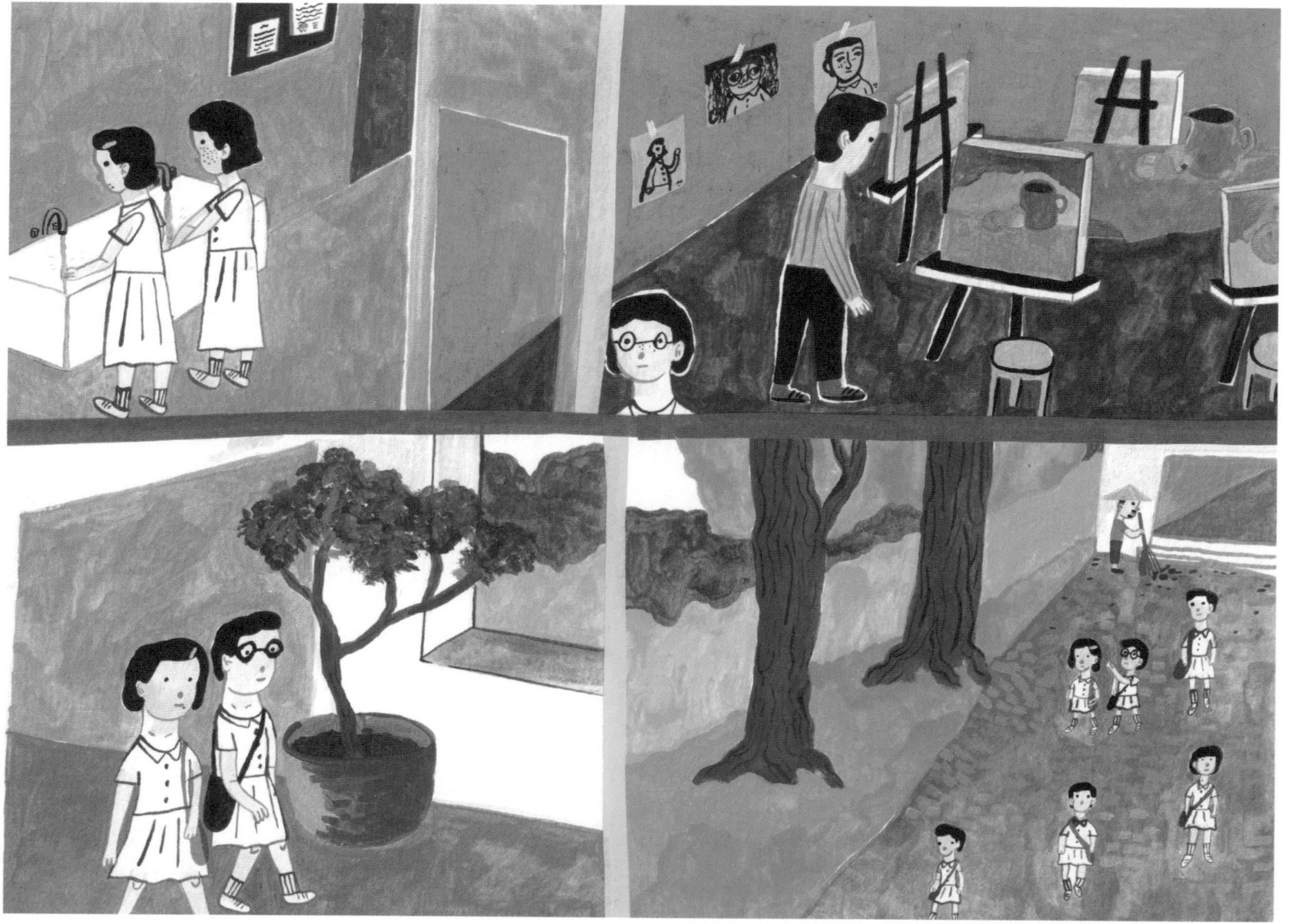

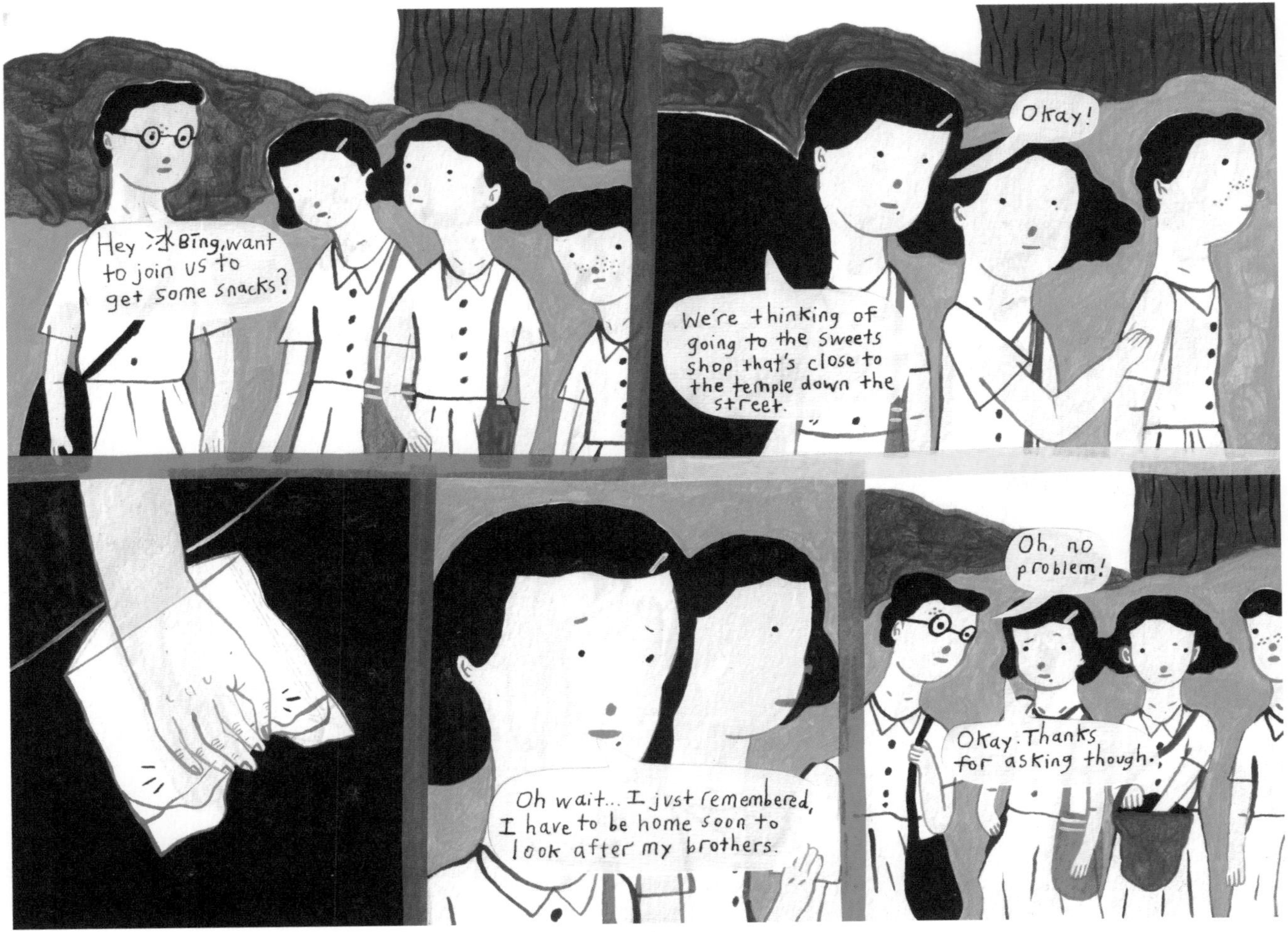
Hey 冰 Bīng, want to join us to get some snacks?
We're thinking of going to the sweets shop that's close to the temple down the street.
Okay!
Oh wait... I just remembered, I have to be home soon to look after my brothers.
Oh, no problem!
Okay. Thanks for asking though.

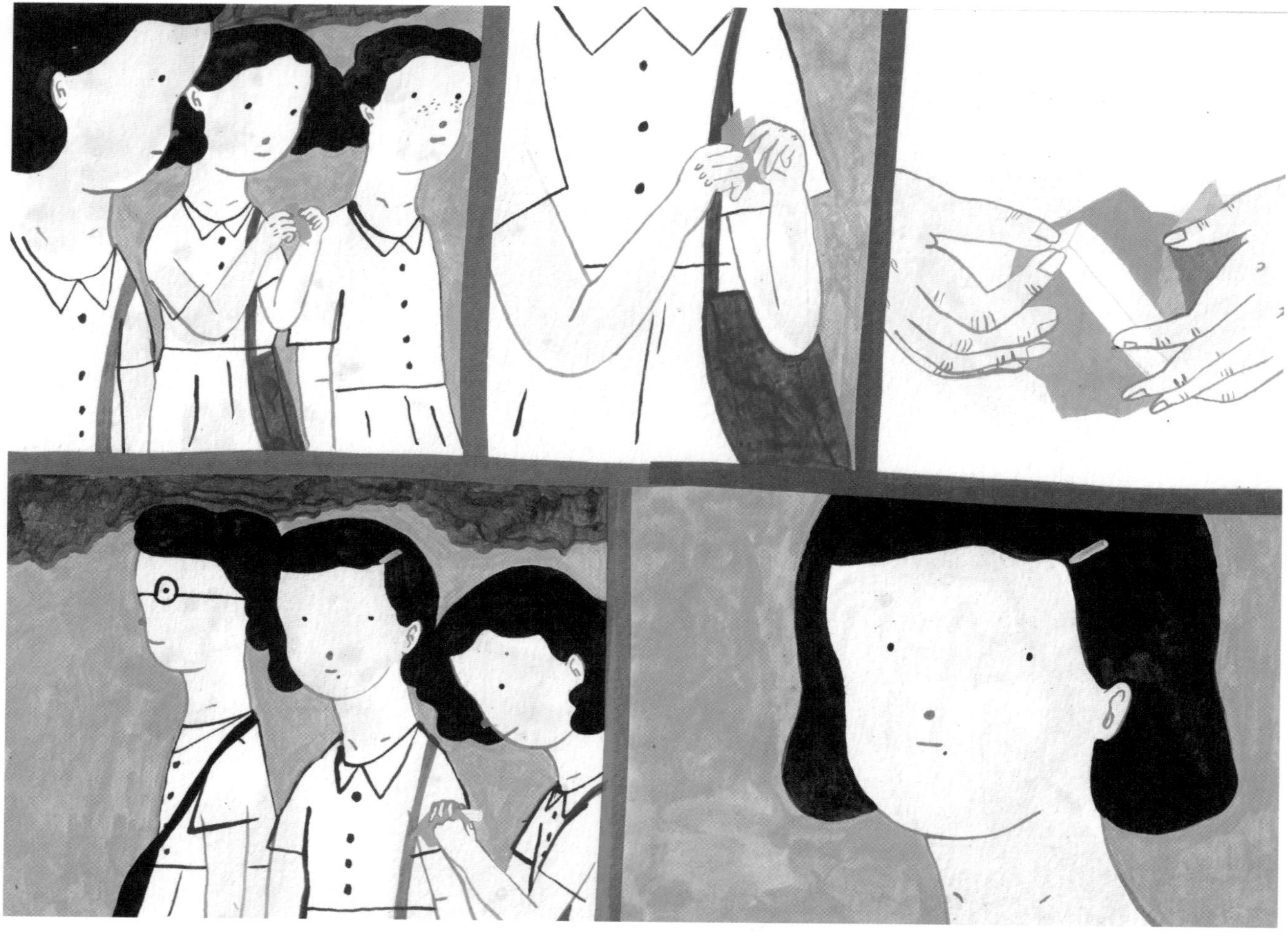

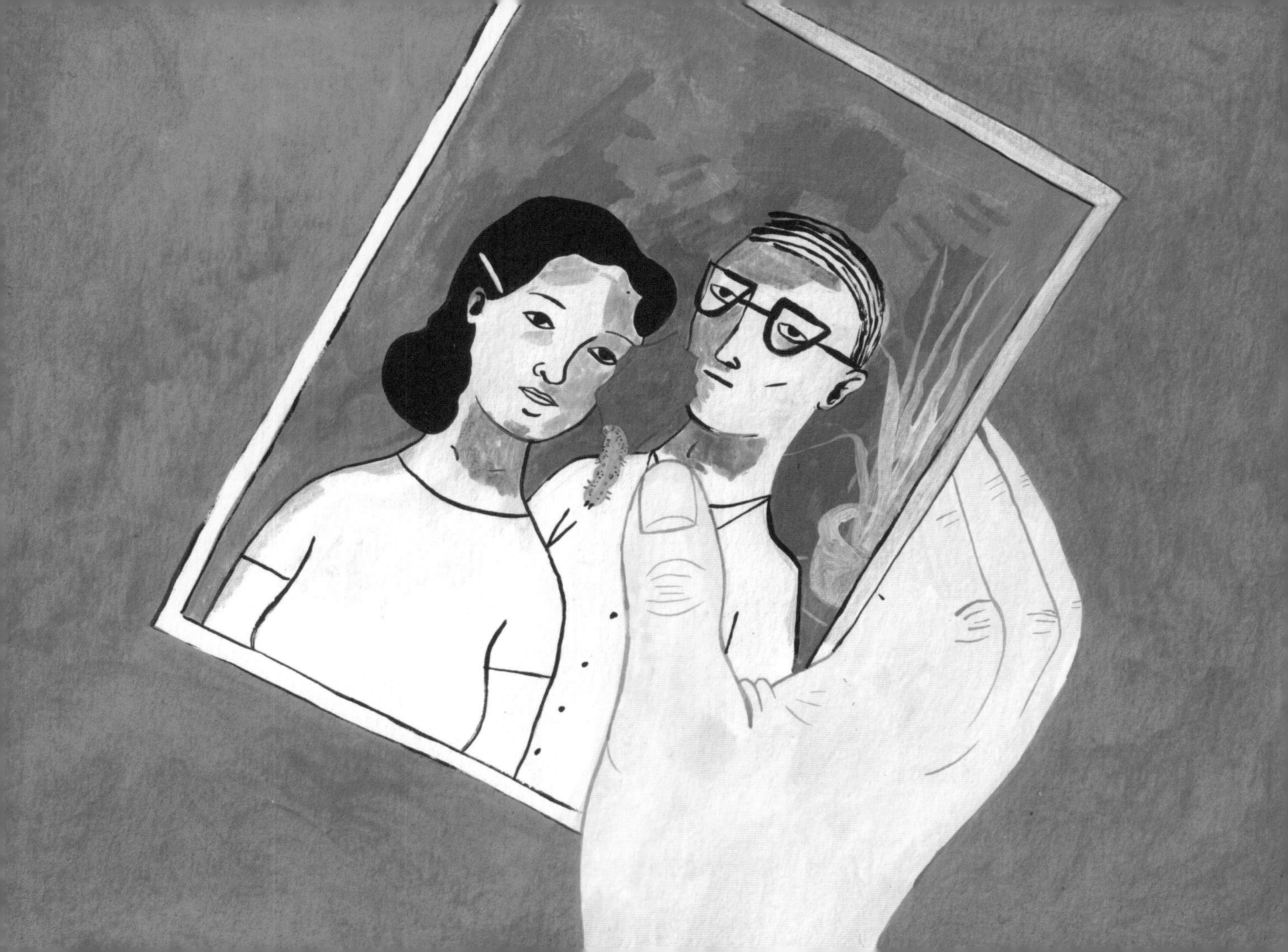

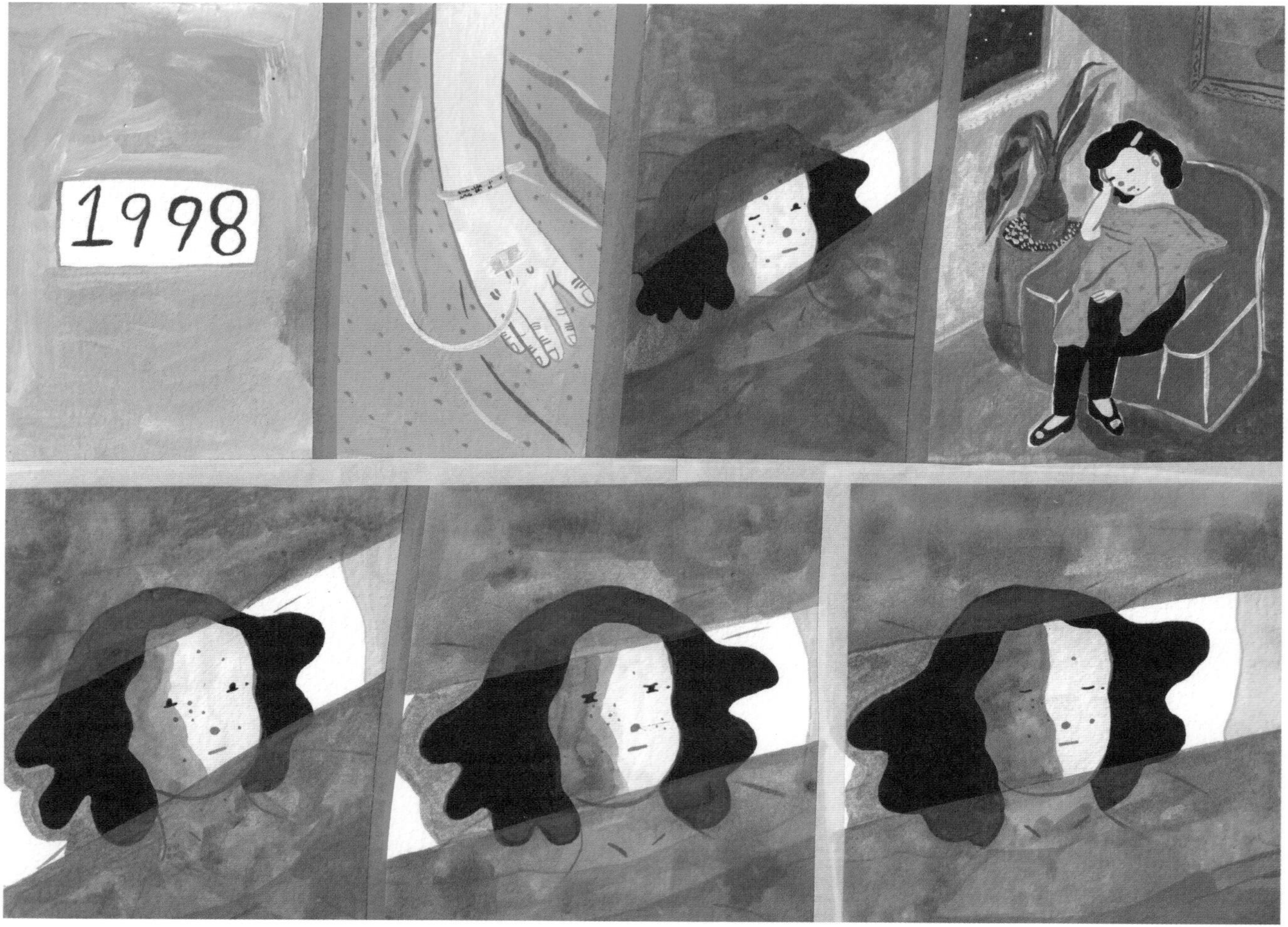
1998

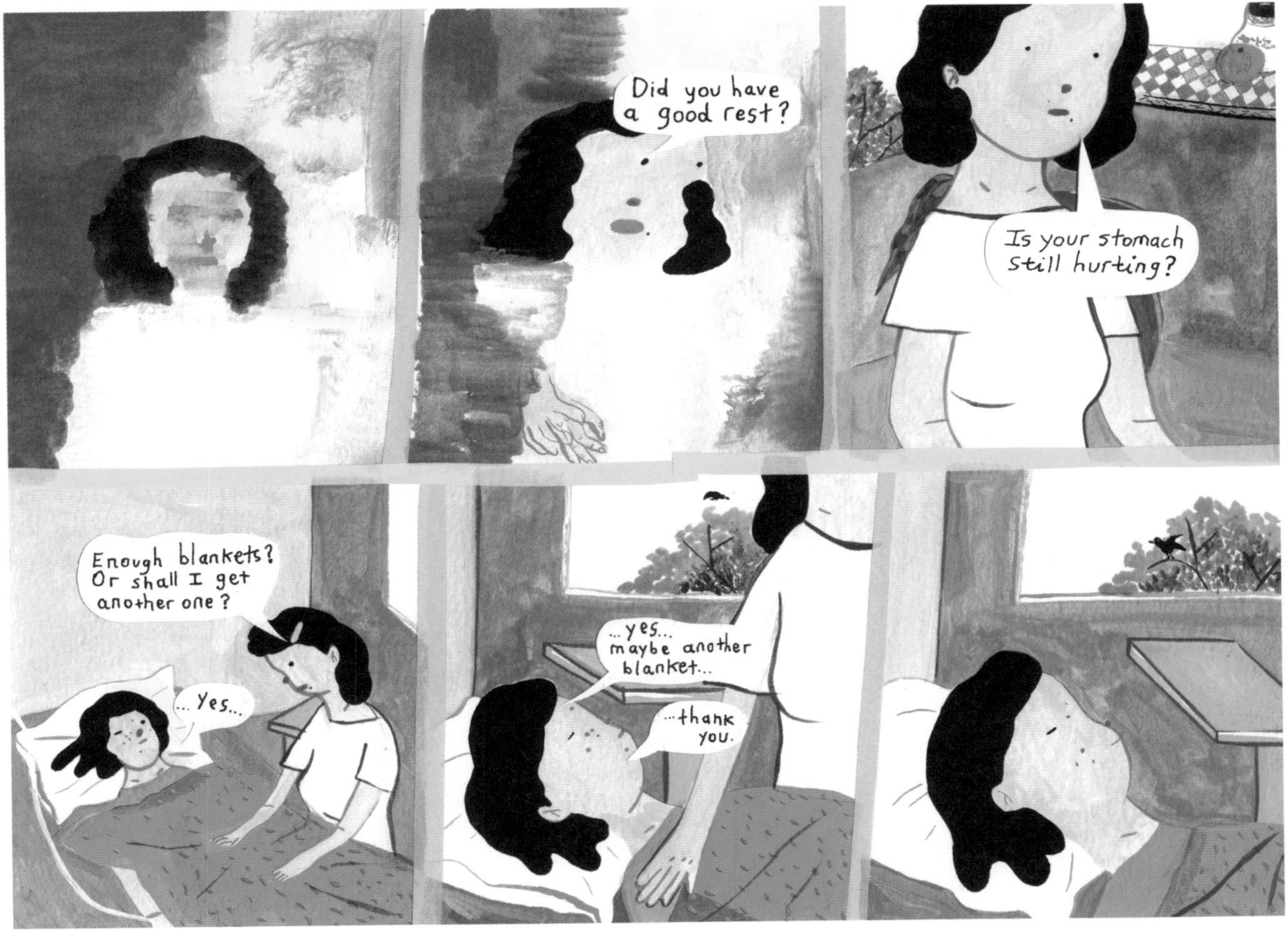
Did you have a good rest?
Is your stomach still hurting?
Enough blankets? Or shall I get another one?
... yes...
... yes... maybe another blanket...
... thank you.

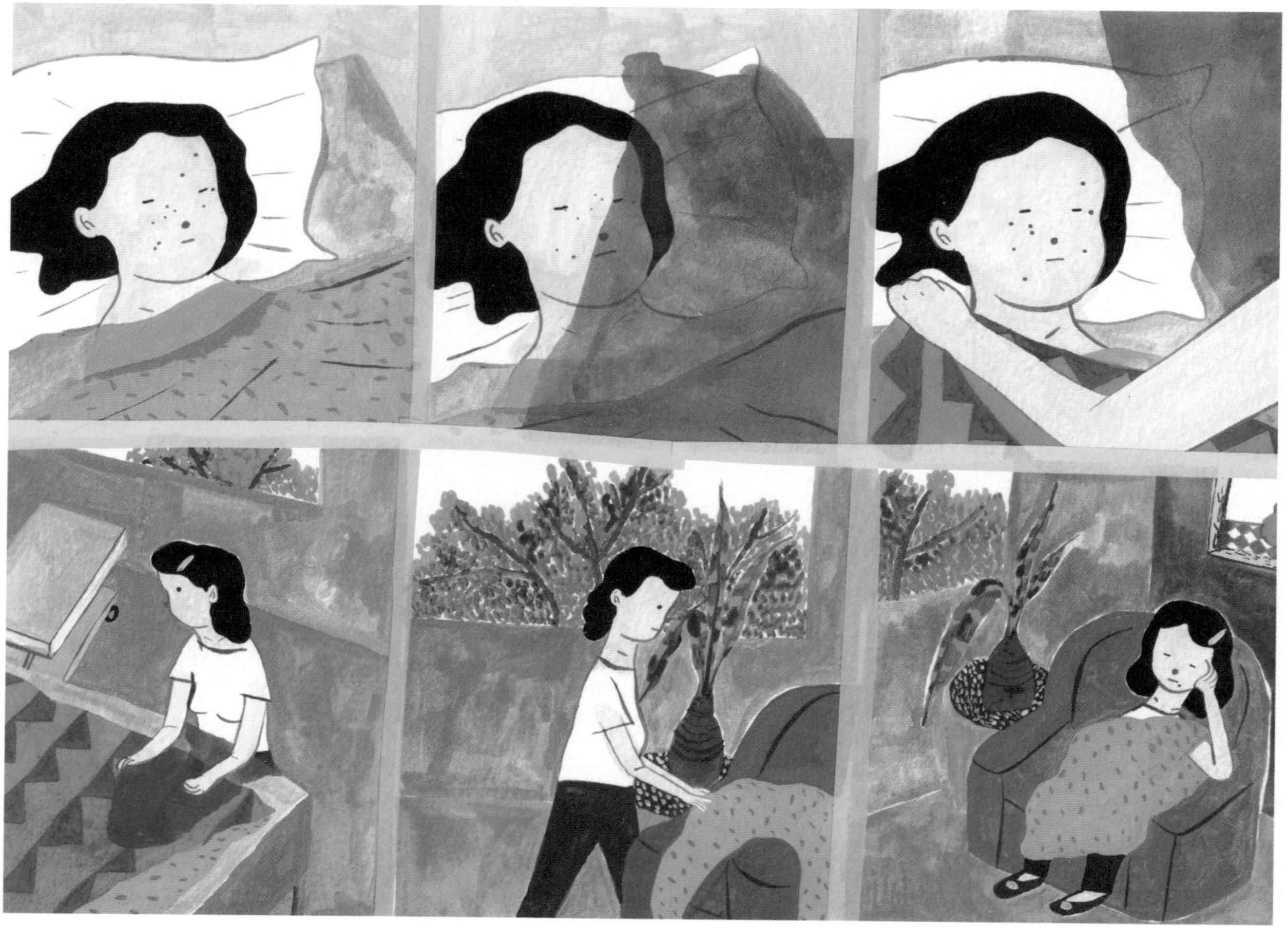

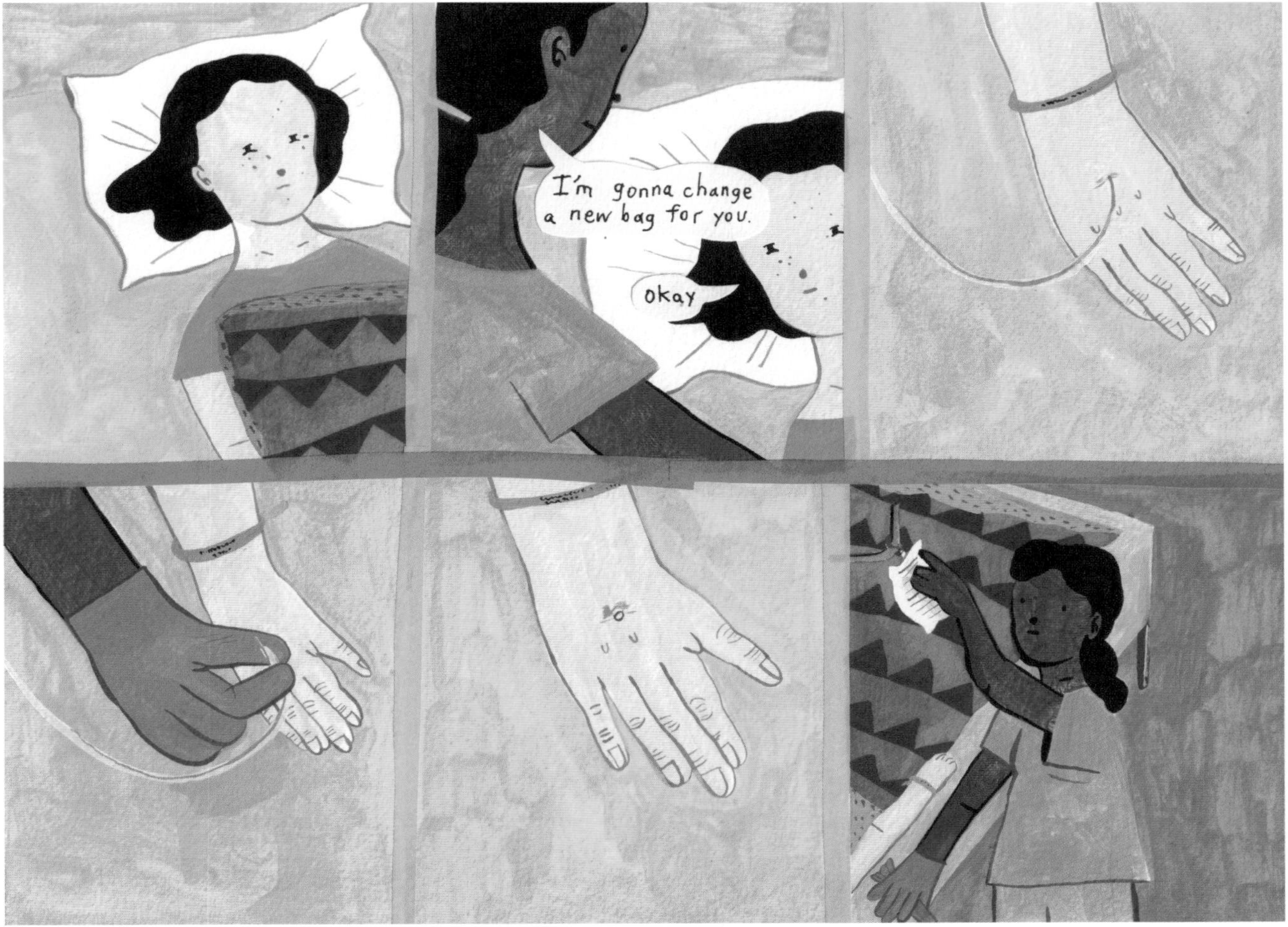
I'm gonna change a new bag for you.
okay

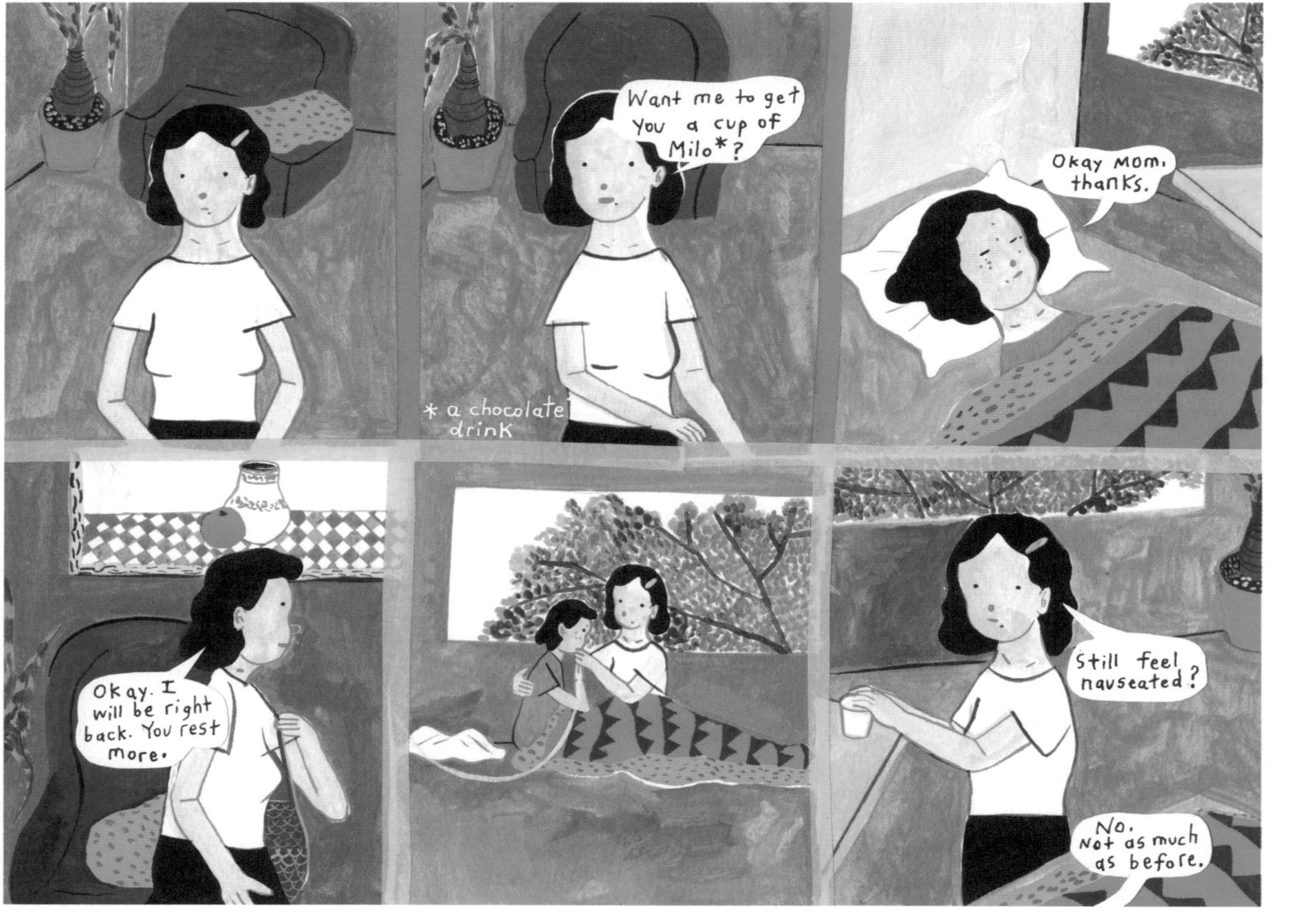
Want me to get you a cup of Milo*?
* a chocolate drink
Okay Mom, thanks.
Okay. I will be right back. You rest more.
Still feel nauseated?
No. Not as much as before.

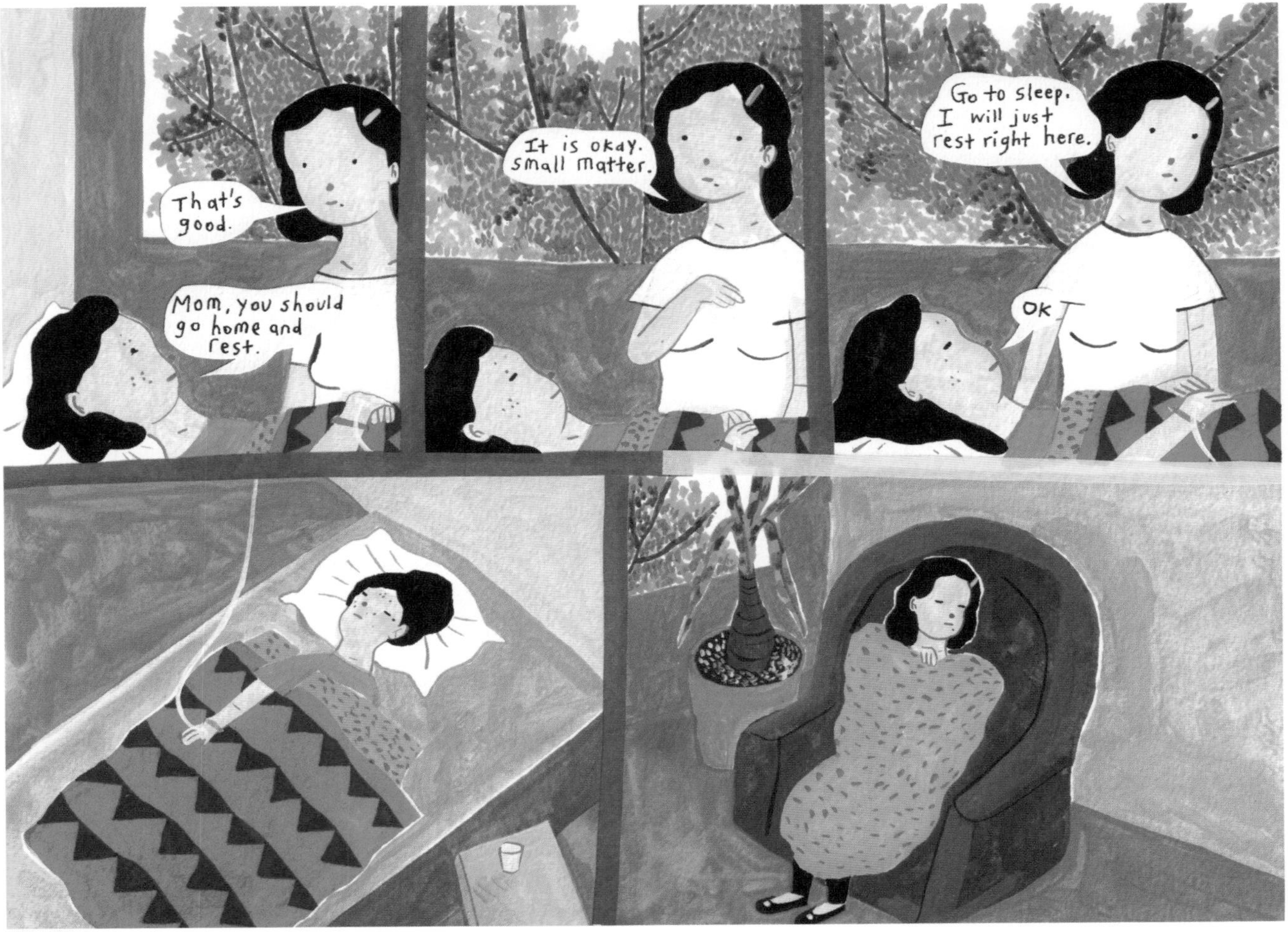
Mom, you should go home and rest.
That's good.
It is okay. small matter.
Go to sleep. I will just rest right here.
OK

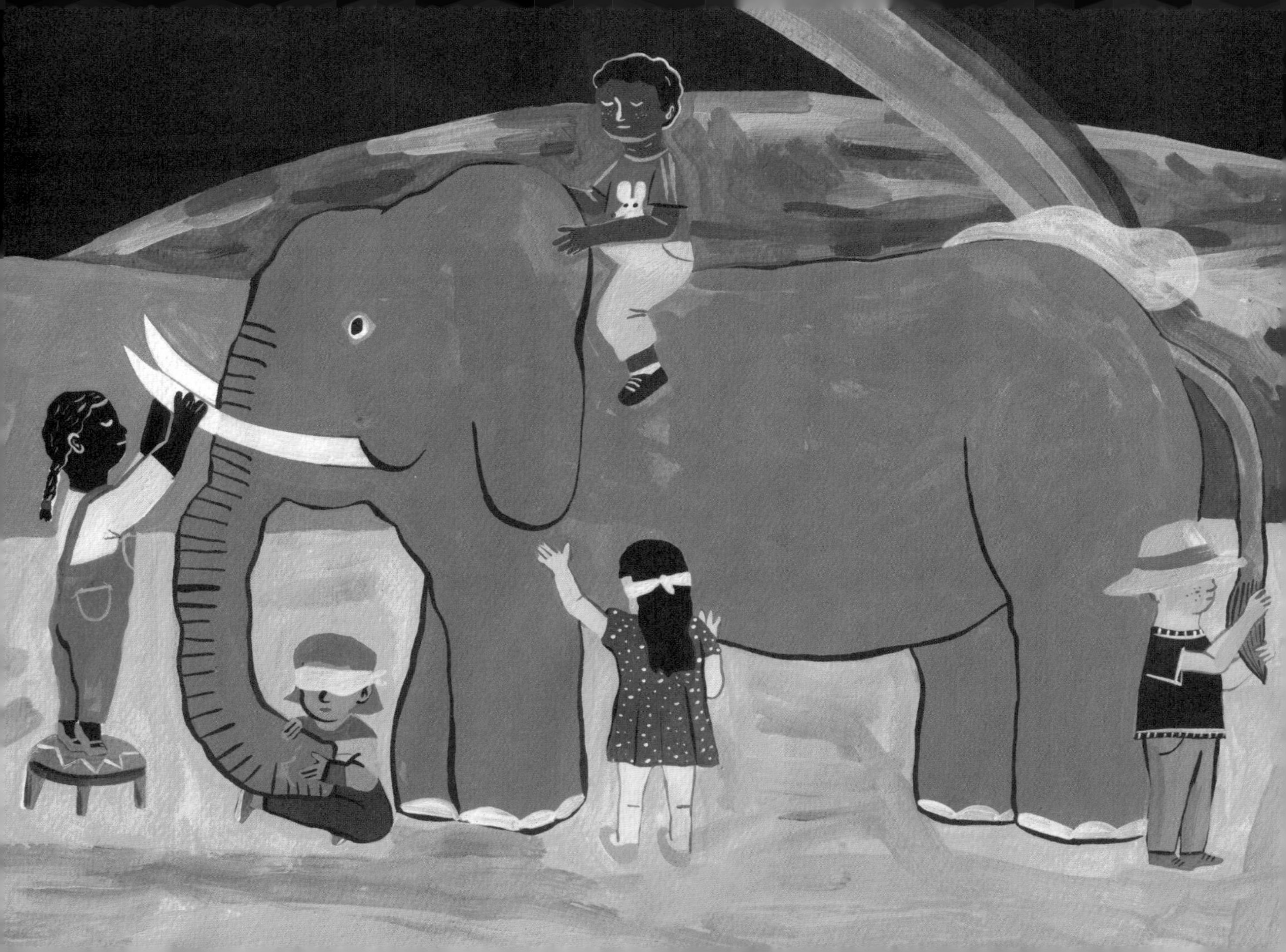

2032

妹Mèi

I wonder what it was like for her mom, in those days.

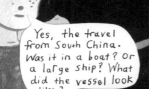

Yes, the travel from South China. Was it in a boat? Or a large ship? What did the vessel look like?

Hmm mmm.

Was she alone? Or was someone with her? How old was she even?

Did she feel safe?

Guess that's a luxury they did not have.

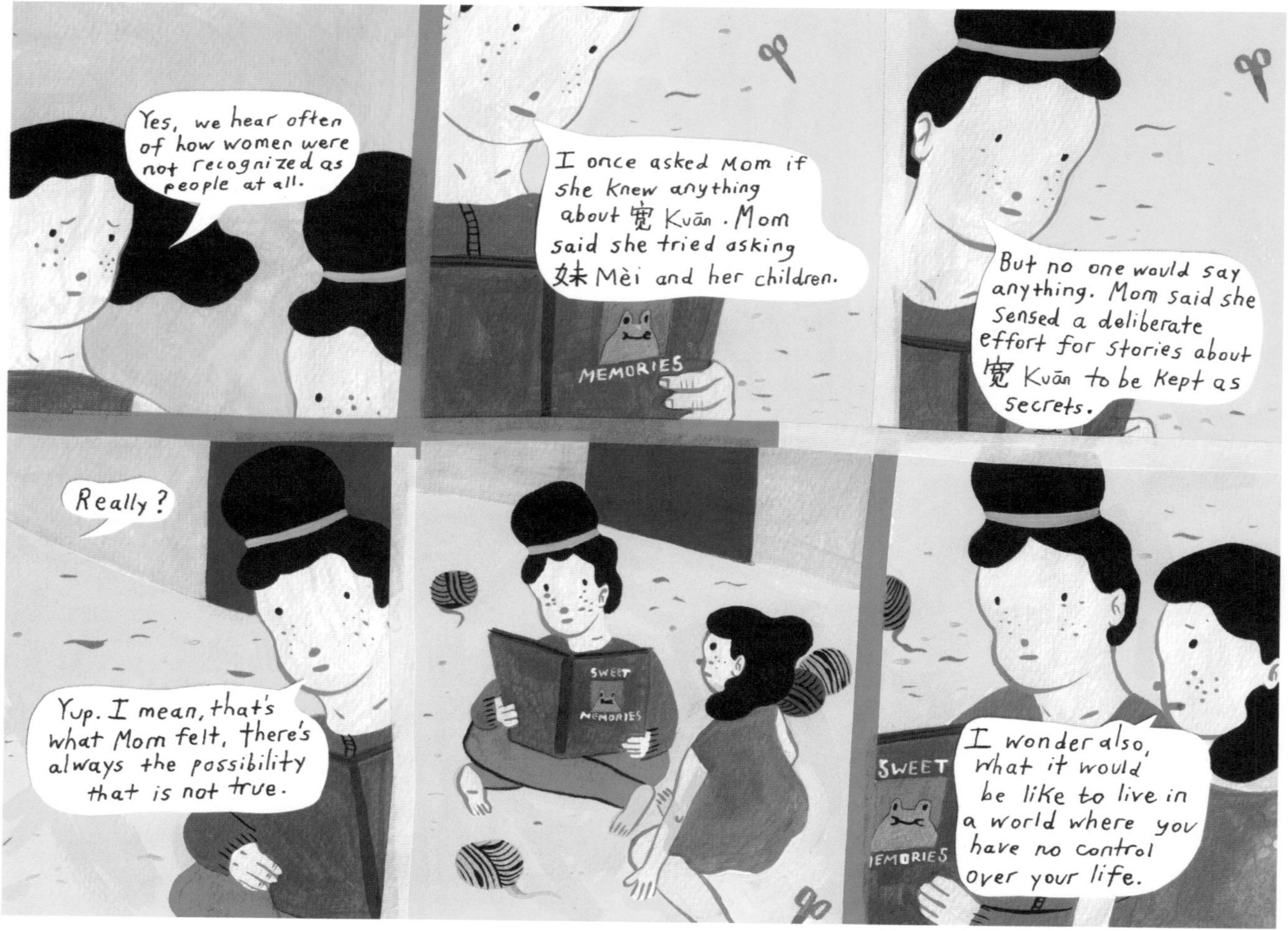
Yes, we hear often of how women were not recognized as people at all.
I once asked Mom if she knew anything about 宽 Kuān. Mom said she tried asking 妹 Mèi and her children.
But no one would say anything. Mom said she sensed a deliberate effort for stories about 宽 Kuān to be kept as secrets.
Really?
Yup. I mean, that's what Mom felt, there's always the possibility that is not true.
SWEET MEMORIES
I wonder also, what it would be like to live in a world where you have no control over your life.

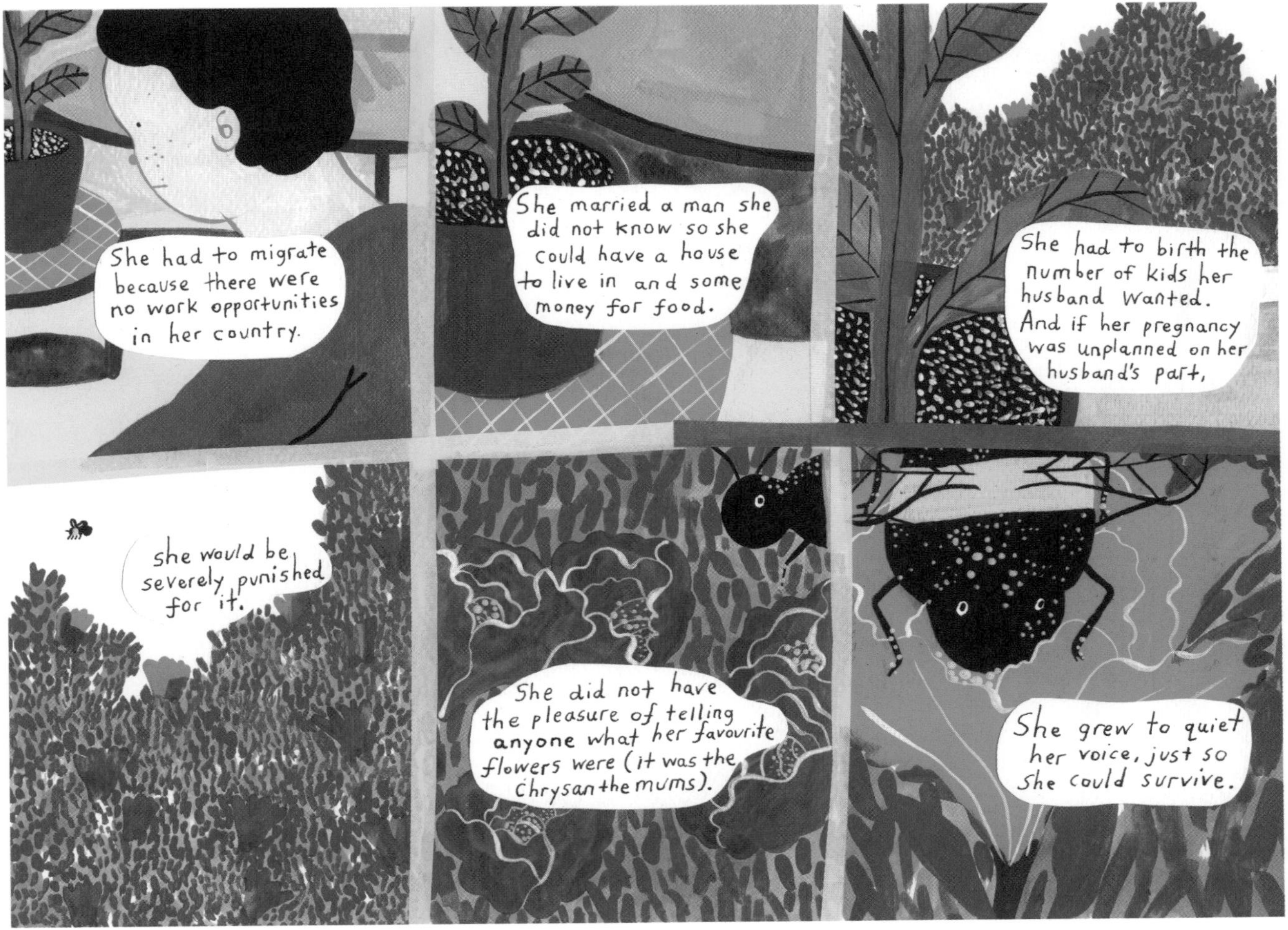
She had to migrate because there were no work opportunities in her country.
She married a man she did not know so she could have a house to live in and some money for food.
She had to birth the number of kids her husband wanted. And if her pregnancy was unplanned on her husband's part,
she would be severely punished for it.
She did not have the pleasure of telling **anyone** what her favourite flowers were (it was the chrysanthemums).
She grew to quiet her voice, just so she could survive.

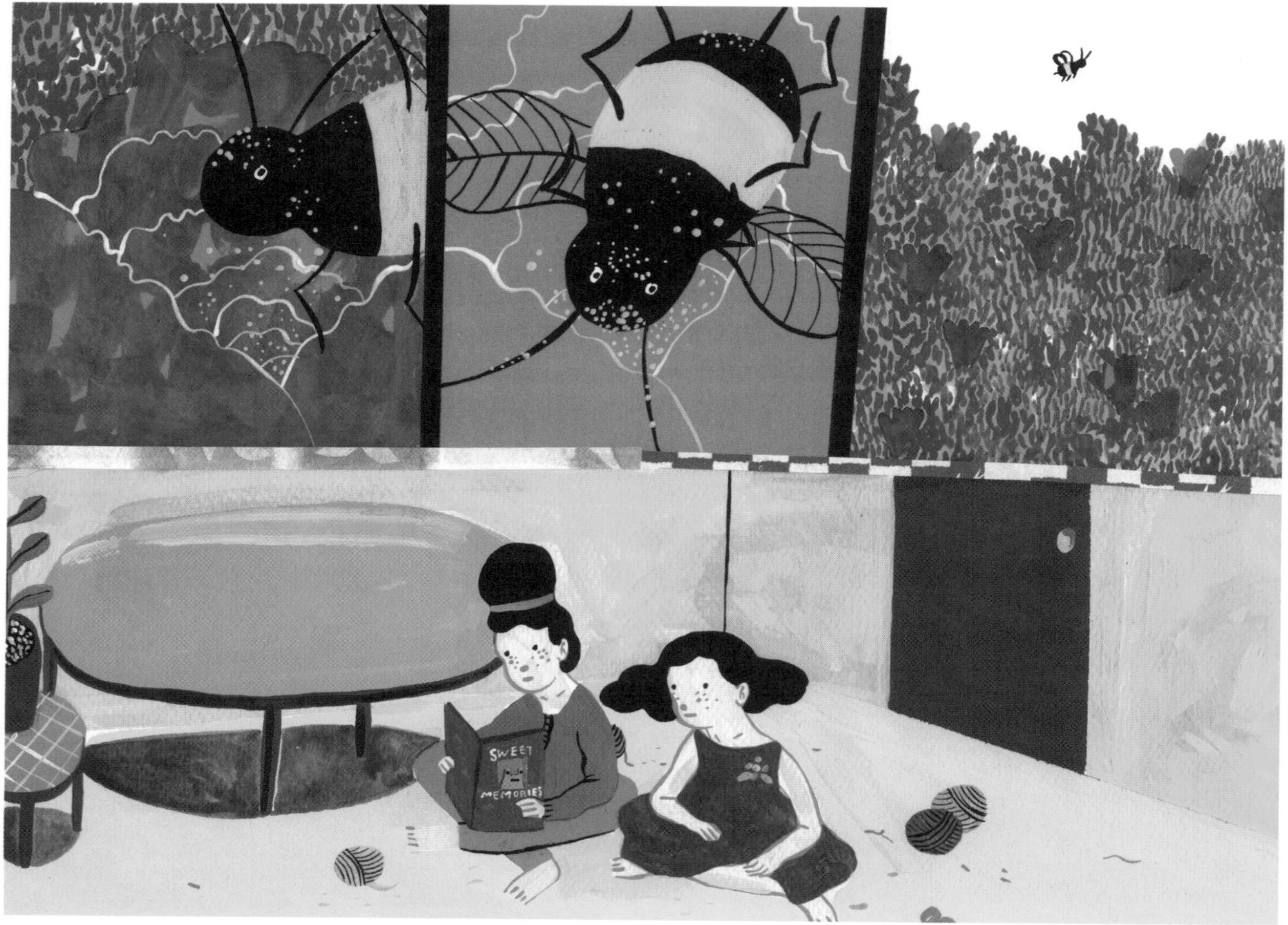
SWEET
MEMORIES

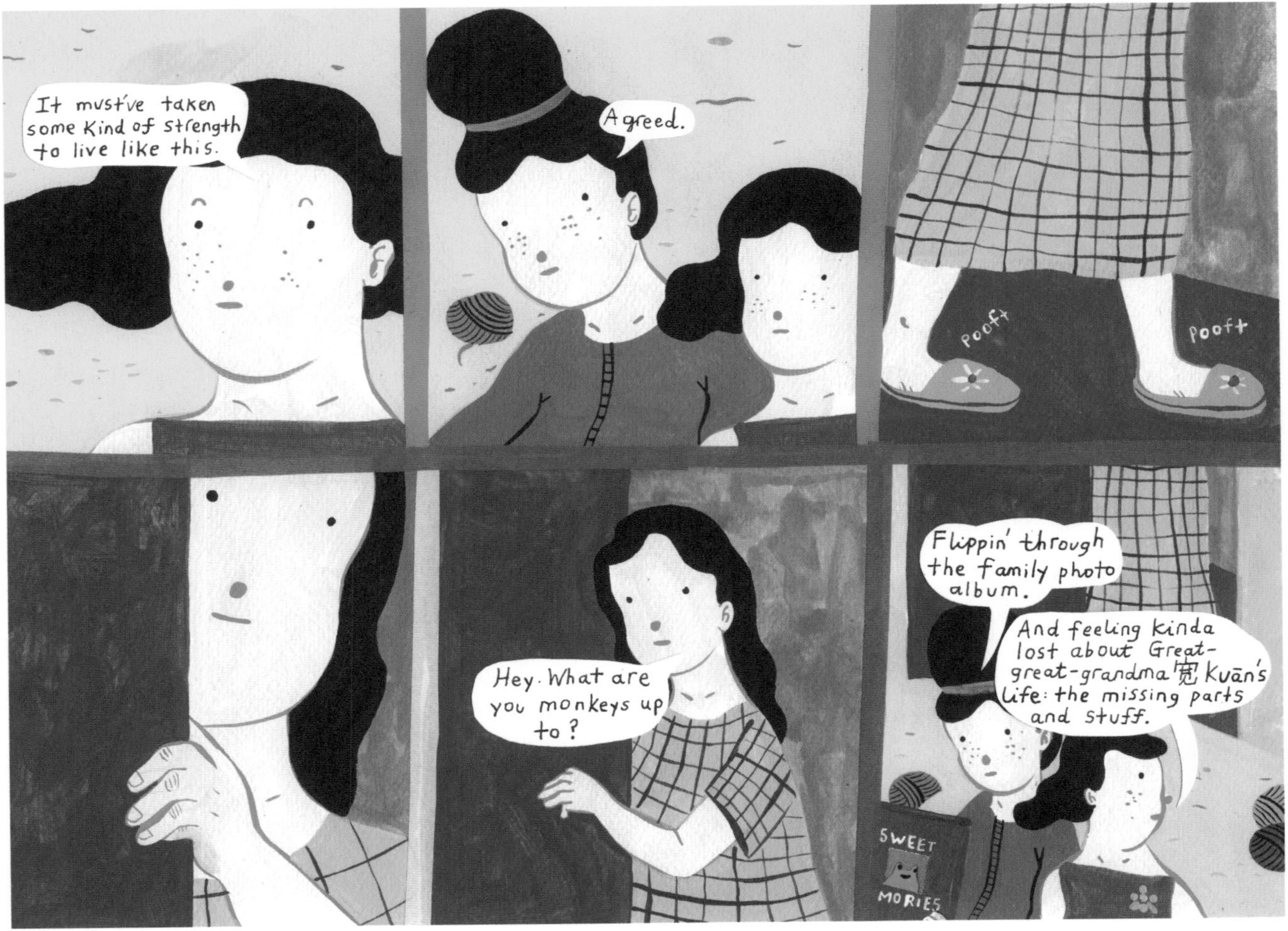
It must've taken some Kind of strength to live like this.
Agreed.
pooft
pooft
Hey. What are you monkeys up to?
Flippin' through the family photo album.
And feeling kinda lost about Great-great-grandma 宽 Kuān's life: the missing parts and stuff.
SWEET MORIES

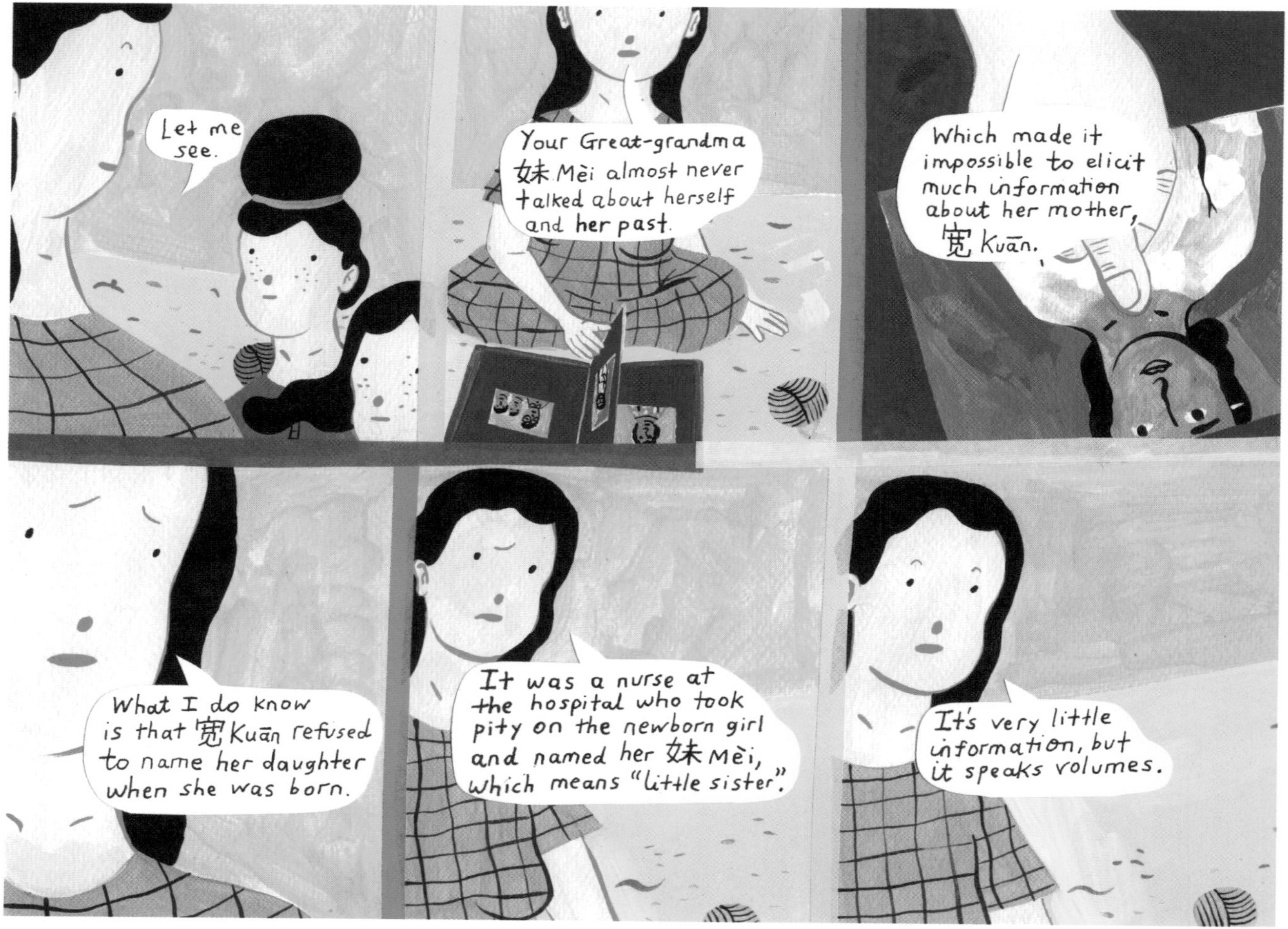
Let me see.
Your Great-grandma 妹 Mèi almost never talked about herself and **her past**.
Which made it impossible to elicit much information about her mother, 宽 Kuān.
What I do know is that 宽 Kuān refused to name her daughter when she was born.
It was a nurse at the hospital who took pity on the newborn girl and named her 妹 Mèi, which means "little sister".
It's very little information, but it speaks volumes.

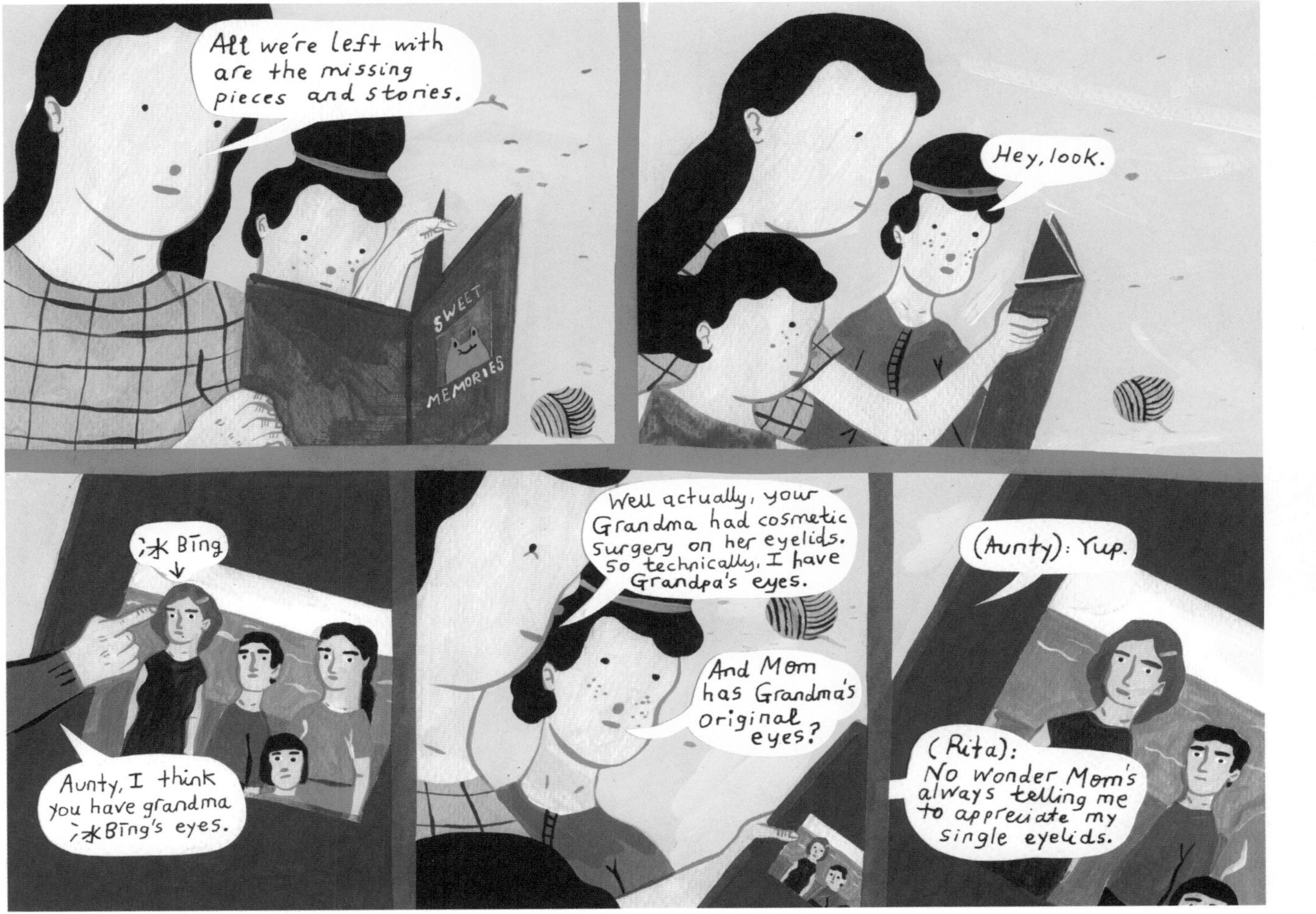

All we're left with are the missing pieces and stories.
Hey, look.
冰 Bīng
Aunty, I think you have grandma 冰 Bīng's eyes.
Well actually, your Grandma had cosmetic surgery on her eyelids. So technically, I have Grandpa's eyes.
And Mom has Grandma's original eyes?
(Aunty): Yup.
(Rita): No wonder Mom's always telling me to appreciate my single eyelids.
SWEET MEMORIES

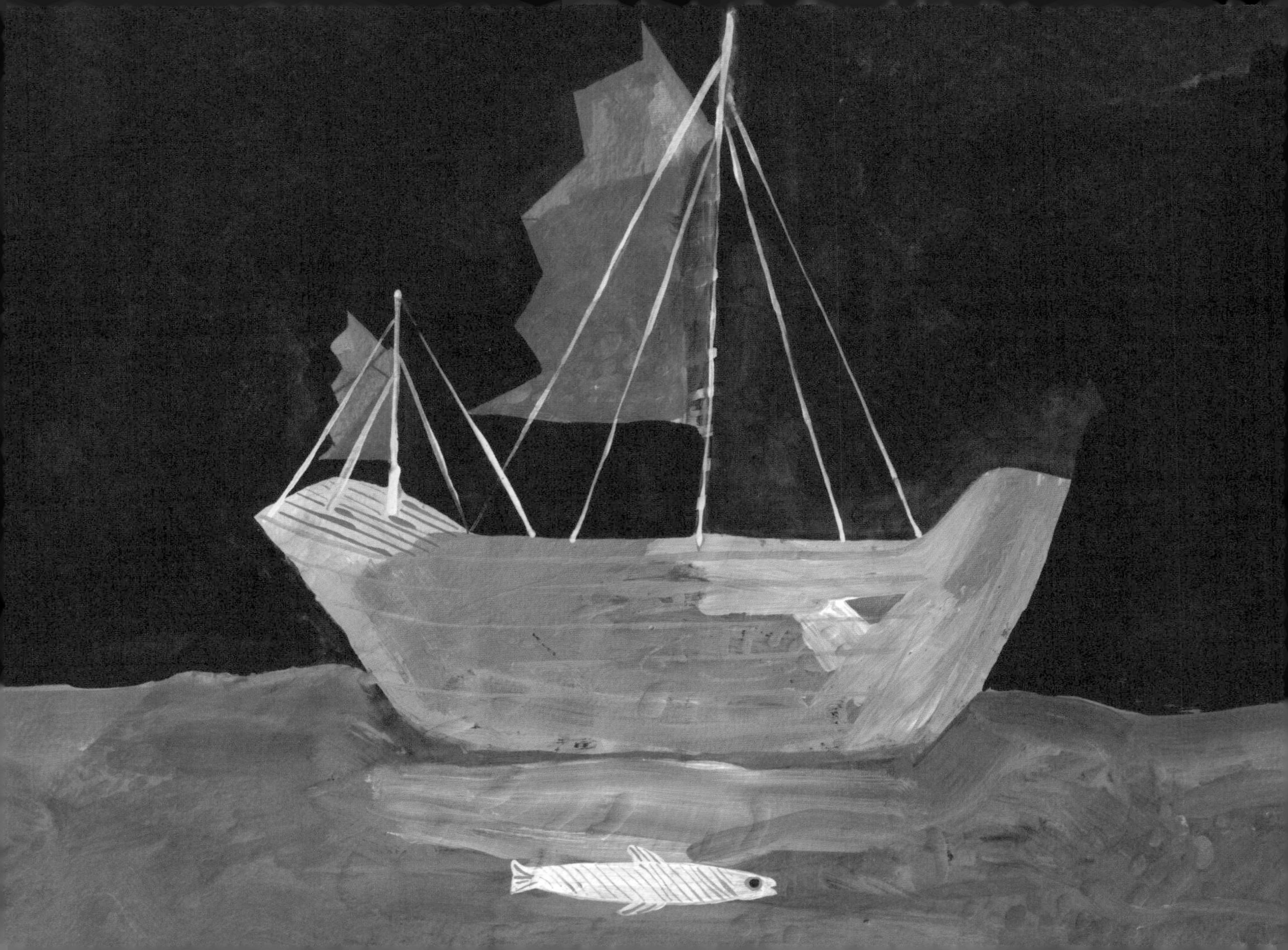

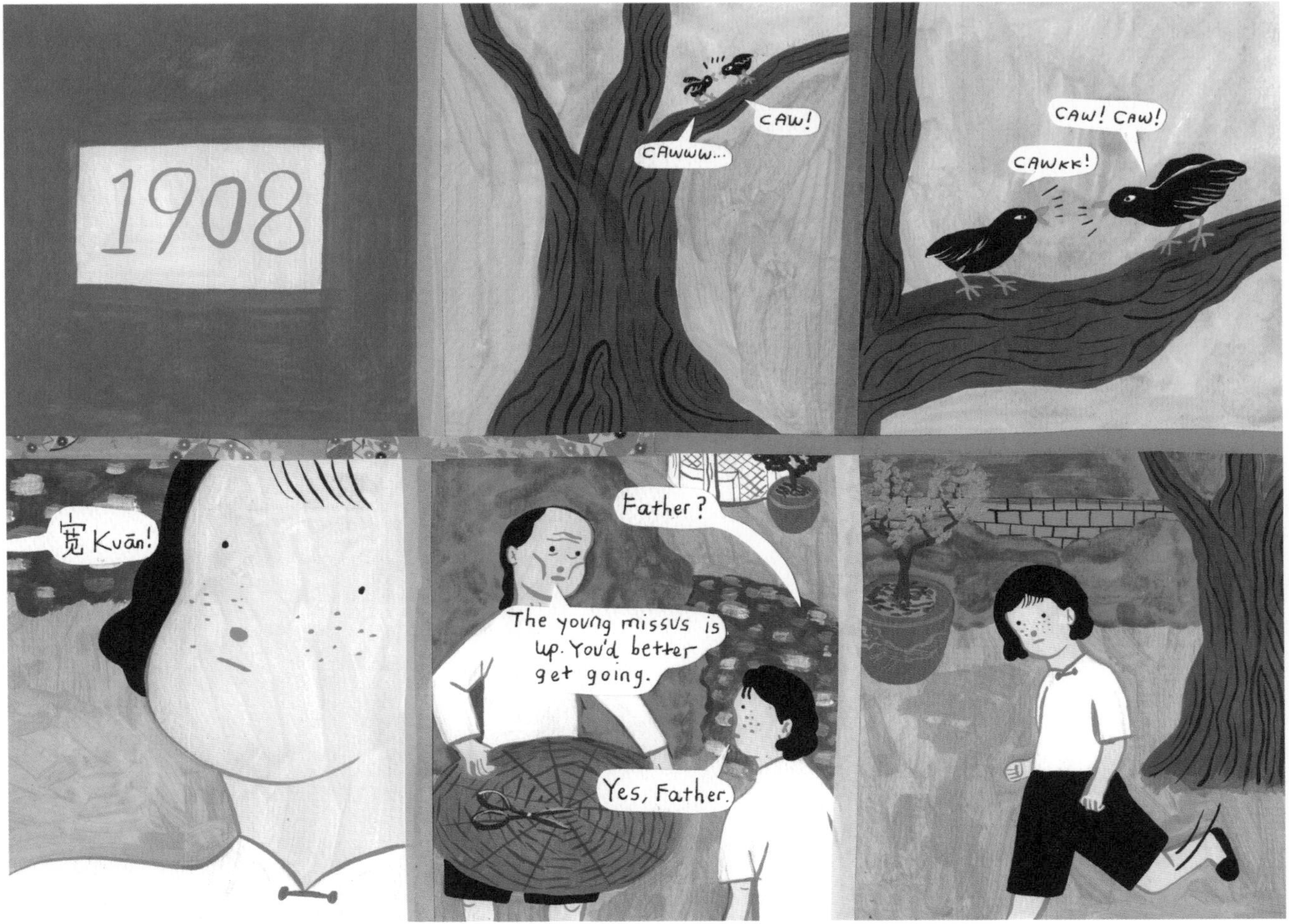
1908
CAWWW...
CAW!
CAW! CAW!
CAWKK!
宽 Kuān!
Father?
The young missus is up. You'd better get going.
Yes, Father.

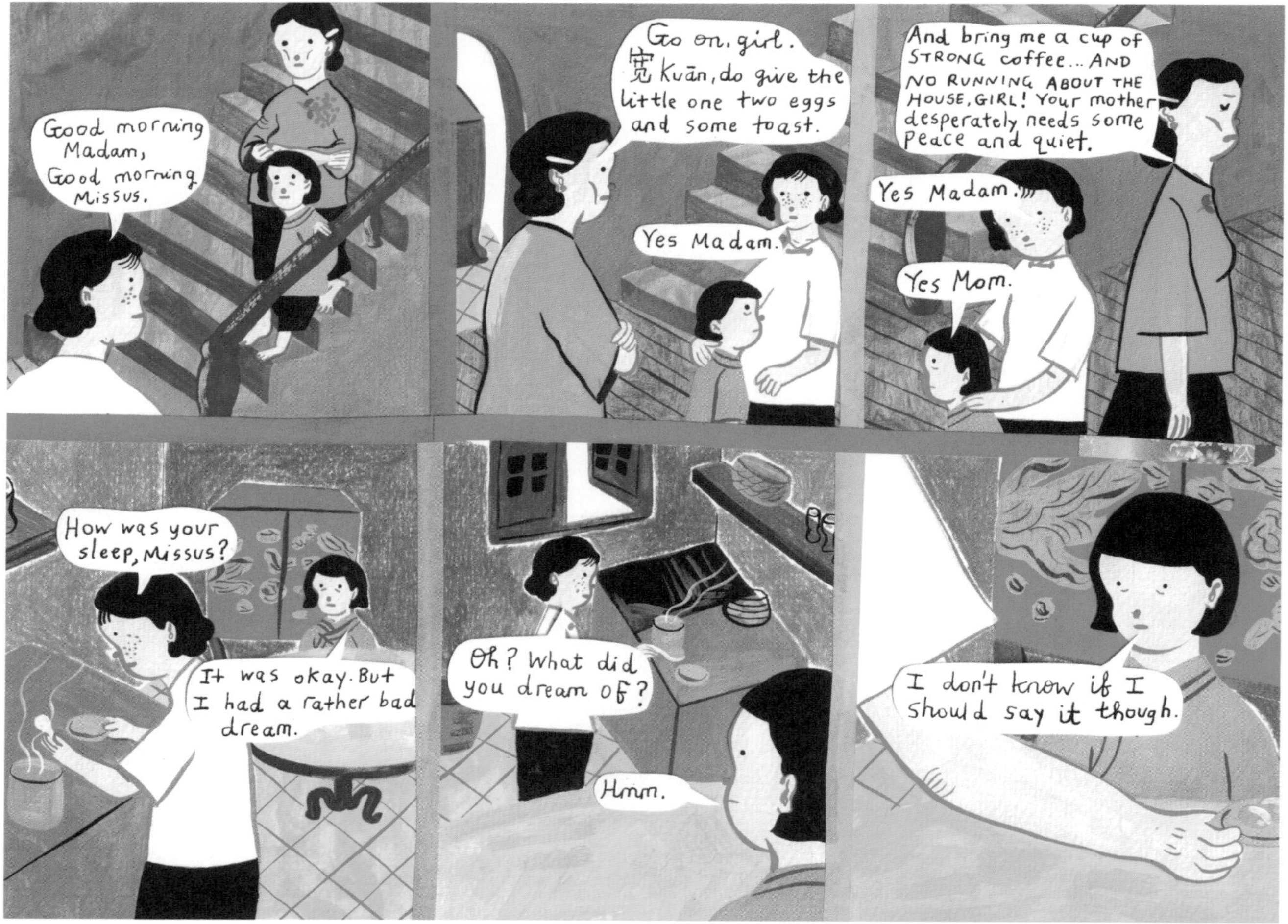
Good morning Madam, Good morning Missus.
Go on, girl. 宽 Kuān, do give the little one two eggs and some toast.
Yes Madam.
And bring me a cup of STRONG coffee... AND NO RUNNING ABOUT THE HOUSE, GIRL! Your mother desperately needs some peace and quiet.
Yes Madam.
Yes Mom.
How was your sleep, Missus?
It was okay. But I had a rather bad dream.
Oh? What did you dream of?
Hmm.
I don't know if I should say it though.

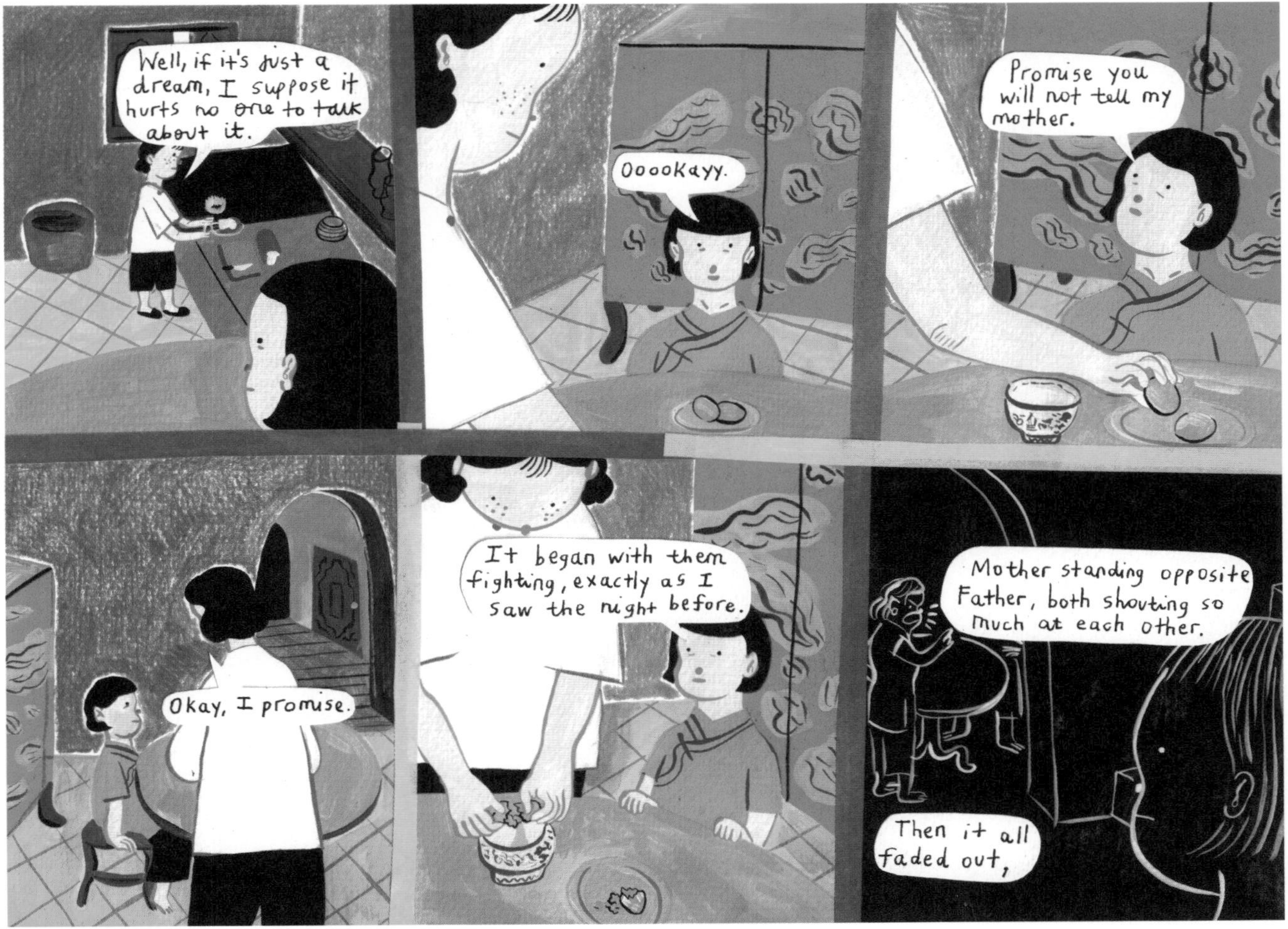
Well, if it's just a dream, I suppose it hurts no one to talk about it.
Ooookayy.
Promise you will not tell my mother.
Okay, I promise.
It began with them fighting, exactly as I saw the night before.
Mother standing opposite Father, both shouting so much at each other.
Then it all faded out,

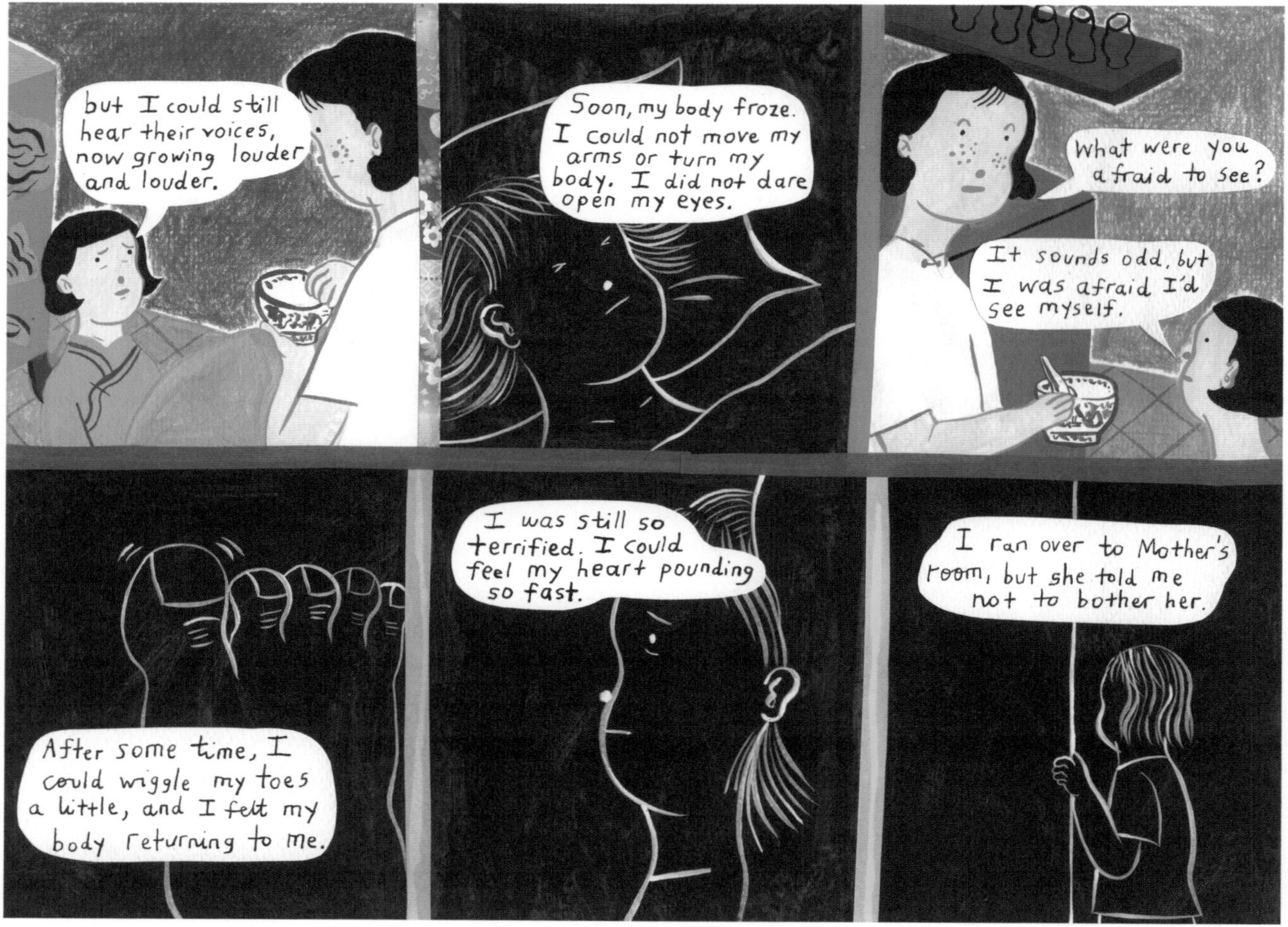
but I could still hear their voices, now growing louder and louder.
Soon, my body froze. I could not move my arms or turn my body. I did not dare open my eyes.
What were you afraid to see?
It sounds odd, but I was afraid I'd see myself.
After some time, I could wiggle my toes a little, and I felt my body returning to me.
I was still so terrified. I could feel my heart pounding so fast.
I ran over to Mother's room, but she told me not to bother her.

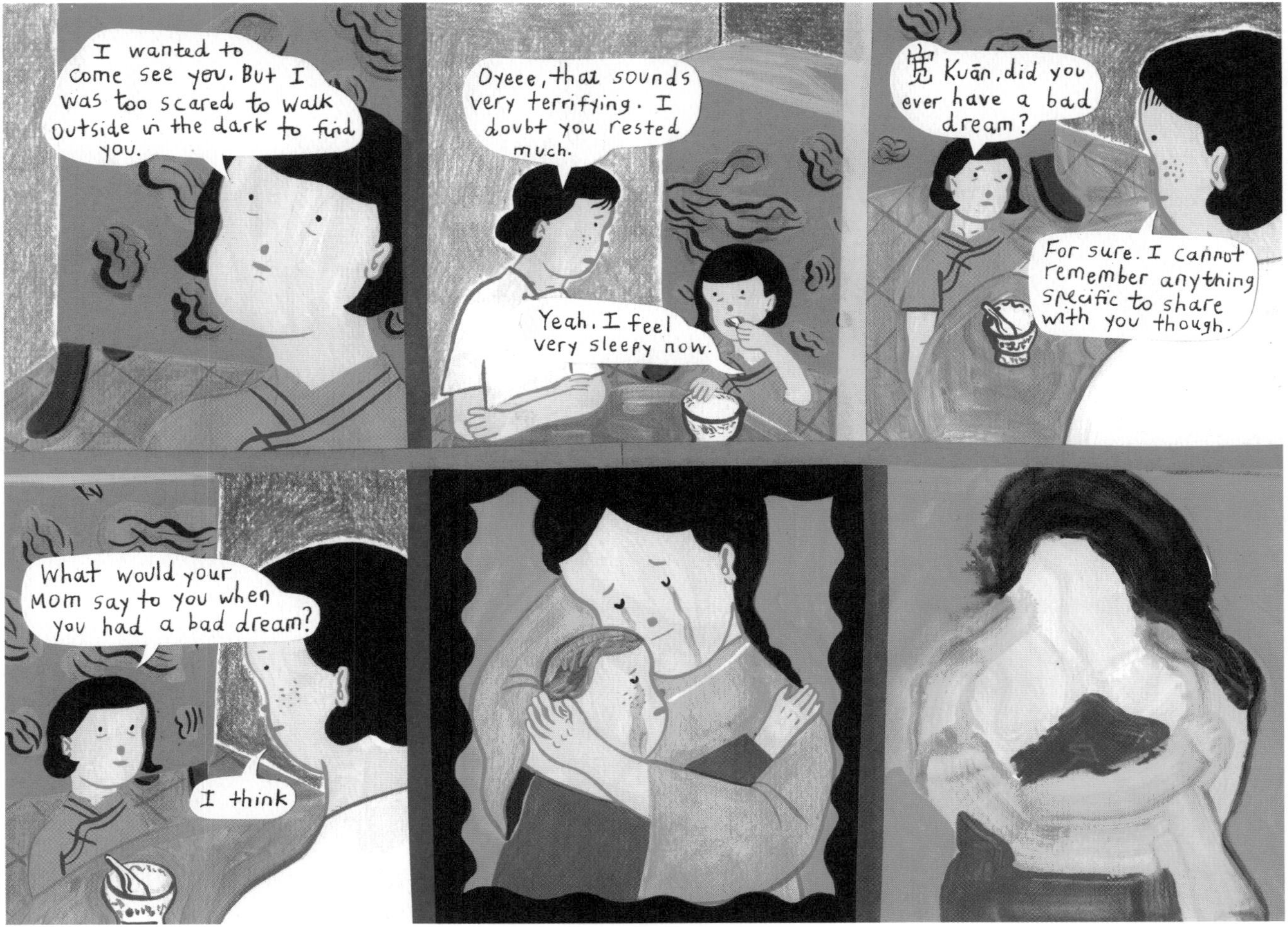
I wanted to come see you. But I was too scared to walk outside in the dark to find you.
Oyeee, that sounds very terrifying. I doubt you rested much.
Yeah. I feel very sleepy now.
宽 Kuān, did you ever have a bad dream?
For sure. I cannot remember anything specific to share with you though.
What would your Mom say to you when you had a bad dream?
I think

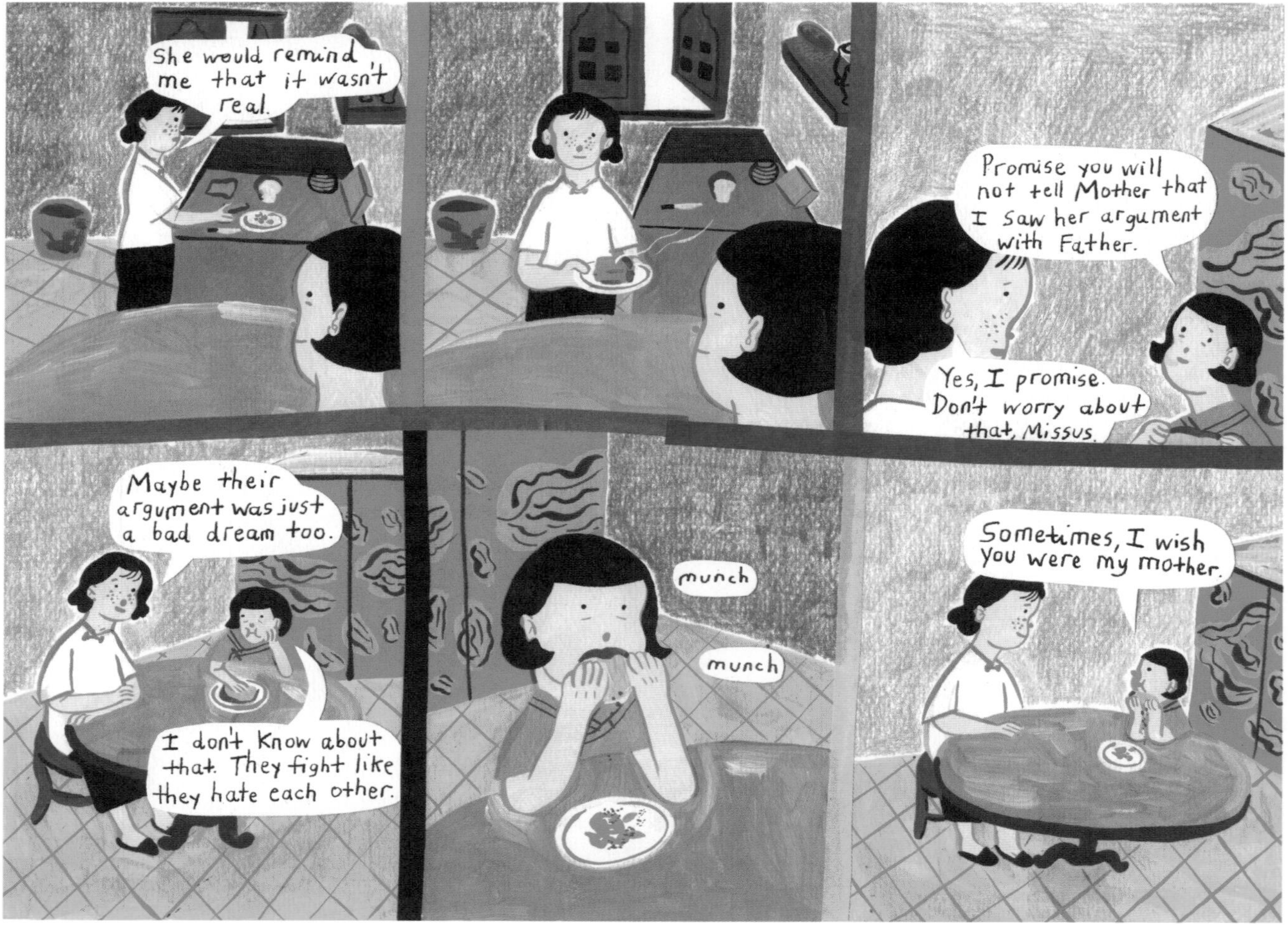
She would remind me that it wasn't real.
Promise you will not tell Mother that I saw her argument with Father.
Yes, I promise. Don't worry about that, Missus.
Maybe their argument was just a bad dream too.
I don't know about that. They fight like they hate each other.
munch
munch
Sometimes, I wish you were my mother.

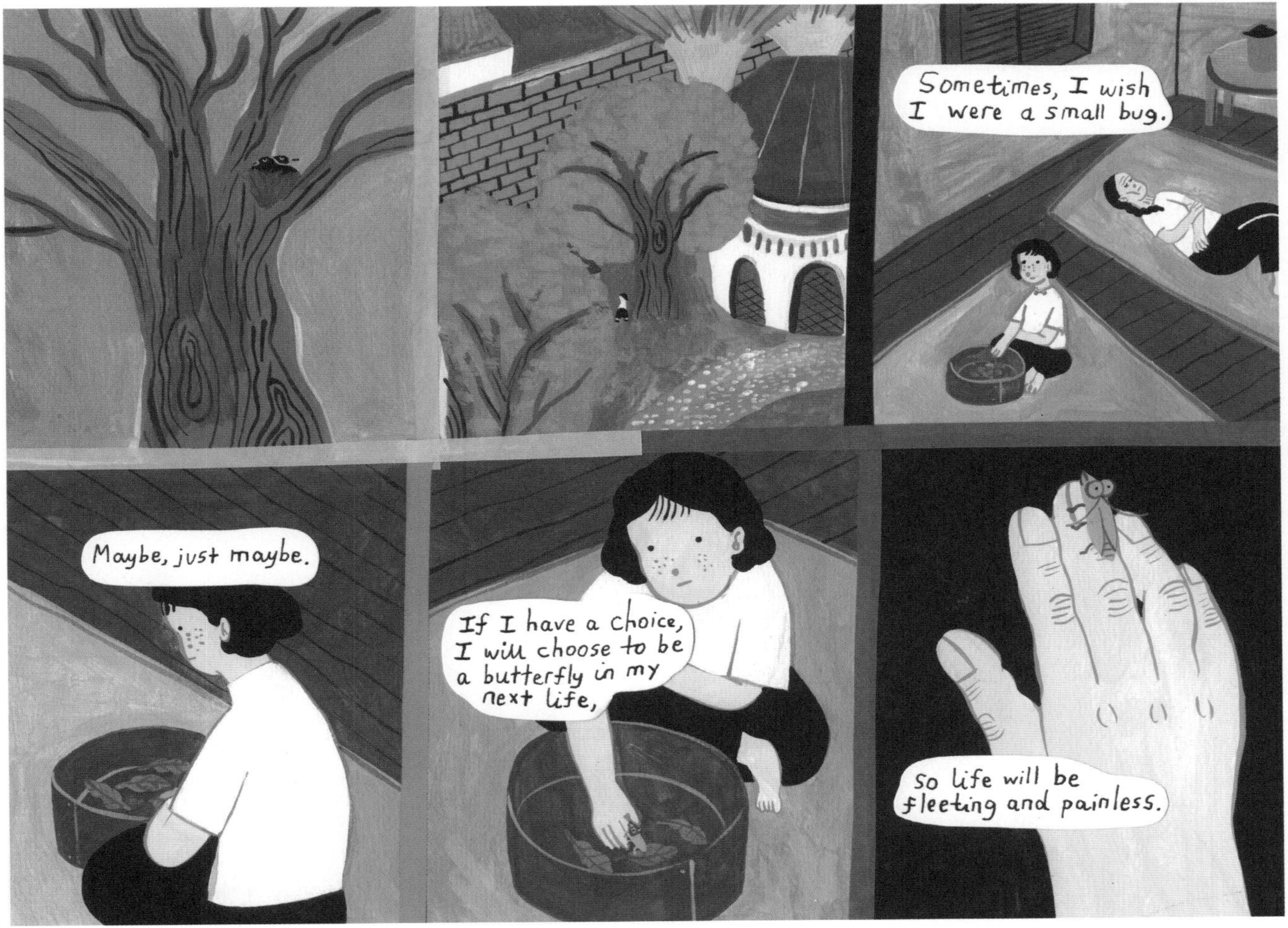
Sometimes, I wish I were a small bug.
Maybe, just maybe.
If I have a choice, I will choose to be a butterfly in my next life,
so life will be fleeting and painless.

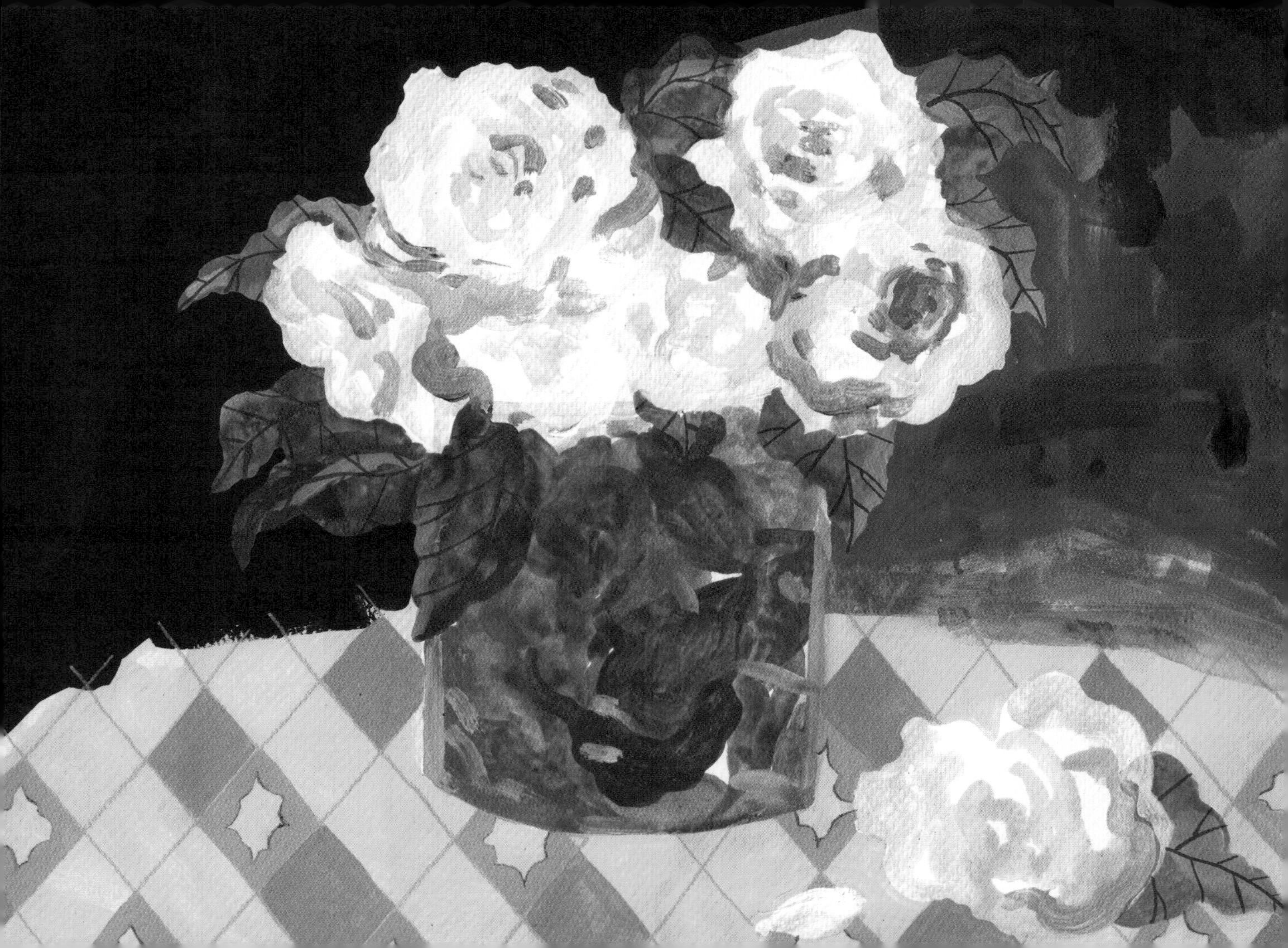

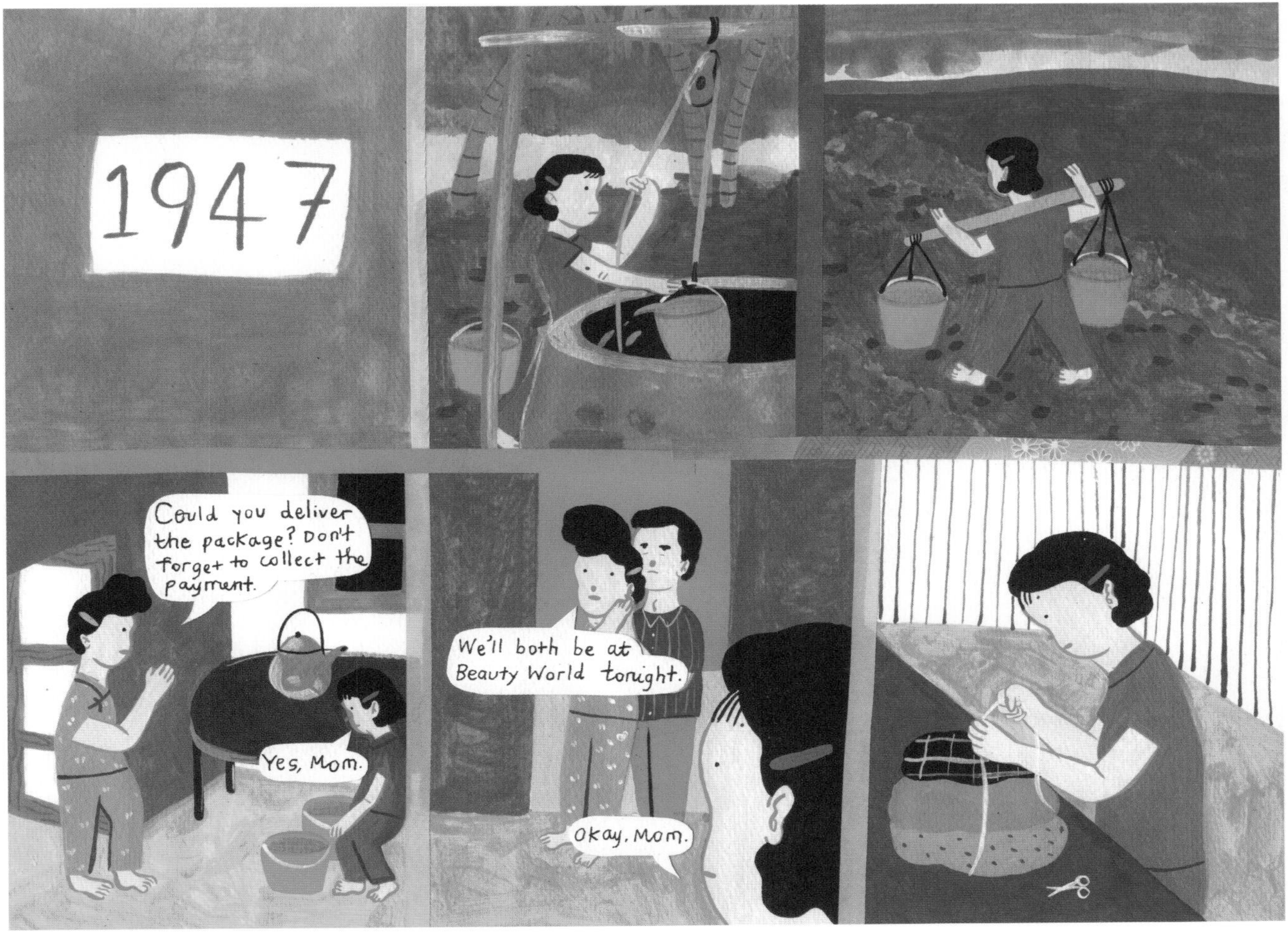
1947
Could you deliver the package? Don't forget to collect the payment.
Yes, Mom.
We'll both be at Beauty World tonight.
Okay, Mom.

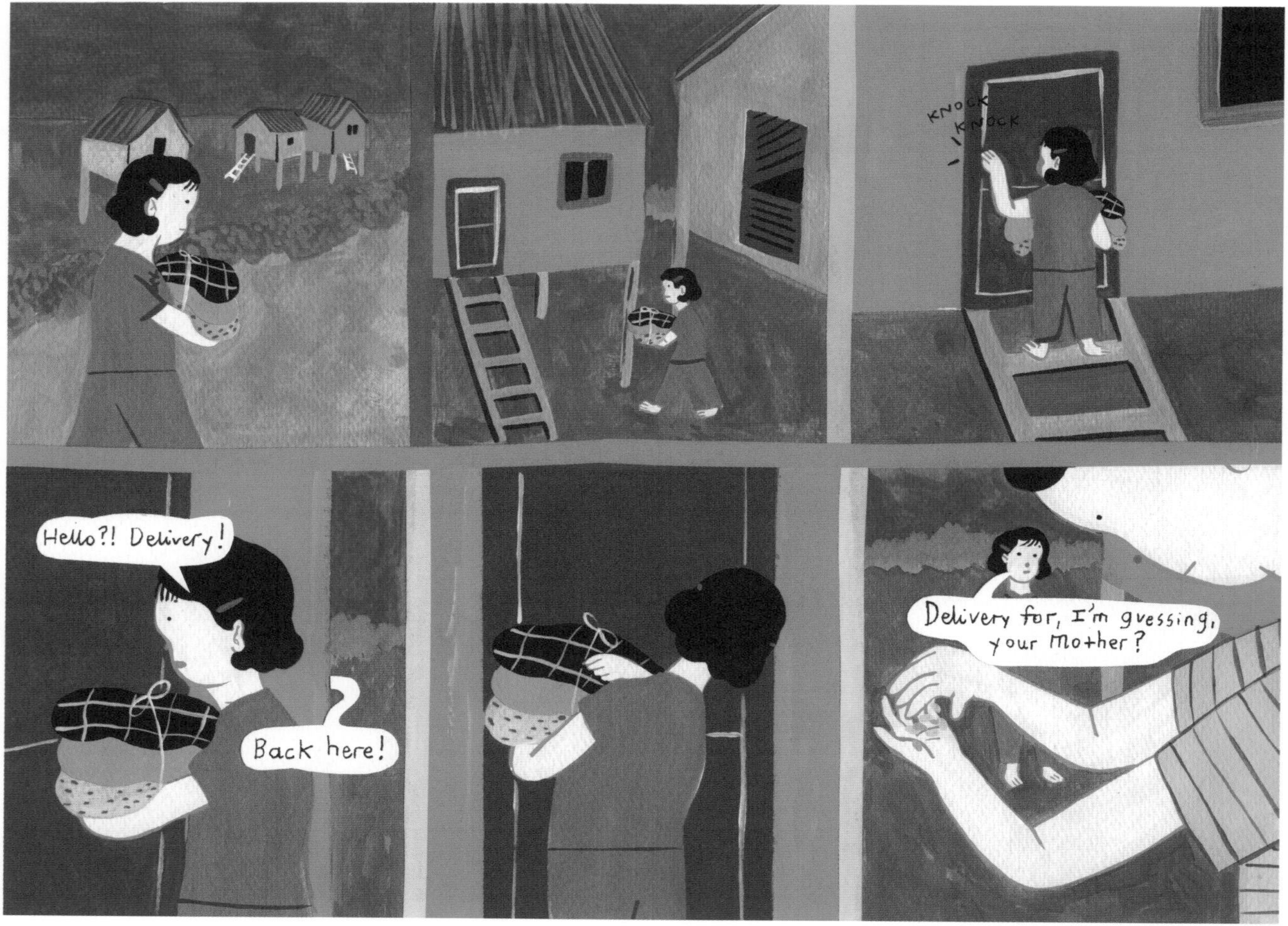
KNOCK KNOCK
Hello?! Delivery!
Back here!
Delivery for, I'm guessing, your mother?

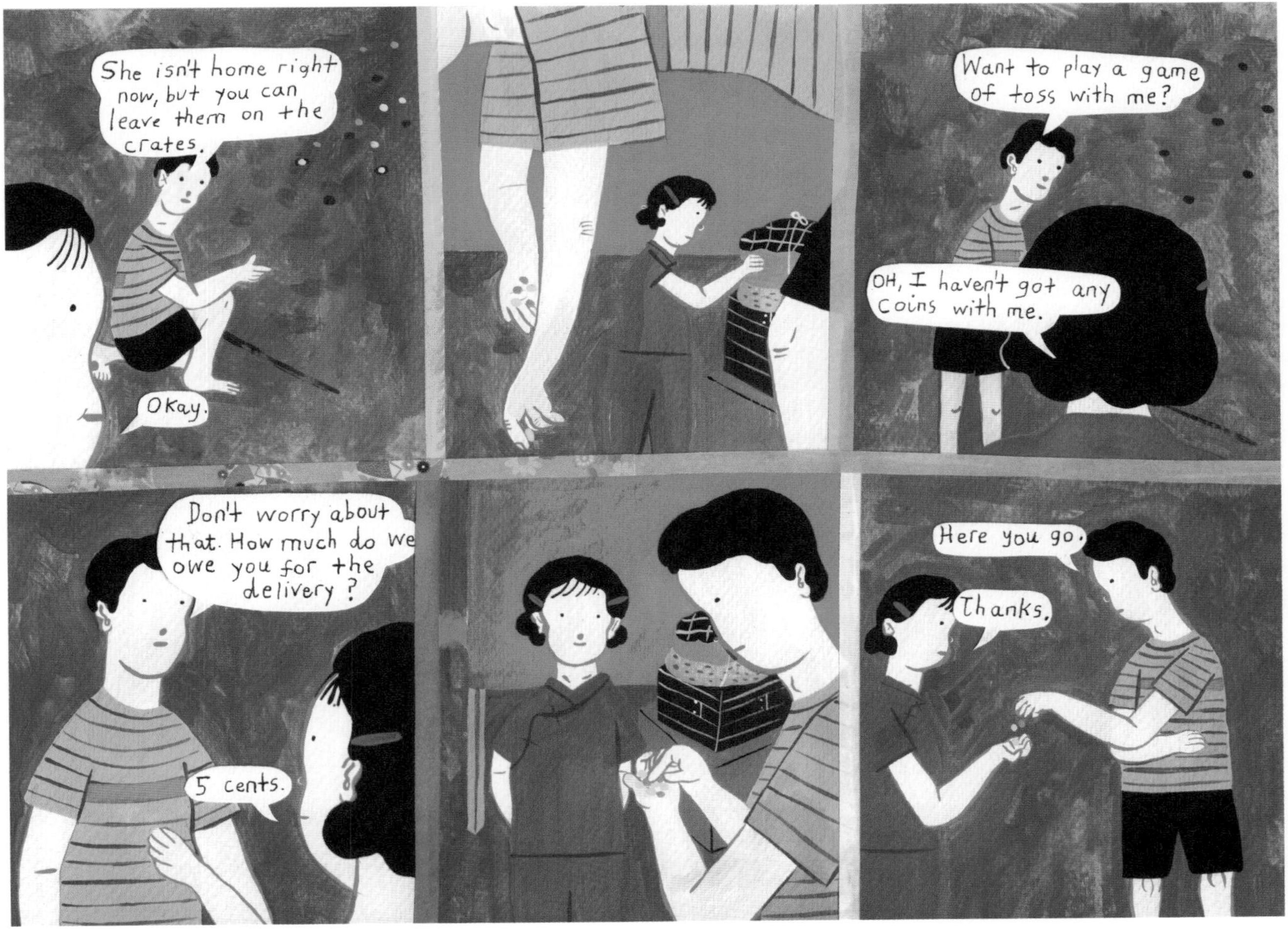
She isn't home right now, but you can leave them on the crates.
Okay.
Want to play a game of toss with me?
OH, I haven't got any coins with me.
Don't worry about that. How much do we owe you for the delivery?
5 cents.
Here you go.
Thanks.

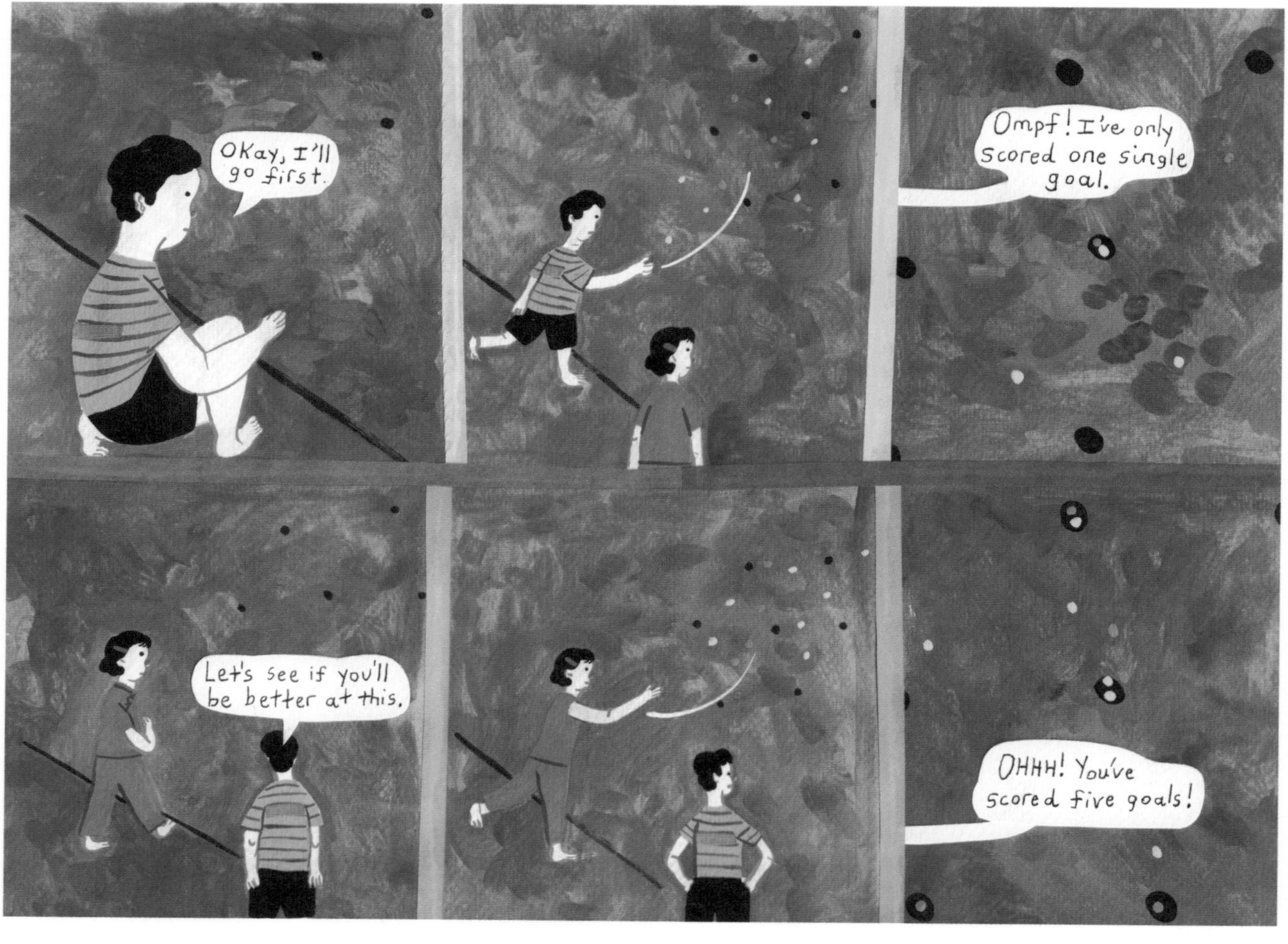
Okay, I'll go first.
Ompf! I've only scored one single goal.
Let's see if you'll be better at this.
OHHH! You've scored five goals!

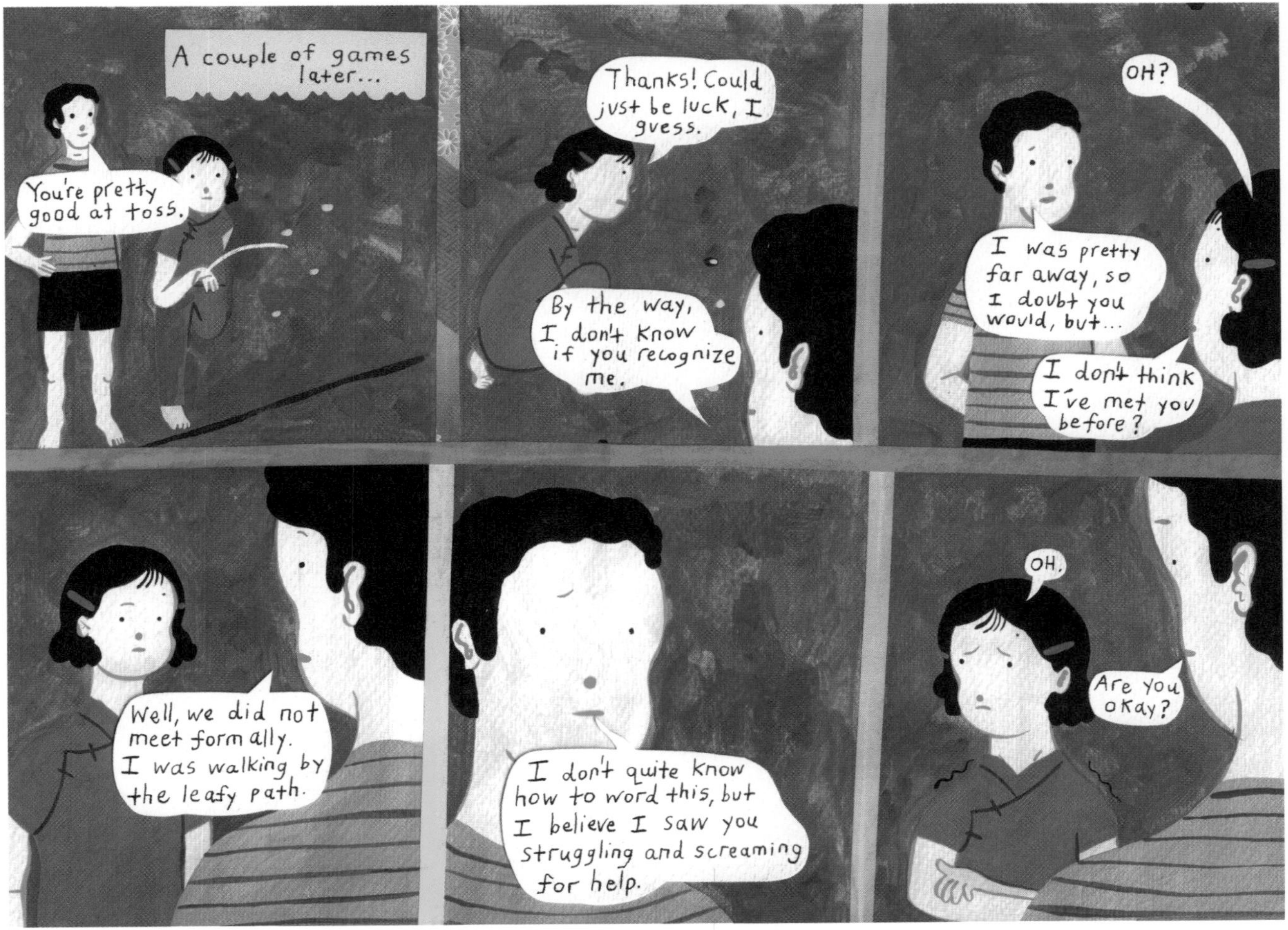
A couple of games later...
You're pretty good at toss.
Thanks! Could just be luck, I guess.
By the way, I don't know if you recognize me.
OH?
I was pretty far away, so I doubt you would, but...
I don't think I've met you before?
Well, we did not meet formally. I was walking by the leafy path.
I don't quite know how to word this, but I believe I saw you struggling and screaming for help.
OH.
Are you okay?

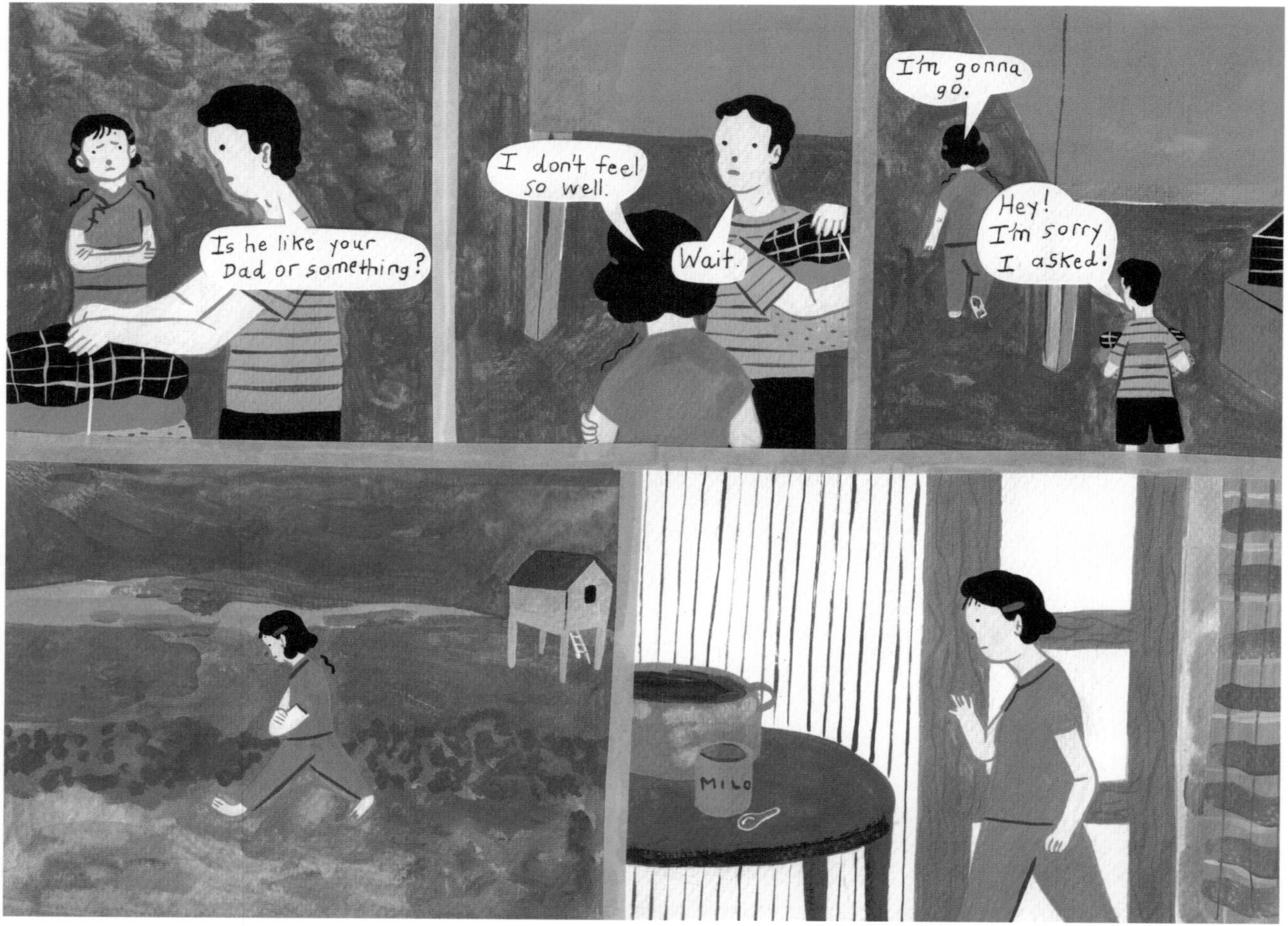
Is he like your Dad or something?
I don't feel so well.
Wait.
I'm gonna go.
Hey! I'm sorry I asked!
MILO

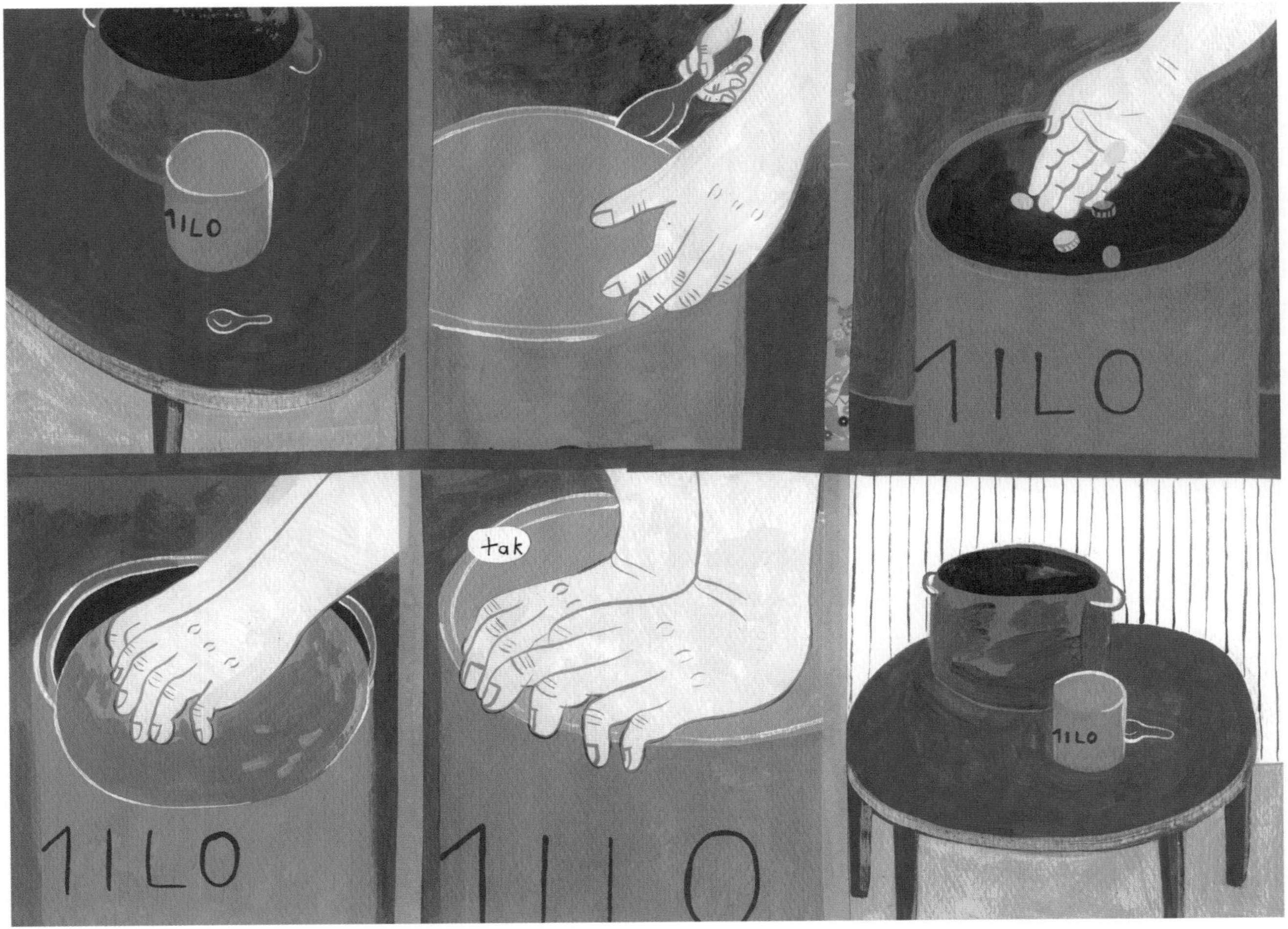
tak

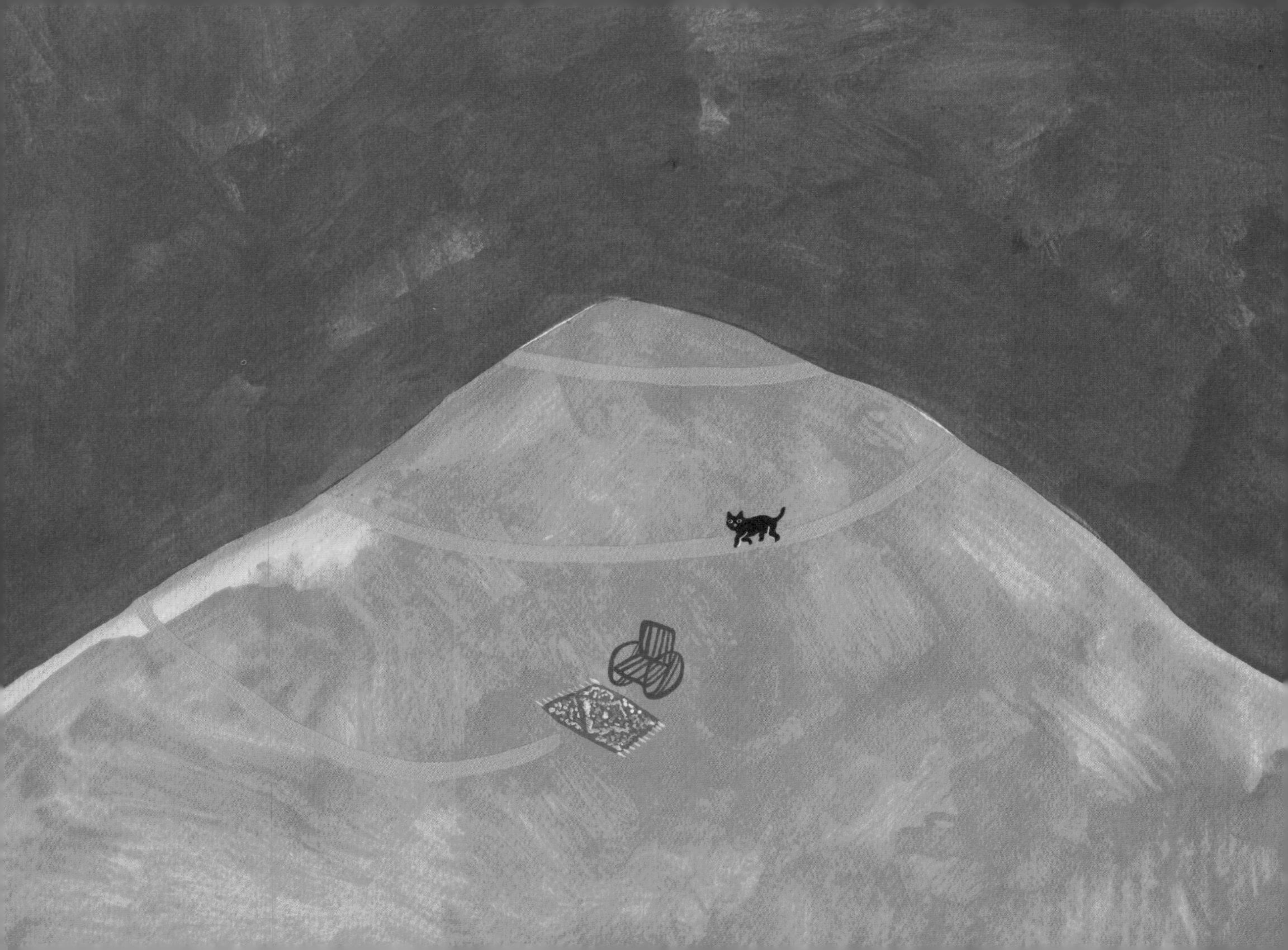

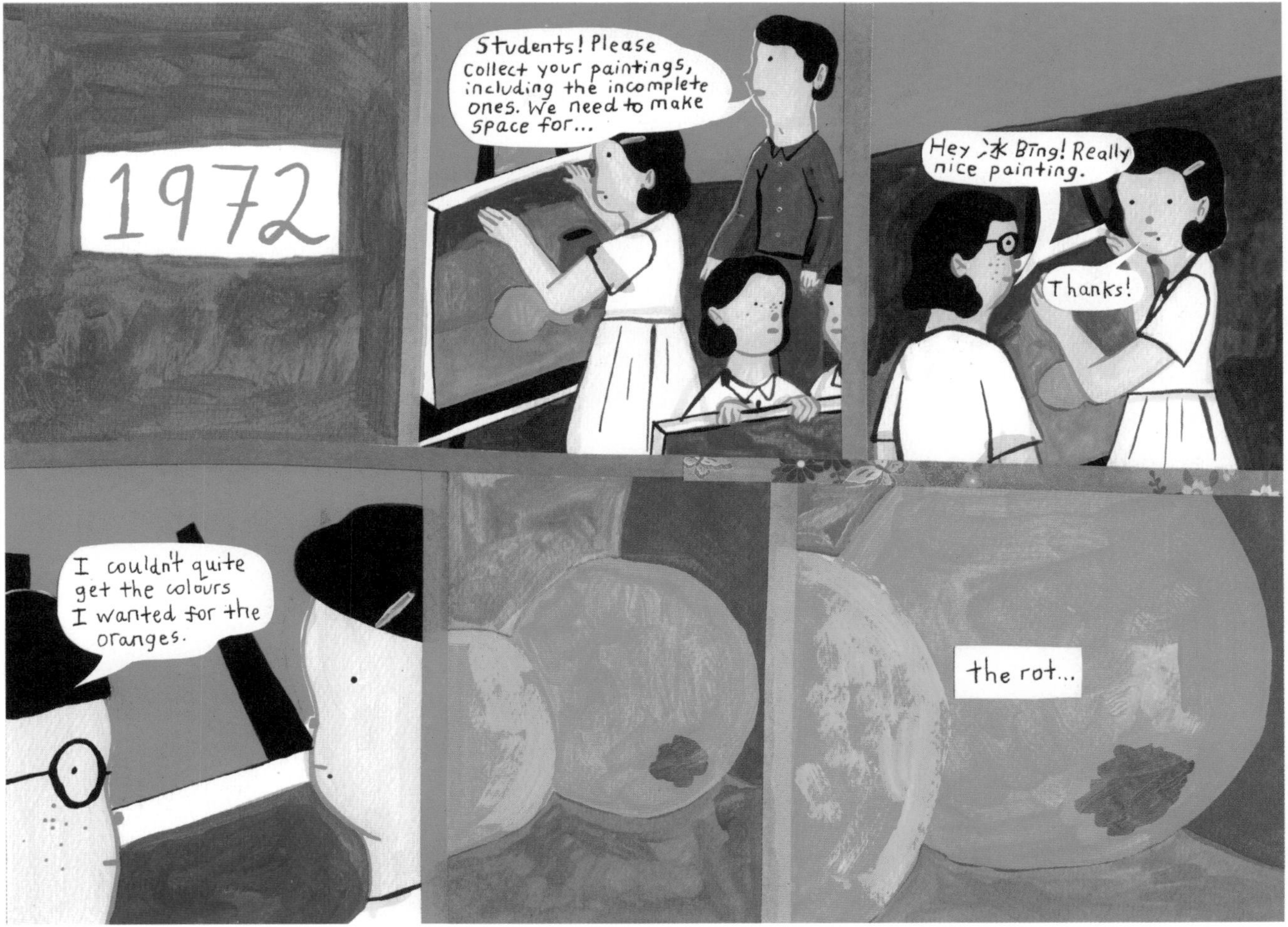

1972
Students! Please collect your paintings, including the incomplete ones. We need to make space for...
Hey 冰 Bīng! Really nice painting.
Thanks!
I couldn't quite get the colours I wanted for the oranges.
the rot...

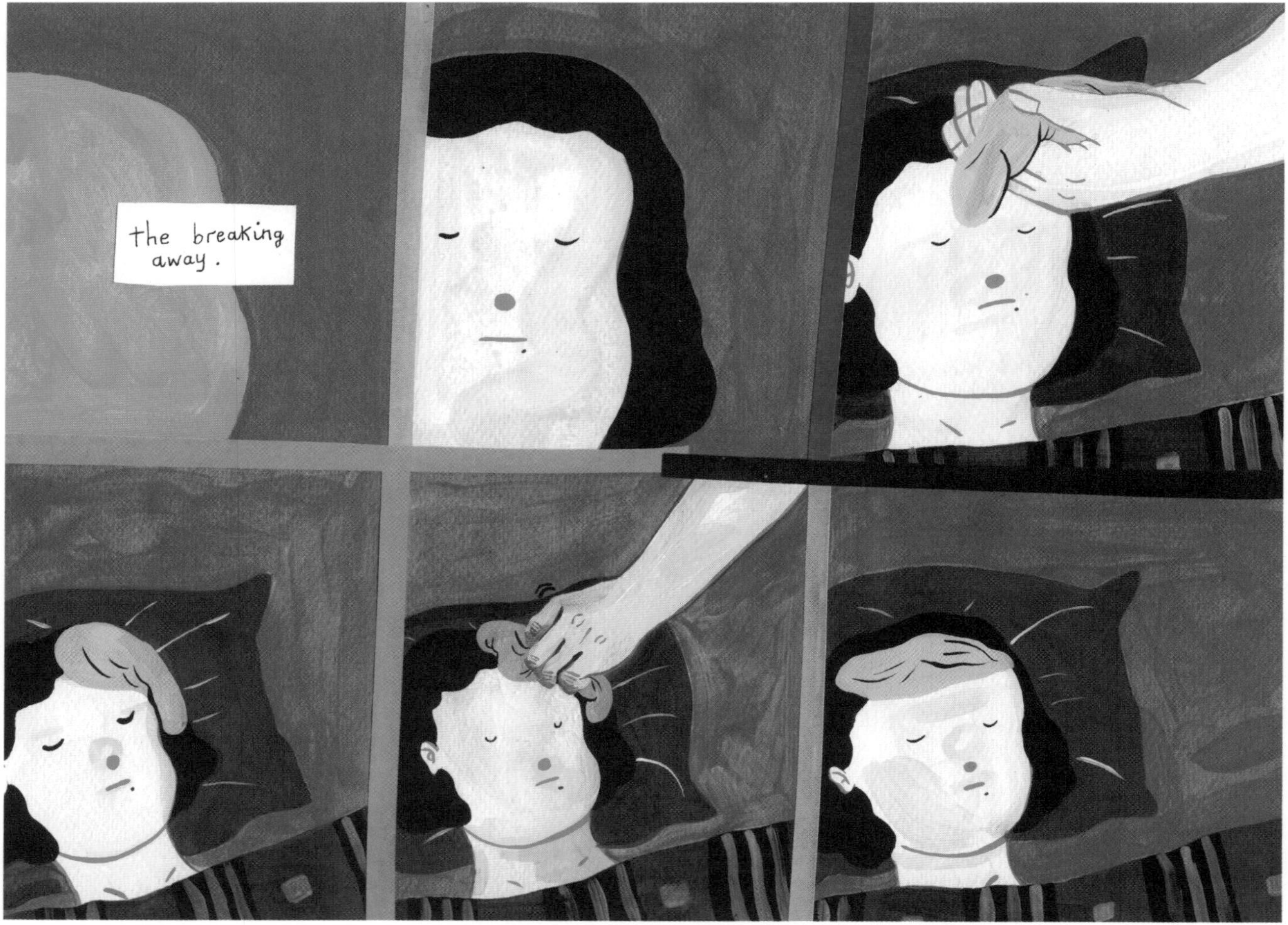
the breaking away.

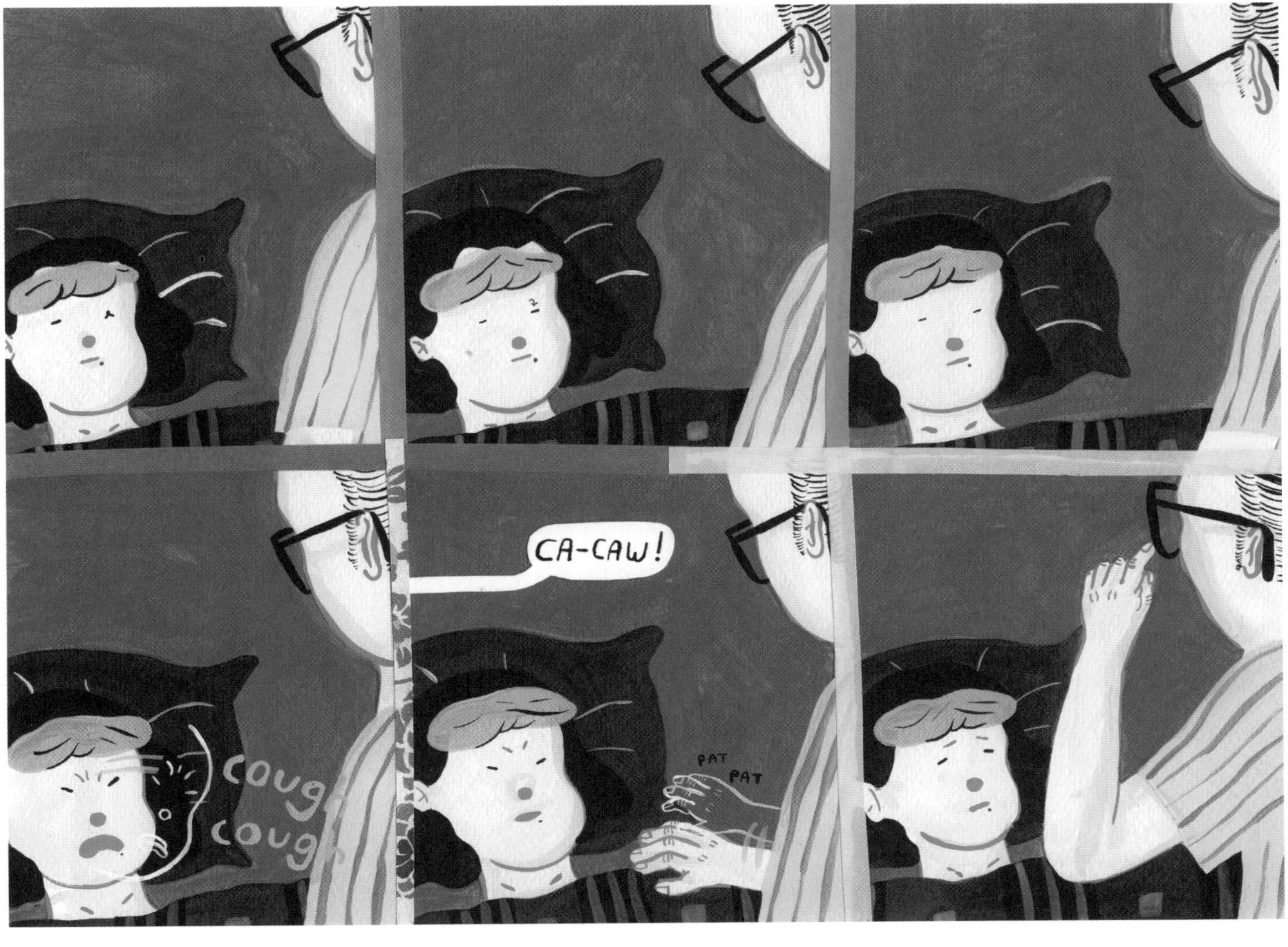
cough
cough
CA-CAW!
PAT
PAT

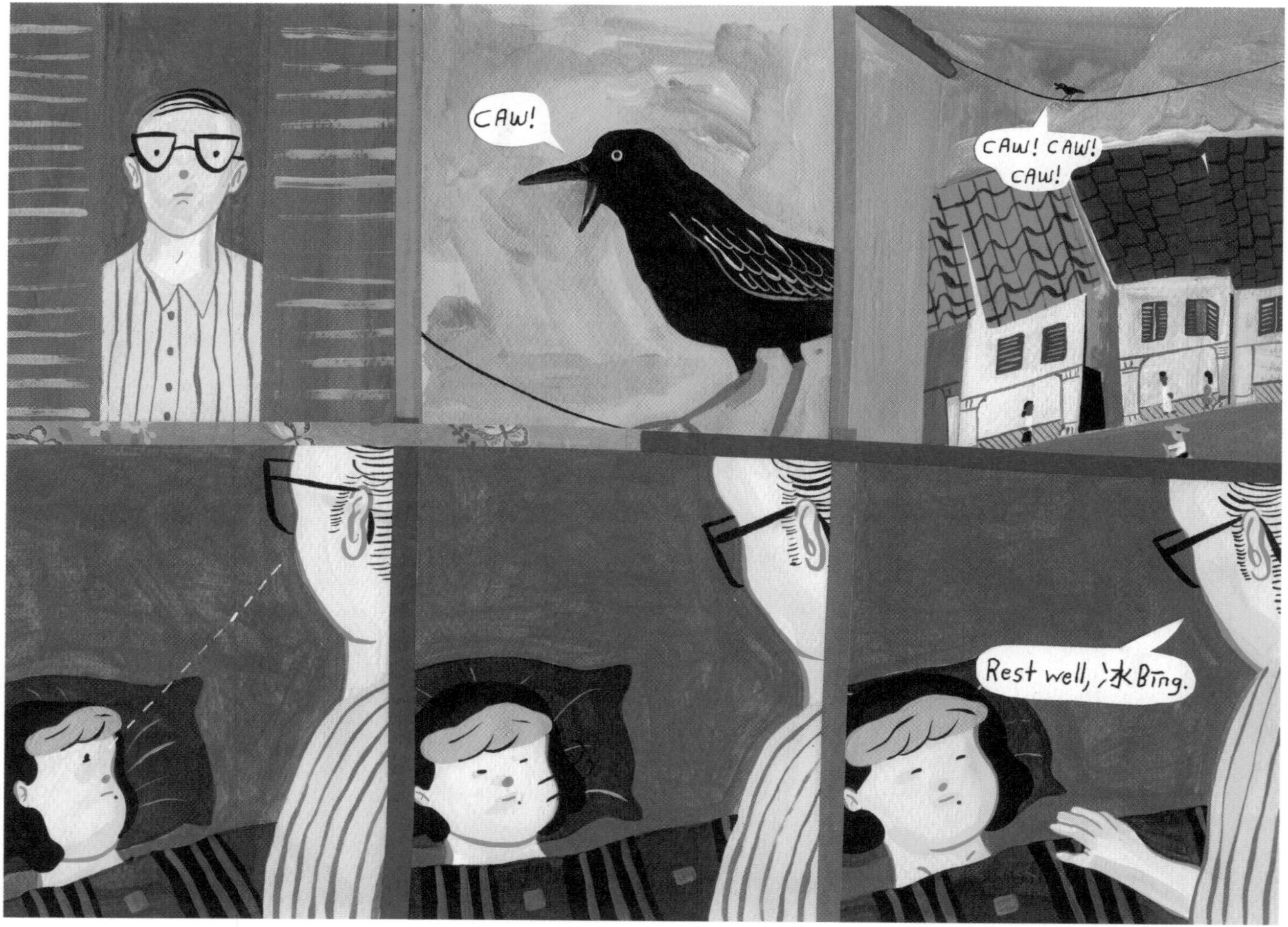
CAW!
CAW! CAW! CAW!
Rest well, 冰Bing.

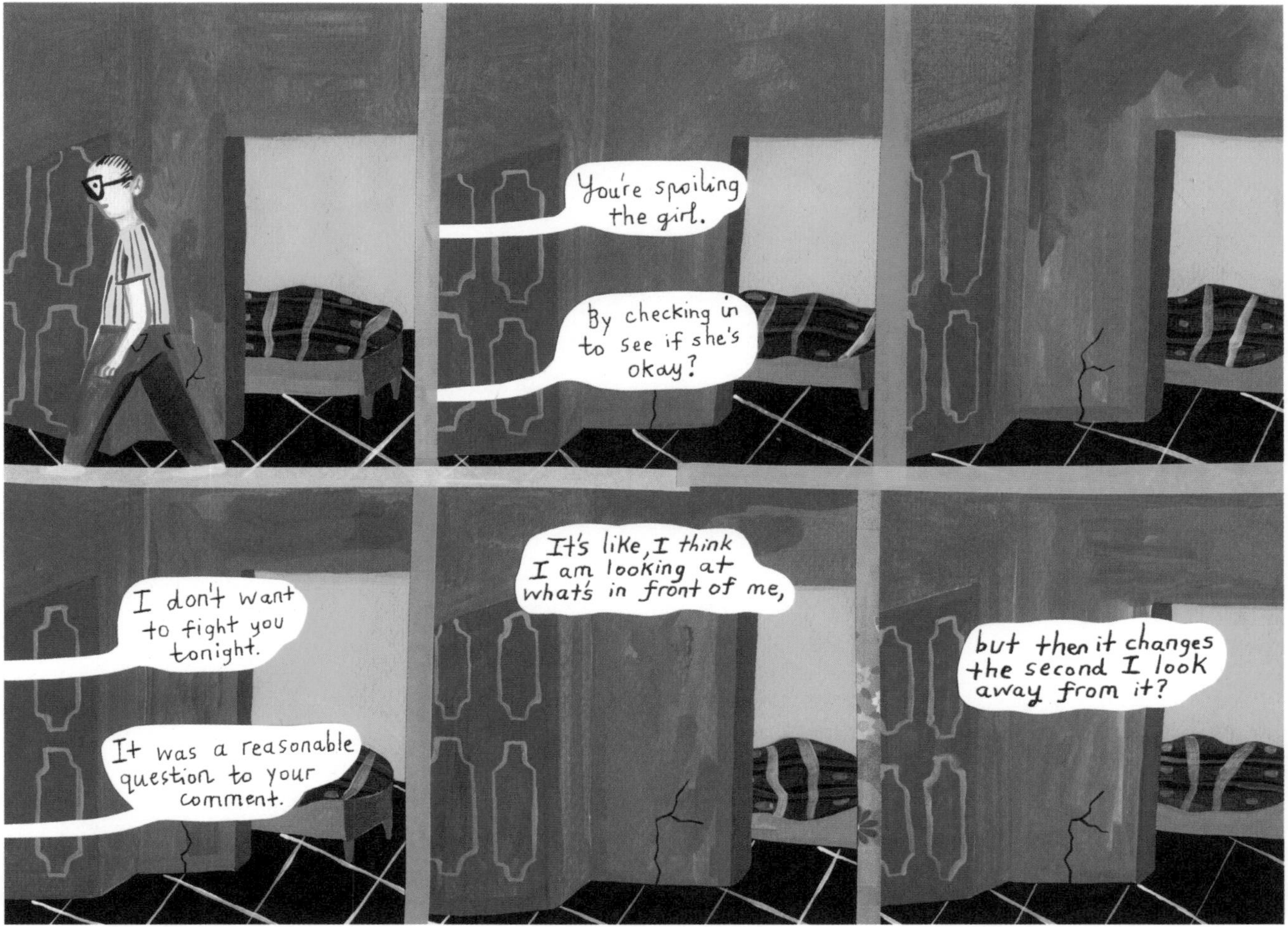
You're spoiling the girl.
By checking in to see if she's okay?
I don't want to fight you tonight.
It was a reasonable question to your comment.
It's like, I think I am looking at what's in front of me,
but then it changes the second I look away from it?

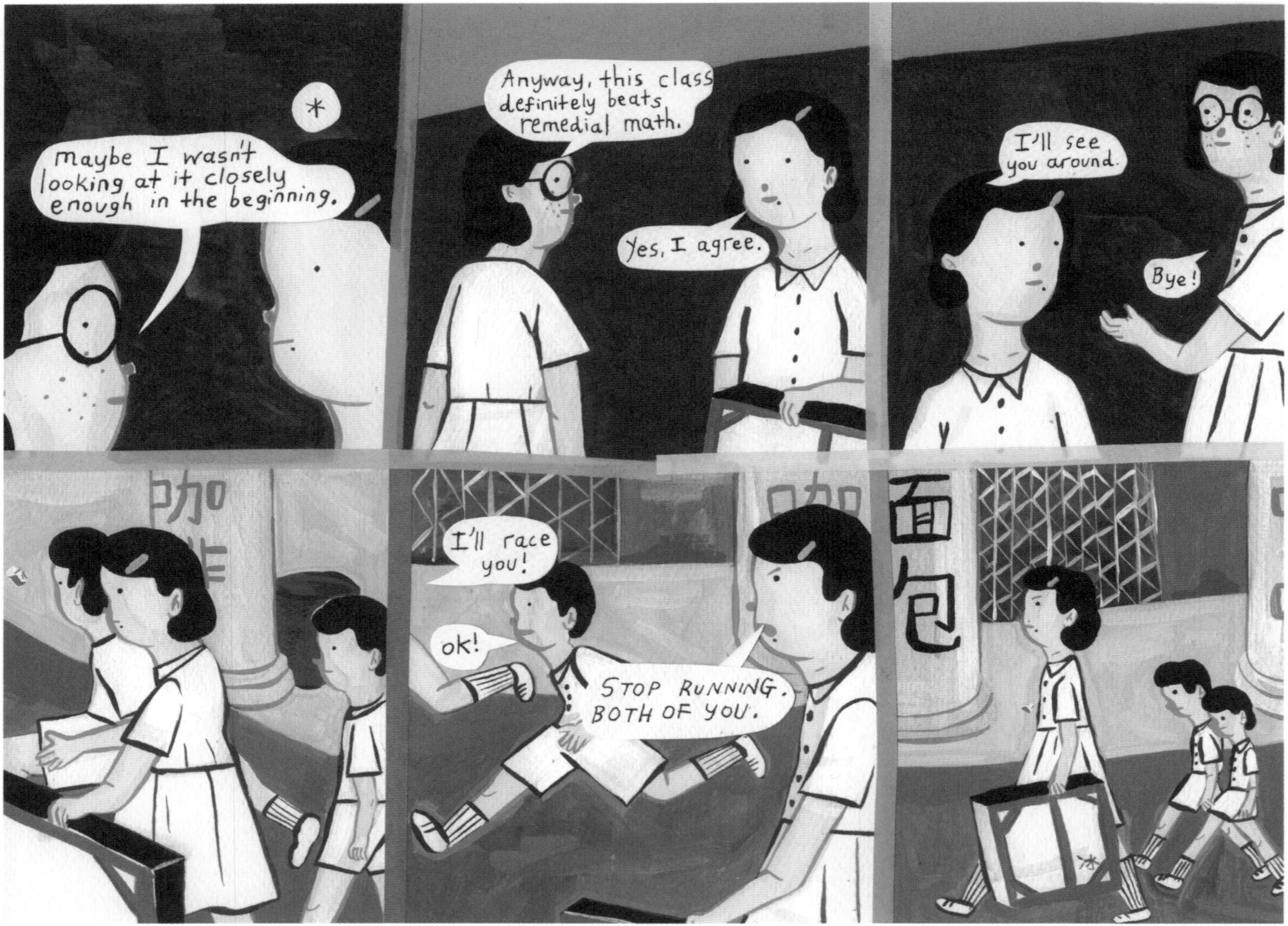
*
maybe I wasn't looking at it closely enough in the beginning.
Anyway, this class definitely beats remedial math.
Yes, I agree.
I'll see you around.
Bye!
咖
I'll race you!
ok!
STOP RUNNING. BOTH OF YOU.
面
包

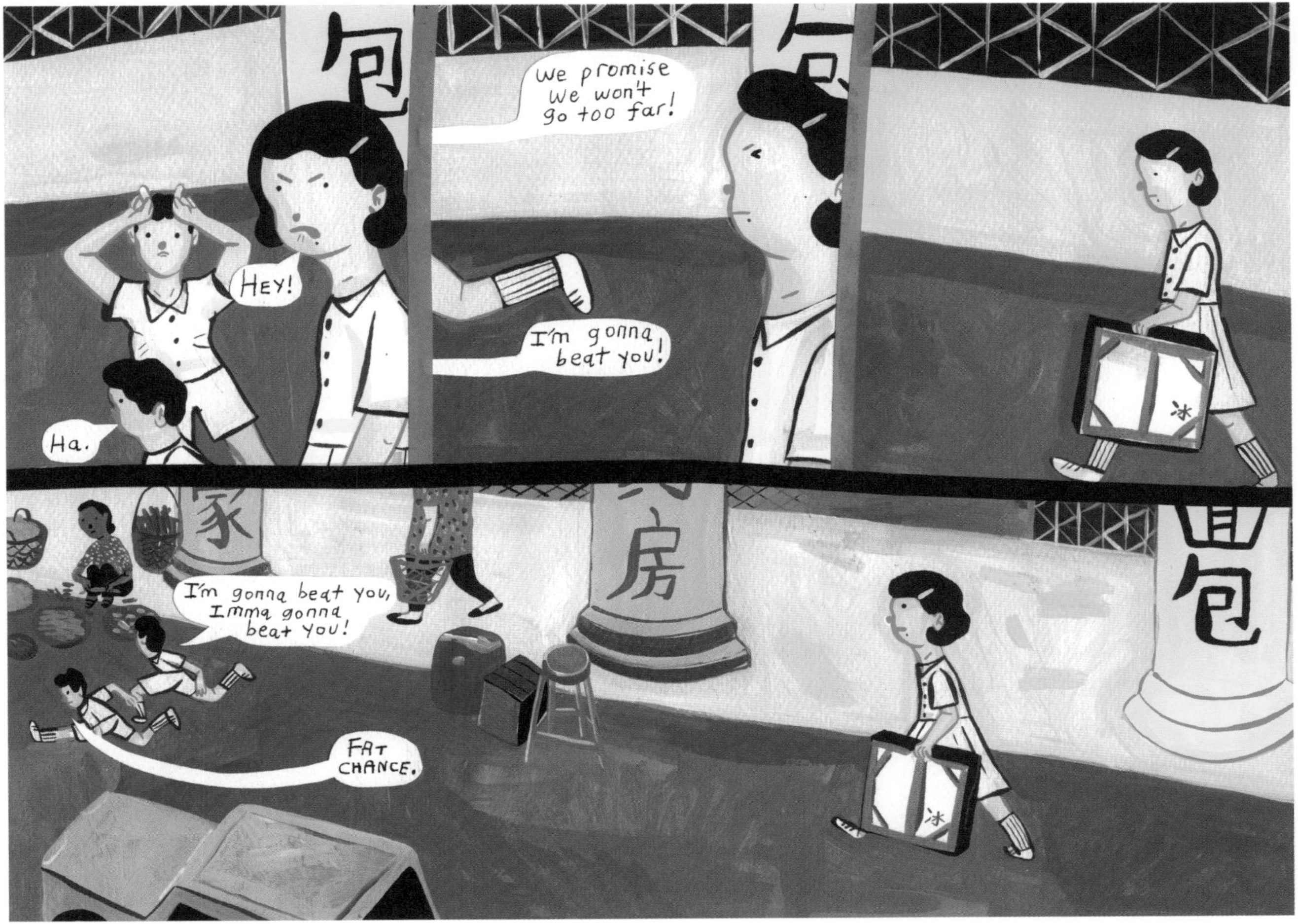

包
HEY!
Ha.
We promise we won't go too far!
I'm gonna beat you!
冰
家
房
I'm gonna beat you, Imma gonna beat you!
FAT CHANCE.
包
冰

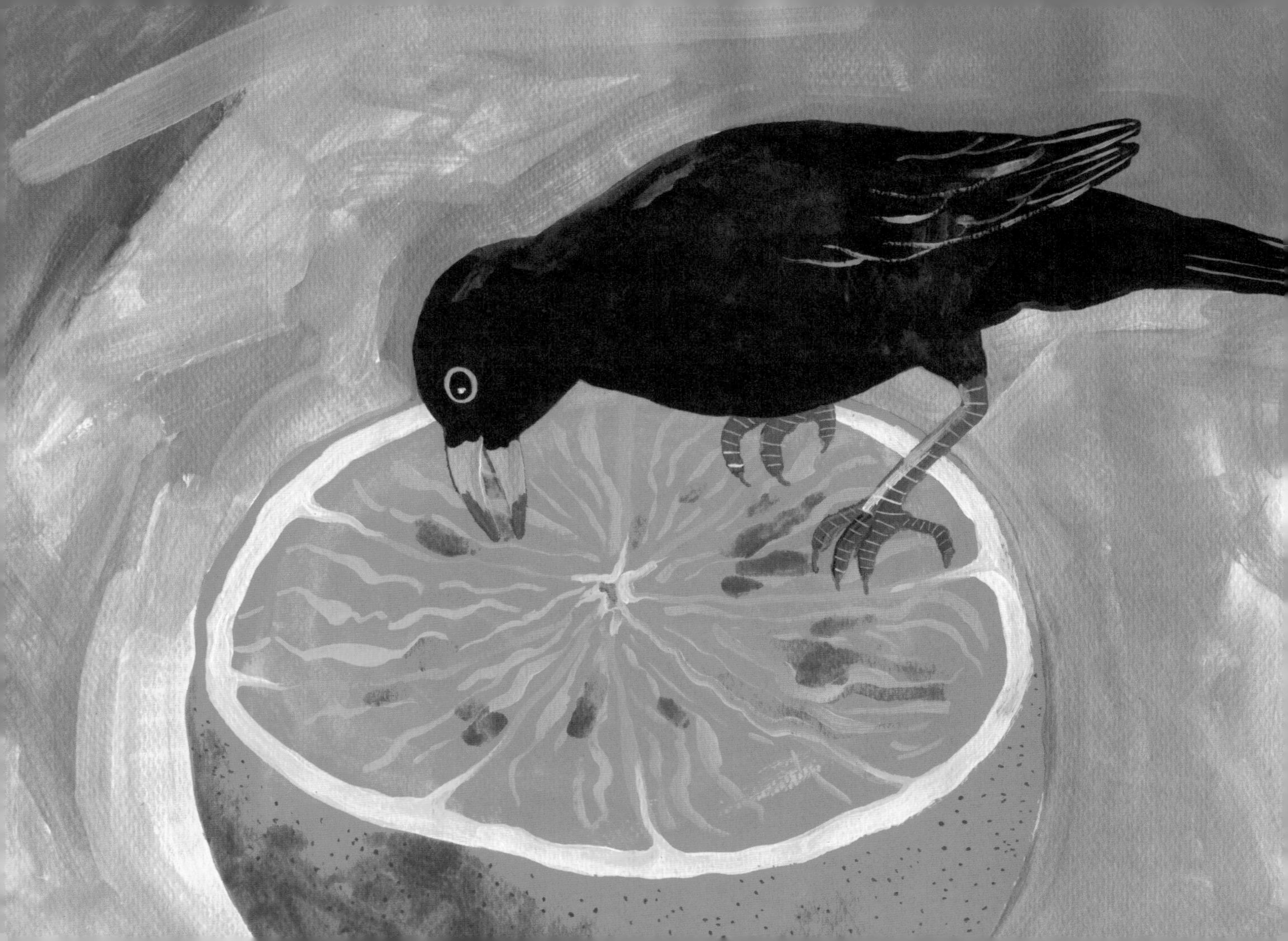

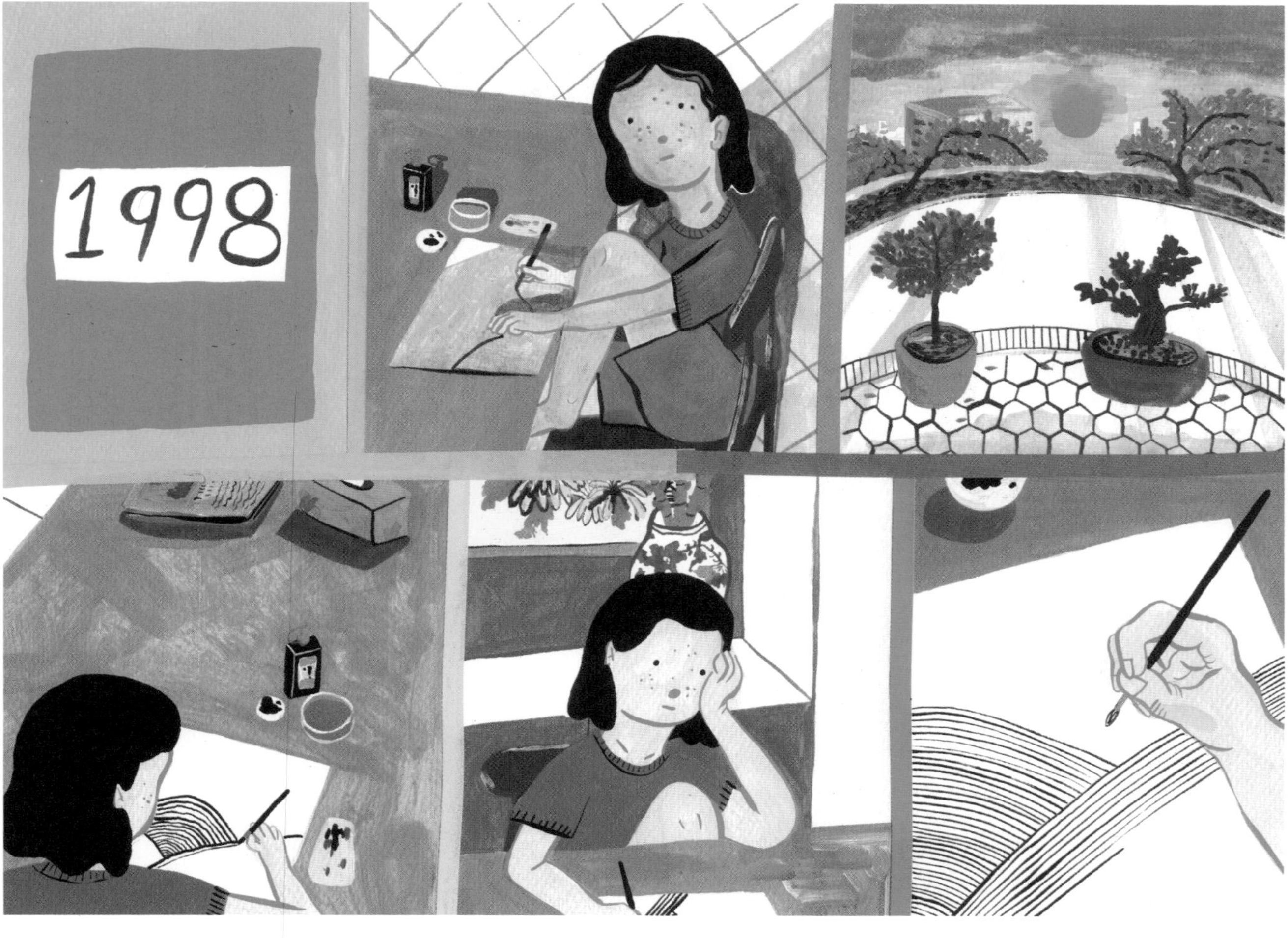
1998

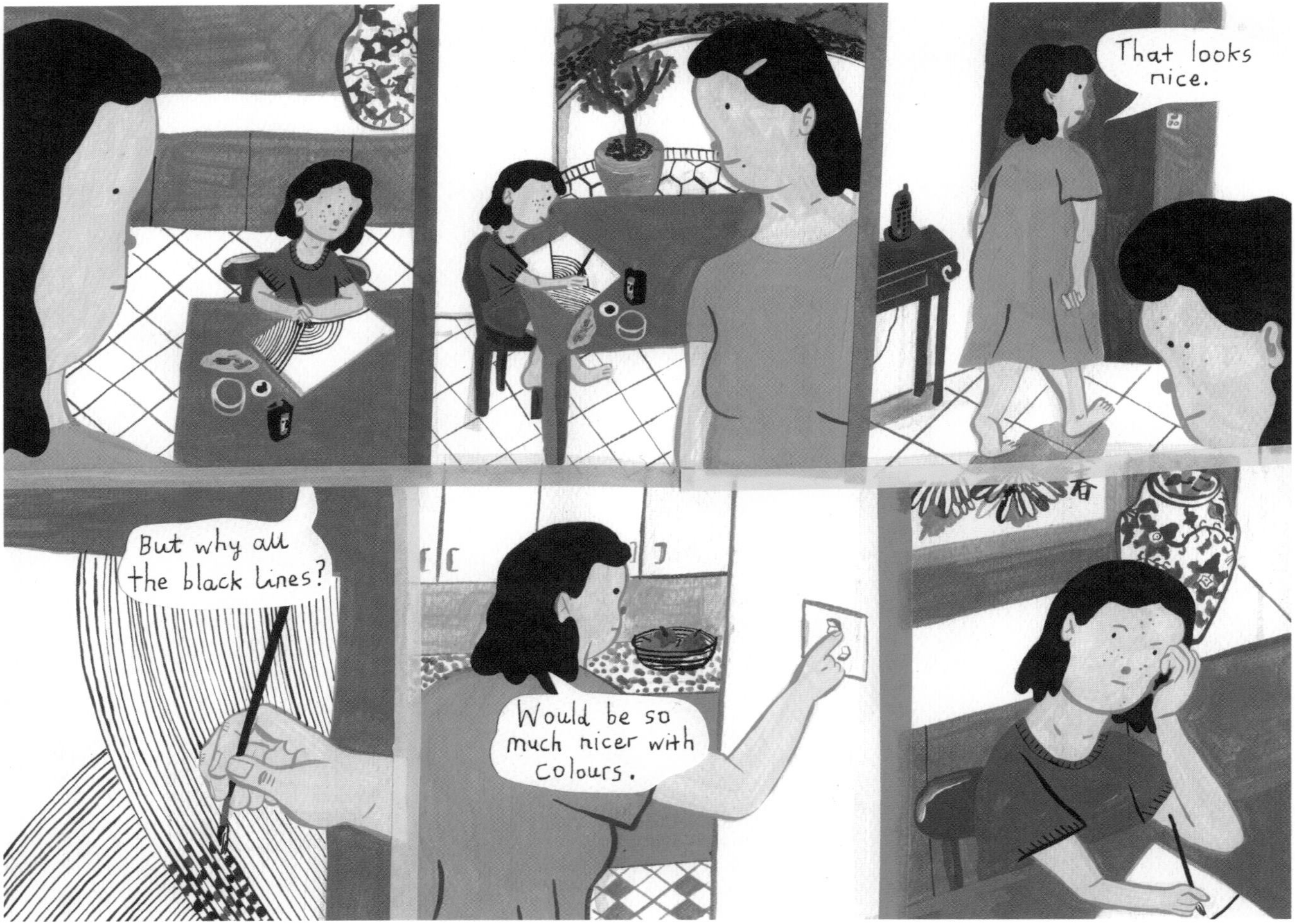
That looks nice.
But why all the black lines?
Would be so much nicer with colours.

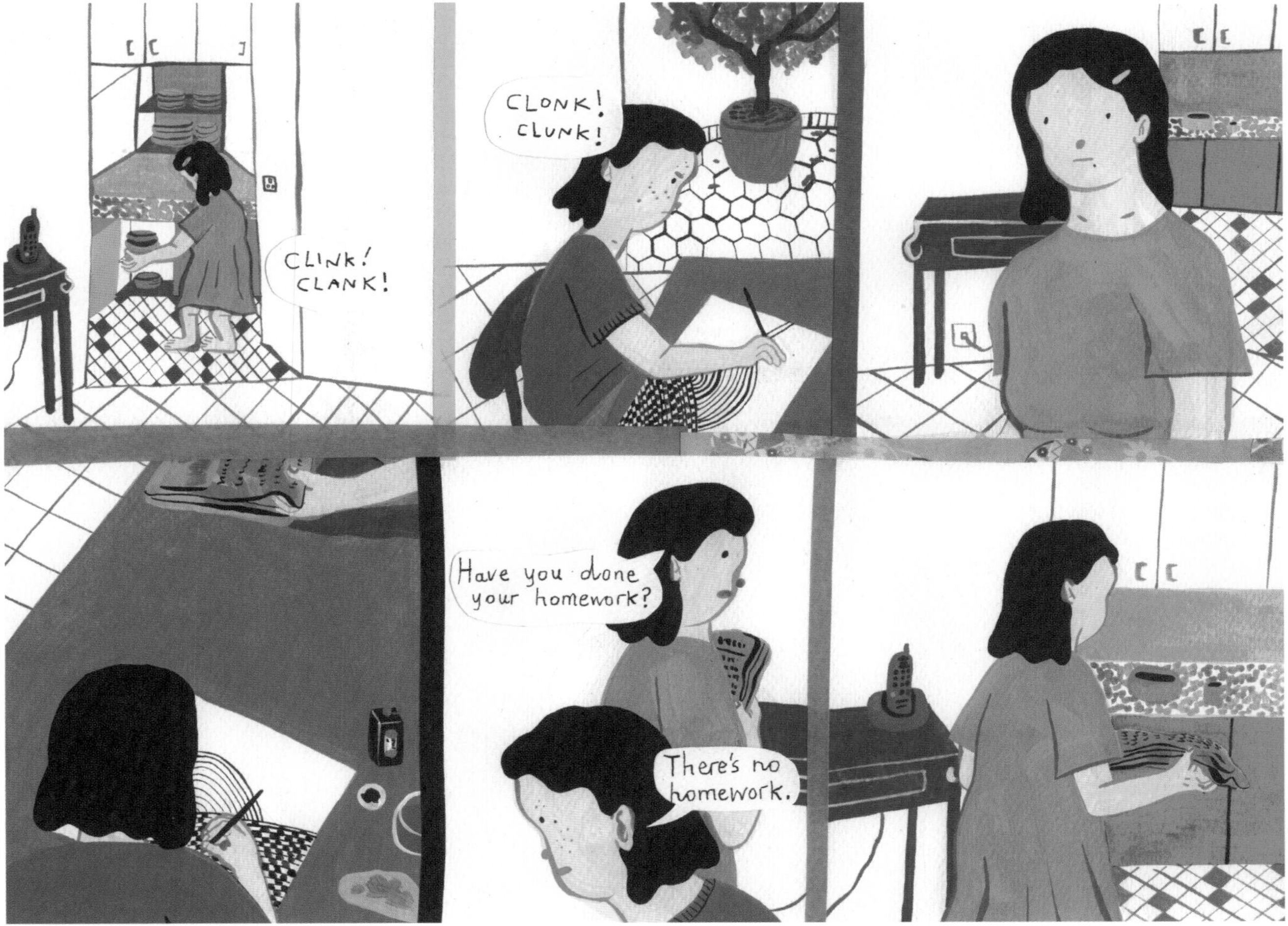
CLINK! CLANK!
CLONK! CLUNK!
Have you done your homework?
There's no homework.

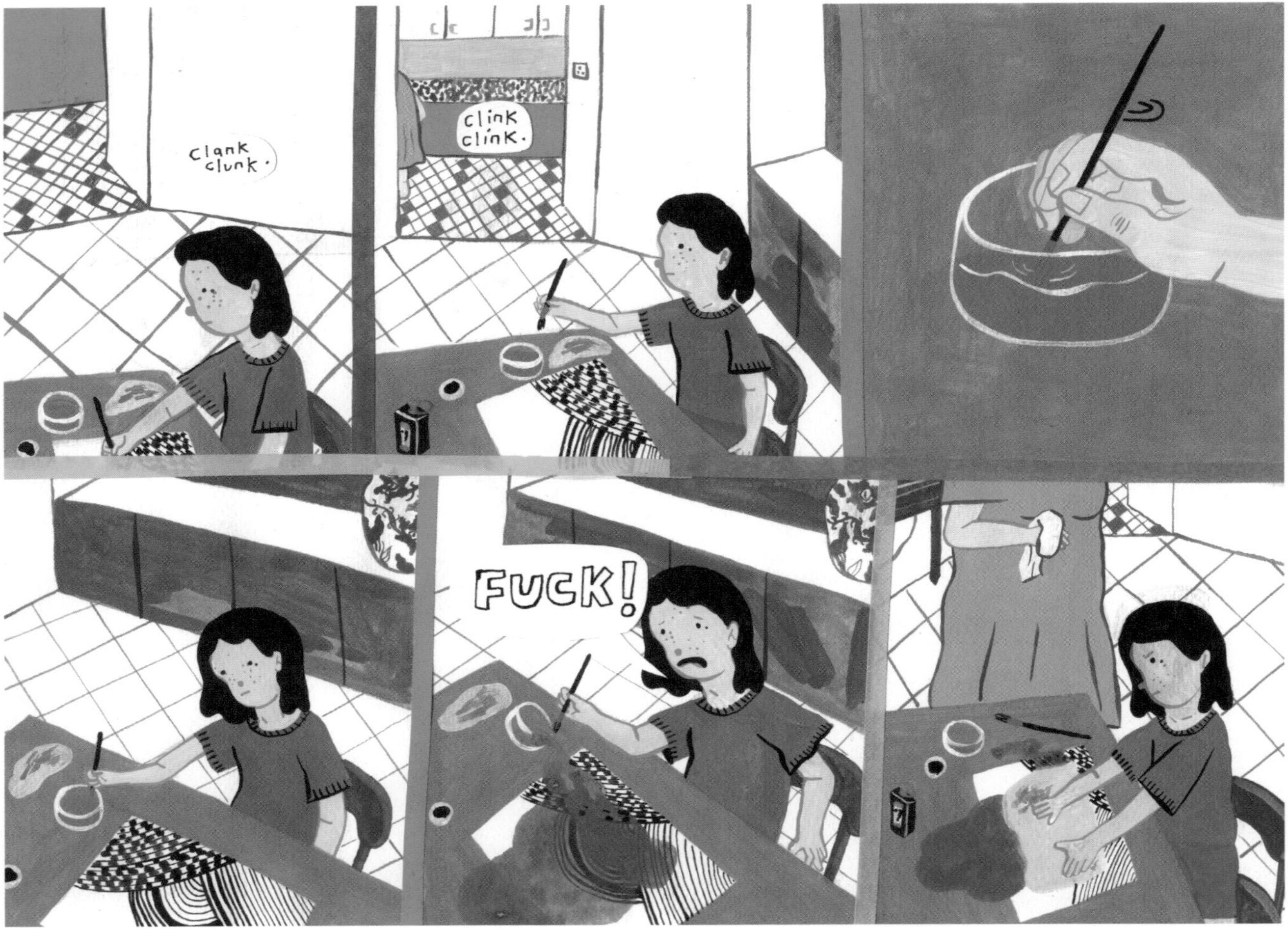
clank clunk.
clink clink.
FUCK!

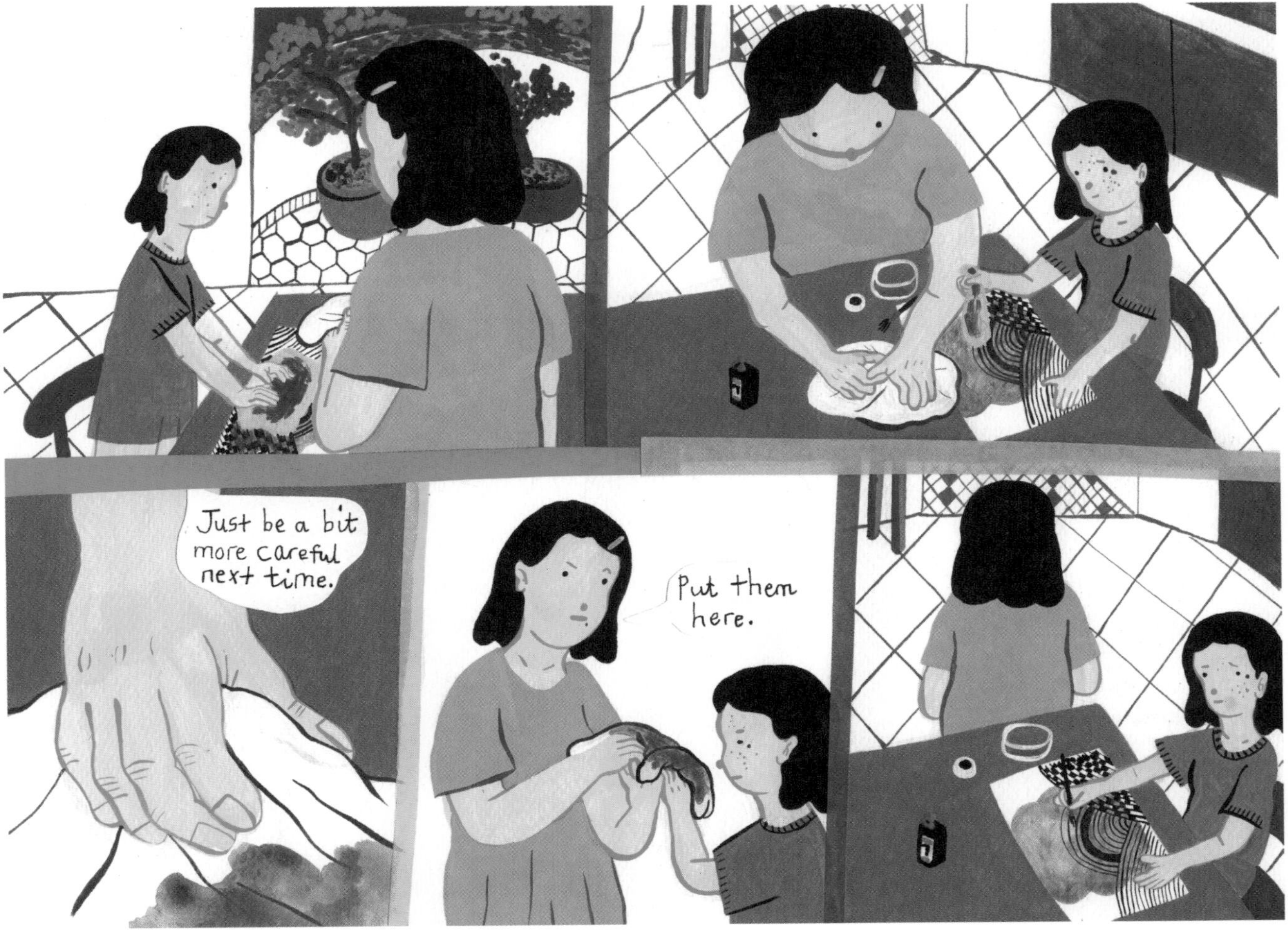
Just be a bit more careful next time.
Put them here.

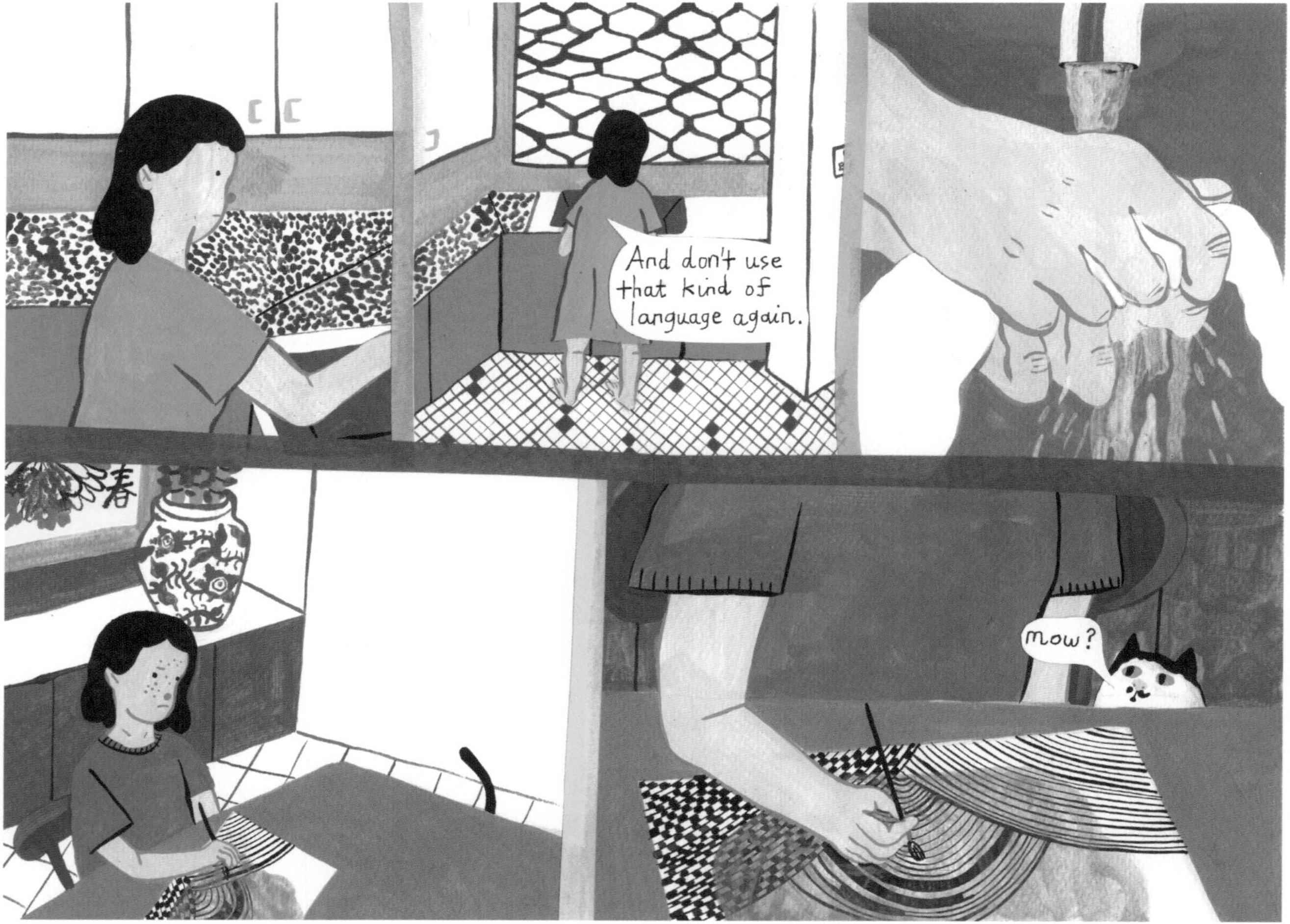
And don't use that kind of language again.
春
mow?

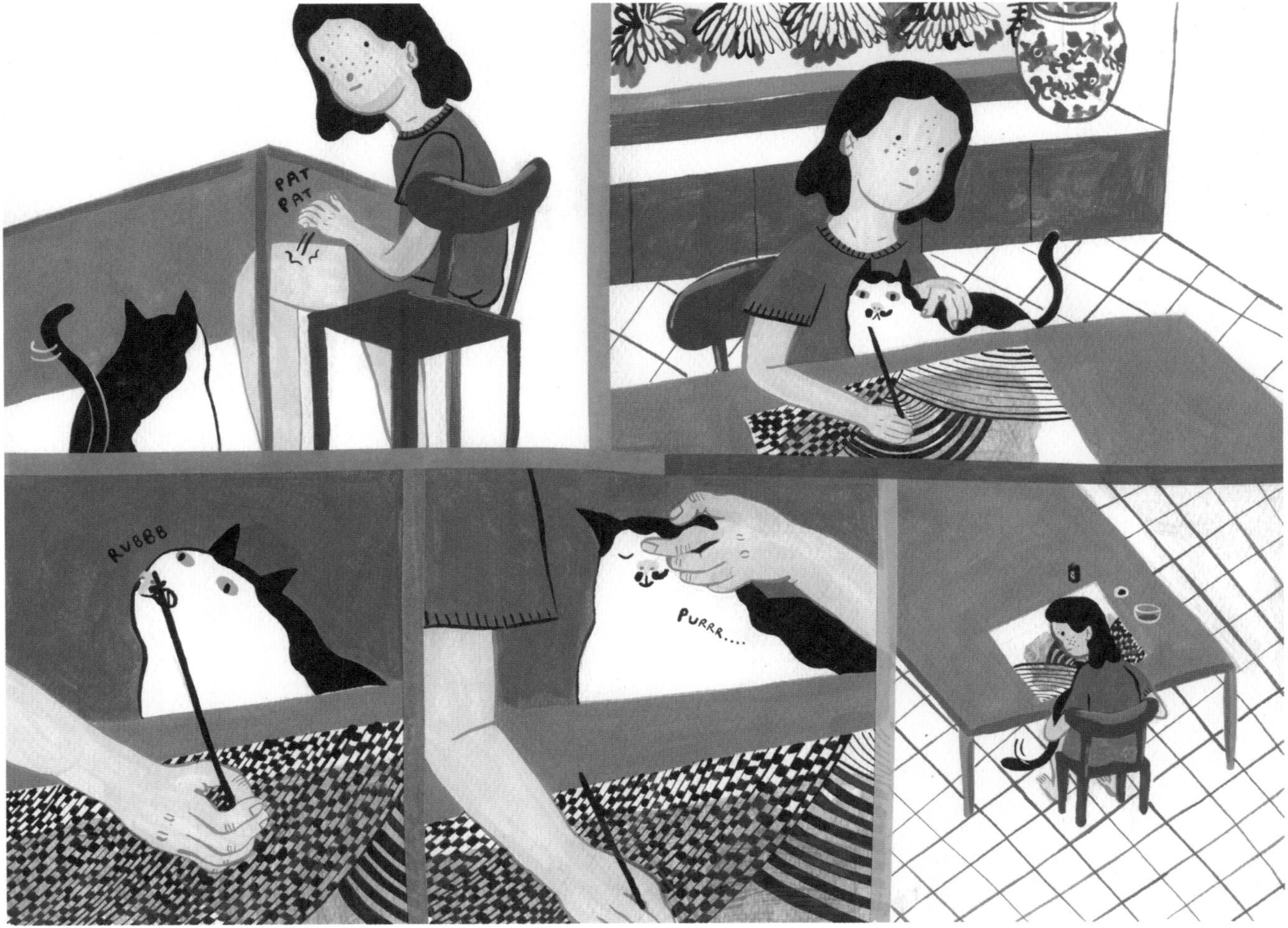
PAT
PAT
RUBBB
PURRR....

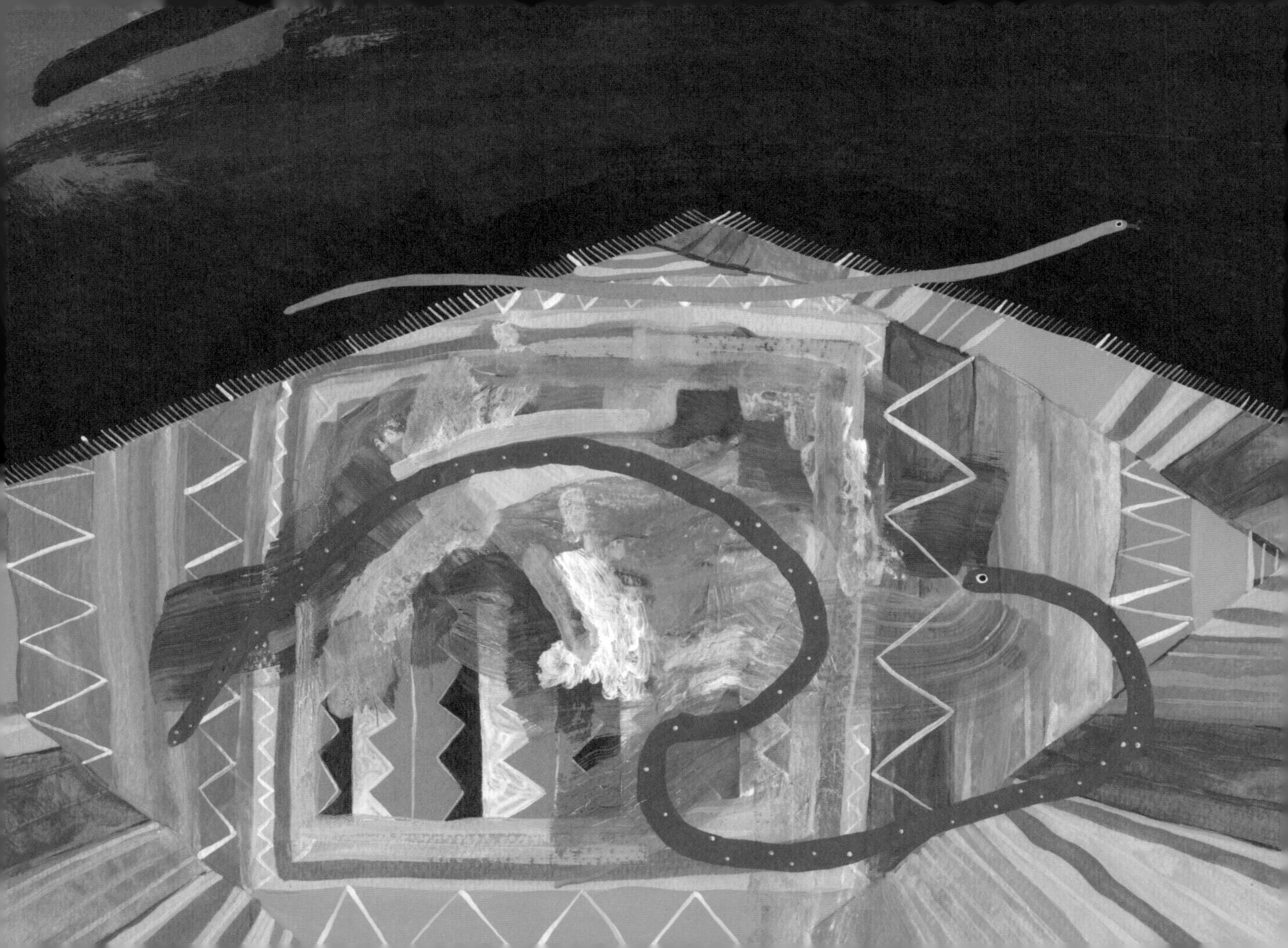

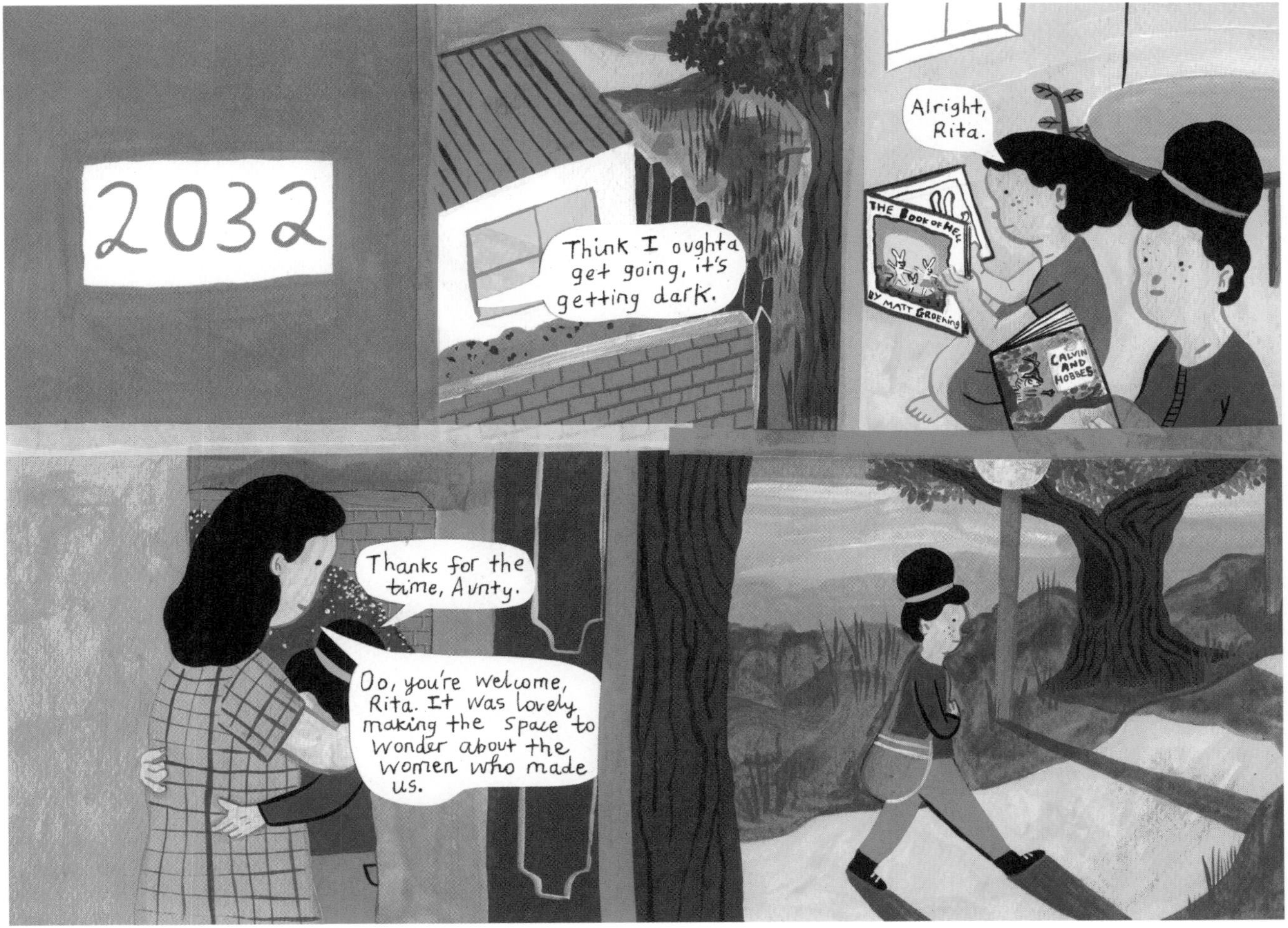
2032
Think I oughta get going, it's getting dark.
Alright, Rita.
THE BOOK OF HELL
BY MATT GROENING
CALVIN AND HOBBES
Thanks for the time, Aunty.
Oo, you're welcome, Rita. It was lovely making the space to wonder about the women who made us.

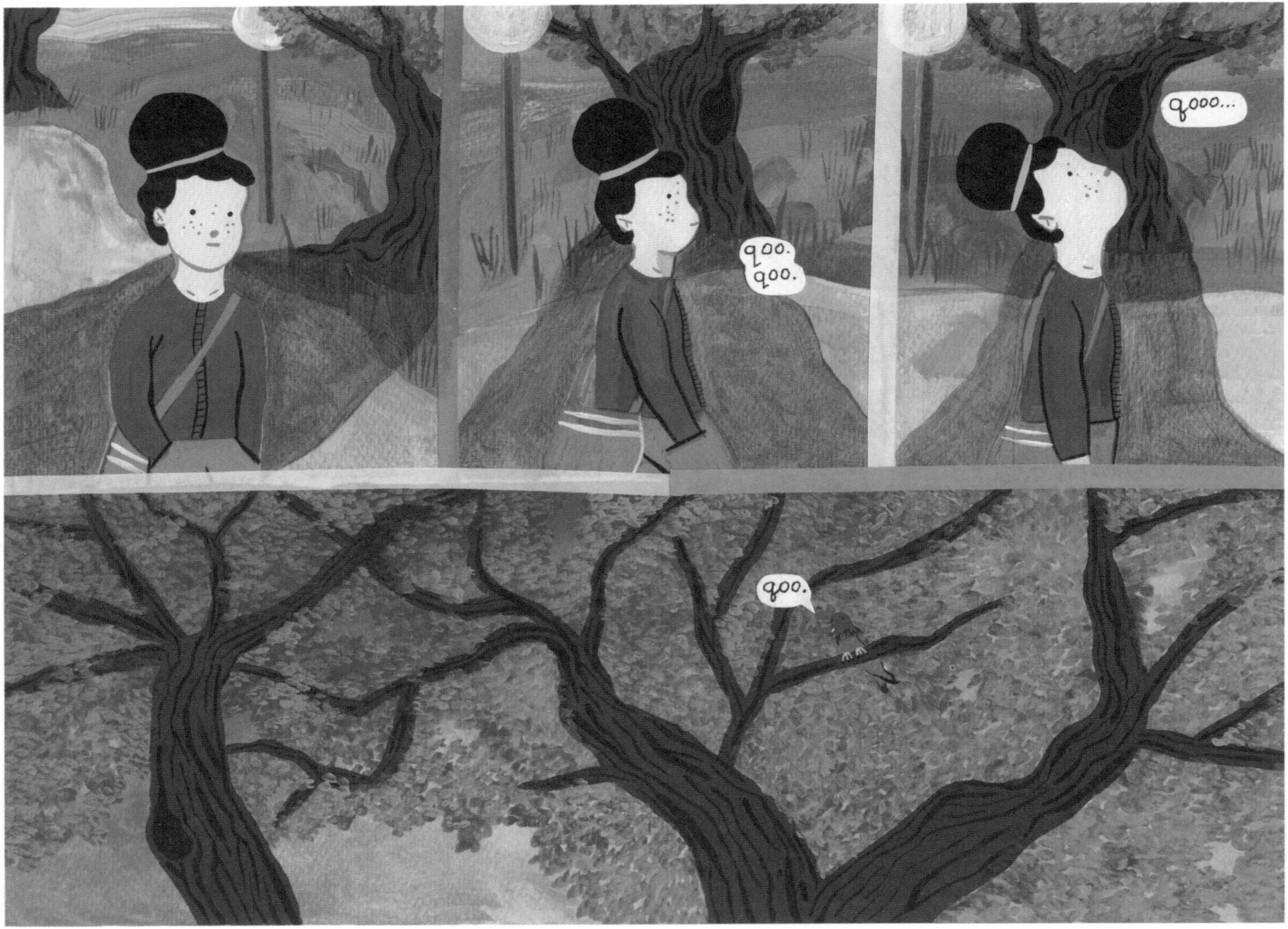
qoo.
qoo.
qooo...
qoo.

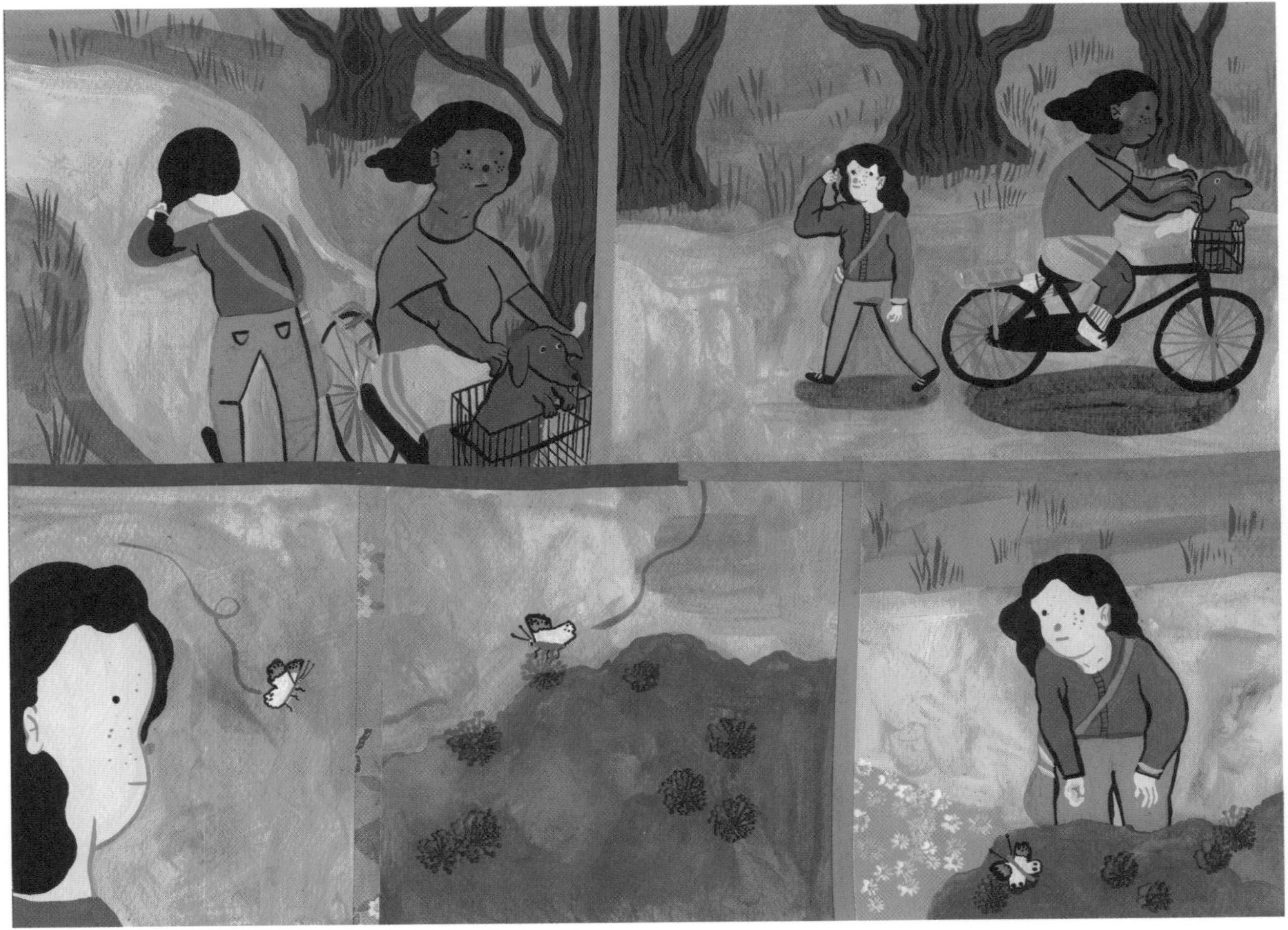

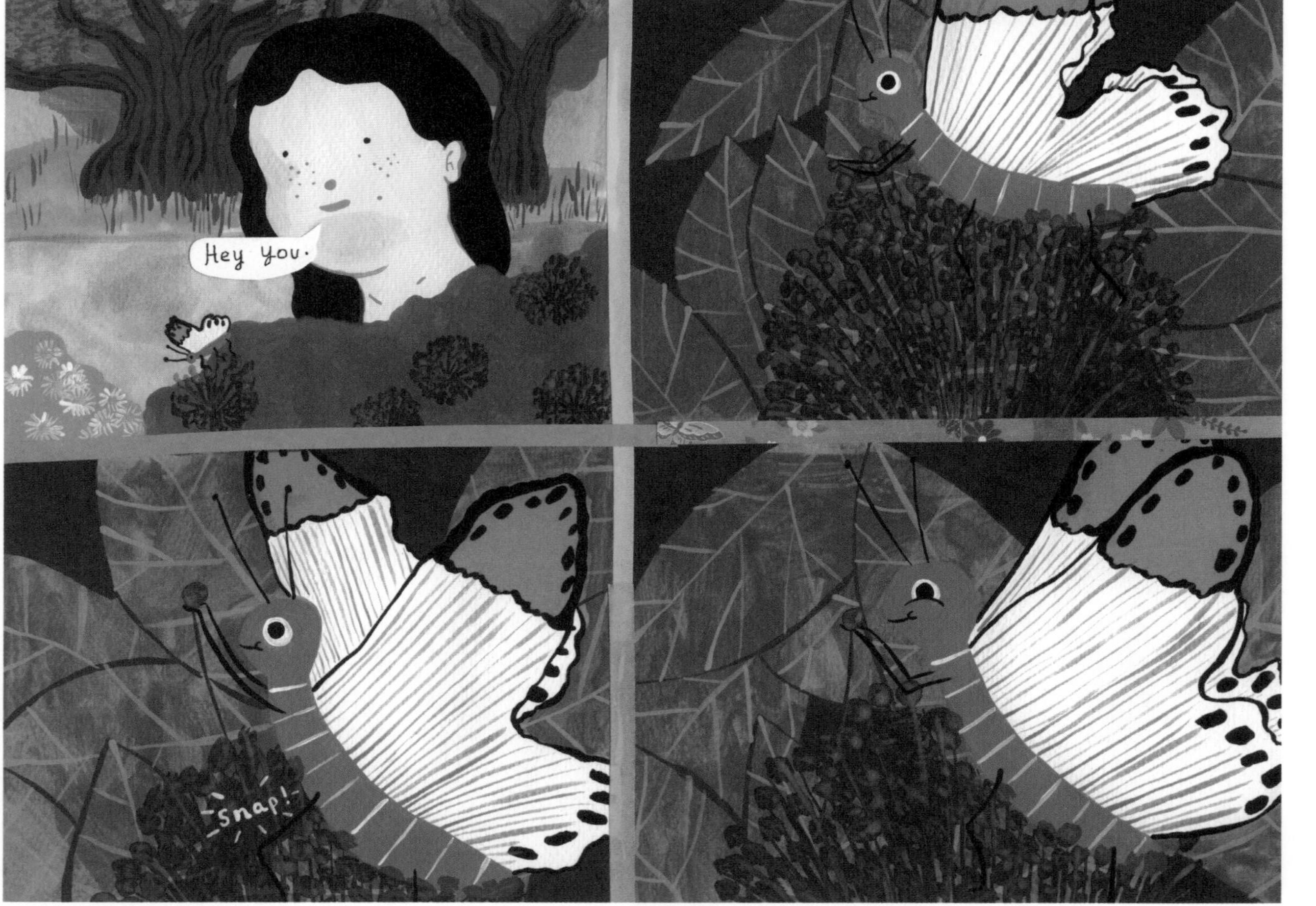
Hey you.
Snap!

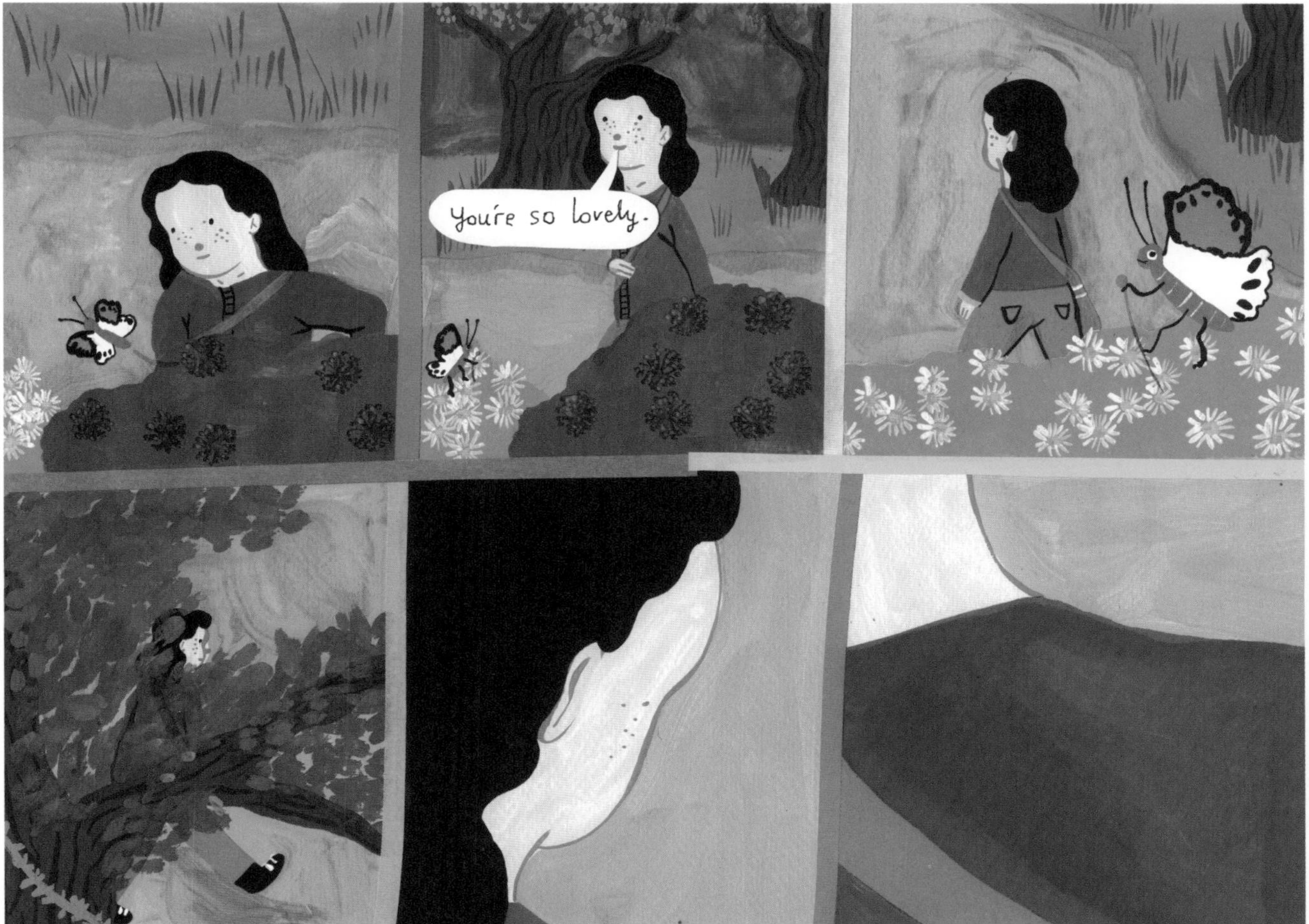
You're so lovely.

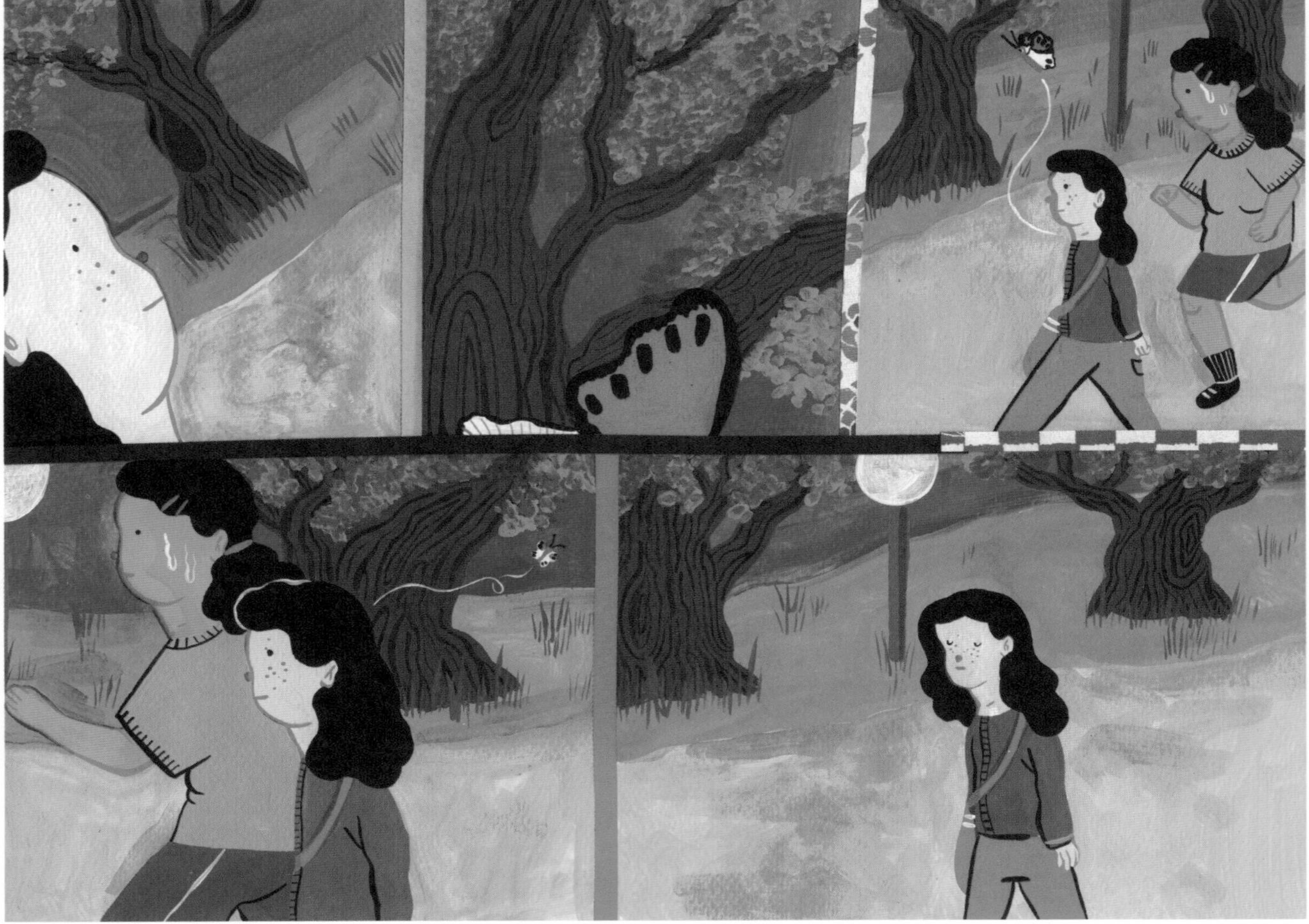

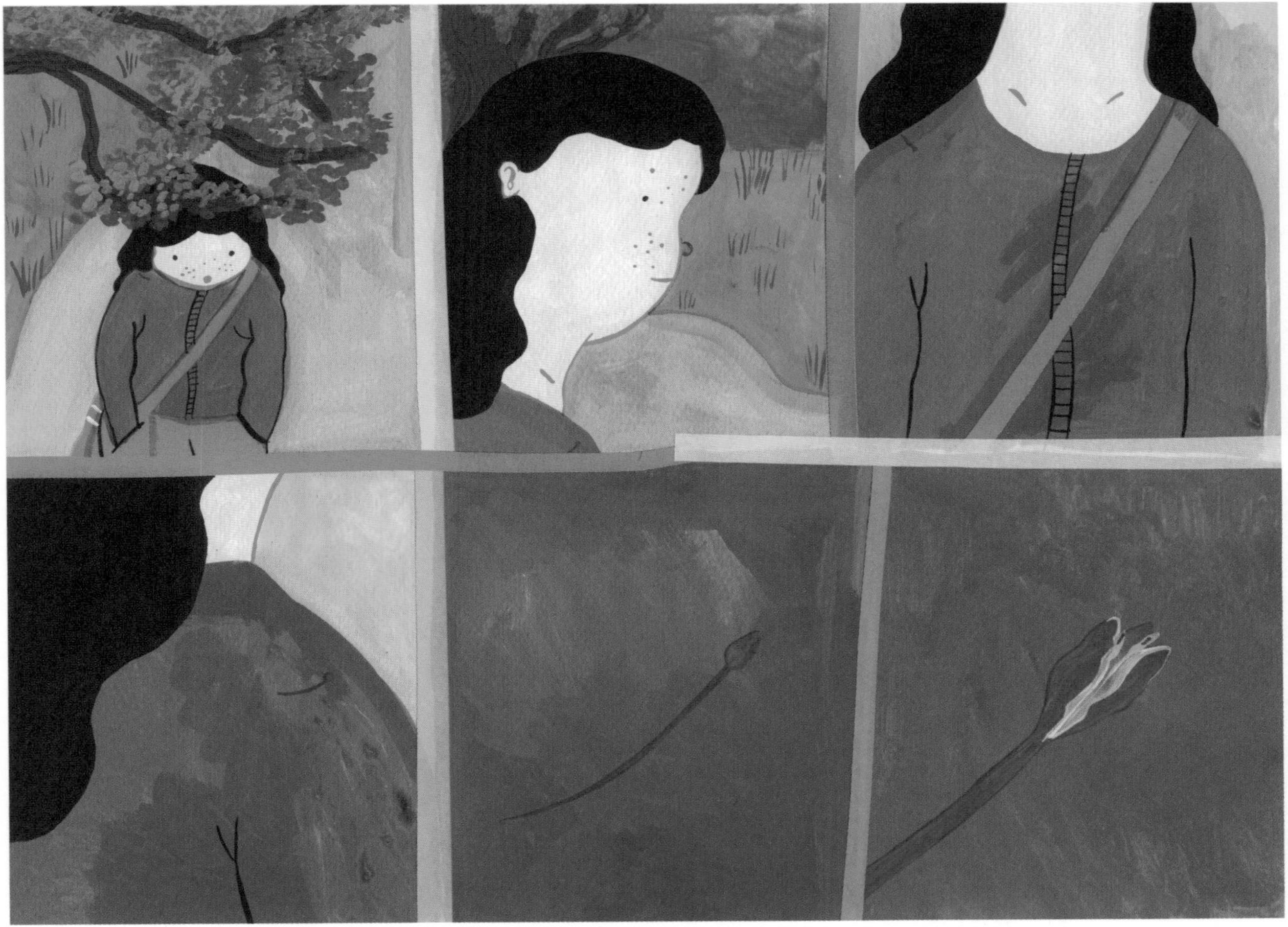

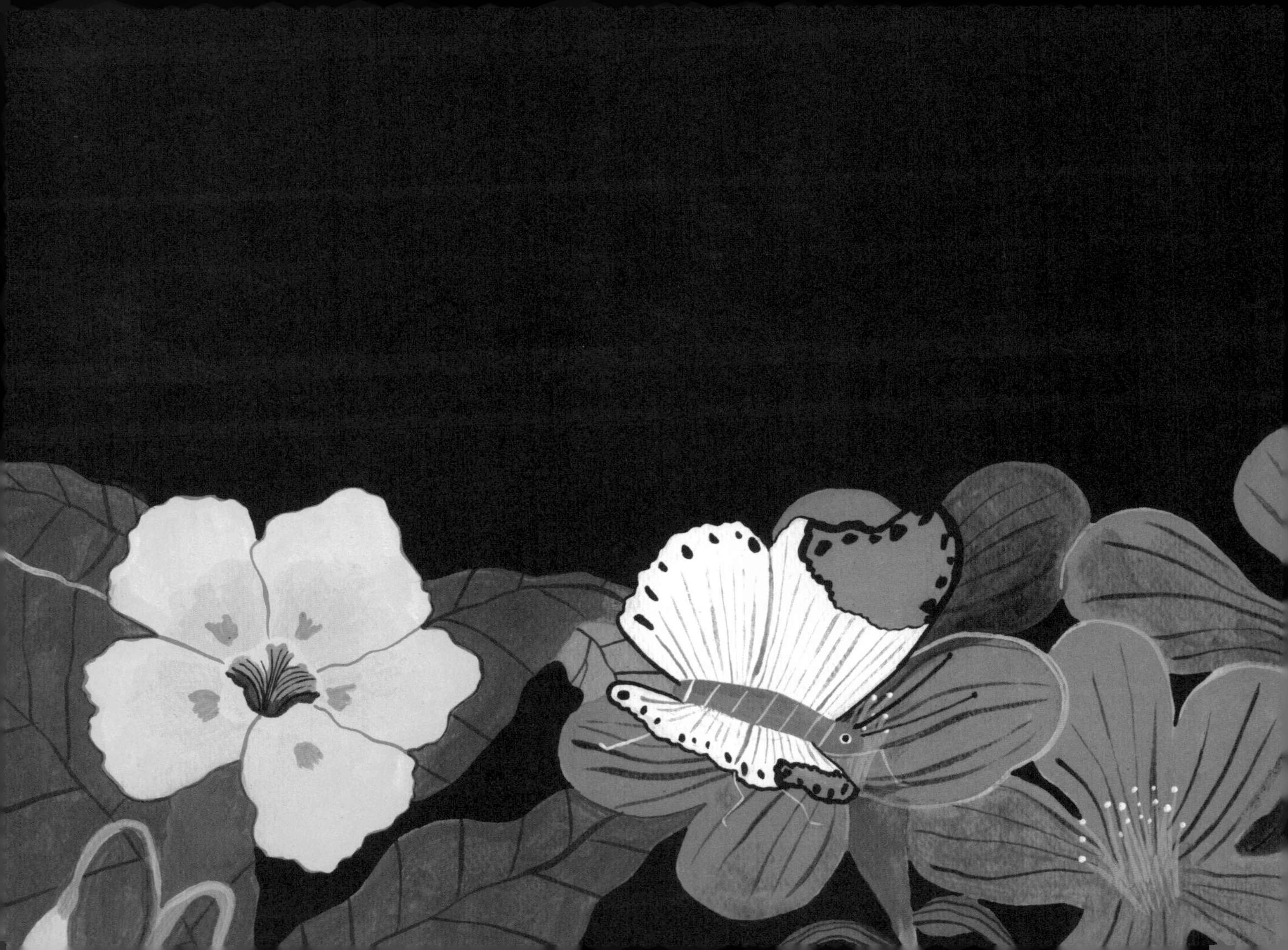

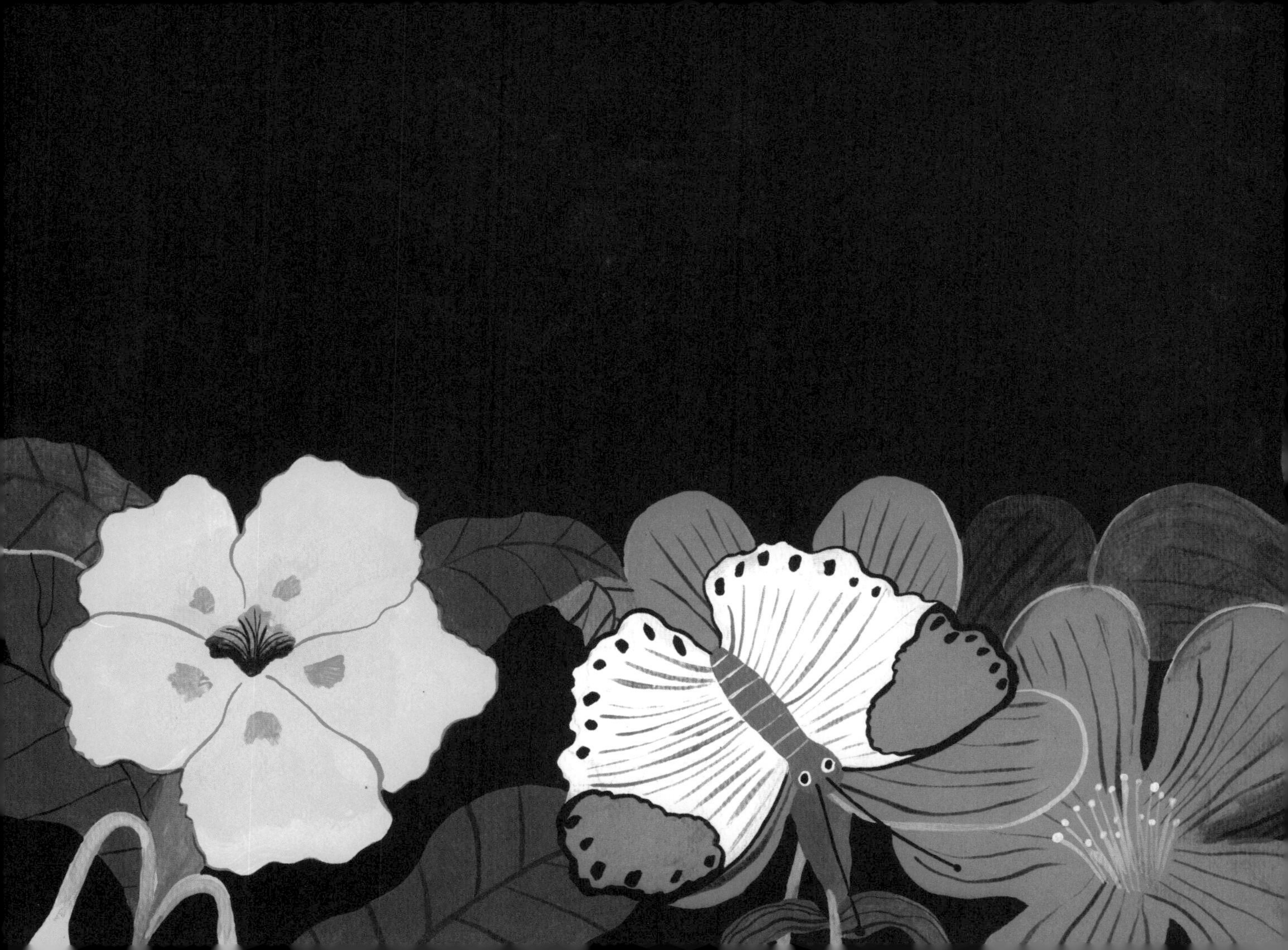

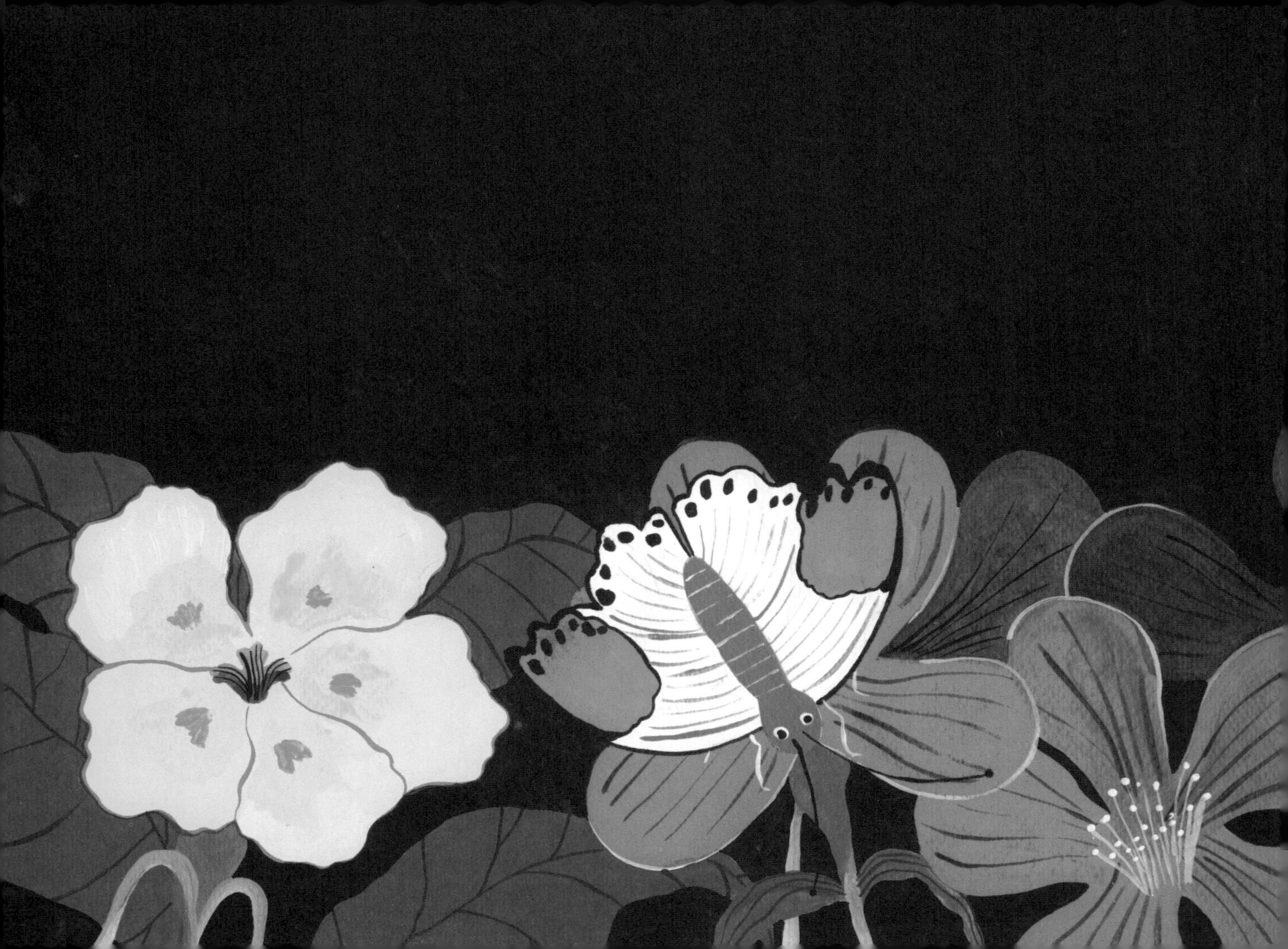

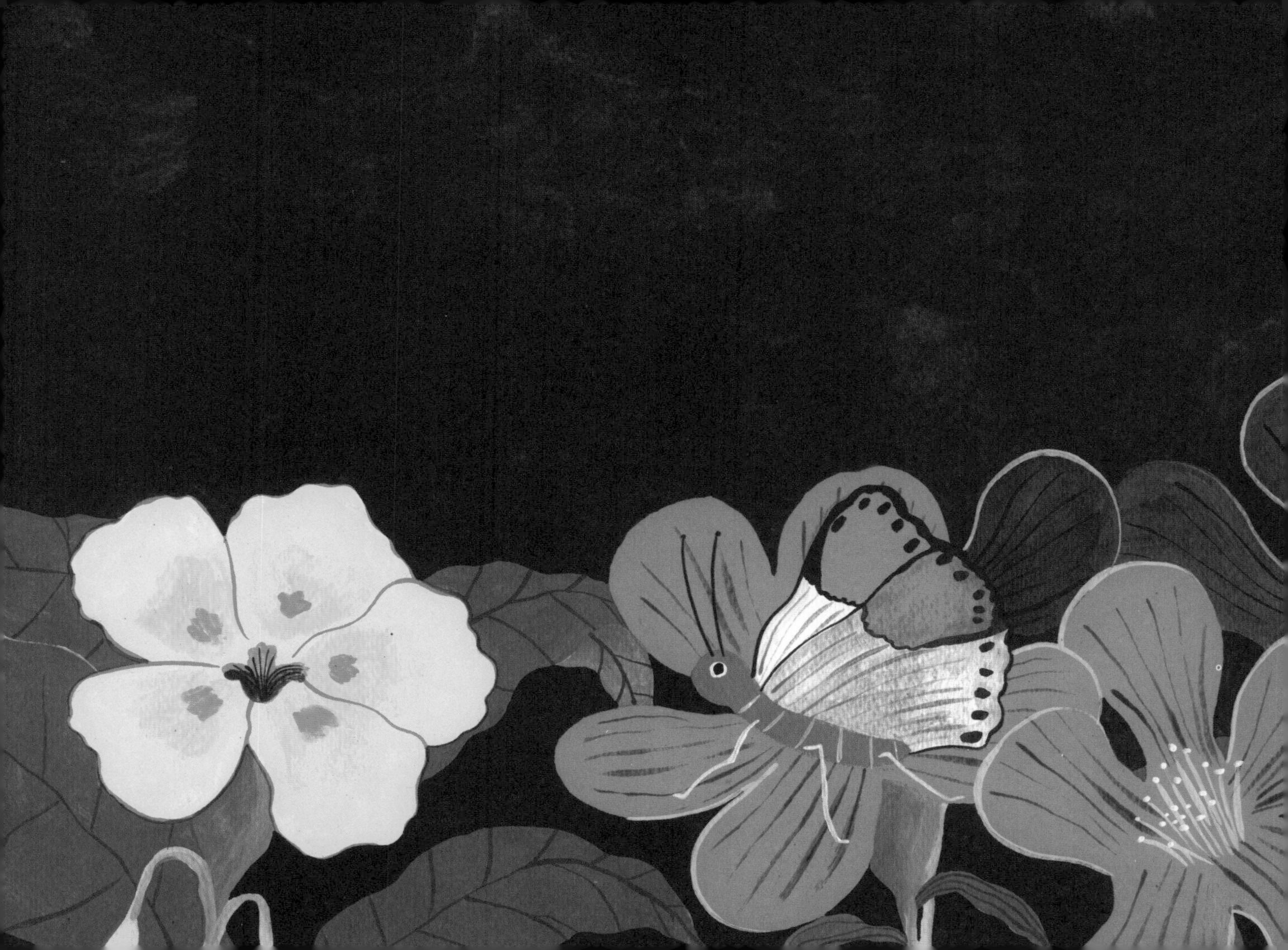

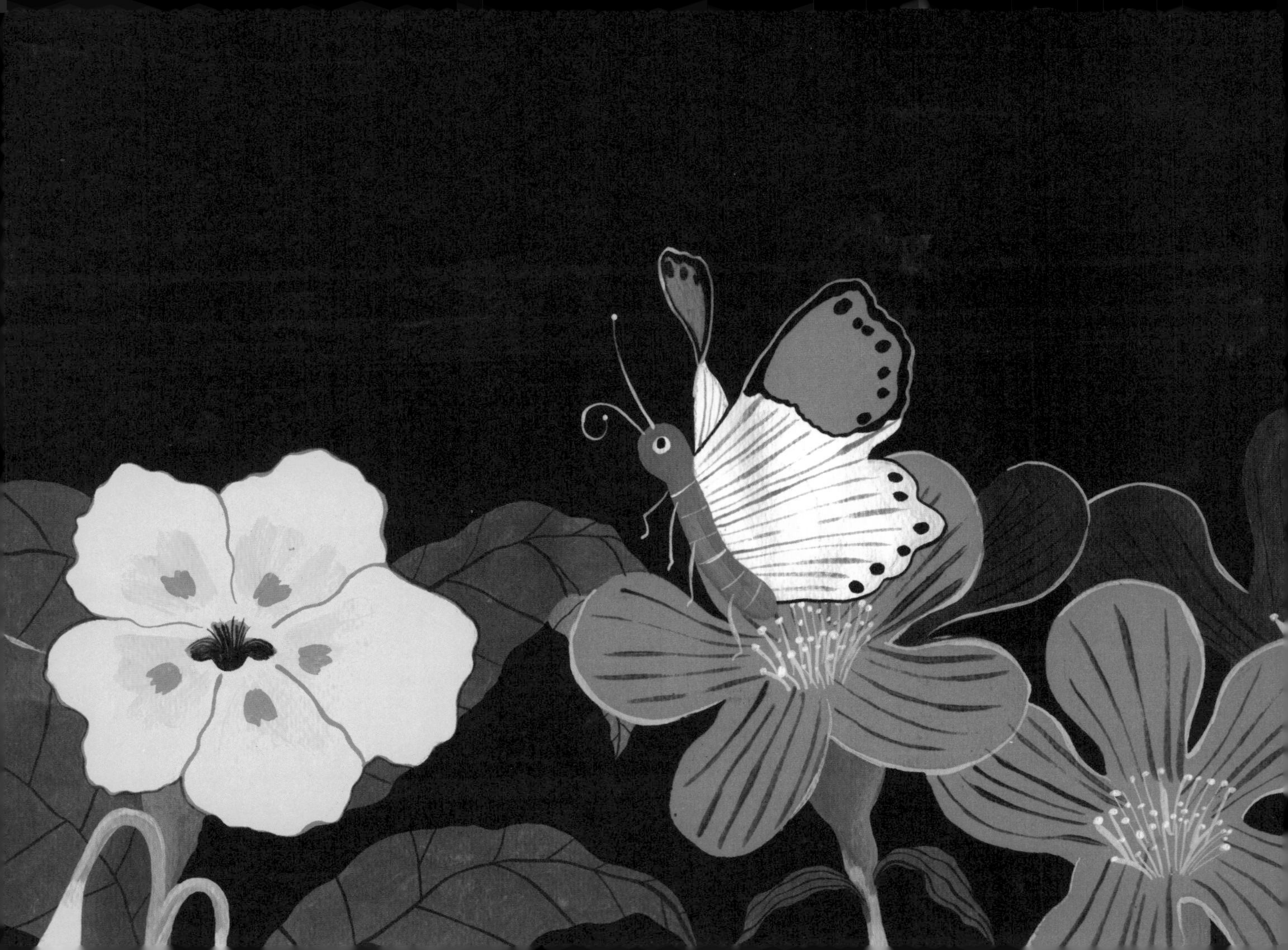

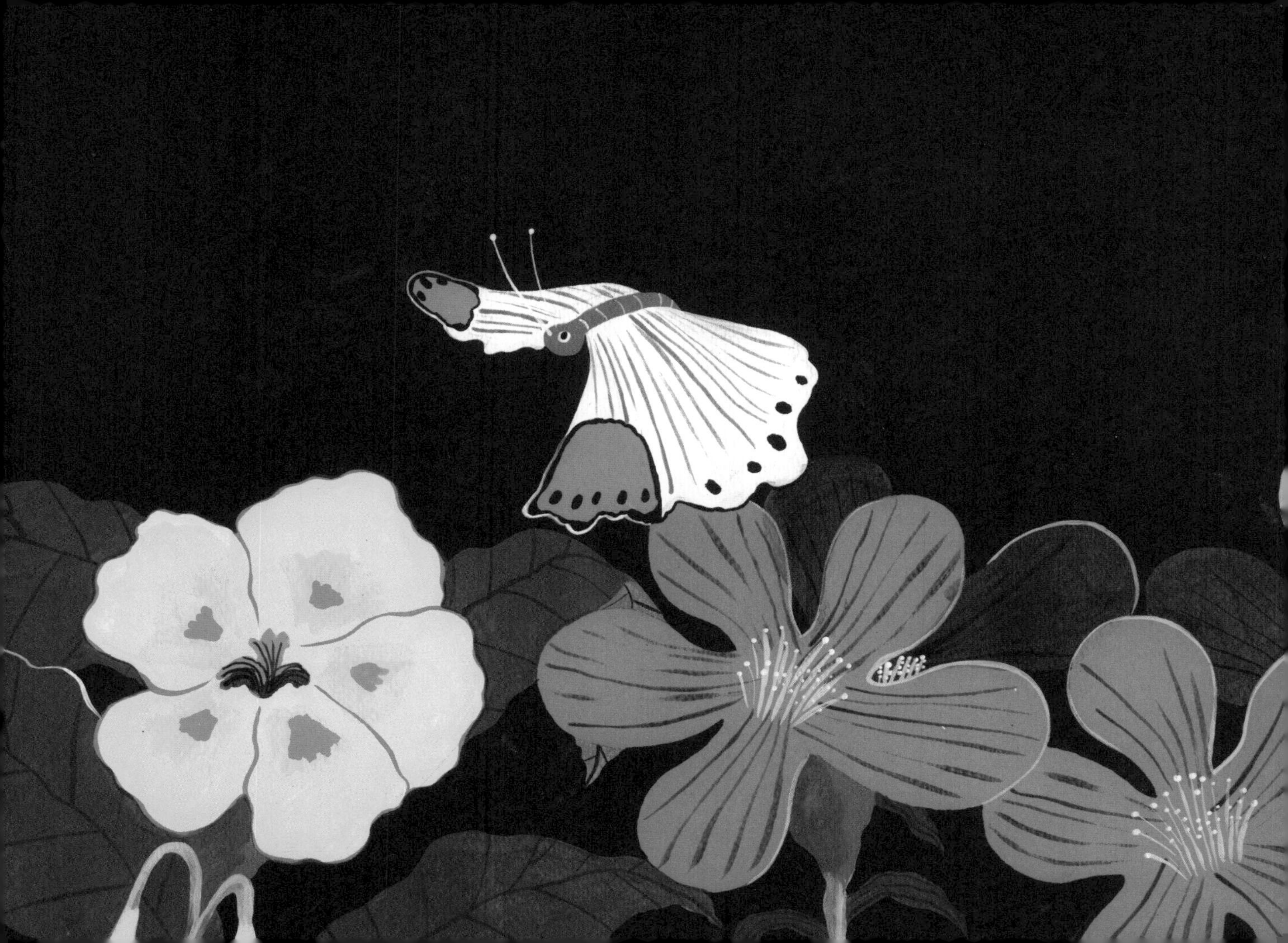

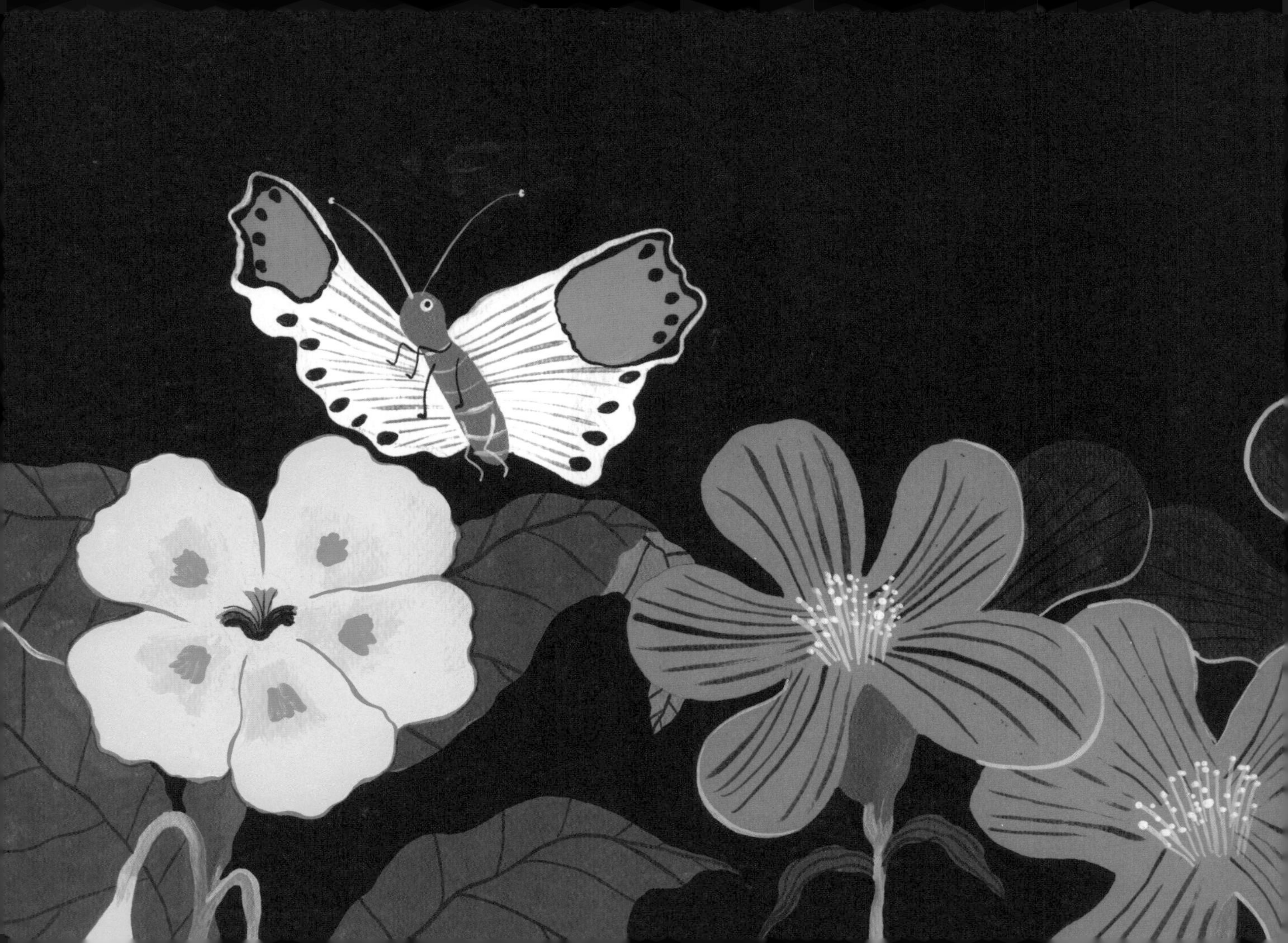

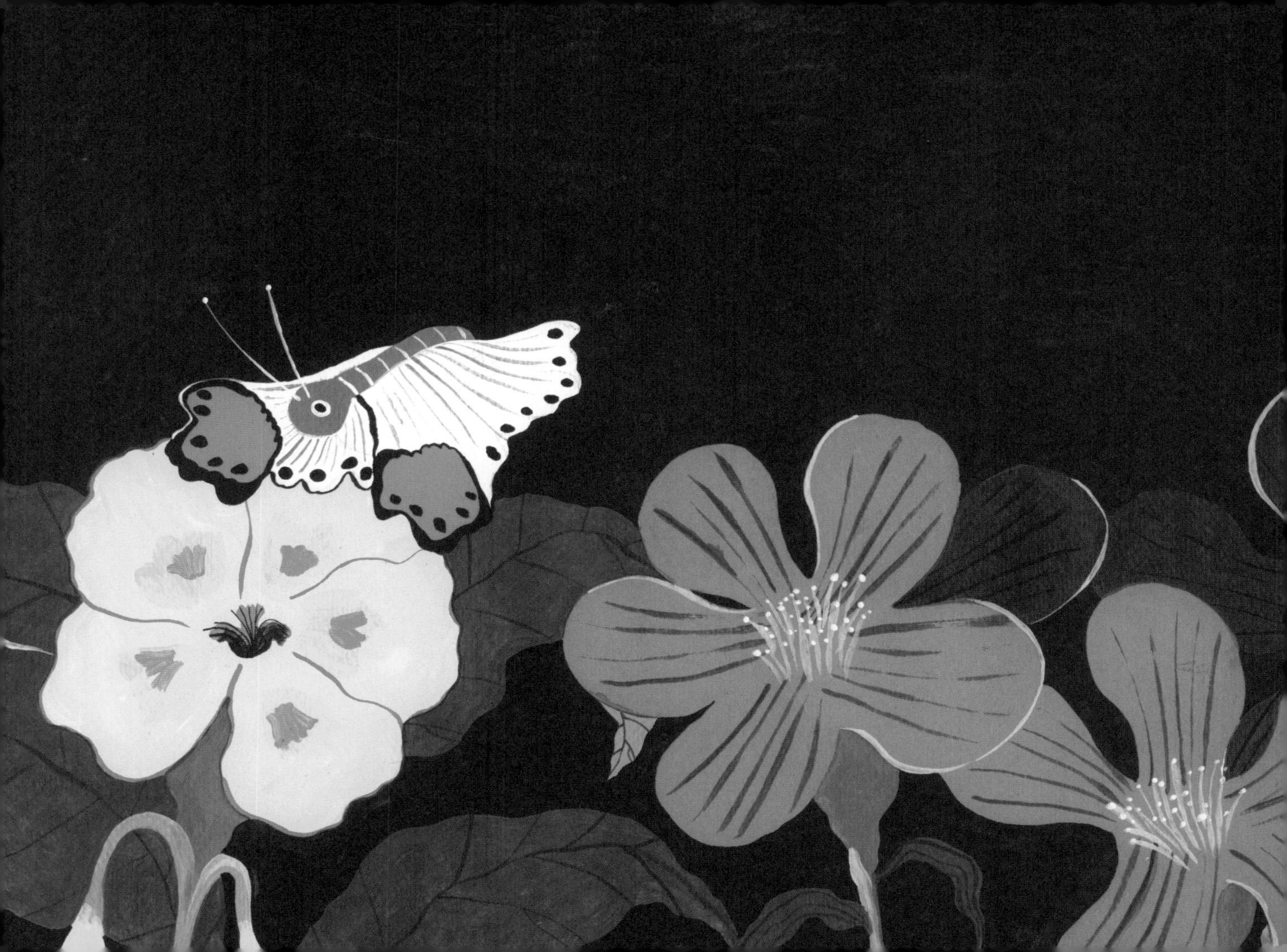

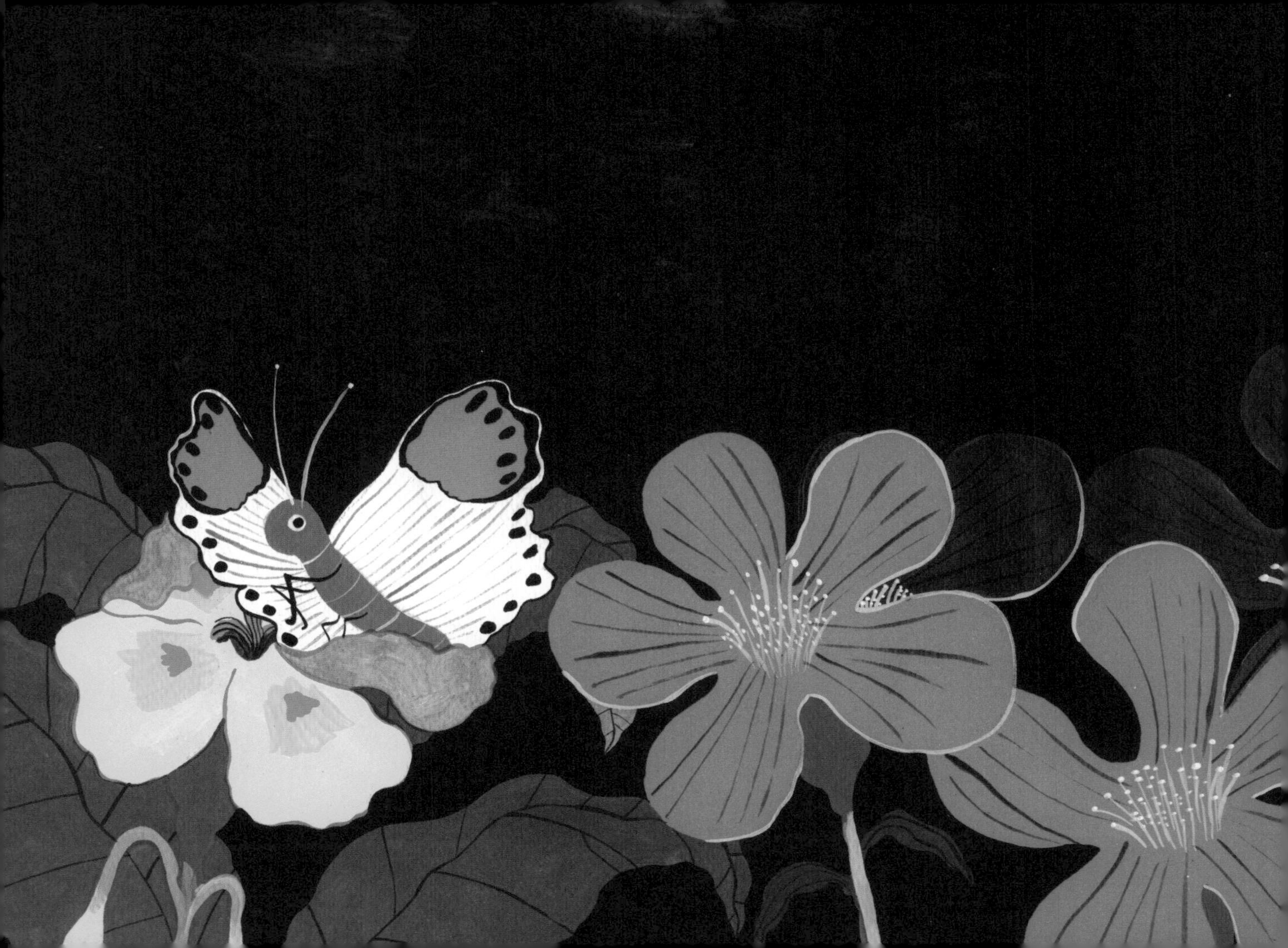

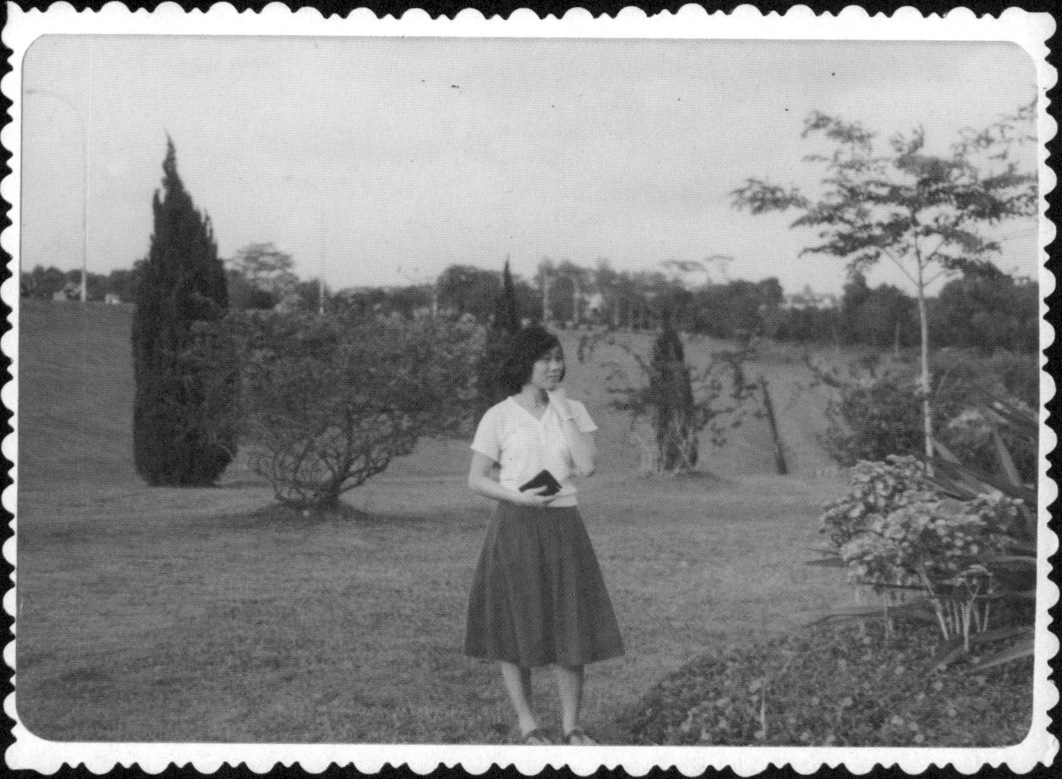

My mother 冰 Bīng. Photo taken in 1978.

Weng Pixin (or Pix for short) was born in 1983 and grew up in sunny Singapore, an island city located along the equator. She loves night time rainfalls, reading non-fiction books, and eavesdropping on sing-song conversations of the toads who live right below her apartment.

As a child, Pixin's father used to tell her stories- stories that reflected his curious nature. When Pix began making art, she wanted to express that same curious nature in her semi-autobiographical comics.

Her first book, Sweet Time, was published by Drawn & Quarterly in 2020.